Beginning Ruby

From Novice to Professional

Peter Cooper

Beginning Ruby: From Novice to Professional

Copyright © 2007 by Peter Cooper

ISBN-13 (pbk): 978-1-59059-766-8

ISBN-10 (pbk): 1-59059-766-4

Printed and bound in the United States of America 9 8 7 6 5 4 3 2

Lead Editors: Jonathan Gennick, Keir Thomas
Technical Reviewers: Tim Fletcher, Peter Marklund
Editorial Board: Steve Anglin, Ewan Buckingham, Gary Cornell, Jason Gilmore, Jonathan Gennick,
    Jonathan Hassell, James Huddleston, Chris Mills, Matthew Moodie, Dominic Shakeshaft, Jim Sumser,
    Keir Thomas, Matt Wade
Project Manager: Beth Christmas
Copy Edit Manager: Nicole Flores
Copy Editor: Susannah Davidson Pfalzer
Assistant Production Director: Kari Brooks-Copony
Production Editor: Lori Bring
Compositor: Gina Rexrode
Proofreader: Nancy Sixsmith
Indexer: Julie Grady
Artist: April Milne
Cover Designer: Kurt Krames
Manufacturing Director: Tom Debolski

Distributed to the book trade worldwide by Springer-Verlag New York, Inc., 233 Spring Street, 6th Floor, New York, NY 10013. Phone 1-800-SPRINGER, fax 201-348-4505, e-mail orders-ny@springer-sbm.com, or visit http://www.springeronline.com.

For information on translations, please contact Apress directly at 2855 Telegraph Avenue, Suite 600, Berkeley, CA 94705. Phone 510-549-5930, fax 510-549-5939, e-mail info@apress.com, or visit http://www.apress.com.

The source code for this book is available to readers at http://www.apress.com in the Source Code/ Download section.

For Laura

Contents at a Glance

PART 1 ■ ■ ■ Foundations and Scaffolding

PART 2 ■ ■ ■ The Core of Ruby

PART 3 ■ ■ ■ Ruby Online

Contents

PART 1 ■■■ Foundations and Scaffolding

PART 2 ■ ■ ■ The Core of Ruby

PART 3 ■ ■ ■ **Ruby Online**

Foreword

here is a nice mountain in japan.

this one's just a meadow with a horse taking it easy.

oh, nice! a bowl of curry! so delicious...

why the lucky stiff

http://whytheluckystiff.net/

About the Author

PETER COOPER is an experienced Ruby developer and trainer, and editor of Ruby Inside (http://www.rubyinside.com/), the most popular Ruby news blog. Until 2007 he was primarily a Ruby trainer and developer, but is now the full-time owner and developer of Feed Digest (http://www.feeddigest.com/), a Ruby- and Rails-powered RSS feed processing and redistribution service that serves more than 200 million requests per month and was recently profiled by *Business 2.0* magazine.

Since 2004 Peter has developed many commercial Web sites using Ruby on Rails, the Ruby-based Web framework. In addition, he created Code Snippets (http://www.bigbold.com/snippets/), one of the Web's largest public code repositories, and Congress, an online chat client using Ajax and Ruby on Rails technologies.

In addition to development work, Peter has written professionally about various development techniques and tools, with more than 100 bylines since 1998. He was co-editor of WebDeveloper.com, and worked on iBoost.com and Webpedia.com during the dot-com boom.

He lives in Lincolnshire, England, with his girlfriend. In his limited spare time he enjoys hiking, camping, and exploring.

About the Technical Reviewers

TIM FLETCHER is 22 years old and lives in Winchester, England, on a student placement with IBM. He likes Ruby because it's fun. He has no children or pets, but an admirable younger sister called Sophie. When not writing code, he loves to read, eat, sleep, and ski as much as possible.

PETER MARKLUND has extensive experience with and expertise in object orientation, Web development, relational databases, and testing, and has been doing Web development with Java and Tcl since 2000. He was one of the core developers of the OpenACS open source Web framework. In late 2004, he was introduced to Ruby on Rails and has since helped develop an online community and a CRM system with Rails. Peter is working as a Ruby on Rails freelancer and is also helping organize events for the Ruby on Rails developer community in Stockholm. Peter has a personal blog at http://marklunds.com, where he shares Rails tips with other developers.

Acknowledgments

It is often said that writing is a lonely task, but it's not until you write a book that you realize the process has to be anything *but* lonely. Without the help and reassurance of the large team of people backing this book, and backing me personally, this book could not have been written.

My first thanks go to Keir Thomas, who approached me with the idea of writing a Ruby book. He gave me great freedom over the scope and specification of the book and was the most essential piece of the puzzle in getting the book approved and everything sorted out in the early stages.

Beth Christmas of Apress deserves a special thanks for her superb project management and constant reassurance during the writing of this book. Without her schedules and assurance that everything was on track, I would have been a nervous wreck.

Jonathan Gennick, Tim Fletcher, and Peter Marklund deserve much praise for their seemingly unending reading and rereading of this book's chapters throughout the various stages of their development. As a newcomer to Ruby, Jonathan provided some especially interesting insights that have served to make the book even better for Ruby newcomers to read.

I'd also like to praise Susannah Davidson Pfalzer for her diligent approach to copy editing this book by fixing my pronouns, removing my overuse of words like "however" and "therefore," and generally making it possible to read the book without going insane. As this is my first book for Apress, I have depended on Susannah's deep knowledge of Apress customs a great deal.

Naturally, thanks go to all of those I directly worked with on the book, whether they're from Apress or independent. In no particular order: Jonathan Gennick, Keir Thomas, Beth Christmas, Tim Fletcher, Peter Marklund, Susannah Davidson Pfalzer, Jason Gilmore, Lori Bring, Nancy Sixsmith, and why the lucky stiff.

Separately from the book itself, I have to give thanks to many in the Ruby community for either working alongside me, producing tools I've used, or just making the Ruby language more appealing in general. In no particular order: why the lucky stiff (for an unforgettable foreword), Yukihiro "Matz" Matsumoto, Jamie van Dyke, Amy Hoy, Evan Weaver, Geoffrey Grosenbach, Obie Fernandez, Damien Tanner, Chris Roos, Martin Sadler, Zach Dennis, Pat Toner, Pat Eyler, Hendy Irawan, Ian Ozsvald, Nic Williams, Shane Vitarana, Josh Catone, Alan Bradburne, Jonathan Conway, Alex MacCaw, Benjamin Curtis, and David Heinemeier Hansson. I am anxious I've missed some names, so if you're missing from this list, I humbly apologize.

Those in my personal life have also supported me a great deal by putting up with my weird work hours and annoying habits, and by asking questions about the book, feeding me, or just being there to talk to. In this regard I'd like to thank—again in no particular order—Laura Craggs, Clive Cooper, Ann Cooper, David Sculley, Ed Farrow, Michael Wong, Bob Pardoe, Dave Hunt, Chris Ueland, Kelly Smith, Graham Craggs, Lorraine Craggs, and Robert Smith. Laura Craggs deserves a special mention for having had to put up with me nearly 24 hours a day during the writing of this book; she is amazing.

Big thanks are due to John Joyce, for his extremely diligent reading and errata reports. If you want someone to go through your book with a fine toothed comb, he is definitely the right man for the job. Thanks!

Last, it's necessary to thank *you*, the reader, for choosing to buy this book, for if no one bought this book, these acknowledgements and the efforts of many people during the writing of this book would have been wasted. Thank you!

Introduction

I wanted to minimize my frustration during programming, so I want to minimize my effort in programming. That was my primary goal in designing Ruby. I want to have fun in programming myself.

—Yukihiro Matsumoto (Matz), creator of Ruby

Ruby is a "best of breed" language that has been assembled from the best and most powerful programming features found in its predecessors.

—Jim White

Ruby makes me smile.

—Amy Hoy (slash7.com)

Ruby is a fun toy. It's also a serious programming language. Ruby is the jolly uncle who keeps the kids entertained, but who puts in solid 12-hour days at the construction site during the week. To hundreds of thousands of programmers, Ruby has become a good friend, a trusted servant, and has revealed a new way of thinking about programming and software development.

Like the guitar, it's often claimed that Ruby is an easy language to learn and a hard one to master. I'd agree, with some provisions. If you don't know any programming languages already, Ruby will be surprisingly easy to learn. If you already know some languages such as PHP, Perl, BASIC, C, or Pascal, some of the concepts in Ruby will already be familiar to you, but the different perspective Ruby takes with problem solving will probably throw you at first. Like the differences between spoken languages, Ruby differs from most other programming languages not only by syntax, but by culture, grammar, and customs. In fact, Ruby has more in common with more esoteric languages such as LISP and Smalltalk than with better-known languages such as PHP and C++.

While Ruby's roots might be different from other languages, it's heavily used and respected in many industries. Companies that use or support Ruby in one way or another include such prestigious names as Sun Microsystems, Intel, Microsoft, Apple, and Amazon.com. The Ruby on Rails Web framework is a system for developing Web applications that uses Ruby as its base language, and it powers hundreds of large Web sites. Ruby is also used as a generic language from the command prompt, much like Perl.

Grammarians, biochemists, database administrators, and thousands of other professionals and hobbyists use Ruby to make their work easier. Ruby is a truly international language with almost unlimited application.

This book is designed to cater both to people new to programming and those with programming experience in other languages. Ruby's culture is different enough from other languages that most of this book will be of use to both groups. Any large sections that can be skipped by already proficient programmers are noted in the text. In any case, I'd suggest that all programmers at least speed-read the sections that might seem obvious to them, as there are some surprising ways in which Ruby is different from what you've done before.

When reading this book be prepared for a little informality, some quirky examples, and a heavy dose of pragmatism. Ruby is an extremely pragmatic language, less concerned with formalities and more concerned with ease of development and valid results. From time to time I'll show you how you can do things the "wrong" way in Ruby, merely for illustrative purposes, but mostly you'll be working with code that does things "the Ruby way." When I started to learn Ruby I learned primarily by example, and with a language as original and idiomatic as Ruby, it's the easiest way to pick up good habits for the future. However, there's always "more than one way to do it," so if you think some code in this book could be rewritten in a different way that fits in more with your way of thinking, try it out!

As you start this book, be prepared to think in new ways, and to feel motivated to start coding for both fun and profit. Ruby has helped a lot of jaded developers become productive once again, and whether you're a beginner to programming or one of those jaded programmers, it's almost inevitable that you'll see how Ruby can be both fun and productive for you.

Last, if you're coming from other modern scripting languages such as Perl, PHP, or Python, you might want to jump to Appendix A before reading Chapter 1. It covers the key differences between Ruby and other scripting languages, which might help you move through the initial chapters of this book more easily.

Good luck, and I hope you enjoy this book. I'll see you in Chapter 1.

PART 1

■■■

Foundations and Scaffolding

This section is where the foundations of your Ruby knowledge will be laid. By the end of this section you'll be able to develop a complete, though basic, Ruby program. You'll learn how to get Ruby working, what object orientation is, how to develop some basic programs, and about the data types and control structures Ruby uses and can operate on. Finally, I'll walk you through creating a small program from start to finish.

—

■■■

## CHAPTER 1

Let's Get It Started: Installing Ruby

Ruby is a popular programming language, but not many computers understand it by default. This chapter takes you through the steps necessary to get Ruby working on your computer.

As an open source language, Ruby has been converted (or "ported," as is the technical term) to run on many different computer platforms and architectures. This means that if you develop a Ruby program on one machine, it's likely you'll be able to run it without any changes on a different machine. You can use Ruby, in one form or another, on all the following operating systems and platforms:

- Microsoft Windows 95, 98, XP, and Vista (all varieties)

- Mac OS X (all varieties)

- Linux (all varieties)

- MS-DOS

- BSDs (including FreeBSD and OpenBSD)

- BeOS

- Acorn RISC OS

- OS/2

- Amiga

- Symbian Series 60 cell phones

- Any platform for which a Java Virtual Machine exists (using JRuby, rather than the official Ruby interpreter)

■**Caution** Some specifics of Ruby vary between platforms, but much of the code in this book (particularly in the earlier chapters) runs on all versions. When we begin to look at more complex code, such as external libraries and interfacing between Ruby and other systems, you should be prepared to make changes in your code or accept that you won't have access to every feature. However, if you're using Windows, Linux, or Mac OS X on an x86 architecture, almost everything will work as described in this book.

Before you can start playing with Ruby, you need to get your computer to understand the Ruby language by installing an implementation of Ruby on your system, which I'll cover first.

Installing Ruby

Typically, when you install Ruby onto your computer, you'll get the "Ruby interpreter," the program that understands other programs written in the Ruby language, along with a wealth of extensions and libraries to make your Ruby more fully featured. However, some installers, such as the Windows installer covered in the following section, include source code editors and more easily accessible documentation, whereas other implementations might not. Fortunately, any extras included by one distribution and not another are always available separately to install later.

To satisfy the majority of readers without referring to external documentation, I'm providing full instructions for installing and using Ruby on Windows, Mac OS X, and Linux, along with links to Ruby implementations for other platforms. In each case, I provide instructions to check that the installation is successful before sending you on to the programming fun in Chapter 2.

Windows

Ruby was initially designed for use under Unix and Unix-related operating systems such as Linux, but Windows users have access to an excellent "one-click installer," which installs Ruby, a horde of extensions, a source code editor, and various documentation, in "one click." Ruby on Windows is as reliable and useful as it is on other operating systems, and Windows makes a good environment for developing Ruby programs.

To get up and running as quickly as possible, follow these steps:

1. Open a Web browser and go to `http://www.ruby-lang.org/en/downloads/`.

2. Scroll down to "Ruby on Windows," about halfway down the page.

3. In the "Ruby on Windows" section, you'll see a few links for different versions of Ruby you can download for Windows. Ideally you want to download the file at the link that's highest in the list that's referred to as a "One-Click Installer." At the time of writing, this is version 1.8.5.

4. Click the link you found in step 3 and save it to your desktop.

5. Once download has completed, look on your desktop for the Ruby EXE file you just downloaded, and double-click it to load the installer.

6. If Windows gives you a "Security Error" box, click the "Run" button to give your approval.

7. A typical installation program appears with some instructions. On the initial screen, click "Next."

8. Work your way through the installation screens. Leave the boxes checked to install the text editors SciTE and FreeRIDE, and the Ruby package manager RubyGems (more on that in Chapter 7). Unless you have a specific reason not to, let the installation program install Ruby in its default location of c:\ruby and its default program group.

9. Installation takes place when you see a stream of filenames flying up your screen. Wait several minutes for the installation process to complete and enjoy the view. There are a lot of files to install!

10. Installation is complete when the installation program says "Installation Complete" and the "Next" button is clickable. Click the "Next" button, then click "Finish" to exit the installation program.

If Ruby installed correctly, congratulations! Go to the "Start" menu and then the "Programs" or "All Programs" menu. There should be a Ruby program group that contains icons for FreeRIDE, SciTE, an uninstaller, and other bits and pieces. To test that your Ruby installation works correctly for Chapter 2, you need to load the program listed as "fxri – Interactive Ruby Help & Console," so click this entry and wait for the program to load. If the program loads successfully, you'll see a screen that looks somewhat like that in Figure 1-1.

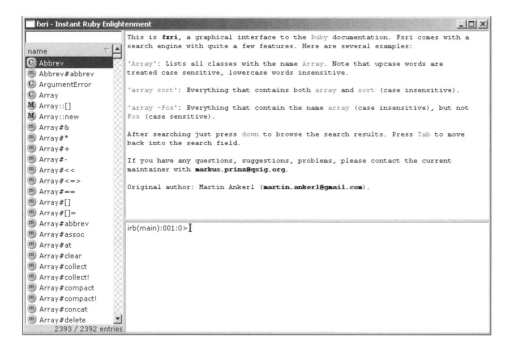

Figure 1-1. *The fxri interactive Ruby program*

If fxri started properly, then Ruby is installed correctly. Congratulations! Lastly, you need to be familiar with running Ruby and its associated utilities from the command prompt, so go to the "Start" menu, then "Run," and type **cmd** into the box and click "OK" ("Command Prompt" might also be in your "Programs" menu under "Accessories"). You should be presented with a command prompt, like that in Figure 1-2.

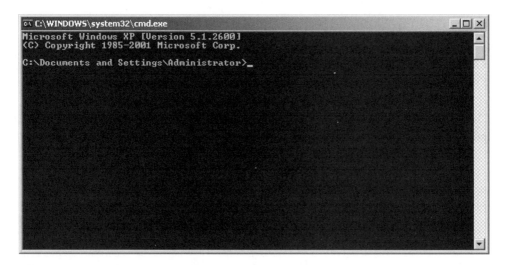

Figure 1-2. *The Microsoft Windows command prompt*

Throughout this book, commands that can be used at the command prompt will be given. This is because using a command prompt such as this is a standard technique in operating systems such as Linux and OS X. For example, in Chapter 7 we'll look at installing extra features (libraries) for Ruby, and the command prompt will be used for this. Therefore, it's necessary for you to know how to access it and run programs.

If you type **irb** at this prompt and press Enter, you should see something like the following:

```
irb(main):001:0>
```

If you see the preceding line, everything is set up correctly, and you can type **exit** and press Enter to be returned to the command prompt.

Now you can move on to Chapter 2 and start to play with the Ruby language itself.

Apple Mac OS X

Unlike Windows, most modern Apple machines running Mac OS X come with a version of Ruby already installed, which means you can get started straight away. Mac OS X Panther (10.3.x) comes with Ruby 1.8.2 by default, and OS X Tiger (10.4.x) comes with Ruby 1.8.4.

Note It's likely that OS X Leopard, due to be released in 2007, will come with the latest version of Ruby, so if you're running that operating system, unavailable at the time of writing, you might already be set to go!

Most of the code in this book works fine with Ruby 1.8.2 or higher, so if you're running Mac OS X Panther or Tiger, you don't need to do anything special. To find out which version of OS X you're running, click the "Apple" menu at the top left of your screen and select "About This Mac." If the version of OS X is later than 10.3, you should have Ruby installed already.

Tip If you're using OS X Tiger (10.4.x), use Apple's Software Update to upgrade to the latest version of OS X, as Apple improved Ruby distribution included in OS X from version 10.4.6 onward. Without this upgrade, you might need to reinstall Ruby manually to get some extensions, such as Ruby on Rails, to work correctly. Although this isn't a concern for the first two sections of this book, it could cause you some confusion later on.

Testing for a Preinstalled Version of Ruby

If you're using OS X Panther or OS X Tiger, you can check whether Ruby is installed by using the Terminal application. Double-click "Macintosh HD" (or whatever your hard drive is called) and go to the Applications folder on your drive. Once in Applications, go to the Utilities folder, where you'll find an application called Terminal. Double-click its icon to start it. If Terminal starts correctly, you'll see a screen similar to that in Figure 1-3.

Once you're in the Terminal, you're at what's called the *command prompt* or *shell*. You're talking directly with your computer, in a technical sense, when you type. The computer will execute the commands that you type immediately once you press Enter.

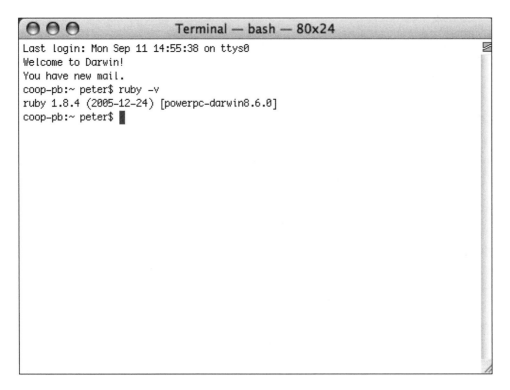

Figure 1-3. *The Mac OS X Terminal in OS X Tiger with a working Ruby installed and tested*

To see if Ruby is installed, type the following at the command prompt from within Terminal *(be sure to press Enter afterward)*:

```
ruby -v
```

If successful, you should see a result, as shown in Figure 1-3, that says what version of Ruby you're running (which should, ideally, be 1.8.2 or greater). If this works, try to run the Ruby interactive interpreter called "irb" by typing the following at the command prompt:

```
irb
```

If you get a result as shown in Figure 1-3, you're ready to go and can move to Chapter 2. If you need to install a newer version of Ruby on OS X, continue to the next section.

Installing Ruby on OS X

There are a few ways to install Ruby on OS X. You can install from a prepackaged installation, by using a package manager such as Fink or DarwinPorts, or by compiling the Ruby source directly. If you already use Fink or DarwinPorts, then refer to their respective sites for further information, but otherwise you'll find it easier to use a prebuilt installation package.

One of the most popular installation packages is called Locomotive, and is available at http://locomotive.raaum.org/.

As a regular DMG OS X file, you can install it like any other OS X application (on both PPC and x86 architectures). Unlike some installers, Locomotive includes Ruby on Rails and LightTPD. These tools aren't immediately useful, unless you're planning to do some Ruby on Rails development right away, but which you'll be glad of by the end of this book.

Installing Ruby from Source on Mac OS X

Installing Ruby directly from source code on OS X is similar to Linux, so continue on to the later Linux section entitled "Installing Ruby From Source Code." Please note that versus installing a package such as Locomotive, when you install Ruby by source, all you get is Ruby. You need to install components such as Rails separately later.

▓**Note** To compile the Ruby sources on OS X, you need to install the Xcode developer tools that come with OS X.

Linux

As an open source programming language, Ruby is already installed with many Linux distributions. It's not universal though, but you can check if Ruby is installed by following the instructions in the next section. If this fails, there are further instructions to help you install it.

Checking If Ruby Is Installed on Linux

Try to run the Ruby interpreter from the command prompt (or terminal window), as follows:

```
ruby -v
```

If Ruby is installed, it will give an output such as the following:

```
ruby 1.8.2 (2004-12-25) [i686-linux]
```

This means that Ruby 1.8.2 is installed on the machine. This book requires 1.8.2 as a bare minimum, so if the version is less than 1.8.2 you'll need to continue onward in this chapter and install a more recent version of Ruby. However, if Ruby appears to be installed and up to date, try to run the irb interactive Ruby interpreter, as follows:

```
irb
```

■Tip On some systems, irb might have a slightly different name. For example, on Ubuntu it can sometimes be called irb1.8, and you'll need to run it as such. To find it, you can use `find / -name "irb" -maxdepth 4`.

Once you've run irb, you should get the following output:

```
irb(main):001:0>
```

If running irb results in a similar output, you can move on to Chapter 2. (You might wish to type **exit** and press Enter to get back to the command line!) Otherwise, read on to install a new version of Ruby.

Installing Ruby with a Package Manager

The installation procedure for Ruby on Linux varies between different Linux distributions. Some distributions, such as Gentoo, Debian, and Red Hat, provide "package managers" to make installation of programs easy. Others require that you install directly from source or install a package manager beforehand.

If you're comfortable with using `emerge`, `rpm`, or `apt-get,` you can install Ruby quickly with the following methods:

- *RPM*: Download Ruby RPMs and install with `rpm -Uhv ruby-*.rpm`

- *Gentoo*: Use `emerge` as follows: `emerge ruby`

- *Debian*: Use `apt-get`: `sudo apt-get install ruby`

- *Ubuntu*: Use `apt-get` as with Debian. You might also need to install irb explicitly. In the case of Ruby 1.8, this line should work:

  ```
  sudo apt-get install ruby ruby1.8 ruby1.8-dev rdoc ri irb
  ```

If one of these methods works for you, try to run Ruby and irb as shown in the preceding section, and progress to Chapter 2 if you're ready. Alternatively, you can search your distribution's package repository for Ruby, as the name for the Ruby package in your distribution might be nonstandard or changing over time. However, if all else fails, you can install Ruby directly from its source code in the next section.

Installing Ruby from Source Code

Installing Ruby from its source code is a great option if you don't mind getting your hands dirty. The process is similar on all forms of Unix (not just Linux). Here are the basic steps:

1. Make sure that your Linux distribution is able to build applications from source by searching for the "make" and "gcc" tools. From the terminal you can use `which gcc` and `which make` to see if the development tools are installed. If not, you need to install these development tools.

2. Open a Web browser and go to `http://www.ruby-lang.org/`.

3. Click the "Download Ruby" link on the right-hand side of the page. If the page's design has changed, look for a link to "downloading Ruby."

4. On the download page, click the link to the stable version of the "Ruby Source Code." At the time of writing this is "ruby-1.8.5." This downloads the `tar.gz` file containing the source code for the latest stable version of Ruby.

5. Uncompress the `tar.gz` file. If you're at a command prompt or terminal window, go to the same directory as the `ruby-1.x.x.tar.gz` file and run `tar xzvf ruby-1.x.x.tar.gz` (where `ruby-1.x.x.tar.gz` is the name of the file you just downloaded).

6. Go into the Ruby folder that was created during decompression. If you're not using a command prompt at this stage, open a terminal window and go to the directory.

7. Run `./configure` to generate the Makefile and `config.h` files.

8. Run `make` to compile Ruby from source. This might take awhile.

9. Run `make install` to install Ruby to its correct location on the system. You need to do this as a superuser (such as root), so you might need to run it as `sudo make install` and type in the root password.

10. If there are errors by this stage, read the README file that accompanies the source code files for pointers. Otherwise, try to see what version of Ruby is now installed with `ruby -v`.

If the expected version of Ruby appears at this point, you're ready to move to Chapter 2 and begin programming. If you get an error complaining that Ruby can't be found, or the wrong version of Ruby is installed, the place where Ruby was installed to might not be in your path (the place your operating system looks for files to run). To fix this, scroll up and find out exactly where Ruby was installed (usually `/usr/local/bin` or `/usr/bin`) and add the relevant directory to your path. The process to do this varies by distribution and shell type, so refer to your Linux documentation on changing your path.

Once you can check which version of Ruby is running and it's 1.8.2 or over, and you can run irb and get a Ruby interpreter prompt, your Ruby installation is complete (for now!) and you can move on to Chapter 2.

Other Platforms

If you're not using Windows, Mac OS X, or Linux, you can still use Ruby if your computer's platform and architecture are listed at the start of this chapter. If you're a user of an uncommon platform, I assume you have basic knowledge of how to install applications on your system, so I simply provide the links to the following different installation programs:

- *MS-DOS*: `http://ftp.ruby-lang.org/pub/ruby/binaries/djgpp/`.

- *FreeBSD*: Various versions of Ruby are available as standard ports.

- *OS/2*: `http://hobbes.nmsu.edu/pub/os2/dev/misc/ruby-181.zip`.

- *BeOS*: Ruby is installable in the same manner as with Linux, as described earlier.

- *Linspire or Lindows*: As a Linux distribution, you can use the same instructions as for Linux, earlier.

- *Symbian Series 60*: `http://developer.symbian.com/main/tools/opensrc/ruby/index.jsp`.

- *Java Virtual Machines (JVMs)*: `http://jruby.codehaus.org/`.

- *Other Unix versions*: Refer to "Installing Ruby from Source Code" in the preceding Linux section for instructions that are reasonably distribution generic.

In many cases, the versions of Ruby for some operating systems might be out of date or unsupported. If this is the case, and you're confident about being able to compile your own version of Ruby directly from the Ruby source code, the source code is available to download from `http://www.ruby-lang.org/en/20020102.html`.

To test that Ruby is installed sufficiently to continue with this book, you want to check which version of Ruby is installed by asking Ruby for its version, as follows:

```
ruby -v
```

You also need access to Ruby's interactive prompt irb. You access this simply by running irb (if it's in your path) as follows:

```
irb
```

If neither Ruby nor irb work without complaint, you need to seek assistance for your specific platform. Appendix C provides a list of useful resources.

Summary

In this chapter we've focused on making sure Ruby is properly installed and that you can run the irb tool that you'll be using over the next several chapters.

Although Ruby is an easy language to learn and develop with, it's easy to become overwhelmed with the administration of Ruby itself, its installation, and its upgrades. As Ruby is a language constantly in development, it's likely that points covered in this chapter will go out of date, or easier ways to install Ruby might come along for your platform.

An important part of being a Ruby developer is being able to use the resources the Ruby community makes available, and being able to find help directly as time goes by. The Ruby community can provide quick help in most cases, and a number of resources to try are available in Chapter 5 and Appendix C.

## CHAPTER 2

Programming == Joy: A Whistle-Stop Tour of Ruby and Object Orientation

Programming is both a science and an art. Telling computers what to do with computer programs requires being able to think as both a scientist and an artist. Being an artist is essential for coming up with big ideas and being flexible enough to take unique approaches. Being a scientist is essential to understanding how and why certain methodologies need to be taken into account, and to approach testing and debugging from a logical perspective, rather than an emotional one.

Luckily, you don't need to be an artist or a scientist already. As with training the body, doing programming "exercises" and thinking about how to solve problems trains the mind to make you a better programmer. Anyone can learn to program. The only things that can stand in the way are a lack of commitment or confusing programming languages. Ruby is one of the easiest programming languages to learn, so that leaves commitment. Programming should be fun, even joyful, and if you're enjoying yourself, commitment comes naturally.

By the time you reach the end of this chapter, I hope you can get a taste of the joy that lies ahead with the knowledge of a powerful, yet deceptively simple programming language, and begin to feel excited about a future of programming nirvana!

■Note This chapter does not follow an instructional format as the following chapters do. Instead I'll just go from concept to concept quickly to give you a feel for Ruby as a language before getting down to the details later.

Baby Steps

In Chapter 1, you focused on installing Ruby so that your computer can understand the language. At the end of the chapter, you loaded a program called irb. Microsoft Windows users ran an application called fxri. fxri and irb provide similar functions, so when I refer to irb, as it's officially known, be aware that you can use fxri instead if you're using Microsoft Windows.

irb: Interactive Ruby

irb stands for "Interactive Ruby." "Interactive" means that as soon as you type something, your computer will *immediately* attempt to process it. So if you typed in the "print 'Hello, world!' 10 times" source code from the previous chapter into irb and pressed Enter, you'd immediately see the results. Sometimes this sort of environment is called an *immediate* or *interactive* environment.

■**Note** If you cannot remember how to load irb or fxri, refer to the section of Chapter 1 dedicated to your computer's operating system.

Start irb (or fxri) and make sure a prompt appears, like so:

```
irb(main):001:0>
```

This prompt is not as complex as it looks. All it means is that you're in the irb program, you're typing your first line (001), and you're at a *depth* of 0. You don't need to place any importance on the depth element at this time.

Type this after the preceding prompt and press Enter:

```
1 + 1
```

The result should come back quickly: 2. The entire process looks like this:

```
irb(main):001:0> 1 + 1
=> 2
irb(main):002:0>
```

Ruby is now ready to accept another command from you.

As a new Ruby programmer, you'll spend a lot of time in irb testing concepts and building up insights into Ruby. It provides the perfect environment for tweaking and testing the language, as you cannot do any real damage from within irb. If you explicitly ask

Ruby to erase files on your drive, of course, that can happen, but you're not susceptible to crashing your computer or harming other programs.

irb's interactive environment also gives you the benefit of immediate feedback—an essential tool when learning. Rather than writing a program in a text editor, saving it, getting the computer to run it, and then looking through the errors to see where you went wrong, you can just type in small snippets of code, hit Enter, and immediately see what happens.

If you want to experiment further, try other arithmetic such as 100 * 5, 57 + 99, or 10 – 50 (note that the division symbol/operator on a computer is the forward slash "/").

Ruby Is English for Computers

Computers can understand languages, though in a rather different fashion to how most people do. Being logical devices that cannot understand subtlety or ambiguity, languages such as English and French aren't appealing to computers. Computers require languages with logical structures and a well-defined *syntax* so that there's a logical clarity in what you're telling the computer to do.

Clarity is required because almost everything you relay to the computer while programming is an *instruction* (or *command*). Instructions are the basic building blocks of all programs, and for the computer to perform (or *execute*) them properly, the programmer's intentions must be clear and precise. Many hundreds of these instructions are tied together into *programs* that perform certain tasks, which means there's little room for error.

You also need to consider that other programmers might need to maintain computer programs you've written. This won't be the case if you're just programming for fun, but it's important that your programs are easy to understand, so you can understand them when you come back to them later on.

Why Ruby Makes a Great Programming Language

Although English would make a bad programming language, due to its ambiguity and complexity, Ruby can feel surprisingly English-like at times. Ruby is just one of hundreds of programming languages, but it's special because it *feels* a lot like a natural language to many programmers, while having the clarity required by computers. Consider this example code:

```
10.times do print "Hello, world!" end
```

Read through this code aloud (it helps, really!). It doesn't flow quite as well as English, but the meaning should be immediately clear. It asks the computer to "10 times" "print" "Hello, world!" to the screen. It works. If you've got irb running, type in the preceding code and press Enter to see the results:

```
Hello, world!Hello, world!Hello, world!Hello, world!Hello, world!Hello, world!
Hello, world!Hello, world!Hello, world!Hello, world!
```

■**Note** Experienced programmers might wonder why there's no semicolon at the end of the previous code example. Unlike many other languages, such as Perl, PHP, C, or C++, a semicolon is not needed at the end of lines in Ruby (although it won't hurt if you do use one). This can take a little while to get used to at first, but for new programmers it makes Ruby even easier to learn.

Here's a much more complex example:

```
User.find_by_email('me@privacy.net').country = 'Belgium'
```

This code is nowhere near as obvious as the "Hello, world!" example, but you should still be able to take a good guess at what it does. First, it tells the computer you want to work with a concept called User. Next, it tries to find a user with a specified e-mail address. Last, it takes the user's country information and changes it to Belgium. Don't worry about how the data is stored for users at this point; that comes later.

This is a reasonably advanced example, but demonstrates a single concept from a potentially complex application where you can deal with different concepts such as "users." By the end of this chapter you'll see how you can create your own real-life concepts in Ruby and operate upon them in a similar way to this example. Your code can be as easy to read as English too.

Trails for the Mind

Learning can be a fun activity in its own right, but merely reading about something won't make you an expert at it. I've read a few cookbooks, but this doesn't seem to improve my cooking when I attempt it from time to time. The missing ingredient is experimentation and testing, as without these your efforts are academic, at best.

With this in mind, it's essential to get into the mood of experimenting and testing from day one of using Ruby. Throughout the book I'll ask you to try out different blocks of code and to play with them to see if you get the results you want. You'll occasionally surprise yourself, sometimes chase your code into dead ends, and often want to pull out your hair (if you have any, of course!). Whatever happens, all good programmers learn from experimentation, and you can only master a language and programming concepts by experimenting as you go along. Trust me, it's fun!

This book will lead you through a forest of code and concepts, but without testing and proving the code is correct to yourself, you can quickly become lost. Use irb and the other tools I'll cover frequently and experiment with the code as much as possible so that the knowledge will stick.

Type in the following code at your irb prompt and press Enter:

```
print "test"
```

The result is, simply:

```
test
=> nil
```

Logically, `print "test"` results in test being printed to the screen. However, the second line is the result of your code as an expression (more about these in Chapter 3). This is because almost everything in Ruby is an expression. However, `print` displays data to the screen rather than return any value as an expression, so you get `nil`. More about this in Chapter 3.

Let's try something else:

```
print "2+2 is equal to" + 2 + 2
```

This command seems logical on the surface. If `2 + 2` is equal to `4` and you're adding that to the end of `"2+2 is equal to"`, you should get `"2+2 is equal to 4"`, right? Unfortunately, you get this error instead:

```
TypeError: can't convert Fixnum into String
        from (irb):45:in `+'
        from (irb):45
        from :0
```

Ruby complains when you make an error, and here it's complaining that you can't convert a number into a string (where a "string" is a collection of text, such as this very sentence). Numbers and strings can't be mixed in this way. Deciphering the reason isn't important yet, but experiments such as this along the way will help you learn and remember more about Ruby than reading this book alone. When an error like this occurs, you can use the error message as a clue to the solution, whether you find it in this book, on the Internet, or by asking another developer.

An interim solution to the preceding problem would be to do this:

```
print "2+2 is equal to "
print 2 + 2
```

Or this:

```
print "2+2 is equal to ", 2 + 2
```

Let's try one more example. What about 10 divided by 3?

```
irb(main):002:0> 10 / 3
=> 3
```

Computers are *supposed* to be precise, but anyone with basic arithmetic skills will know that 10 divided by 3 is 3.33 recurring, rather than 3!

The reason for the curious result is that, by default, Ruby assumes a number such as 10 or 3 to be an *integer*—a whole number. Arithmetic with integers in Ruby gives integer results, so it's necessary to provide Ruby with a *floating point* number (a number with decimal places) to get a floating point answer such as 3.33. Here's an example of how to do that:

```
Irb(main):001:0> 10.0 / 3
=> 3.3333333333333
```

Unobvious outcomes such as these make testing not only a good learning tool, but an essential process in larger programs.

That's enough of the errors for now though. Let's make something useful!

Turning Ideas into Ruby Code

Part of the artistry of programming is in being able to turn your ideas into computer programs. Once you become proficient with a programming language, you can turn your ideas directly into code. However, before you can do this, you need to see how Ruby understands real-world concepts itself, and how you can relay your ideas into a form that Ruby appreciates.

How Ruby Understands Concepts with Objects and Classes

Ruby is an *object-oriented* programming language. In the simplest sense, this means that your Ruby programs can define and operate upon concepts in a real-world fashion. Your program can contain concepts such as "people," "boxes," "tickets," "maps," or any other concept you want to work with. Object-oriented languages make it easy to implement these concepts in a way that you can create *objects* based upon them. As an object-oriented language, Ruby can then act upon and understand the relationships between these concepts in any way you define.

For example, you might want to create an application that can manage the booking of tickets for sports events. The concepts involved include "events," "people," "tickets," "venues," and so forth. Ruby lets you put these concepts directly into your programs, create *object instances* of them (instances of an "event" might be the Super Bowl or the final of the 2010 World Cup), and perform operations upon and define relationships between them. With all these concepts in your program, you can quickly relate "events" to "venues" and "tickets" to "people," meaning that your code presents a logical system from the outset.

If you haven't programmed much before, the idea of taking real-life concepts and using them directly in a computer program might seem like an obvious way to make software development easier. However, object orientation is a reasonably new idea in software development (the concept was developed in the 1960s, but it only became popular in mainstream programming in the 1990s). With non–object-oriented languages, the programmer has less flexibility in handling concepts and the relationships between them and will have a lot of overhead to deal with.

The Making of a Man

Let's jump directly into some source code demonstrating a simple concept, a person:

```
class Person
  attr_accessor :name, :age, :gender
end
```

Ruby seemed a lot like English before, but it doesn't seem much like English when defining concepts. Let's go through it step by step:

```
class Person
```

This line is where you start to define the concept of a "person." When we define concepts in Ruby (or in most other object-oriented languages, for that matter) we call them *classes*. A *class* is the definition of a single type of object. Class names in Ruby always start with a capital letter, so your programs will end up with classes with names like User, Person, Place, Topic, Message, and so forth.

```
attr_accessor :name, :age, :gender
```

The preceding line provides three *attributes* for the Person class. An individual person has a name, an age, and a gender, and this line creates those attributes. attr stands for "attribute," and accessor roughly means "make these attributes accessible to be set and changed." This means that when you're working with a Person object in your code, you can change that person's name, age, and gender (or, more accurately, its name, age, and gender *attributes*).

```
end
```

The end line should be of obvious utility. It matches up with the class definition on the first line and tells Ruby that you're no longer defining the Person class.

To recap, a class defines a concept (such as a Person), and an object is a single thing based on a class (such as a "Chris" or a "Mrs. Smith").

So let's experiment with our Person class. Go to your irb prompt and type in the Person class found earlier. Your efforts should look like this:

```
irb(main):001:0> class Person
irb(main):002:1> attr_accessor :name, :age, :gender
irb(main):003:1> end
=> nil
irb(main):004:0>
```

You'll notice that the digit at the end of each irb prompt line changed when you were entering the class code. The reason for this is that when you pressed Enter for the class Person line, Ruby knew that you were now within a class structure, defining a class, rather than typing code to be processed immediately. The 1 represents that you're at a *depth* of 1 of nested concepts. If this doesn't make sense to you now, don't worry, as I'll be covering this in more detail later.

Once you've finished your class definition and Ruby has processed it, nil is returned, because defining a class results in no return value, and nil is Ruby's way of representing "nothing." As there were no errors, your Person class now exists within Ruby, so let's do something with it:

```
person_instance = Person.new
=> #<Person:0x358ea8>
```

What the first line does is create a "new" instance of the Person class, so you're creating a "new person," and assigning it to person_instance—a placeholder representing the new person, known as a *variable*. The second line is Ruby's response to creating a new person and isn't important at this stage. The 0x358ea8 bit will be different from computer to computer, and only represents an internal reference that Ruby has assigned to the new person. You don't have to take it into account at all.

Let's immediately do something with person_instance:

```
person_instance.name = "Robert"
```

In this basic example you refer to person_instance's name attribute and give it a value of "Robert". You've just given your person a name. The Person class has two other attributes: age and gender. Let's set those:

```
person_instance.age = 52
person_instance.gender = "male"
```

Simple. You've given `person_instance` a basic identity. What about printing out the person's name back to the screen?

```
puts person_instance.name
```

`Robert` appears when you press Enter. Try the same with the age and the gender.

■**Note** In previous examples, you've used `print` to put things on the screen. In the preceding example you used `puts`. The difference between `print` and `puts` is that `puts` automatically moves the output cursor to the next line, whereas `print` continues printing text onto the same line as the previous time. Generally you'll want to use `puts`, but I used `print` to make the earlier examples more intuitive to read out loud.

Basic Variables

In the previous section you created a person and assigned that person to a *variable* (computer terminology for a "placeholder") called `person_instance`.

Variables are an important part of programming, and they're easy to understand, especially if you have the barest of knowledge of algebra. Consider this:

```
x = 10
```

This code assigns the value 10 to the variable x. x now equals 10, and you can do things like this:

```
x * 2
```

Variables in Ruby can contain any concept that Ruby understands, such as numbers, text, and other data structures I'll cover throughout this book. In the previous section, `person_instance` was a variable that referred to an object instance of the `Person` class, much like x is a variable containing the number 10. More simply, consider `person_instance` as a name that refers to a particular, unique `Person` object.

When you want to store something and use it over multiple lines within a program, you'll use variables as temporary storage places for the data you're working with.

From People to Pets

Previously, you created a simple class (Person), created an object of that class, assigned it as the person_instance variable, and gave it an identity (you called it "Robert") that you queried. If these concepts seem simple to you, well done—you understand the bare basics of object orientation! If not, reread the previous section and make sure you follow along on your computer, but also read this section, as I'm going to go into a little more depth.

You started out with a Person class, but now you need something a bit more complex, so let's create some "pets" to live inside Ruby. You'll create some cats, dogs, and snakes. The first step is to define the classes. You could do something like this:

```
class Cat
  attr_accessor :name, :age, :gender, :color
end

class Dog
  attr_accessor :name, :age, :gender, :color
end

class Snake
  attr_accessor :name, :age, :gender, :color
end
```

It's just like creating the Person class, but multiplied for the three different animals. You could continue on by creating animals with code such as lassie = Dog.new or sammy = Snake.new, and setting the attributes for the pets with code such as lassie.age = 12 or sammy.color = "Green". Type in the preceding code and give it a try if you like.

However, creating the classes in this way would miss out on one of the best features of object-oriented programming: inheritance.

Inheritance allows different classes to relate to one another and group concepts by their similarities. In this case, cats, dogs, and snakes are all pets. Inheritance allows you to create a "parent" Pet class, and then let your Cat, Dog, and Snake classes *inherit* the features that all pets have.

Almost everything in real life exists in a similar structure to your classes. Cats can be pets, which are, in turn, animals; which are, in turn, living things; which are, in turn, objects that exist in the universe. A hierarchy of classes exists everywhere, and object-oriented languages let you define those relationships in code.

Note Chapter 6 features a helpful diagram showing the concept of inheritance between different forms of life such as Mammals, Plants, and so forth.

Structuring Your Pets Logically

Now that we've come up with some ideas to improve our code, let's retype it from scratch. To totally cleanse out and reset what you're working on, you can restart irb. irb doesn't remember information between the different times you use it. So restart irb (to exit irb, type **exit** and press Enter) and rewrite the class definitions like so:

```
class Pet
  attr_accessor :name, :age, :gender, :color
end

class Cat < Pet
end

class Dog < Pet
end

class Snake < Pet
end
```

■**Note** In the code listings in this chapter, any code that's within classes is indented, as with the attr_ accessor line in the preceding Pet class. This is only a matter of style, and it makes the code easier to read. When you type it into irb it's not necessary to replicate the effect. You can simply type what you see. Once you start using a text editor to write longer programs, you'll want to indent your code to make it easier to read too, but it's not important yet.

First you create the Pet class and define the name, age, gender, and color attributes available to Pet objects. Next, you define the Cat, Dog, and Snake classes that inherit from the Pet class. This means that cat, dog, and snake objects will all have the name, age, gender, and color attributes, but because the functionality of these attributes is inherited from the Pet class, the functionality doesn't have to be created specifically in each class. This makes the code easier to maintain and update if you wanted to store more information about the pets, or if you wanted to add another type of animal.

What about attributes that aren't relevant to every animal? What if you wanted to store the length of snakes, but didn't want to store the length of dogs or cats? Luckily inheritance gives you lots of benefits with no downside. You can still add class-specific code wherever you want. Reenter the Snake class like so:

```
class Snake < Pet
  attr_accessor :length
end
```

The Snake class now has a length attribute. However, this is added to the attributes Snake has inherited from Pet, so Snake has name, age, gender, color, and length attributes, whereas Cat and Dog only have the first four attributes. You can test this, like so (some output lines removed for clarity):

```
irb(main):001:0> snake = Snake.new
irb(main):002:0> snake.name = "Sammy"
irb(main):003:0> snake.length = 500
irb(main):004:0> lassie = Dog.new
irb(main):005:0> lassie.name = "Lassie"
irb(main):006:0> lassie.age = 20
irb(main):007:0> lassie.length = 10
```

```
NoMethodError: undefined method `length=' for #<Dog:0x32fddc @age=20,
@name="Lassie">
```

Here you created two dogs and a snake. You gave the snake a length of 500, before trying to give one of your dogs a length of 10 (the units aren't important). Trying to give the dog a length results in an error of undefined method 'length=' because you only gave the Snake class the length attribute.

Try playing with the other attributes and creating other "pets." Try using attributes that don't exist and see what the error messages are.

Controlling Your Pets

So far you've been creating classes and objects with various changeable attributes. Attributes are data related to individual objects. A snake can have a length, a dog can have a name, and a cat can be of a certain color. What about the *instructions* I spoke of earlier? How do you give your objects instructions to perform? You define *methods* for each class.

Methods are important in Ruby. They make objects *do* things. For example, you might want to add a bark method to your Dog class, which, if called on a Dog object, prints "Woof!" to the screen. You could write it like so:

```
class Dog < Pet
  def bark
    puts "Woof!"
  end
end
```

After entering this code, any dogs you create can now bark. Let's try it out:

```
irb(main):0> a_dog = Dog.new
irb(main):0> a_dog.bark
```

```
Woof!
```

Eureka! You'll notice that the way you make the dog bark is simply by referring to the dog (a_dog, in this case) and putting a period (".") followed by the bark method's name, whereupon your dog "barks." Let's dissect exactly what happened.

First, you added a bark method to your Dog class. The way you did this was by *defining* the method. To define a method, you use the word def followed by the name of the method you wish to define. This is what the def bark line means. It means "I'm defining the bark method within this class until I say end." The following line then simply puts the word "Woof!" on the screen, and the last line of the method ends the definition of that method. The last end ends the class definition (this is why indentation is useful, so you can see which end lines up with which definition). The Dog class then contains a new method called bark, as you used earlier.

Think about how you would create methods for the other Pet classes or the Pet class itself. Are there any methods that are generic to all pets? If so, they'd go in the Pet class. Are there methods specific to cats? They'd go in the Cat class.

Everything Is an Object

In this chapter we've looked at how Ruby can understand concepts in the form of classes and objects. We created virtual cats and dogs, gave them names, and triggered their methods (the bark method, for example). These basic concepts form the core of object-oriented programming, and you'll use them constantly throughout this book. Dogs and cats are merely an example of the flexibility object orientation offers, but the concepts we've used so far could apply to most concepts, whether we're giving a "ticket" a command to change its price or a "user" a command to change his or her password. Begin to think of the programs you want to develop in terms of their general concepts and how you can turn them into classes you can manipulate with Ruby.

Among even object-oriented programming languages, Ruby is reasonably unique in that almost *everything* in the language is an object, even the concepts relating to the language itself. Consider the following line of code:

```
puts 1 + 10
```

If you typed this into irb and pressed Enter, you'd see the number 11 in response. You've asked Ruby to print the result of 1 + 10 to the screen. It seems simple enough, but believe it or not, this simple line uses *two objects*. 1 is an object, as is 10. They're objects of class Fixnum, and this built-in class has methods already defined to perform operations upon numbers, such as addition and subtraction.

We've considered how concepts can be related to different classes. Our pets make a good example. However, even defining the concepts that programmers use to write computer programs as classes and objects makes sense. When you write a simple sum such as 2 + 2, you expect the computer to add two numbers together to make 4. In its object-oriented way, Ruby considers the two numbers in the sum (2 and 2) to be number objects. 2 + 2 is merely shorthand for asking the first number object to add the second number object to itself. In fact, the + sign is actually an addition *method*!

You can prove that everything in Ruby is an object by asking things of which class they're a member. In the pet example earlier, you could have made a_dog tell you what class it's a member of with the following code:

```
puts a_dog.class
```

```
Dog
```

class isn't a method you created yourself, such as the bark method, but one that Ruby supplies by default to all objects. This means that you can ask any object of which class it's a member by using its class method. So when you try puts a_dog.class, you get the result Dog.

What about if you ask a number what its class is? Try it out:

```
puts 2.class
```

```
Fixnum
```

The number 2 is an object of the Fixnum class. This means that all Ruby has to do is implement the logic and code for adding numbers together in the Fixnum class, much like you created the bark method for your Dog class, and then Ruby will know how to add any two numbers together! Better than that, though, is that you can then add your own methods to the Fixnum class and process numbers in any way you see fit.

Kernel Methods

Kernel is a special class (actually, a *module*—but don't worry about that till Chapter 6!) whose methods are made available in every class and scope throughout Ruby. You've used a key method provided by Kernel already.

Consider the puts method. You've been using the puts method to print data to the screen, like so:

```
puts "Hello, world!"
```

However, unlike the methods on your own classes, puts isn't prefixed by the name of a class or object upon which to complete the method. It would seem logical that the full command should be something like Screen.puts or Display.puts, as puts places text on the screen. However, in reality, puts is a method made available from the Kernel module—a special type of class packed full of standard, commonly used methods, making your code easier to read and write.

■**Note** The Kernel module in Ruby has no relationship to kernels in operating systems or the Linux kernel. As with a kernel and its operating system, the Kernel module is part of Ruby's "core," but there is no connection beyond that.

When you type puts "Hello, world!", Ruby can tell that there's no class or object involved, so it looks through its default, predefined classes and modules for a method called puts, finds it in the Kernel module, and does its thing. When you see lines of code where there's no obvious class or object involved, take time to consider where the method call is going.

To guarantee that you're using the Kernel puts method, you can refer to it explicitly, although this is rarely done with puts:

```
Kernel.puts "Hello, world!"
```

Passing Data to Methods

Asking a dog to bark or asking an object its class is simple with Ruby. You simply refer to a class or object and follow it with a period and the name of the method, such as a_dog.bark, 2.class, or Dog.new. However, there are situations where you don't want to issue a simple command, but you want to associate some data with it too. The `puts` method is one example. Let's refer to it explicitly:

```
Kernel.puts "Hello, world!"
```

```
Hello, world!
```

With the `puts` method, you need to *pass* the data you want to print to the screen, which is why `"Hello, world!"` is placed after the method name.

Although you can follow a method call directly with the data associated with that method, this is only a shortcut, and becomes cumbersome when you want to tie a number of methods together (as you'll do later in this chapter). To make the relationship between the method and the data entirely clear, the usual practice is to surround the data in brackets (parentheses) after the method call, like so:

```
Kernel.puts("Hello, world!")
```

This means exactly the same thing, and works in exactly the same way, as `puts "Hello, world!"`, which is only different because of two shortcuts:

1. `puts` is a method of the `Kernel` module that is included and searched by default, so usually you won't need to use `Kernel.puts` to refer to it.

2. `puts` takes only one *argument* (that is, a discrete item of data being *passed* to a method—also often called a *parameter*) and is rarely followed by other methods or logic, so parentheses are not strictly necessary. Often, however, parentheses are required, as in many situations omitting them leaves the code vague and imprecise.

Therefore, all these lines of code are functionally equivalent:

```
Kernel.puts("Hello, world!")
Kernel.puts "Hello, world!"
puts("Hello, world!")
puts "Hello, world!"
```

In each case, the data `"Hello, world!"` is being passed to `Kernel.puts`, but the style used to do so is different. As you work through some of the examples in this chapter, try experimenting with different ways of printing the data to the screen by using parentheses and/or using the `Kernel` module directly.

Using the Methods of the String Class

You've played with dogs and numbers, but lines of text (*strings*) can be interesting to play with too:

```
puts "This is a test".length
```

14

You've asked the string "This is a test", which is an object of the String class (confirm this with "This is a test".class), to print its length onto the screen using the length method. The length method is available on all strings, so you can replace "This is a test" with any text you want and you'll get a valid answer.

Asking a string for its length isn't the only thing you can do. Consider this:

```
puts "This is a test".upcase
```

THIS IS A TEST

The String class has many methods, which I'll cover in the next chapter, but experiment with some of the following: capitalize, downcase, chop, hash, next, reverse, sum, or swapcase. Table 2-1 demonstrates some of the methods available to strings.

Table 2-1. *The Results of Using Different Methods on the String* "Test"

Expression	Output
"Test" + "Test"	TestTest
"Test".capitalize	Test
"Test".downcase	test
"Test".chop	Tes
"Test".hash	-98625764
"Test".next	Tesu
"Test".reverse	tseT
"Test".sum	416
"Test".swapcase	tEST
"Test".upcase	TEST
"Test".upcase.reverse	TSET
"Test".upcase.reverse.next	TSEU

Some of the examples in Table 2-1 are obvious, such as changing the case of the text or reversing it, but the last two examples are of particular interest. Rather than processing one method against the text, you process two or three in succession. The reason you can do this is that methods will return the original object after it's been adjusted by the method, so you have a fresh String object upon which to process another method. "Test".upcase results in the string TEST being returned, upon which the reverse method is called, resulting in TSET, upon which the next method is called, which "increments" the last character, resulting in TSEU.

In the next chapter we'll be looking at strings more deeply, but the concept of chaining methods together to get quick results is an important one in Ruby. You can read the preceding examples aloud and they make sense. Not many other programming languages can give you that level of instant familiarity!

Using Ruby Without Object Orientation

So far in this chapter we've looked at several reasonably complex concepts. With some programming languages, object orientation is almost an afterthought, and beginners' books for these languages don't cover object orientation until readers understand the basics of the language (particularly with Perl and PHP, popular Web development languages). However, this doesn't work for Ruby because Ruby is a *pure* object-oriented language, and you can gain significant advantages over users of other languages by understanding these concepts right away.

Ruby has its roots in other languages though. Ruby has been heavily influenced by languages such as Perl and C, both usually considered procedural non–object-oriented languages (although Perl has some object-oriented features). As such, even though almost everything in Ruby is an object, you can use Ruby in the same way as a non–object-oriented language if you like, even if it's less than ideal.

A common demonstration program for a language such as Perl or C involves creating a *subroutine* (essentially a sort of method that has no associated object or class) and calling it, much like you called the bark method on your Dog objects. Here's a similar program, written in Ruby:

```
def dog_barking
  puts "Woof!"
end

dog_barking
```

This looks a lot different from your previous experiments. Rather than defining a method within a class, you're defining it on its own. The method is very general and doesn't appear to be tied to any particular class or object. Instead, it stands alone. In a language such as Perl or C, this method would be called a *procedure, function*, or *sub-function*, as *method* is a word generally used to refer to an action that can take place upon an object.

After the method is defined—it's still called a method, even though other languages would consider it to be a subroutine or function—it becomes available to use immediately without using a class or object name, like how `puts` is available without referring directly to the `Kernel` module. You call the method simply by using its name on its own, as on the last line of the preceding example. Typing in the preceding code into irb results in the `dog_barking` method being called, giving the following result:

```
Woof!
```

Like `Kernel.puts`, however, the `dog_barking` method does end up under a class. In Ruby, almost everything's an object, and that includes the magical space where classless methods end up! Understanding exactly where isn't important at this stage, but it's always useful to bear Ruby's object-oriented ways in mind even when you're trying not to use object-oriented techniques!

■**Note** If you want to experiment, you'll find `dog_barking` at `Object.dog_barking`.

Summary

In this chapter you've learned about several important concepts not only for programming in Ruby, but for programming in general. If these concepts seem logical to you already, you're well on the way to being a solid Ruby developer. Let's recap the main concepts before moving on:

- *Class*: A class is a definition of a concept in an object-oriented language such as Ruby. We created classes called `Pet`, `Dog`, `Cat`, `Snake`, and `Person`. Classes can inherit features from other classes, but still have unique features of their own.

- *Object*: An object is a single instance of a class (or, as can be the case, an instance of a class itself). An object of class `Person` is a single person. An object of class `Dog` is a single dog. Think of objects as real-life objects. A class is the classification, whereas an object is the actual object or "thing" itself.

- *Object orientation*: Object orientation is the approach of using classes and objects to model real-world concepts in a programming language, such as Ruby.

- *Variable*: In Ruby, a variable is a placeholder for a single object, which may be a number, string, list, or an instance of a class that you have defined, such as, in this chapter, a `Pet`.

- *Method*: A method represents a set of code (containing multiple commands and statements) within a class and/or an object. For example, our `Dog` class objects had a `bark` method that printed "Woof!" to the screen. Methods can also be directly linked to classes, as with `fred = Person.new`, where `new` is a method that creates a new object based upon the `Person` class. Methods can also accept data—known as arguments or parameters—included in parentheses after the method name, as with `puts("Test")`.

- *Arguments/parameters*: The data passed to methods in parentheses (or, as in some cases, following the method name without parentheses, as in `puts "Test"`).

- *Kernel*: Some methods don't require a class name to be usable, such as `puts`. These are usually built-in, common methods that don't have an obvious connection to any classes. Many of these methods are included in Ruby's `Kernel` module, a module that provides functions that work from anywhere within Ruby code without being explicitly referred to.

- *Experimentation*: One of the most fulfilling things about programming is that you can turn your dreams into reality. The amount of skill you need varies with your dreams, but generally if you want to develop a certain type of application or service, you can give it a try. Most software comes from necessity or a dream, so keeping your eyes and ears open for things you might want to develop is important. It's even more important when you first get practical knowledge of a new language, as you are while reading this book. If an idea crosses your mind, break it down into the smallest components that you can represent as Ruby classes and see if you can put together the building blocks with the Ruby you've learned so far. Your programming skills can only improve with practice.

In the next few chapters we're going to move through looking at the topics briefly passed over in this chapter in more detail.

■ ■ ■

## CHAPTER 3

Ruby's Building Blocks: Data, Expressions, and Flow Control

Computer programs spend nearly all their time manipulating data. We type in words, phrases, and numbers; listen to music; and watch videos, while the computer performs calculations, makes decisions, and relays information to us. To write computer programs, it's essential to understand the basics of data and how to manipulate it. Naturally, Ruby keeps it simple.

This chapter looks at some of the basic forms of data that Ruby supports, along with how to work with and manipulate them. The topics covered in this chapter will provide the majority of the foundation of knowledge on which your future Ruby programs will be developed.

Numbers and Expressions

At the lowest level, computers are entirely number-based, with everything represented by streams of numbers. A language such as Ruby insulates you from the internal workings of the computer, and numbers in Ruby are used for mostly the same things that you use numbers for in real life, such as counting, logical comparisons, arithmetic, and so on. Let's look at how you can use numbers in these ways in Ruby and how to *do* something with them.

Basic Expressions

When programming, an *expression* is a combination of numbers, operators (such as + or -), and variables that, when understood by the computer, result in an answer of some form. For example, these are all expressions:

```
5
1 + 2
"a" + "b" + "c"
100 - 5 * (2 - 1)
x + y
```

The top four expressions all work right away with irb (try them out now!) and get the answers you'd expect from such basic operations (1 + 2 results in 3, "a" + "b" + "c" results in abc, and so on). Brackets (parentheses) work the same way as with regular arithmetic. Anything inside brackets is calculated first (or, more technically, given higher *precedence*).

■**Note** You can work through all the topics in this chapter using irb, the immediate Ruby interpreter. If you get stuck at any point, simply leave irb by typing **exit** at any time, and start irb again as demonstrated in Chapter 1.

Expressions are used regularly throughout all computer programs, and not just with numbers. However, an understanding of how expressions and operations work with numbers immediately translates into a basic knowledge of how they work with text, lists, and other items too.

Variables

In Chapter 2 we ran through a multitude of concepts, including variables. Variables are placeholders or references for objects, including numbers, text, or any objects you've chosen to create. For example:

```
x = 10
puts x
```

10

Here you *assign* the numeric value of 10 to a variable called x. You can name variables however you like, with only a few limitations. Variable names must be a single unit (no spaces!); must start with either a letter or an underscore; must contain only letters, numbers, or underscores; and are case sensitive. Table 3-1 demonstrates variable names that are valid and invalid.

Table 3-1. *Valid and Invalid Variable Names*

Variable Name	Valid Or Invalid?
x	Valid
y2	Valid
_x	Valid
7x	Invalid (starts with a digit)
this_is_a_test	Valid
this is a test	Invalid (not a single word)
this'is@a'test!	Invalid (contains invalid characters: ', @, and !)
this-is-a-test	Invalid (looks like subtraction)

Variables are important because they allow you to write and use programs that work upon varying data. For example, consider a small program that has the sole job of subtracting two numbers:

```
x = 100
y = 10
puts x - y
```

```
90
```

If the code was written simply as puts 100 - 10, you'd get the same result, but it's not as flexible. Using variables, you can get the values for x and y from the user, a file, or some other source. The only logic is the subtraction.

As variables are placeholders for values and data, they can also be assigned the results of an expression (such as x = 2 - 1) and be used in expressions themselves (such as x - y + 2). Here's a more complex example:

```
x = 50
y = x * 100
x += y
puts x
```

```
5050
```

Step through the example line by line. First you set x to equal 50. You then set y to the value of x * 100 (50 * 100 or 5000). Next you add y to x before printing the result, 5050, to the screen. It makes sense, but the third line isn't obvious at first. Adding y to x looks more logical if you say x = x + y rather than x += y. This is another Ruby shortcut. Because the act of a variable performing an operation upon itself is so common in programming, you can shorten x = x + y to x += y. The same works for other operations too, such as multiplication and division, with x *= y and x /= y being valid too. A common way to increase a variable's value by 1 is x += 1, which is shorthand for x = x + 1.

Comparison Operators and Expressions

A program without logic is merely a calculator. Computers don't just perform single operations on data. They also use logic to determine the correct course of action. A basic form of logic is to use *comparison operators* within expressions to make decisions.

Consider a system that demands the user be over a certain age:

```
age = 10
puts "You're too young to use this system" if age < 18
```

If you try this code, you'll see "You're too young to use this system" because you print the text to the screen only when the value of age is under 18. Let's make something more complex:

```
age = 24
puts "You're a teenager" if age > 12 && age < 20
```

This code results in no response because someone aged 24 is not a teenager. However, if age were to be between 13 or 19, the message would appear. This is a case where two small expressions (age > 12 and age < 20) are joined together with &&, meaning "and." Reading expressions such as this aloud is the best way to understand them. Print the text if age is larger than 12 *and* age is smaller than 20.

To get the opposite effect you can use the word unless:

```
age = 24
puts "You're NOT a teenager" unless age > 12 && age < 20
```

This time you'd get the message that you're not a teenager with your age of 24. This is because unless means the opposite of if. You display the message *unless* the age is in the teenage range.

■Note Another cute technique offered by Ruby is the `between?` method that returns `true` or `false` if the object is between or equal to two supplied values. For example: `age.between?(12, 20)`

You can also test for equality:

```
age = 24
puts "You're 24!" if age == 24
```

Notice that the "equals" concept is represented in two different ways, given two different meanings. On the first line you're saying that age equals 24, meaning you want age to contain the number 24. However, on the second line, you're asking if age "is equal to" 24. In the first case you're *demanding*, and in the second case you're *asking*. This difference results in different operators to prevent confusion. Therefore, the equality operator is == and the assignment operator is just =. A full list of comparison operators for numbers is shown in Table 3-2.

Table 3-2. *A Full List of Number Comparison Operators in Ruby*

Comparison	Meaning
x > y	Greater than.
x < y	Less than.
x == y	Equal to.
x >= y	Greater than *or* equal to.
x <= y	Less than *or* equal to.
x <=> y	Comparison. Returns 0 if x and y are equal, 1 if x is higher, -1 if y is higher.
x != y	Not equal to.

As you saw earlier, it's possible to group multiple expressions into a single expression, as with the following:

```
puts "You're NOT a teenager" unless age > 12 && age < 20
```

&& is used to enforce that *both* age > 12 and age < 20 are true. However, you can also check whether one *or* the other is true by using ||, as so:

```
puts "You're either very young or very old" if age > 80 || age < 10
```

Chaining together multiple comparisons is also possible with a clever use of parentheses:

```
puts "You're a working age man" if gender == "male" && (age >= 18 && age <= 65)
```

This example checks if gender is equal to "male" and if age is between 18 and 65.

Looping Through Numbers with Blocks and Iterators

Nearly all programs require certain operations to be repeated over and over again to accomplish a result. It'd be extremely inefficient (and inflexible!) to write a program to count through numbers like this:

```
x = 1
puts x
x += 1
puts x
x += 1
puts x
...
...
```

What you want to do in these situations is to implement a *loop*, a mechanism that makes the program use the same code over and over. Here's a basic way to implement a loop:

```
5.times do puts "Test" end
```

```
Test
Test
Test
Test
Test
```

First, you take the number 5. Next, you call the times method, common to all numbers in Ruby. Rather than pass data to this method, you pass it more code: the code between do and end. The times method then uses the code five times in succession, producing the preceding five lines of output.

Another way to write this is with curly brackets instead of do and end. Although do and end are encouraged for multiple-line code blocks, curly brackets make the code easier to read on a single line. Therefore, this code works in exactly the same way:

```
5.times { puts "Test" }
```

You'll be using this style for single lines of code from here on, but will be using do and end for longer blocks of code. This is a good habit to pick up, as it's the style nearly all professional Ruby developers follow (although there are always exceptions to the rule).

In Ruby, one mechanism to create a loop is called an *iterator*. An iterator is something that progresses through a list of items one by one. In this case it loops, or *iterates*, through five steps, resulting in five lines of "Test." Other iterators are available for numbers, such as the following:

```
1.upto(5) { ...code to loop here... }
10.downto(5) { ...code to loop here... }
0.step(50, 5) { ...code to loop here... }
```

The first example counts from 1 "up to" 5. The second example counts from 10 "down to" 5. The last example counts up from 0 to 50 in steps of 5, because you're using the step method on the number 0.

What isn't obvious is how to get hold of the number being iterated upon at each step of the way so that you can do something with it in the looped code. What if you wanted to print out the current iteration number? How could you develop a counting program with these iterators? Simply, you *pass* the state of the iteration to the looped code as a parameter, like so:

```
1.upto(5) { |number| puts number }
```

```
1
2
3
4
5
```

The easiest way to understand it is that the code between do and end is the code being looped upon. At the start of that code, the number from the "1 up to 5" count is sent down a chute into a variable called number. You can visualize the "chute" with the bars surrounding number. This is how parameters are passed into blocks of code that don't have specific names (unlike methods on classes and objects, which have names). In the preceding line of code, you ask Ruby to count from 1 to 5. It starts with 1, which is passed into the code block and displayed with `puts`. This is repeated for the numbers 2 through 5, resulting in the output shown.

Note that Ruby (and irb) doesn't (usually, there are exceptions!) care whether you spread your code over multiple lines or not. For example, this code works in exactly the same way as that in the previous example:

```
1.upto(5) do |number|
  puts number
end
```

Floating Point Numbers

In Chapter 2 you ran a test where you divided 10 by 3, like so:

```
puts 10 / 3
```

```
3
```

The result is 3, although the actual answer should be 3.33 recurring. The reason for this is that, by default, Ruby considers any numbers without a floating point (also known as a decimal point) to be an integer—a whole number. When you say 10 / 3, you're asking Ruby to divide two *integers*, and Ruby gives you an integer as a result. Let's refine the code slightly:

```
puts 10.0 / 3.0
```

```
3.33333333333
```

Now you get the desired result. Ruby is now working with number objects of the `Float` class, and returns a `Float`, giving you the level of precision you'd expect.

There might be situations where you don't have control over the incoming numbers, but you still want to have them treated as floats. Consider a situation where a user enters two numbers to be divided, and the numbers require a precise answer:

```
x = 10
y = 3
puts x / y
```

```
3
```

Both input numbers are integers, so the result is an integer, as before. Luckily, integers have a special method that converts them to floats on the fly. You'd simply rewrite the code like this:

```
x = 10
y = 3
puts x.to_f / y.to_f
```

```
3.33333333333
```

In this situation, when you reach the division, both x and y are converted to their floating point number equivalents using the Integer class's to_f method. Similarly, floating point numbers can be converted back in the other direction, to integers, using to_i:

```
puts 5.7.to_i
```

```
5
```

We'll look at this technique used in other ways in the section "Converting Between Classes," later in this chapter.

Constants

Earlier you looked at separating data and logic with variables, concluding that there's rarely a need for data to be a direct part of a computer program. This is true in most cases, but consider some values that never change—the value of pi, for example. These nonchanging values are called *constants*, and can also be represented in Ruby by a variable name beginning with a capital letter:

```
Pi = 3.141592
```

If you enter the preceding line into irb and then try to change the value of Pi, it'll let you do it, but you'll get a warning:

```
Pi = 3.141592
Pi = 500
```

```
(irb): warning: already initialized constant Pi
```

Ruby gives you full control over the value of constants, but the warning message gives out a clear message. In the future, Ruby might enforce tighter control over constants, so respect this style of usage and try not to reassign constants mid-program.

The eagle-eyed reader might recall that in Chapter 2 you referred to classes by names such as Dog and Cat, beginning with capital letters. This is because once a class is defined, it's a constant part of the program and therefore acts as a constant too.

Text and Strings

If numbers are the most basic type of data that a computer can process, text is the next rung on the data ladder. Text is used everywhere, especially in communicating with users. In this section you'll find out how to manipulate text to your heart's content.

String Literals

We've used strings already, in some of our earlier code examples, like so:

```
puts "Hello, world!"
```

A string is a collection of textual characters (including digits, letters, whitespace, and symbols) of any length. All strings in Ruby are objects of the String class, as you can discover by calling a string's class method and printing the result:

```
puts "Hello, world!".class
```

```
String
```

When a string is embedded directly into code, using quotation marks as earlier, the construction is called a *string literal*. This differs from a string whose data comes from a remote source, such as a user typing in text, a file, or the Internet. Any text that's pre-embedded within a program is a string literal.

Like numbers, strings can be included in operations, added to, and compared against. You can also assign strings to variables:

```
x = "Test"
y = "String"
puts "Success!" if x + y == "TestString"
```

```
Success!
```

There are several other ways of including a string literal within a program. For example, you might want to include multiple lines of text. Using quotation marks is only viable for a single line, but if you want to span multiple lines, try this:

```
x = %q{This is a test
of the multi
line capabilities}
```

In this example, the quotation marks have been replaced with %q{ and }. You don't have to use curly brackets, though. You can use < and >, (and), or simply two other delimiters of your choice, such as ! and !. This code works in exactly the same way:

```
x = %q!This is a test
of the multi
line capabilities!
```

However, the important thing to remember is that if you use exclamation marks as your delimiter, then any exclamation marks in the text you're quoting will cause this technique to go awry. If delimiter characters are present in your string, your string literal will end early and Ruby will consider your remaining text erroneous. Choose your delimiters wisely!

Another way to build up a long string literal is by using a *here document*, a concept found in many other programming languages. It works in a similar way to the previous example, except that the delimiter can be many characters long. Here's an example:

```
x = <<END_MY_STRING_PLEASE
This is the string
And a second line
END_MY_STRING_PLEASE
```

In this case, << marks the start of the string literal and is followed by a delimiter of your choice. The string literal then starts from the next new line and finishes when the delimiter is repeated again on a line on its own. Using this method means that you're unlikely to run into any problems with choosing a bad delimiter, as long as you're creative!

String Expressions

Using the + symbol *concatenates* (joins together) the two strings "Test" and "String" to produce "TestString", meaning that the following comparison is true, which then writes "Success!" to the screen:

```
puts "Success!" if "Test" + "String" == "TestString"
```

Likewise, you can *multiply* strings. For example, let's say you want to replicate a string five times, like so:

```
puts "abc" * 5
```

```
abcabcabcabcabc
```

You can also perform "greater than" and "less than" comparisons:

```
puts "x" > "y"
```

```
false
```

```
puts "y" > "x"
```

```
true
```

■**Note** "x" > "y" and "y" > "x" are expressions that, by using a comparison operator, result in true or false outcomes.

In this situation, Ruby compares the numbers that represent the characters in the string. As was mentioned previously, characters are stored as numbers inside your computer's memory. Every letter and symbol has a value, called an *ASCII value*. These values aren't particularly important, but they do mean you can do comparisons between letters, and even longer strings, in this way. If you're interested to learn what value a particular character has, find out like so:

```
puts ?x
```

```
120
```

```
puts ?A
```

```
65
```

A question mark followed by a character returns an integer matching the position of that character in the *ASCII table*, a standard for representing characters as values.

You can achieve the inverse by using the String class's chr method. For example:

```
puts ?x
puts 120.chr
```

```
120
x
```

■Note Explaining more about the ASCII character set here is beyond the scope of this book, but there are many resources on the Web if you wish to learn more. One excellent resource is http://en.wikipedia.org/wiki/ASCII.

Interpolation

In previous examples, you've printed the results of your code to the screen with the puts method. However, your results have had little explanation. If a random user came along and used your code, it wouldn't be obvious what's going on, as they won't be interested in reading your source code. Therefore, it's essential to provide user-friendly output from your programs. You'll go back to using numbers for this example:

```
x = 10
y = 20
puts "#{x} + #{y} = #{x + y}"
```

```
10 + 20 = 30
```

It's kindergarten-level math, but the result highlights an interesting capability. You can embed expressions (and even logic) directly into strings. This process is called *interpolation*. In this situation, interpolation refers to the process of inserting the result of an expression into a string literal. The way to interpolate within a string is to place the expression within #{ and } symbols. An even more basic example demonstrates:

```
puts "100 * 5 = #{100 * 5}"
```

```
100 * 5 = 500
```

The #{100 * 5} section interpolates the result of 100 * 5 (500) into the string at that position, resulting in the output shown. Examine this code:

```
puts "#{x} + #{y} = #{x + y}"
```

You first interpolate the value of x, then the value of y, and then the value of x added to y. You surround each section with the relevant mathematical symbols, and hey presto, you get a complete mathematical equation:

```
10 + 20 = 30
```

You can interpolate other strings too:

```
x = "cat"
puts "The #{x} in the hat"
```

```
The cat in the hat
```

Or if you want to get clever:

```
puts "It's a #{"bad " * 5}world"
```

```
It's a bad bad bad bad bad world
```

In this instance you interpolate a repetition of a string, `"bad "`, five times. It's certainly a lot quicker than typing it!

Interpolation also works within strings used in assignments:

```
my_string = "It's a #{"bad " * 5}world"
puts my_string
```

```
It's a bad bad bad bad bad world
```

It's worth noting that you could achieve the same results as the preceding results by placing the expressions outside the strings, without using interpolation. For example:

```
x = 10
y = 20
puts x.to_s + " + " + y.to_s + " = " + (x + y).to_s
puts "#{x} + #{y} = #{x + y}"
```

The two `puts` lines result in the same output. The first uses string concatenation (+) to join several different strings together. The numbers in x and y are converted to strings with their to_s method. However, the second `puts` line uses interpolation, which doesn't require the numbers to be converted to strings explicitly.

String Methods

We've looked at using strings in expressions, but you can do a lot more with strings than adding them together or multiplying them. As you experimented in Chapter 2, you can use a number of different methods on a string. Table 3-3 provides a recap of the string methods you looked at in Chapter 2.

Table 3-3. *The Results of Using Different Methods on the String* "Test"

Expression	Output
"Test" + "Test"	TestTest
"Test".capitalize	Test
"Test".downcase	test
"Test".chop	Tes
"Test".hash	-98625764
"Test".next	Tesu
"Test".reverse	tseT
"Test".sum	416
"Test".swapcase	tEST
"Test".upcase	TEST
"Test".upcase.reverse	TSET
"Test".upcase.reverse.next	TSEU

In each example in Table 3-3, you're using a method that the string offers, whether it's concatenation, conversion to upper case, reversal, or merely incrementing the last letter. You can *chain* methods together, as in the final example of the table. First, you create the "Test" string literal, then you convert it to upper case, returning TEST, then you reverse *that*, returning TSET, and then you increment the last letter of *that*, returning TSEU.

Another method you used in Chapter 2 was length, like so:

```
puts "This is a test".length
```

```
14
```

These methods are useful, but they don't let you do anything particularly impressive with your strings. Let's move on to playing directly with the text itself.

Regular Expressions and String Manipulation

When working with strings at an advanced level, it becomes necessary to learn about *regular expressions*. A regular expression is, essentially, a search query, and not to be confused with the expressions we've discussed already in this chapter. If you type **ruby** into your favorite search engine, you'd expect information about Ruby to appear. Likewise, if your regular expression is ruby and you run that query against, say, a long string, you'd expect any matches to be returned. A regular expression, therefore, is a string that describes a pattern for matching elements in other strings.

■**Note** This section provides only a brief introduction to regular expressions. Regular expressions are a major branch of computer science, and many books and Web sites are dedicated to their use. Ruby supports the majority of standard regular expression syntax, so non–Ruby-specific knowledge about regular expressions obtained from elsewhere can still prove useful in Ruby.

Substitutions

One thing you'll often want to do is substitute something within a string for something else. Take this example:

```
puts "foobar".sub('bar', 'foo')
```

```
foofoo
```

In this example you use a method on the string called sub, which substitutes the first instance of the first parameter 'bar' with the second parameter 'foo', resulting in foofoo. sub only does one substitution at a time, on the first instance of the text to match, whereas gsub does multiple substitutions at once, as this example demonstrates:

```
puts "this is a test".gsub('i', '')
```

```
ths s a test
```

Here you've substituted all occurrences of the letter 'i' with an empty string. What about more complex patterns? Simply matching the letter 'i' is not a true example of a regular expression. For example, let's say you want to replace the first two characters of a string with 'Hello':

```
x = "This is a test"
puts x.sub(/^../, 'Hello')
```

```
Hellois is a test
```

In this case, you make a single substitution with sub. The first parameter given to sub isn't a string but a regular expression—forward slashes are used to start and end a regular expression. Within the regular expression is ^... The ^ is an *anchor*, meaning the regular expression will match from the beginning of any lines within the string. The two periods each represent "any character." In all, /^../ means "any two characters immediately after the start of a line." Therefore, Th of "This is a test" gets replaced with Hello.

Likewise, if you want to change the last two letters, you can use a different anchor:

```
x = "This is a test"
puts x.sub(/..$/, 'Hello')
```

```
This is a teHello
```

This time the regular expression matches the two characters that are anchored to the end of any lines within the string.

■Note If you want to anchor to the absolute start or end of a string, you can use \A and \Z respectively, whereas ^ and $ anchor to the starts and ends of lines.

Iteration with a Regular Expression

Previously, you used iterators to move through sets of numbers, counting from 1 to 10 for example. What if you want to iterate through a string and have access to each section of it separately? scan is the iterator method you require:

```
"xyz".scan(/./) { |letter| puts letter }
```

```
x
y
z
```

scan lives up to its name. It scans through the string looking for anything that matches the regular expression passed to it. In this case, you've supplied a regular expression that looks for a single character at a time. That's why you get x, y, and z separately in the output. Each letter is fed to the block, assigned to letter, and printed to the screen. Try this more elaborate example:

```
"This is a test".scan(/../) { |x| puts x }
```

```
Th
is
 i
s
a
te
st
```

This time you're scanning for two characters at a time. Easy! Scanning for all characters results in some weird output, though, with all the spaces mixed in. Let's adjust our regular expression to match only letters and digits, like so:

```
"This is a test".scan(/\w\w/) { |x| puts x }
```

```
Th
is
is
te
st
```

Within regular expressions there are special characters that are denoted with a backslash, and they have special meanings. \w means "any alphanumeric character or an underscore." There are many others, as illustrated in Table 3-4.

Table 3-4. *Basic Special Characters and Symbols Within Regular Expressions*

Character	Meaning
^	Anchor for the beginning of a line
$	Anchor for the end of a line
\A	Anchor for the start of a string
\Z	Anchor for the end of a string
.	Any character
\w	Any letter, digit, or underscore
\W	Anything that \w doesn't match
\d	Any digit
\D	Anything that \d doesn't match (non-digits)
\s	Whitespace (spaces, tabs, newlines, and so on)
\S	Non-whitespace (any visible character)

Using the knowledge from Table 3-4, you can easily extract numbers from a string:

```
"The car costs $1000 and the cat costs $10".scan(/\d+/) do |x|
  puts x
end
```

```
1000
10
```

You've just gotten Ruby to extract meaning from some arbitrary English text! The scan method was used as before, but you've given it a regular expression that uses \d to match any digit, and the + that follows \d makes \d match as many digits in a row as possible. This means it matches both 1000 and 10, rather than just each individual digit at a time. To prove it, try this:

```
"The car costs $1000 and the cat costs $10".scan(/\d/) do |x|
  puts x
end
```

So + after a character in a regular expression means *match one or more* of that type of character. There are other types of modifiers, and these are shown in Table 3-5.

Table 3-5. *Regular Expression Character and Sub-Expression Modifiers*

Modifier	Description
*	Match zero or more occurrences of the preceding character, and match as many as possible.
+	Match one or more occurrences of the preceding character, and match as many as possible.
*?	Match zero or more occurrences of the preceding character, and match as *few* as possible.
+?	Match one or more occurrences of the preceding character, and match as *few* as possible.
?	Match either one or none of the preceding character.
{x}	Match x occurrences of the preceding character.
{x,y}	Match at least x occurrences and at most y occurrences.

The last important aspect of regular expressions you need to understand at this stage is *character classes*. These allow you to match against a specific set of characters. For example, you can scan through all the vowels in a string:

```
"This is a test".scan(/[aeiou]/) { |x| puts x }
```

[aeiou] means "match any of a, e, i, o, or u." You can also specify ranges of characters inside the square brackets, like so:

```
"This is a test".scan(/[a-m]/) { |x| puts x }
```

```
h
i
i
a
e
```

This scan matches all lowercase letters between a and m.

Regular expressions can be complex and confusing, and entire books larger than this one have been dedicated to them. Most coders only need to understand the basics, as the more-advanced techniques will become apparent with time, but they're a powerful tool when you experiment with, and master, them.

You'll be using, and expanding upon, all the techniques covered in this section in code examples throughout the rest of the book.

Matching

Making substitutions and extracting certain text from strings is useful, but sometimes you merely want to check whether a certain string matches against the pattern of your choice. You might want to establish quickly if a string contains any vowels:

```
puts "String has vowels" if "This is a test" =~ /[aeiou]/
```

In this example, =~ is another form of operator, a *matching* operator. If the string matches the regular expression following the operator, then the expression is true. You can, of course, do the opposite:

```
puts "String contains no digits" unless "This is a test" =~ /[0-9]/
```

This time you're saying that *unless* the range of digits from 0 to 9 matches against the test string, tell the user that there are no digits in the string.

It's also possible to use a method called match, provided by the String class. Whereas =~ returns true or false depending on whether the regular expression matches the string, match provides a lot more power. Here's a basic example:

```
puts "String has vowels" if "This is a test".match(/[aeiou]/)
```

It looks almost the same as the earlier example. However, because `match` doesn't require a regular expression as an argument, it converts any string supplied into a regular expression, so this works in the same way:

```
puts "String has vowels" if "This is a test".match("[aeiou]")
```

This functionality is useful if the regular expression is supplied by a user, or loaded in from a file or other external source rather than hard coded.

In regular expressions, if you surround a section of the expression with parentheses (and), the data matched by that section of the regular expression is made available separately from the rest. `match` lets you access this data:

```
x = "This is a test".match(/(\w+) (\w+)/)
puts x[0]
puts x[1]
puts x[2]
```

```
This is
This
is
```

`match` returns a `MatchData` object that can be accessed like an array. The first element contains the data matched by the entire regular expression. However, each successive element contains that which was matched by each referenced section of the regular expression. In this example, the first (`\w+`) matched `This` and the second (`\w+`) matched `is`.

Note Matching can be more complex than this, but I'll be covering more-advanced uses in the next chapter when you put together your first full Ruby program.

Arrays and Lists

So far in this chapter, you've created single instances of number and string objects and manipulated them. After a while, it becomes necessary to create collections of these objects and to work with them as a list. In Ruby, you can represent ordered collections of objects using *arrays*.

Basic Arrays

Here's a basic array:

```
x = [1, 2, 3, 4]
```

This array has four elements. Each element is an integer, and is separated by commas from its neighboring elements. All the elements are contained within square brackets.

Elements can be accessed by their index (their position within the array). To access a particular element, an array, or a variable containing an array, is followed by the index contained within square brackets. This is called an *element reference*. For example:

```
x = [1, 2, 3, 4]
puts x[2]
```

```
3
```

As with most programming languages, the indexing for Ruby's arrays starts from 0, so the first element of the array is element 0, and the second element of the array is element 1, and so on. In our example, this means x[2] is addressing what we'd call the third element of the array, which in this case is an object representing the number 3. To change an element, you can simply assign it a new value or manipulate it as you've manipulated numbers and strings earlier in this chapter:

```
x[2] += 1
puts x[2]
```

```
4
```

Or:

```
x[2] = "Fish" * 3
puts x[2]
```

```
FishFishFish
```

Arrays don't need to be set up with predefined entries or have elements allocated manually. You can create an empty array like so:

```
x = []
```

The array is empty, and trying to address, say, x[5] results in nothing being returned. You can add things to the end of the array by *pushing* data into it, like so:

```
x = []
x << "Word"
```

After this, the array contains a single element: a string saying "Word". With arrays, << is the operator for pushing an item onto the end of an array. You can also use the push method, which is equivalent.

You can also remove entries from an array one by one. Traditionally, arrays act as a "first in, first out" system where items can be pushed onto the end but also *popped* from the end (*popping* is the process of retrieving items from the end of the array and removing them at the same time).

```
x = []
x << "Word"
x << "Play"
x << "Fun"
puts x.pop
puts x.pop
puts x.length
```

```
Fun
Play
1
```

You push "Word", "Play", and "Fun" into the array held in x, and then display the first "popped" element on screen. Elements are popped from the end of the array, so Fun comes out first. Next comes Play. For good measure, you then print out the length of the array at that point, using the aptly named length method (size works too and gives exactly the same result), which is 1 because "Word" is still present in the array.

Another useful feature is that if an array is full of strings, you can join all the elements together into one big string by calling the join method on the array:

```
x = ["Word", "Play", "Fun"]
puts x.join
```

```
WordPlayFun
```

The `join` method can take an optional parameter that's placed between each element in the resulting string:

```
x = ["Word", "Play", "Fun"]
puts x.join(', ')
```

```
Word, Play, Fun
```

This time you join the array elements together, but between each set of elements you place a comma and a space. This results in cleaner output.

Splitting Strings into Arrays

In the section relating to strings, you used `scan` to iterate through the contents of the string looking for characters that matched patterns you expressed as regular expressions. With `scan` you used a block of code that accepted each set of characters and displayed them on the screen. However, if you use scan *without* a block of code, it returns an array of all the matching parts of the string, like so:

```
puts "This is a test".scan(/\w/).join(',')
```

```
T,h,i,s,i,s,a,t,e,s,t
```

First you define a string literal, then you scan over it for alphanumeric characters (using `/\w/`), and finally you join the elements of the returned array together with commas.

What if you don't want to scan for particular characters, but instead want to *split* a string into multiple pieces? You can use the `split` method, and tell it to split a string into an array of strings on the periods, like so:

```
puts "Short sentence. Another. No more.".split(/\./).inspect
```

```
["Short sentence", " Another", " No more"]
```

There are a couple of important points here. First, if you'd used . in the regular expression rather than \., you'd be splitting on every character rather than on full stops because . represents "any character" in a regular expression. Therefore, you have to *escape* it by prefixing it with a backslash (*escaping* is the process of specifically denoting a character to make its meaning clear). Second, rather than joining and printing out the sentences, you're using the inspect method to get a tidier result.

The inspect method is common to almost all built-in classes in Ruby and it gives you a textual representation of the object. For example, the preceding output shows the result array in the same way that you might create an array yourself. inspect is incredibly useful when experimenting and debugging!

split is also happy splitting on newlines, or multiple characters at once, to get a cleaner result:

```
puts "Words   with   lots of    spaces".split(/\s+/).inspect
```

```
["Words", "with", "lots", "of", "spaces"]
```

With Ruby and some regular expressions, you're never far from solving any text-processing problem!

Array Iteration

Iterating through arrays is simple and uses the each method. The each method goes through each element of the array and passes it as a parameter to the code block you supply. For example:

```
[1, "test", 2, 3, 4].each { |element| puts element.to_s + "X" }
```

```
1X
testX
2X
3X
4X
```

Although each iterates through elements of an array, you can also convert an array on the fly using the `collect` method:

```
[1, 2, 3, 4].collect { |element| element * 2 }
```

```
[2, 4, 6, 8]
```

`collect` iterates through an array element by element, and assigns to that element the result of any expression within the code block. In this example you multiply the value of the element by 2.

Programmers who have come from less dynamic and possibly non–object-oriented languages might see these techniques as being quite modern. It's possible to do things "the old-fashioned way" with Ruby if required:

```
a = [1, "test", 2, 3, 4]
i = 0

while (i < a.length)
  puts a[i].to_s + "X"
  i += 1
end
```

This works in a similar way to the each example from earlier, but loops through the array in a way more familiar to traditional programmers (from languages such as C or BASIC). However, it should be immediately apparent to anyone why iterators, code blocks, and methods such as each and `collect` are preferable with Ruby, as they make the code significantly easier to read and understand.

Other Array Methods

Arrays have a lot of interesting methods, some of which I'll cover in this section.

Array Addition and Concatenation

If you have two arrays, you can quickly combine their results into one:

```
x = [1, 2, 3]
y = ["a", "b", "c"]
z = x + y
puts z.inspect
```

```
[1, 2, 3, "a", "b", "c"]
```

Array Subtraction and Difference

You can also compare two arrays by subtracting one against the other. This technique removes any elements from the main array that are in both arrays:

```
x = [1, 2, 3, 4, 5]
y = [1, 2, 3]
z = x - y
puts z.inspect
```

```
[4, 5]
```

Check for an Empty Array

If you're about to iterate over an array, you might want to check if it has any items yet. You could do this by checking if `array.size` or `array.length` is larger than 0, but a more popular shorthand is to use `empty?`:

```
x = []
puts "x is empty" if x.empty?
```

```
x is empty
```

Check an Array for a Certain Item

The `include?` method returns `true` if the supplied parameter is in the array, and `false` otherwise:

```
x = [1, 2, 3]
puts x.include?("x")
puts x.include?(3)
```

```
false
true
```

Access the First and Last Elements of the Array

Accessing the first and last elements of an array is easy with the `first` and `last` methods:

```
x = [1, 2, 3]
puts x.first
puts x.last
```

```
1
3
```

If you pass a numeric parameter to `first` or `last`, you'll get that number of items from the start or the end of the array:

```
x = [1, 2, 3]
puts x.first(2).join("-")
```

```
1-2
```

Reverse the Order of the Array's Elements

Like a string, an array can be reversed:

```
x = [1, 2, 3]
puts x.reverse.inspect
```

```
[3, 2, 1]
```

Hashes

Arrays are collections of objects, and so are hashes. However, hashes have a different storage format and way to define each object within the collection. Rather than having an assigned position in a list, objects within a hash are given a *key* that points to them. It's more like a dictionary than a list, as there's no guaranteed order, but just simple links between keys and values. Here's a basic hash with two entries:

```
dictionary = { 'cat' => 'feline animal', 'dog' => 'canine animal' }
```

The variable storing the hash is `dictionary`, and it contains two entries, as you can prove:

```
puts dictionary.size
```

```
2
```

One entry has a key of `cat` and a value of `feline animal`, while the other has a key of `dog` and a value of `canine animal`. Like arrays, you use square brackets to reference the element you wish to retrieve. For example:

```
puts dictionary['cat']
```

```
feline animal
```

As you can see, a hash can be viewed as an array that has names for elements instead of position numbers. You can even change values in the same way as an array:

```
dictionary['cat'] = "fluffy animal"
puts dictionary['cat']
```

```
fluffy animal
```

■Note It won't be immediately useful to you, but it's worth noting that both keys and values can be objects of any type. Therefore, it's possible to use an array (or even another hash) as a key. This might come in useful when you're dealing with more complex data structures in future.

Basic Hash Methods

As with arrays, hashes have many useful methods that you'll look at in this section.

Iterating Through Hash Elements

With arrays, you can use the each method to iterate through each element of the array. You can do the same with hashes. However, as hashes use keys for each element, there's no guaranteed order of response:

```
x = { "a" => 1, "b" => 2 }
x.each { |key, value| puts "#{key} equals #{value}" }
```

```
a equals 1
b equals 2
```

The each iterator method for a hash passes two parameters into the code block: first, a key, and second, the value associated with that key. In this example, you assign them to variables called key and value and use string interpolation to display their contents on screen.

Retrieving Keys

Sometimes you might not be interested in the values within a hash, but want to get a feel for what the hash contains. A great way to do this is to look at the keys. Ruby gives you an easy way to see the keys in any hash immediately, using the keys method:

```
x = { "a" => 1, "b" => 2, "c" => 3 }
puts x.keys.inspect
```

```
["a", "b", "c"]
```

keys returns an array of all the keys in the hash, and if you're ever in the mood, values will return an array of all the values in the hash too. Generally, however, you'll look up values based on a key.

Deleting Hash Elements

Deleting hash elements is easy with the delete method. All you do is pass in a key as a parameter and the element is removed:

```
x = { "a" => 1, "b" => 2 }
x.delete("a")
puts x.inspect
```

```
{"b"=>2}
```

Deleting Hash Elements Conditionally

Let's say you want to delete any hash elements whose value is below a certain figure:

```
x = { "a" => 100, "b" => 20 }
x.delete_if { |key, value| value < 25 }
puts x.inspect
```

```
{"a"=>100}
```

Hashes Within Hashes

It's possible to have hashes (or, indeed, any sort of object) within hashes, and even arrays within hashes, within hashes! Because everything is an object and hashes and arrays can contain any other objects, there exists the ability to create giant tree structures with hashes and arrays. Here's a demonstration:

```
people = {
  'fred' => {
    'name' => 'Fred Elliott',
    'age' => 63,
    'gender' => 'male',
    'favorite painters' => ['Monet', 'Constable', 'Da Vinci']
  },
  'janet' => {
    'name' => 'Janet S Porter',
```

```
    'age' => 55,
    'gender' => 'female'
  }
}

puts people['fred']['age']
puts people['janet']['gender']
puts people['janet'].inspect
```

```
63
female
{"name"=>"Janet S Porter", "gender"=>"female", "age"=>55}
```

Although the structure of the hash looks a little confusing at first, it becomes reasonably easy when you break it down into sections. The 'fred' and 'janet' sections are simple hashes of their own, but they're wrapped up into another giant hash assigned to people. In the code that queries the giant hash, you simply chain the lookups on top of each other, as with puts people['fred']['age']. First it gets people['fred'], which returns Fred's hash, and then you request ['age'] from that, yielding the result of 63.

Even the array embedded within Fred's hash is easy to access:

```
puts people['fred']['favorite painters'].length
puts people['fred']['favorite painters'].join(", ")
```

```
3
Monet, Constable, Da Vinci
```

These techniques are used more, and explained in more depth, in following chapters.

Flow Control

In this chapter you've used comparisons, together with if and unless, to perform different operations based upon the circumstances. if and unless work well on single lines of code, but when combined with large sections of code become even more powerful. In this section you'll be looking at how Ruby lets you control the *flow* of your programs with these and other constructs.

if and unless

The first use of if within this chapter used this demonstration:

```
age = 10
puts "You're too young to use this system" if age < 18
```

If the value of age is under 18, the string is printed to the screen. The following code is equivalent:

```
age = 10
if age < 18
  puts "You're too young to use this system"
end
```

It looks similar, but the code to be executed if the expression is true is contained between the if expression and end, instead of the if expression being added onto the end of a single line of code. This construction makes it possible to put any number of lines of code in between the if statement and the end line:

```
age = 10
if age < 18
  puts "You're too young to use this system"
  puts "So we're going to exit your program now"
  exit
end
```

It's worth noting that unless can work in exactly the same way because unless is just the opposite of if:

```
age = 10
unless age >= 18
  puts "You're too young to use this system"
  puts "So we're going to exit your program now"
  exit
end
```

It's possible to nest logic too, as in this example:

```
age = 19
if age < 21
  puts "You can't drink in most of the United States"
  if age >= 18
    puts "But you can in the United Kingdom!"
  end
end
```

if and unless also supply the else condition, used to delimit lines of code that you want to be executed if the main expression is false:

```
age = 10
if age < 18
  puts "You're too young to use this system"
else
  puts "You can use this system"
end
```

?:, The Ternary Operator

The ternary operator makes it possible for an expression to contain a mini if/else statement. It's construction that's entirely optional to use, and some developers are oblivious to its existence. However, because it can be useful to produce more compact code, it's worth learning early. Let's dive in with an example:

```
age = 10
type = age < 18 ? "child" : "adult"
puts "You are a " + type
```

The second line contains the ternary operator. It starts by assigning the result of an expression to the variable, type. The expression is age < 18 ? "child" : "adult". The structure is as follows:

```
<condition> ? <result if condition is true> : <result if condition is false>
```

In our example, age < 18 returns as true, so the first result, "child", is returned and assigned to type. However, if age < 18 were to be false, "adult" would be returned.

Consider an alternative:

```
age = 10
type = 'child' if age < 18
type = 'adult' unless age < 18
puts "You are a " + type
```

The double comparison makes it harder to read. Another alternative is to use the multiline if/else option:

```
age = 10
if age < 18
  type = 'child'
else
```

```
  type = 'adult'
end
puts "You are a " + type
```

The ternary operator shows its immediate benefit in its conciseness, and as it can be used to build expressions on a single line, you can use it easily in calls to methods or within other expressions where `if` statements would be invalid. Consider this even simpler version of the first example from this section:

```
age = 10
puts "You are a " + (age < 18 ? "child" : "adult")
```

elsif and case

Sometimes it's desirable to make several comparisons with the same variable at the same time. You could do this with the `if` statement, as covered previously:

```
fruit = "orange"
color = "orange" if fruit == "orange"
color = "green" if fruit == "apple"
color = "yellow" if fruit == "banana"
```

If you want to use `else` to assign something different if `fruit` is not equal to either orange, apple, or banana, it will quickly get messy, as you'd need to create an `if` block to check for the presence of any of these words, and then perform the same comparisons as earlier. An alternative is to use `elsif`, meaning "else if":

```
fruit = "orange"
if fruit == "orange"
  color = "orange"
elsif fruit == "apple"
  color = "green"
elsif fruit == "banana"
  color = "yellow"
else
  color = "unknown"
end
```

`elsif` blocks act somewhat like `else` blocks, except that you can specify a whole new comparison expression to be performed, and if none of those match, you can specify a regular `else` block to be executed.

A variant of this technique is to use a case block. Our preceding example, with a case block, becomes the following:

```ruby
fruit = "orange"
case fruit
  when "orange"
    color = "orange"
  when "apple"
    color = "green"
  when "banana"
    color = "yellow"
  else
    color = "unknown"
end
```

This code is similar to the if block, except that the syntax is a lot cleaner. A case block works by processing an expression first, and then by finding a contained when block that matches the result of that expression. If no matching when block is found, then the else block within the case block is executed instead.

case has another trick up its sleeve. As all Ruby expressions return a result, you can make the previous example even shorter:

```ruby
fruit = "orange"
color = case fruit
  when "orange"
    "orange"
  when "apple"
    "green"
  when "banana"
    "yellow"
  else
    "unknown"
end
```

In this example, you use a case block, but you assign the result of whichever inner block is executed directly to color.

while and until

In previous sections, you've performed loops using iterator methods, like so:

```ruby
1.upto(5) { |number| puts number }
```

```
1
2
3
4
5
```

However, it's possible to loop code in other ways. while and until allow you to loop code based on the result of a comparison made on each loop:

```
x = 1
while x < 100
  puts x
  x = x * 2
end
```

```
1
2
4
8
16
32
64
```

In this example, you have a while block that denotes a section of code that is to be repeated over and over while the expression x < 100 is satisfied. Therefore, x is doubled loop after loop and printed to the screen. Once x is 100 or over, the loop ends.

until provides the opposite functionality, looping until a certain condition is met:

```
x = 1
until x > 99
  puts x
  x = x * 2
end
```

It's also possible to use while and until in a single line setting, as with if and unless:

```
i = 1
i = i * 2 until i > 1000
puts i
```

```
1024
```

The value of i is doubled over and over until the result is over 1,000, at which point the loop ends.

Code Blocks

Code blocks have been used in several code examples in this chapter. For example:

```
x = [1, 2, 3]
x.each { |y| puts y }
```

```
1
2
3
```

The each method accepts a single code block as a parameter. The code block is defined within the { and } symbols, or within do and end delimiters:

```
x = [1, 2, 3]
x.each do |y|
  puts y
end
```

The code between { and } or do and end is a code block, essentially an anonymous, nameless method or function. This code is passed to the each method that then runs the code block for each element of the array.

You can write methods of your own to handle code blocks. For example:

```
def each_vowel(&code_block)
  %w{a e i o u}.each { |vowel| code_block.call(vowel) }
end

each_vowel { |vowel| puts vowel }
```

```
a
e
i
o
u
```

each_vowel accepts a code block, as designated by the ampersand (&) before the variable name code_block in the method definition. It then iterates over each vowel in the literal array %w{a e i o u} and uses the call method on code_block to execute the code block once for each vowel, passing in the vowel variable as a parameter each time.

■Note Code blocks passed in this way result in objects that have many methods of their own, such as call. Remember, almost everything in Ruby is an object!

An alternate technique is to use the yield method, which automatically detects any passed code block and passes control to it:

```ruby
def each_vowel
  %w{a e i o u}.each { |vowel| yield vowel }
end

each_vowel { |vowel| puts vowel }
```

This example is functionally equivalent to the last, although it's less obvious what it does because you see no code block being accepted in the function definition. Which technique you choose to use is up to you.

■Note Only one code block can be passed at any one time. It's not possible to accept two or more code blocks as parameters to a method. However, code blocks may accept none, one, or more parameters themselves.

It's also possible to store code blocks within variables, using the lambda method:

```ruby
print_parameter_to_screen = lambda { |x| puts x }
print_parameter_to_screen.call(100)
```

```
100
```

As with accepting a code block into a method, you use the `lambda` object's `call` method to execute it, as well as to pass any parameters in.

■**Note** The term *lambda* is used due to its popularity elsewhere and in other programming languages. You can certainly continue to call them code blocks, and they are sometimes referred to as `Procs`.

Other Useful Building Blocks

So far in this chapter, we've covered the primary built-in data classes of numbers, strings, arrays, and hashes. These few types of objects can get you a long way and will be used in all your programs. You'll be looking at objects more in depth in Chapter 6, but before you get that far there are a few other important points you need to look at first.

Dates and Times

A concept that's useful to represent within many computer programs is time, in the form of dates and times. Ruby provides a class called `Time` to handle these concepts.

Internally, `Time` stores times as a number of microseconds since the Unix time epoch: January 1st, 1970 00:00:00 Greenwich Mean Time (GMT)/Coordinated Universal Time (UTC). This makes it easy to compare times using the standard comparison operators, such as ‹ and ›.

Let's look at how to use the `Time` class:

```
puts Time.now
```

```
Tue Mar 27 00:00:00 +0100 2007
```

`Time.now` creates an instance of class `Time` that's set to the current time. However, because you're trying to print it to the screen, it's converted into the preceding string.

You can manipulate time objects by adding and subtracting numbers of seconds to them. For example:

```
puts Time.now
puts Time.now - 10
puts Time.now + 86400
```

```
Tue Mar 27 00:00:00 +0100 2007
Tue Mar 26 23:59:50 +0100 2007
Tue Mar 28 00:00:00 +0100 2007
```

In the first example you print the current time, and then the current time minus 10 seconds, and then the current time with 86,400 seconds (exactly one day) added on. Because times are so easy to manipulate, some developers extend the Fixnum class with some helper methods to make manipulating dates easier:

```
class Fixnum
  def seconds
    self
  end
  def minutes
    self * 60
  end
  def hours
    self * 60 * 60
  end
  def days
    self * 60 * 60 * 24
  end
end

puts Time.now
puts Time.now + 10.minutes
puts Time.now + 16.hours
puts Time.now - 7.days
```

```
Tue Mar 27 00:00:00 +0100 2007
Tue Mar 27 00:10:00 +0100 2007
Tue Mar 27 16:00:00 +0100 2007
Mon Mar 19 23:00:00 +0000 2007
```

Don't worry if this code seems confusing and unfamiliar, as we'll be covering this type of technique more in the following chapters. Do note, however, the style used in the final `puts` statements. It's easy to manipulate dates with these helpers!

The `Time` class also allows you to create `Time` objects based on arbitrary dates:

```
Time.local(year, month, day, hour, min, sec, msec)
```

The preceding code creates a `Time` object based on the current (local) time zone. All arguments from `month` onward are optional and take default values of 1 or 0. You can specify months numerically (between 1 and 12), or as three-letter abbreviations of their English names.

```
Time.gm(year, month, day, hour, min, sec, msec)
```

The preceding code creates a `Time` object based on GMT/UTC. Argument requirements are the same as for `Time.local`.

```
Time.utc(year, month, day, hour, min, sec, msec)
```

The preceding code is identical to `Time.gm`, although some might prefer this method's name.

You can also convert `Time` objects to an integer representing the number of seconds since the Unix time epoch:

```
Time.gm(2007, 05).to_i
```

```
1177977600
```

Likewise, you can convert epoch times back into `Time` objects. This technique can be useful if you want to store times and dates in a file or a format where only a single integer is needed rather than an entire `Time` object:

```
epoch_time = Time.gm(2007, 5).to_i
t = Time.at(epoch_time)
puts t.year, t.month, t.day
```

```
2007
5
1
```

As well as demonstrating the conversions of times between `Time` objects and epoch times, this code shows that `Time` objects also have methods that can be used to retrieve certain sections of a date/time. A list of these methods is shown in Table 3-6.

Table 3-6. *Time Object Methods Used to Access Date/Time Attributes*

Method	What the Method Returns
hour	A number representing the hour in 24-hour format (21 for 9 p.m., for example).
min	The number of minutes past the hour.
sec	The number of seconds past the minute.
usec	The number of microseconds past the second (there are 1,000,000 microseconds per second).
day	The number of the day in the month.
mday	Synonym for the day method, considered to be "month" day.
wday	The number of the day in terms of the week (Sunday is 0, Saturday is 6).
yday	The number of the day in terms of the year.
month	The number of the month of the date (11 for November, for example).
year	The year associated with the date.
zone	Returns the name of the time zone associated with the time.
utc?	Returns `true` or `false` depending on if the time/date is in the UTC/GMT time zone or not.
gmt?	Synonym for the `utc?` method for those who prefer to use the term GMT.

Note that these methods are for retrieving attributes from a date or time, and cannot be used to set them. If you want to change elements of a date or time, you'll either need to add or subtract seconds, or construct a new `Time` object using `Time.gm` or `Time.local`.

■**Note** In Chapter 16 you'll look at a Ruby library called *Chronic* that lets you specify dates and times in a natural, English language style and have them converted to valid `Time` objects.

Large Numbers

A common story that's told about the invention of the game of chess revolves around large numbers. A powerful king demanded a game he could play in his spare time, and a poor mathematician devised the game of chess for him. The king loved the game and offered the mathematician anything he would like as a reward. The mathematician said that he'd like rice, distributed on his chessboard. He wanted one grain on the first square, two on the second square, four on the third square, and so on, double the amount from square to square, until the board was full. The king thought the mathematician to be a fool, as he saw how few grains it took to fill the first row of the board.

Let's create a simulation of this situation with Ruby using an iterator and some interpolation:

```
rice_on_square = 1
64.times do |square|
  puts "On square #{square + 1} are #{rice_on_square} grain(s)"
  rice_on_square *= 2
end
```

You get the following results:

```
On square 1 are 1 grain(s)
On square 2 are 2 grain(s)
On square 3 are 4 grain(s)
On square 4 are 8 grain(s)
On square 5 are 16 grain(s)
On square 6 are 32 grain(s)
On square 7 are 64 grain(s)
On square 8 are 128 grain(s)
[Results for squares 9 through 61 trimmed for brevity..]
On square 62 are 2305843009213693952 grain(s)
On square 63 are 4611686018427387904 grain(s)
On square 64 are 9223372036854775808 grain(s)
```

By square 64, you're up to placing many trillions of grains of rice on each square! The story ends with the king realizing his position and unable to fulfill his promise. However, it proves that Ruby is able to deal with extremely large numbers, and unlike many other programming languages, there are no inconvenient limits.

Other languages often have limitations on the size of numbers that can be represented. Commonly this is 32 binary bits, resulting in a limit on values to roughly 4.2 billion in languages that enforce 32-bit integers. Most operating systems and computer architectures also have similar limitations. Ruby, on the other hand, seamlessly converts between numbers that the computer can handle natively (that is, with ease) and those that require more work. It does this with different classes, one called Fixnum that represents easily managed smaller numbers, and another, aptly called Bignum, that represents "big" numbers Ruby needs to manage internally. On most systems, the boundary is the number 1,073,741,823—you can find it by experimenting in irb:

```
puts 1073741823.class
```

```
Fixnum
```

```
puts 1073741824.class
```

```
Bignum
```

If you don't get exactly the same results, don't worry. Ruby will handle Bignums and Fixnums for you, and you can perform arithmetic and other operations without any problems. Results might vary depending on your system's architecture, but as these changes are handled entirely by Ruby, there's no need to worry.

Ranges

Sometimes it's useful to be able to store the concept of a list, instead of its actual contents. For example, if you want to represent all the letters between A and Z, you could begin to create an array, like so:

```
x = ['A', 'B', 'C', 'D', 'E' .. and so on.. ]
```

It'd be nice, though, merely to store the concept of "everything between A and Z." With a *range*, you can do that. A range is represented in this way:

```
('A'..'Z')
```

On its own, it's not much use, but the Range class offers a simple way to convert a range into an array with to_a. This one-line example demonstrates:

```
('A'..'Z').to_a.each { |letter| print letter }
```

It's compact, but it does the job. It converts the range 'A' to 'Z' into an array with 26 elements, each one containing a letter of the alphabet. It then iterates over each element using each, which you first used in the previous section on arrays, and passes the value into letter, which is then printed to the screen.

Note As you've used print, rather than puts, the letters are printed one after another on the same line, whereas puts starts a new line every time it's used.

It might also be useful to test if something is included in the set of objects specified by the range. For example, with your ('A'..'Z') range, you can check to see if R is within the range, using the include method, like so:

```
print "R is within A to Z!" if ('A'..'Z').include?('R')
```

```
R is within A to Z!
```

Being a lowercase letter, however, "r" is not:

```
print "R is within A to Z!" if ('A'..'Z').include?('r')
```

```
=> nil
```

You can also use ranges as array indices to select multiple elements at the same time:

```
a = [2, 4, 6, 8, 10, 12]
puts a[1..3].inspect
```

```
[4, 6, 8]
```

Similarly, you can use them to set multiple elements at the same time:

```
a[1..3] = ["a", "b", "c"]
puts a.inspect
```

```
[2, "a", "b", "c", 10, 12]
```

You can use ranges with objects belonging to many different classes, including ones you create yourself.

Symbols

Among mainstream languages, *symbols* are reasonably unique to Ruby (although LISP and Erlang do have similar concepts). They're powerful and are used by most professional Ruby developers, so they're worth learning about, although they tend to confuse most new users. Let's jump straight into an illustrative example:

```ruby
current_situation = :good
puts "Everything is fine" if current_situation == :good
puts "PANIC!" if current_situation == :bad
```

```
Everything is fine
```

In this example, :good and :bad are symbols. Symbols don't contain values or objects, like variables do. Instead, they're used as a consistent name within code. For example, in the preceding code you could easily replace the symbols with strings, like so:

```ruby
current_situation = "good"
puts "Everything is fine" if current_situation == "good"
puts "PANIC!" if current_situation == "bad"
```

This gives the same result, but isn't as efficient. In this example, every mention of "good" and "bad" creates a new object stored separately in memory, whereas symbols are single reference values that are only initialized once. In the first code example, only :good and :bad exist, whereas in the second example you end up with the full strings of "good", "good", and "bad" taking up memory.

Symbols also result in cleaner code in many situations. Often you'll use symbols to give method parameters a name. Having varying data as strings and fixed information as symbols results in easier-to-read code.

You might want to consider symbols to be literal constants that have no value, but whose name is the most important factor. If you assign the :good symbol to a variable, and compare that variable with :good in future, you'll get a match. This makes symbols useful in situations where you don't necessarily want to store an actual value, but a concept or an option.

Symbols are particularly useful when creating hashes and you want to have a distinction between keys and values. For example:

```ruby
s = { :key => 'value' }
```

This technique can also be useful when there's a specification or consistency in which key names to use:

```
person1 = { :name => "Fred", :age => 20, :gender => :male }
person2 = { :name => "Laura", :age => 23, :gender => :female }
```

Many methods provided by Ruby classes use this style to pass information into that method (and often for return values). You'll see examples of this construction throughout this book.

Converting Between Classes

Numbers, strings, symbols, and other types of data are just objects belonging to various classes. Numbers belong to Fixnum, Bignum, Float, and/or Integer classes. Strings are objects of the String class, symbols are objects of the Symbol class, and so on.

In most cases, you can convert objects between the different classes, so a number can become a string and a string can become a number. Consider the following:

```
puts "12" + "10"
puts 12 + 10
```

```
1210
22
```

The first line joins two strings, which happen to contain representations of numbers, together, resulting in 1210. The second line adds two numbers together, resulting in 22.

However, converting these objects to representations in different classes is possible:

```
puts "12".to_i + "10".to_i
puts 12.to_s + 10.to_s
```

```
22
1210
```

The tables have been turned with the to_ methods. The String class provides the to_i and to_f methods to convert a string to an object of class Integer or Float respectively. The String class also offers to_sym, which converts a string into a symbol. Symbols provide the inverse, with a to_s method to convert them into strings.

Likewise, the number classes support to_s to convert themselves into textual representations, as well as to_i and to_f to convert to and between integers and floats.

Summary

In this chapter, you've looked at the key building blocks of all computer programs—data, expressions, and logic—and discovered how to implement them with Ruby. The topics in this chapter provide a critical foundation for every other chapter in this book, as almost every future line of your Ruby code will contain an expression, an iterator, or some sort of logic.

■**Note** It's important to remember that due to the depth of Ruby, I haven't tried to cover every single combination of classes and methods here. There's more than one way to do anything in Ruby, and we've looked at the easiest routes first, before moving on to more advanced techniques later in the book.

You have not yet exhausted the different types of data within Ruby. Objects and classes, as covered in Chapter 2, are actually types of data too, although they might appear not to be. In Chapter 6 you'll directly manipulate objects and classes in a similar way to how you've manipulated the numbers and strings in this chapter, and the bigger picture will become clear.

Before moving on to Chapter 4, where you'll develop a full, but basic, Ruby program, let's reflect on what you've covered so far:

- *Variables*: We already covered these in Chapter 2, but extended our knowledge of them in this chapter. They're placeholders that can hold an object, from numbers, to text, to arrays, to objects of your own creation.

- *Operator*: Something that's used in an expression to manipulate objects such as + (plus), - (minus), * (multiply), and / (divide). You can also use operators to do comparisons, such as with <, >, and &&.

- *Integer*: A whole number, such as 5 or 923737.

- *Float*: A number with a decimal portion, such as 1.0 or 3.141592.

- *Character*: A single letter, digit, unit of space, or typographic symbol.

- *String*: A collection of characters such as "Hello, world!" or "Ruby is cool."

- *Constant*: A variable with a fixed value. Constant variable names begin with a capital letter.

- *Iterator*: A special method such as `each`, `upto`, or `times` that steps through a list element by element. This process is called iteration, and `each`, `upto`, and `times` are *iterator methods*.

- *Interpolation*: The mixing of expressions into strings.

- *Array*: A collection of objects or values with a defined, regular order.

- *Hash*: A collection of objects or values associated with keys. A key can be used to find its respective value inside a hash, but items inside a hash have no specific order. It's a lookup table, much like the index of a book or a dictionary.

- *Regular expression*: A way to describe patterns in text that can be matched and compared against.

- *Flow control*: The process of managing which sections of code to execute based on certain conditions and states.

- *Code block*: A section of code, often used as an argument to an iterator method, that has no discrete name and that is not a method itself, but that can be called and handled by a method that receives it as an argument. Code blocks can also be stored in variables as objects of the `Proc` class.

- *Range*: The representation for an entire range of values between a start and an end point.

- *Symbol*: A Ruby symbol is a unique reference. Symbols don't contain values, as variables do, but can be used to maintain a consistent reference within code. They can be considered constants without values.

Now it's time to put together some of these basic elements and develop a fully working program in Chapter 4.

CHAPTER 4

■■■

Developing a Basic Ruby Application

Up to this point we've focused on covering the basics of the Ruby language and looking at how it works at the ground level. In this chapter we'll move into the world of real software development and develop a full, though basic, Ruby application with a basic set of features. Once we've developed and tested the basic application, we'll look at different ways to extend it to become more useful. On our way we'll cover some new facets of development that haven't been mentioned so far in this book.

First, we're going to look at the basics of source code organization before moving on to actual programming.

Working with Source Code Files

So far in this book we've focused on using the irb immediate Ruby prompt to learn about the language. However, for developing anything you wish to reuse over and over, it's essential to store the source code in a file that can be stored on disk (or sent over the Internet, kept on CD, and so forth).

The mechanism by which you create and manipulate source code files on your system varies by operating system and personal preference. On Windows, you might be familiar with the included Notepad software for creating and editing text files. At a Linux prompt, you might be using vi, Emacs, or pico/nano. Mac users have TextEdit at their disposal. Whatever you use, you need to be able to create new files and save them as plain text so that Ruby can use them properly. In the next few sections, you're going to look at some specific tools available on each platform that tie in well with Ruby development.

Creating a Test File

The first step to developing a Ruby application is to get familiar with your text editor. Here's some guidance for each major platform.

If you're already familiar with text editors and how they relate to writing and saving source code, skip down to the section entitled "The Test Source Code File."

Windows

If you followed the instructions in Chapter 1 for downloading and installing Ruby, you'll have two text editors called SciTE and FreeRIDE in the Ruby program group in your "Start" menu. SciTE is a generic source code editing tool, whereas FreeRIDE is a Ruby-specific source code editor, written in Ruby itself. SciTE is a little faster, but FreeRIDE is more than fast enough for general development work and has better integration with Ruby.

Once you load an editor, you're presented with a blank document where you can begin to type Ruby source code (on FreeRIDE you need to use the "File" menu to create a new document). By using the "File" menu, you can also save your source code to the hard drive, as you'll do in the next section. With FreeRIDE, it's also possible to organize multiple files into a single *project*.

Mac OS X

Mac OS X has a number of text editors available. TextMate by MacroMates (`http://www.macromates.com/`), as shown in Figure 4-1, tends to be the most respected in the Ruby community, but it's not free and costs approximately $50. Xcode, included with the OS X Development Tools, is also a viable alternative, but requires that you know how to install and use the development tools (these come on your OS X installation disc). Xcode can also feel quite slow, depending on the specification of your Mac.

Included with OS X for free, however, is TextEdit. You can load TextEdit by going to your `Applications` folder and double-clicking the TextEdit icon. In its default mode, TextEdit isn't a plain text editor, but if you go to the "Format" menu and select "Make Plain Text," you'll be taken to a plain text editing mode that's suitable for editing Ruby source code.

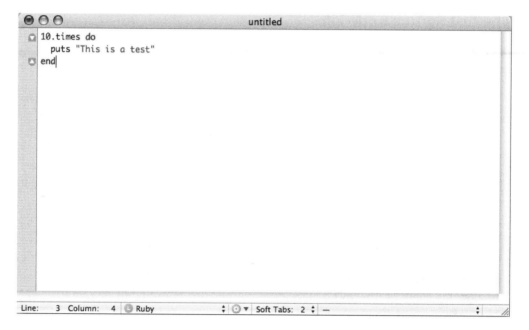

Figure 4-1. *Using TextMate*

At this point you can simply type or paste Ruby code and use the "File" ➤ "Save" menu option to save your text to a location on your drive. It would probably be good to create a folder called ruby within your home folder (the folder on the left that has your username in it) and save your initial Ruby source code there, as this is what the instructions assume in the next section.

Linux

Linux distributions often come with varying text editors, but there will be at least one available. If you're working entirely from the shell or terminal, you might be familiar with vi, Emacs, pico, or nano, and all of these are suitable for editing Ruby source code. If you're using Linux with a graphical interface, you might have Kate (KDE Advanced Text Editor) and/or gedit (GNOME Editor) available. All the preceding are great text and source code editors.

You could also download and install FreeRIDE, a cross-platform source code editor that's specifically designed for Ruby developers. It allows you to run your code with a single click directly from the editor (if you're using the X graphical user interface), and colors in your code in a way that reflects its syntax, which makes it easier to read. You can learn more about FreeRIDE at http://freeride.rubyforge.org/.

At this stage it would be a good idea to create a folder in your home directory called ruby, so that you can save your Ruby code there and have it in an easily remembered place.

The Test Source Code File

Once you've got an environment where you can edit and save text files, enter the following code:

```
x = 2
print "This application is running okay if 2 + 2 = #{x + x}"
```

■**Note** If this code looks like nonsense to you, you've skipped too many chapters. Head back to Chapter 3! This chapter requires full knowledge of everything covered in Chapter 3.

Save the code with a filename of a.rb in a folder or directory of your choice. It's advisable that you create a folder called ruby located somewhere that's easy to find. On Windows this might be directly off of your C drive, and on OS X or Linux this could be a folder located in your home directory.

■**Note** RB is the de facto standard file extension for Ruby files, much like PHP is standard for PHP, TXT is common for text files, and JPG is standard for JPEG images.

Now you're ready to run the code.

Running Your Source Code

Once you've created the basic Ruby source code file, a.rb, you need to get Ruby to execute it. As always, the process by which to do this varies by operating system. Read the particular following section that matches your operating system. If your operating system isn't listed, the OS X and Linux instructions are most likely to match those for your platform.

Whenever this book asks you to "run" your program, this is what you'll be doing each time.

■**Note** Even though you're going to be developing an application in this chapter, there are still times when you'll want to use irb to follow along with the tests or basic theory work throughout the chapter. Use your judgment to jump between these two methods of development. irb is extremely useful for testing small concepts and short blocks of code without the overhead of jumping back and forth between a text editor and the Ruby interpreter.

Windows

If you're using the SciTE or FreeRIDE programs that came with the Ruby installer for Windows, you can run Ruby programs directly from them (see Figure 4-2). In both programs you can press the F5 function key to run your Ruby code. Alternatively you can use the menus ("Tools" ➤ "Go" in SciTe, and "Run" ➤ "Run" in FreeRIDE). However, before you do this, it's important to make sure you have saved your Ruby code. If not, the results might be unpredictable (running old code from a prior save, for example) or you'll be prompted to save your work.

If running the a.rb code gives a satisfactory output in the output view pane (to the right on SciTE, and at the bottom on FreeRIDE), you're ready to move on to the section, "Our Application: A Text Analyzer."

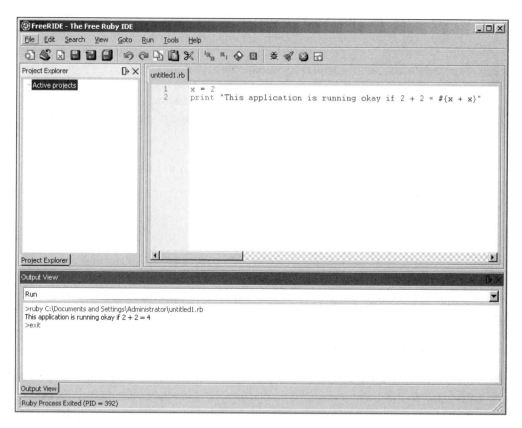

Figure 4-2. *Running code in FreeRIDE on Microsoft Windows (notice the output in the bottom pane)*

Alternatively, you might prefer to run Ruby from the command prompt. To do this, load up the command prompt ("Start" menu ➤ "Run" ➤ Type **cmd** and click "OK"), navigate to the folder containing a.rb using the cd command, and then type **ruby a.rb**.

However, this method is only advised if you understand how to navigate your hard drive from the command prompt. Another option, if you're comfortable with creating short-cuts, is to create a shortcut to the Ruby executable file (`ruby.exe`) and drop your source code file(s) onto it.

Mac OS X

The simplest method to run Ruby applications on Mac OS X is from the Terminal, much in the same way as irb is run. The Terminal was explained in Chapter 1. If you followed the preceding instructions, continue like so:

1. Launch the Terminal (found in `Applications/Utilities`).

2. Use `cd` to navigate to the folder where you placed `a.rb` like so: `cd ~/ruby` . This tells the Terminal to take you to the `ruby` folder located off of your home user folder.

3. Type **ruby a.rb** and press Enter to execute the `a.rb` Ruby script.

4. If you get an error such as `ruby: No such file or directory -- a.rb (LoadError)`, you aren't in the same folder as the `a.rb` source file and need to establish where you have saved it.

If you get a satisfactory response from `a.rb`, you're ready to move on to the section, "Our Application: A Text Analyzer."

Linux and Other Unix-Based Systems

In Linux or other Unix-based systems, you run your Ruby applications from the shell (that is, within a terminal window) in the same way that you ran irb. The process to run irb was explained in Chapter 1, so if you've forgotten how to get that far, you need to recap yourself before continuing like so:

1. Launch your terminal emulator (xterm, for example) so you get a Linux shell/command prompt.

2. Navigate to the directory where you placed `a.rb` using the `cd` command (for example, `cd ~/ruby` takes you to the `ruby` directory located directly under your home directory, usually `/home/yourusernamehere/`).

3. Type **ruby a.rb** and press Enter to make Ruby execute the `a.rb` script.

If you get a satisfactory response from `a.rb`, you're ready to move on.

TEXT EDITORS VS. SOURCE CODE EDITORS

Previously I've stated that source code is basically the same as plain text. This is true, and although you can write your code in a general text editor, some benefits can be obtained by using a specialist source code editor (or a development IDE—Integrated Development Environment).

The FreeRIDE editor is an example of an editor specifically created for Ruby developers. It edits text, as with any other text editor, but offers extended features such as source code highlighting and the ability to run code directly from the editor.

Some developers find source code syntax highlighting an invaluable feature, as it makes their code easier to read. Variable names, expressions, string literals, and other elements of your source code are all given different colors, which makes it easy to pick them out.

Whether you choose a source code editor or a basic text editor depends on your own preference, but it's worth trying both. Many developers prefer the freedom of a regular text editor and then running their Ruby programs from the command line, whereas others prefer to work entirely within a single environment.

FreeRIDE is available from `http://freeride.rubyforge.org/`, and a competing source code editor for Ruby *and* Rails, called RadRails, is available at `http://www.radrails.org/`. It's certainly worth investigating these other editors on your platform in case they fit in more with how you wish to work.

Our Application: A Text Analyzer

The application you're going to develop in this chapter will be a text analyzer. Your Ruby code will read in text supplied in a separate file, analyze it for various patterns and statistics, and print out the results for the user. It's not a 3D graphical adventure or a fancy Web site, but text processing programs are the bread and butter of systems administration and most application development. They can be vital for parsing log files and user-submitted text on Web sites, and manipulating other textual data.

Ruby is well suited for text and document analysis with its regular expression features, along with the ease of use of scan and split, and you'll be using these heavily in your application.

Note With this application you'll be focusing on implementing the features quickly, rather than developing an elaborate object-oriented structure, any documentation, or a testing methodology. I'll be covering object orientation and its usage in larger programs in depth in Chapter 6, and documentation and testing are covered in Chapter 8.

Required Basic Features

Your text analyzer will provide the following basic statistics:

- Character count

- Character count (excluding spaces)

- Line count

- Word count

- Sentence count

- Paragraph count

- Average number of words per sentence

- Average number of sentences per paragraph

In the last two cases, the statistics are easily calculated from each other. That is, once you have the total number of words and the total number of sentences, it becomes a matter of a simple division to work out the average number of words per sentence.

Building the Basic Application

When starting to develop a new program, it's useful to think of the key steps involved. In the past it was common to draw *flow charts* to show how the operation of a computer program would flow, but it's easy to experiment, to change things about, and to remain agile with modern tools, such as Ruby. Let's outline the basic steps as follows:

1. Load in a file containing the text or document you want to analyze.

2. As you load the file line by line, keep a count of how many lines there were (one of your statistics taken care of).

3. Put the text into a string and measure its length to get your character count.

4. Temporarily remove all whitespace and measure the length of the resulting string to get the character count excluding spaces.

5. Split out all the whitespace to find out how many words there are.

6. Split on full stops to find out how many sentences there are.

7. Split on double newlines to find out how many paragraphs there are.

8. Perform calculations to work out the averages.

Create a new, blank Ruby source file and save it as `analyzer.rb` in your Ruby folder. As you work through the next few sections you'll be able to fill it out.

Obtaining Some Dummy Text

Before you start to code, the first step is to get some test data that your analyzer can process. The first chapter of *Oliver Twist* is an ideal piece of text to use, as it's copyright free and easy to obtain. It's also of a reasonable length. You can find the text at `http://www.rubyinside.com/book/oliver.txt` or `http://www.dickens-literature.com/ Oliver_Twist/0.html` for you to copy into a local text file. Save the file in the same folder as where you saved `a.rb` and call it `text.txt`. Your application will read from `text.txt` by default (although you'll make it be more dynamic and able to accept other sources of data later on).

■**Tip** If the preceding Web pages are unavailable at the time of reading, use your favorite search engine to search for "twist workhouse rendered profound thingummy" and you're guaranteed to find it. Alternatively, use any large block of text you can obtain.

If you're using the *Oliver Twist* text and want your results to match up roughly with those given as examples throughout this chapter, make sure you only copy and paste the text including and between these sections:

```
Among other public buildings in a certain town, which for many
reasons it will be prudent to refrain from mentioning
```

And:

```
Oliver cried lustily. If he could have known that he was an
orphan, left to the tender mercies of church-wardens and
overseers, perhaps he would have cried the louder.
```

Loading Text Files and Counting Lines

Now it's time to get coding! The first step is to load the file. Ruby provides a comprehensive set of file manipulation methods via the `File` class. Whereas other languages can make you jump through hoops to work with files, Ruby keeps the interface simple. Here's some code that opens up your `text.txt` file:

```
File.open("text.txt").each { |line| puts line }
```

Type this into analyzer.rb and run the code. If text.txt is in the current directory, the result is that you'll see the entire text file flying up the screen.

You're asking the File class to open up text.txt, and then, much like with an array, you can call the each method on the file directly, resulting in each line being passed to the inner code block one by one, where puts sends the line as output to the screen. (In Chapter 9 you'll look at how file access and manipulation work in more detail, along with better techniques than are used in this chapter!)

Edit the code to look like this instead:

```
line_count = 0
File.open("text.txt").each { |line| line_count += 1 }
puts line_count
```

You initialize line_count to store the line count, then open the file and iterate over each line, while incrementing line_count by 1 each time. When you're done, you print the total to the screen (approximately 121 if you're using the *Oliver Twist* chapter). You have your first statistic!

You've counted the lines, but still don't have access to the contents of the file to count the words, paragraphs, sentences, and so forth. This is easy to fix. Let's change the code a little, and add a variable, text, to collect the lines together as one as we go:

```
text=''
line_count = 0
File.open("text.txt").each do |line|
  line_count += 1
  text << line
end

puts "#{line_count} lines"
```

■**Note** Remember that using { and } to surround blocks is the standard style for single line blocks, but using do and end is preferable for multiline blocks. However, this is a convention rather than a requirement.

Compared to your previous attempt, this code introduces the text variable and adds each line onto the end of it in turn. When the iteration over the file has finished—that is, when you run out of lines—text contains the entire file in a single string ready for you to use.

That's a simple-looking way to get the file into a single string and count the lines, but File also has other methods that can be used to read files more quickly. For example, you can rewrite the preceding code like this:

```
lines = File.readlines("text.txt")
line_count = lines.size
text = lines.join

puts "#{line_count} lines"
```

Much simpler! `File` implements a `readlines` method that reads an entire file into an array, line by line. You can use this both to count the lines and join them all into a single string.

Counting Characters

The second easiest statistic to work out is the number of characters in the file. As you've collected the entire file into the `text` variable, and `text` is a string, you can use the `length` method that all strings supply to get the exact size of the file, and therefore the number of characters.

To the end of the previous code in `analyzer.rb`, add the following:

```
total_characters = text.length
puts "#{total_characters} characters"
```

If you ran `analyzer.rb` now with the *Oliver Twist* text, you'd get output like this:

```
121 lines
6165 characters
```

The second statistic you wanted to get relating to characters was a character total excluding whitespace. If you can remember back to Chapter 3, strings have a `gsub` method that performs a global substitution (like a search and replace) upon the string. For example:

```
"this is a test".gsub(/t/, 'X')
```

```
Xhis is a XesX
```

You can use `gsub` to eradicate the spaces from your `text` string in the same way, and then use the `length` method to get the length of the newly "de-spacified" text. Add the following code to `analyzer.rb`:

```
total_characters_nospaces = text.gsub(/\s+/, '').length
puts "#{total_characters_nospaces} characters excluding spaces"
```

If you run `analyzer.rb` in its current state against the *Oliver Twist* text, the results should be similar to the following:

```
121 lines
6165 characters
5055 characters (excluding spaces)
```

Counting Words

A common feature offered by word processing software is a "word counter." All it does is count the number of complete words in your document or a selected area of text. This information is useful to work out how many pages the document will take up when printed. Many assignments also have requirements for a certain number of words, so knowing the number of words in a piece of text is certainly useful.

You can approach this feature in a couple of ways:

1. Count the number of groups of contiguous letters using `scan`.

2. Split the text on whitespace and count the resulting fragments using `split` and `size`.

Let's look at each method in turn to see what's best. Recall from Chapter 3 that `scan` works by iterating over a string of text and finding certain patterns over and over. For example:

```
puts "this is a test".scan(/\w/).join
```

```
thisisatest
```

In this example, `scan` looked through the string for anything matching `\w`, a special term representing all alphanumeric characters (and underscores), and placed them into an array that you've joined together into a string and printed to the screen.

You can do the same with groups of alphanumeric characters. In Chapter 3 you learned that to match multiple characters with a regular expression, you could follow the character with +. So let's try again:

```
puts "this is a test".scan(/\w+/).join('-')
```

```
this-is-a-test
```

This time, `scan` has looked for all *groups* of alphanumeric characters and placed them into the array that you've then joined together into a string using - as the separation character.

To get the number of words in the string, you can use the `length` or `size` array methods to count the number of elements rather than join them together:

```
puts "this is a test".scan(/\w+/).length
```

4

Excellent! So what about the `split` approach?

The `split` approach demonstrates a core tenet of Ruby (as well as some other languages, particularly Perl) that "There's always more than one way to do it!" Analyzing different methods to solve the same problem is a crucial part of becoming a good programmer, as different methods can vary in their efficacy.

Let's split the string by spaces and get the length of the resulting array, like so:

```
puts "this is a test".split.length
```

4

As it happens, by *default* split will split by whitespace (single or multiple characters of spaces, tabs, newlines, and so on), and that makes this code shorter and easier to read than the scan alternative.

So what's the difference between these two methods? Simply, one is looking for words and returning them to you for you to count, and the other is splitting the string by that which separates words—whitespace—and telling you how many parts the string was broken into. Interestingly, these two approaches can yield different results:

```
text = "First-class decisions require clear-headed thinking."
puts "Scan method: #{text.scan(/\w+/).length}"
puts "Split method: #{text.split.length}"
```

```
Scan method: 7
Split method: 5
```

Interesting! The `scan` method is looking through for all blocks of alphanumeric characters, and, sure enough, there are seven in the sentence. However, if you split by spaces, there are five words. The reason is the hyphenated words. Hyphens aren't "alphanumeric," so `scan` is seeing "first" and "class" as separate words.

Returning to `analyzer.rb`, let's apply what we've learned here. Add the following:

```
word_count = text.split.length
puts "#{word_count} words"
```

Running the complete `analyzer.rb` gets these results:

```
122 lines
6166 characters
5055 characters (excluding spaces)
1093 words
```

Counting Sentences and Paragraphs

Once you understand the logic of counting words, counting the sentences and paragraphs becomes easy. Rather than splitting on whitespace, sentences and paragraphs have different splitting criteria.

Sentences end with full stops, question marks, and exclamation marks. They can also be separated with dashes and other punctuation, but we won't worry about these rare cases here. The split is simple. Instead of asking Ruby to split the text on one type of character, you simply ask it to split on any of three types of characters, like so:

```
sentence_count = text.split(/\.|\?|!/).length
```

The regular expression looks odd here, but the full stop, question mark, and exclamation mark are clearly visible. Let's look at the regular expression directly:

```
/\.|\?|!/
```

The forward slashes at the start and the end are the usual delimiters for a regular expression, so those can be ignored. The first section is `\.` and this represents a full stop.

The reason why you can't just use . without the backslash in front is because . represents "any character" in a regular expression (as covered in Chapter 3), so it needs to be *escaped* with the backslash to identify itself as a literal full stop. This also explains why the question mark is escaped with a backslash, as a question mark in a regular expression usually means "zero or one of the previous character"—also covered in Chapter 3. The ! is not escaped, as it has no other meaning in terms of regular expressions.

The pipes (| characters) separate the three main characters, which means they're treated separately so that split can match one or another of them. This is what allows the split to split on periods, question marks, *and* exclamation marks all at the same time. You can test it like so:

```
puts "Test code! It works. Does it? Yes.".split(/\.|\?|!/).length
```

4

Paragraphs can also be split apart with regular expressions. Whereas paragraphs in a printed book, such as this one, tend not to have any spacing between them, paragraphs that are typed on a computer typically do, so you can split by a double newline (as represented by the special combination \n\n—simply, two newlines in succession) to get the paragraphs separated. For example:

```
text = %q{
This is a test of
paragraph one.

This is a test of
paragraph two.

This is a test of
paragraph three.
}

puts text.split(/\n\n/).length
```

3

Let's add both these concepts to analyzer.rb:

```
paragraph_count = text.split(/\n\n/).length
puts "#{paragraph_count} paragraphs"

sentence_count = text.split(/\.|\?|!/).length
puts "#{sentence_count} sentences"
```

Calculating Averages

The final statistics required for your basic application are the average number of words per sentence, and the average number of sentences per paragraph. You already have the paragraph, sentence, and word counts available in the variables word_count, paragraph_count, and sentence_count, so only basic arithmetic is required, like so:

```
puts "#{sentence_count / paragraph_count} sentences per paragraph (average)"
puts "#{word_count / sentence_count} words per sentence (average)"
```

The calculations are so simple that they can be interpolated directly into the output commands rather than precalculated.

The Source Code So Far

You've been updating the source code as you've gone along, and in each case you've put the logic next to the puts statement that shows the result to the user. However, for the final version of your basic application, it'd be tidier to separate the logic from the presentation a little and put the calculations in a separate block of code before everything is printed to the screen.

There are no logic changes, but the finished source for analyzer.rb looks a little cleaner this way:

```
lines = File.readlines("text.txt")
line_count = lines.size
text = lines.join
word_count = text.split.length
character_count = text.length
character_count_nospaces = text.gsub(/\s+/, '').length
paragraph_count = text.split(/\n\n/).length
sentence_count = text.split(/\.|\?|!/).length

puts "#{line_count} lines"
puts "#{character_count} characters"
```

```
puts "#{character_count_nospaces} characters excluding spaces"
puts "#{word_count} words"
puts "#{paragraph_count} paragraphs"
puts "#{sentence_count} sentences"
puts "#{sentence_count / paragraph_count} sentences per paragraph (average)"
puts "#{word_count / sentence_count} words per sentence (average)"
```

If you've made it this far and everything's making sense, congratulations are due. Let's look at how to extend our application a little further with some more interesting statistics.

Adding Extra Features

Your analyzer has a few basic functions, but it's not particularly interesting. Line, paragraph, and word counts are useful statistics, but with the power of Ruby you can extract significantly more interesting data from the text. The only limit is your imagination, but in this section you'll look at a couple other features you can implement, and how to do so.

Note When developing software it's always worth considering the likelihood of the software being extended or tweaked in the future and planning ahead for the possibility. Many development bottlenecks have occurred when systems were designed too rigidly to cope with changing circumstances!

Percentage of "Useful" Words

Most written material, including this very book, contains a high number of words that, although providing context and structure, are not directly useful or interesting. In the last sentence, the words "that," "and," "are," and "or" are not of particular interest, even if the sentence would make less sense without them.

These words are typically called "stop words," and are often ignored by computer systems whose job is to analyze and search through text, because they aren't words most people are likely to be searching for (as opposed to nouns, for example). Google is a perfect example of this, as it doesn't want to have to store information that takes up space and that's generally irrelevant to searches.

Note For more information about stop words, including links to complete lists, visit `http://en.wikipedia.org/wiki/Stop_words`.

It could be assumed that more "interesting" text, or text by a more proficient author, might have a lower percentage of stop words and a higher percentage of useful or interesting words. You can easily extend your application to work out the percentage of non–stop words in the supplied text.

The first step is to build up a list of stop words. There are hundreds of possible stop words, but you'll start with just a handful. Let's create an array to hold them:

```ruby
stop_words = %w{the a by on for of are with just but and to the my I has some in}
```

This code results in an array of stop words being assigned to the `stop_words` variable.

Tip In Chapter 3, you saw arrays being defined like so: `x = ['a', 'b', 'c']`. However, like many languages, Ruby has a shortcut that builds arrays quickly with string-separated text. This segment can be shorted to the equivalent `x = %w{a b c}`, as demonstrated in the preceding stop word code.

For demonstration purposes, let's write a small, separate program to test the concept:

```ruby
text = %q{Los Angeles has some of the nicest weather in the country.}
stop_words = %w{the a by on for of are with just but and to the my I has some}

words = text.scan(/\w+/)
key_words = words.select { |word| !stop_words.include?(word) }

puts key_words.join(' ')
```

When you run this code, you get the following result:

```
Los Angeles nicest weather country
```

Cool, right? First you put some text into the program, then the list of stop words. Next you get all the words from `text` into an array called `words`. Then you get to the magic:

```ruby
key_words = words.select { |word| !stop_words.include?(word) }
```

This line first takes your array of words, words, and calls the select method with a block of code to process for each word (like the iterators you played with in Chapter 3). The select method is a method available to all arrays and hashes that returns the elements of that array or hash that match the expression in the code block.

In this case, the code in the code block takes each word via the variable word, and asks the stop_words array whether it includes any elements equal to word. This is what stop_words.include?(word) does.

The exclamation mark (!) before the expression negates the expression (an exclamation mark negates any Ruby expression). The reason for this is you *don't* want to select words that *are* in the stop_words array. You want to select words that *aren't*.

In closing, then, you select all elements of words that are *not* included in the stop_words array and assign them to key_words. Don't read on until that makes sense, as this type of single-line construction is common in Ruby programming.

After that, working out the percentage of non–stop words to all words uses some basic arithmetic:

```
((key_words.length.to_f / words.length.to_f) * 100).to_i
```

The reason for the .to_f's is so that the lengths are treated as floating decimal point numbers, and the percentage is worked out more accurately. When you work it up to the real percentage (out of 100), you can convert back to an integer once again.

You'll see how this all comes together in the final version at the end of this chapter.

Summarizing by Finding "Interesting" Sentences

Word processors such as Microsoft Word generally have summarization features that can take a long piece of text and seemingly pick out the best sentences to produce an "at-a-glance" summary. The mechanisms for producing summaries have become more complex over the years, but one of the simplest ways to develop a summarizer of your own is to scan for sentences with certain characteristics.

One technique is to look for sentences that are of about average length and that look like they contain nouns. Tiny sentences are unlikely to contain anything useful, and long sentences are likely to be simply too long for a summary. Finding nouns reliably would require systems that are far beyond the scope of this book, so you could "cheat" by looking for words that indicate the presence of useful nouns in the same sentence, such as "is" and "are" (for example, "Noun is," "Nouns are," "There are x nouns").

Let's assume that you want to throw away two-thirds of the sentences—a third that are the shortest sentences and a third that are the longest sentences—leaving you with an ideal third of the original sentences that are ideally sized for your task.

For ease of development, let's create a new program from scratch, and transfer your logic over to the main application later. Create a new program called summarize.rb and use this code:

```
text = %q{
Ruby is a great programming language. It is object oriented
and has many groovy features. Some people don't like it, but that's
not our problem! It's easy to learn. It's great. To learn more about Ruby,
visit the official Ruby Web site today.
}

sentences = text.gsub(/\s+/, ' ').strip.split(/\.|\?|\!/)
sentences_sorted = sentences.sort_by { |sentence| sentence.length }
one_third = sentences_sorted.length / 3
ideal_sentences = sentences_sorted.slice(one_third, one_third + 1)
ideal_sentences = ideal_sentences.select { |sentence| sentence =~ /is|are/ }
puts ideal_sentences.join(". ")
```

And for good measure run it to see what happens:

```
Ruby is a great programming language. It is object oriented and has many groovy
features
```

Seems like a success! Let's walk through the program.

First, you define the variable text to hold the long string of multiple sentences, much like in analyzer.rb. Next you split text into an array of sentences like so:

```
sentences = text.gsub(/\s+/, ' ').strip.split(/\.|\?|!/)
```

This is slightly different from the method used in analyzer.rb. There is an extra gsub in the chain, as well as strip. The gsub gets rid of all large areas of whitespace and replaces them with a single space (\s+ meaning "one or more whitespace characters"). This is simply for cosmetic reasons. The strip removes all extra whitespace from the start and end of the string. The split is then the same as that used in the analyzer.

Next you sort the sentences by their lengths, as you want to ignore the shortest third and the longest third:

```
sentences_sorted = sentences.sort_by { |sentence| sentence.length }
```

Arrays and hashes have the sort_by method that rearranges them into almost any order you want. sort_by takes a code block as its argument, where the code block is an expression that defines what to sort by. In this case, you're sorting the sentences array. You pass each sentence in as the sentence variable, and choose to sort them by their length, using the length method upon the sentence. After this line, sentences_sorted contains an array with the sentences in length order.

Next you need to get the middle third of the length-sorted sentences in sentences_sorted, as these are the ones you've deemed to be probably the most interesting. To do this you can divide the length of the array by 3, to get the number of elements in a third, and then grab that number of elements from one third into the array (note that you grab one extra element to compensate for rounding caused by integer division). This is done like so:

```
one_third = sentences_sorted.length / 3
ideal_sentences = sentences_sorted.slice(one_third, one_third + 1)
```

The first line takes the length of the array and divides it by 3 to get the quantity that is equal to "a third of the array." The second line uses the slice method to "cut out" a section of the array to assign to ideal_sentences. In this case, assume that the sentences_sorted is 6 elements long. 6 divided by 3 is 2, so a third of the array is 2 elements long. The slice method then cuts *from* element 2 *for* 2 (plus 1) elements, so you effectively carve out elements 2, 3, and 4 (remember that array elements start counting from 0). This means you get the "inner third" of the ideal-lengthed sentences you wanted.

The penultimate line checks to see if the sentence includes the word "is" or "are," and only accepts each sentence if so:

```
ideal_sentences = ideal_sentences.select { |sentence| sentence =~ /is|are/ }
```

It uses the select method, as the "stop word" removal code in the previous section did. The expression in the code block uses a regular expression that matches against sentence, and only returns true if "is" or "are" are present within sentence. This means ideal_sentences now only contains sentences that are in the middle third length-wise *and* contain either "is" or "are."

The final line simply joins the ideal_sentences together with a full stop and space between them to make them readable:

```
puts ideal_sentences.join(". ")
```

Analyzing Files Other Than text.txt

So far your application has the filename text.txt hard-coded into it. This is acceptable, but it'd be a lot nicer if you could specify, when you run the program, what file you want the analyzer to process.

Note This technique is only practical to demonstrate if you're running analyzer.rb from a command prompt or shell, as on Mac OS X or Linux (or Windows if you're using the Windows command prompt). If you're using an IDE on Windows, this section will be read-only for you.

Typically, if you're starting a program from the command line, you can append parameters onto the end of the command and the program processes them. You can do the same with your Ruby application.

Ruby automatically places any parameters that are appended to the command line when you launch your Ruby program into a special array called ARGV. To test it out, create a new script called argv.rb and use this code:

```
puts ARGV.join('-')
```

From the command prompt, run the script like so:

```
ruby argv.rb
```

The result will be blank, but then try to run it like so:

```
ruby argv.rb test 123
```

```
test-123
```

This time the parameters are taken from ARGV, joined together with a hyphen, and displayed on screen. You can use this to replace the reference to text.txt in analyzer.rb by replacing "text.txt" with ARGV[0] or ARGV.first (which both mean exactly the same thing—the first element of the ARGV array). The line that reads the file becomes the following:

```
lines = File.readlines(ARGV[0])
```

To process text.txt now, you'd run it like so:

```
ruby analyzer.rb text.txt
```

You'll learn more about deploying programs and making them friendly to other users, along with ARGV, in Chapter 10.

The Completed Program

You've already got the source for the completed basic program, but it's time to add all the new, extended features from the previous few sections to analyzer.rb to create the final version of your text analyzer.

■**Note** Remember that source code for this book is available in the Source Code/Download area at
http://www.apress.com, so it isn't strictly necessary to type in code directly from the book.

Here we go:

```ruby
# analyzer.rb -- Text Analyzer

stop_words = %w{the a by on for of are with just but and to the my I has some in}
lines = File.readlines("text.txt")
line_count = lines.size
text = lines.join

# Count the characters
character_count = text.length
character_count_nospaces = text.gsub(/\s+/, '').length

# Count the words, sentences, and paragraphs
word_count = text.split.length
sentence_count = text.split(/\.|\?|!/).length
paragraph_count = text.split(/\n\n/).length

# Make a list of words in the text that aren't stop words,
# count them, and work out the percentage of non-stop words
# against all words
all_words = text.scan(/\w+/)
good_words = all_words.select{ |word| !stop_words.include?(word) }
good_percentage = ((good_words.length.to_f / all_words.length.to_f) * 100).to_i

# Summarize the text by cherry picking some choice sentences
sentences = text.gsub(/\s+/, ' ').strip.split(/\.|\?|\!/)
sentences_sorted = sentences.sort_by { |sentence| sentence.length }
one_third = sentences_sorted.length / 3
ideal_sentences = sentences_sorted.slice(one_third, one_third + 1)
ideal_sentences = ideal_sentences.select { |sentence| sentence =~ /is|are/ }

# Give the analysis back to the user
puts "#{line_count} lines"
puts "#{character_count} characters"
puts "#{character_count_nospaces} characters (excluding spaces)"
puts "#{word_count} words"
```

```
puts "#{sentence_count} sentences"
puts "#{paragraph_count} paragraphs"
puts "#{sentence_count / paragraph_count} sentences per paragraph (average)"
puts "#{word_count / sentence_count} words per sentence (average)"
puts "#{good_percentage}% of words are non-fluff words"
puts "Summary:\n\n" + ideal_sentences.join(". ")
puts "-- End of analysis"
```

■Note If you're a Windows user, you might want to replace the ARGV[0] reference with an explicit reference to "text.txt" to make sure it works okay from FreeRIDE or SciTE. However, if you're running the program from the command prompt, it should operate correctly.

Running the completed analyzer.rb with the *Oliver Twist* text now results in an output like so:

```
121 lines
6165 characters
5055 characters (excluding spaces)
1093 words
18 paragraphs
45 sentences
2 sentences per paragraph (average)
24 words per sentence (average)
76% of words are non-fluff words
Summary:

' The surgeon leaned over the body, and raised the left hand.  Think what it is
to be a mother, there's a dear young lamb do.  'The old story,' he said, shaking
his head: 'no wedding-ring, I see.  What an excellent example of the power of
dress, young Oliver Twist was. ' Apparently this consolatory perspective of a
mother's prospects failed in producing its due effect. ' The surgeon had been
sitting with his face turned towards the fire: giving the palms of his hands a
warm and a rub alternately. ' 'You needn't mind sending up to me, if the child
cries, nurse,' said the surgeon, putting on his gloves with great deliberation.
She had walked some distance, for her shoes were worn to pieces; but where
she came from, or where she was going to, nobody knows. ' He put on his hat,
and, pausing by the bed-side on his way to the door, added, 'She was a
good-looking girl, too; where did she come from
-- End of analysis
```

Try `analyzer.rb` with some other text of your choice (a Web page, perhaps) and see if you can make improvements to its features. This application is ripe for improvement with the concepts you'll learn over the next several chapters, so keep it in mind if you're looking for some code to play with.

CODE COMMENTS

You might notice text in source code prefixed with # symbols. These are *comments* and are generally used in programs for the benefit of the original developer(s), along with anyone else that might need to read the source code. They're particularly useful for making notes to remind you of why you took a particular course of action that you're likely to forget in future.

You can place comments in any Ruby source code file on their own lines, or even at the end of a line of code. Here are some valid examples of commenting in Ruby:

```
puts "2+2 = #{2+2}" # Adds 2+2 to make 4
# A comment on a line by itself
```

As long as a comment is on a line by itself, or is the last thing on a line, it's fine. Comment liberally, and your code will be easier to understand.

Summary

In this chapter you developed a complete, basic application that had a set of requirements and desired features. You then extended it with some nonessential, but useful, elaborations. Ruby makes developing quick applications a snap.

The application you've developed in this chapter has demonstrated that if you have a lot of text to process or a number of calculations to do, and you're dreading doing the work manually, Ruby can take the strain.

Chapter 4 marks the end of the practical programming exercises in the first part of this book. Next, in Chapter 5, you'll take a look at the history of Ruby; Ruby's community of developers; the historical reasons behind certain features in Ruby; and learn how to get help from, and become part of, the Ruby community. Code makes up only half the journey to becoming a great programmer!

CHAPTER 5

■ ■ ■

The Ruby Ecosystem

As with almost all other programming languages, Ruby has its own culture and "eco system." Ruby's ecosystem is made up of many thousands of developers, maintainers, documenters, bloggers, and those who help sponsor or fund the development and use of the language.

Some programmers who are new to a language make the mistake that learning about a language's history and community is pointless, but the most successful developers quickly learn about the ecosystem and get involved in it. The motivations behind a language's development and its users can provide significant clues about the best approaches to take when solving problems, and understanding the vocabulary of other developers of that language greatly helps when it comes to looking for help and advice.

This chapter takes a break from the code-focused tutorials to bring you up to speed with how the Ruby world works, the motivations behind the language, as well as the best ways to find help and get involved with the community. If you're new to software development, this chapter will also explain some of the many terms and phrases used by developers relating to software development.

You'll also take a quick look at Ruby's history, Ruby's creator, the processes and terminology that Ruby developers use that make them reasonably unique, and the technologies that have taken Ruby from being relatively unknown to being an important first-class programming language.

Ruby's History

Ruby is relatively young in the world of programming languages, having been first developed in 1993, making it roughly the same age as both Perl and Python. Among the most popular programming languages still in use today, Fortran, for example, was developed in 1953; C was developed in the early 1970s; and BASIC was developed in 1963. However, Ruby's modernness is an asset rather than a downfall. From day one it was designed with object-oriented programming in mind, and its syntax has remained remarkably consistent over time. However, the older languages have been forced to complicate their syntax and change radically to address modern concepts such as object orientation, networks, and graphical environments.

Unlike many languages that are formed out of pure necessity or research, Ruby's birth partly came from a sense of frustration with existing languages. Despite the presence of so many established programming languages, a plucky Japanese computer scientist felt development was becoming ever more complex and tiresome, and decided some fun had to be injected into the world of programming languages.

The Land of the Rising Sun

Ruby began life in Japan as the creation of Yukihiro Matsumoto, known more commonly as "Matz." Unlike that of most language developers, Matz's motivation for Ruby was fun and a principle of "least surprise," in order to improve overall developer productivity. He couldn't find a language that resonated with his mindset, so he took his own outlook about how programming should work and created Ruby (named after the gemstone, but a convenient homage to the Perl programming language).

A longtime object-oriented programming fan, Matz felt it was the best model to adopt, but unlike other languages, such as Perl, object orientation wouldn't be an afterthought, but act as the core foundation for the whole language. Everything would be an object, and methods would fill the roles of the procedures and functions developers had come to expect in older procedural languages. As Matz himself said in a 2001 interview: "I wanted a language that was more powerful than Perl, and more object-oriented than Python. That's why I decided to design my own language."

In December 1995, Matz released the first public alpha version of Ruby, and soon thereafter a community began to form in Japan. However, although Ruby quickly became relatively popular in Japan, it struggled to gain a foothold elsewhere.

■**Note** In software development, the terms *alpha*, *beta*, and *gamma*, among others, are used to denote the development stage of a piece of software. An initial release that's not for general use is often called an alpha. A release that implements most of the required features, but might not be entirely tested or stable, is often called a beta, although this term is becoming muddied by the plethora of Web applications now permanently using the term "beta" on otherwise fully released products and services.

In 1996, the development of Ruby was opened up somewhat, and a small team of core developers and other contributors began to form alongside the more general community of Ruby developers. Ruby 1.0 was released on December 25, 1996. These core developers help Matz develop Ruby and submit their patches (adjustments to the code) and ideas to him. Matz continues to act as a "benevolent dictator" who ultimately controls the direction of the language, despite the ever-widening influence of other developers.

■**Note** Although developing software privately is still common, many projects are now worked upon in a public manner, allowing them to be extended and worked upon by any competent programmer. In many cases this makes it possible for other developers to *fork* the project (taking the existing code and splitting it into their own version), but in practice this is rare.

Ruby's Influences

In developing Ruby, Matz was heavily influenced by the programming languages he was already familiar with. Larry Wall, the developer of the popular Perl language, was a hero of Matz's, and Perl's principle of "There's More Than One Way To Do It" is present in Ruby.

Some languages, such as Python, prefer to provide more rigid structures and to present a clean method for developers to have a small number of options to perform a certain task. Ruby allows its developers to solve problems in any one of many ways. This allows the language great flexibility, and combined with the object-oriented nature of the language, Ruby is extremely customizable.

In terms of its object-oriented nature, Ruby has also been heavily influenced by Smalltalk, a prolific object-oriented language developed in the 1970s. As in Smalltalk, almost everything in Ruby is an object, and Ruby also gives programmers the ability to change many details of the language's operation within their own programs on the fly. This feature is called *reflection*.

To a lesser extent, Python, LISP, Eiffel, ADA, and C++ have also influenced Ruby. These influences demonstrate that Ruby isn't a language that's afraid to take on the best ideas from other languages. This is one of many reasons why Ruby is such a powerful and dynamic language. The implementation of many of these features has also made the migration from other languages to Ruby significantly easier. Learning Ruby means, to a great extent, learning the best features of other programming languages for free. (Refer to Appendix A for a comparison between Ruby and other languages.)

Go West

As a language initially developed for Matz's own use in Japan, the initial documentation was entirely in Japanese, locking most non-Japanese users out. Although it's customary for programming languages to use English for their keywords (such as `print`, `puts`, `if`, and so on) it wasn't until 1997 that the initial English documentation began to be produced.

Matz first began to officially promote the Ruby language in English in late 1998 with the creation of the `ruby-talk` mailing list, still one of the best places to discuss the Ruby language, as well as a useful resource with more than 200,000 messages archived at the list's Web site (`http://blade.nagaokaut.ac.jp/ruby/ruby-talk/index.shtml`).

■Note You can subscribe to `ruby-talk` yourself by sending an e-mail containing "subscribe" followed by your first name and then last name to `ruby-talk-ctl@ruby-lang.org`.

An official English language Web site soon followed in late 1999 with the creation of ruby-lang.org (`http://www.ruby-lang.org/`), which is still Ruby's official English language Web site (see Figures 5-1 and 5-2 for a comparison of the official site between then and now).

Ruby failed to catch on with all but a few ardent developers until 2000 and 2001 (with the main Ruby Usenet newsgroup `comp.lang.ruby` being created in May 2000), and even then the English-speaking Ruby community was tiny. Matz didn't consider this to be important though, and was even surprised that other people found his language useful, having only created it to fit his own way of thinking.

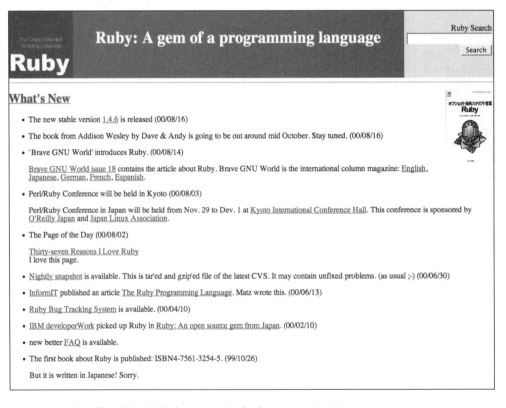

Figure 5-1. *The official English-language Ruby homepage in 2000*

Figure 5-2. *The official Ruby homepage as of late 2006*

However, the exposure of Ruby to the larger audience of software developers continued to be low. IBM published an article with a brief overview of Ruby and an interview with Matz in 2000, and the much-revered *Dr. Dobb's Journal* published an article by Dave Thomas and Andy Hunt with a similar introduction in January 2001.

Despite Ruby's obvious power, it appeared as if Python and PHP were going to win the race to become "the next Perl" as general scripting and Web languages, respectively, up until 2004 (although Ruby was more popular than Python even in 2000). But then everything changed when a young Dane released a tool based upon Ruby that would quickly change the perception of the language in the worldwide development community.

Ruby on Rails

Since 2005 it has become impossible to publish any book or article about Ruby without mentioning *Ruby on Rails*. Ruby on Rails is a Web application framework that has propelled the popularity of Ruby outside of Japan from a humble core of avid developers to hundreds of thousands of developers all now interested in using the language. This section examines Ruby on Rails, explains why it's important, and discusses how its presence has changed the whole dynamic of the Ruby ecosystem.

■**Note** An application framework is a set of conventions, structures, and systems that provide an underlying structure to make application development easier. Ruby on Rails is such a framework for Web application development.

I'll be covering Ruby on Rails development in Chapter 13, but let's first look at the motivation behind the framework and how it has changed the entire Ruby landscape.

Why Rails Came into Existence

37signals (`http://www.37signals.com/`), a successful Web software company, was founded in 1999 initially as a Web design agency that promoted the use of clean, fast, and functional designs over the gee-whiz Flash-based Web sites that were popular at the time. With only two cofounders running the entire company, they quickly realized they needed some tools to help them run their business efficiently. They tried some off-the-shelf software but found nothing that matched their needs, and found most solutions to be bloated and complex. They felt their attitude toward Web design should also be applied to applications, and in mid-2003 decided to develop their own project management tool.

As designers, rather than coders, 37signals turned to the services of David Heinemeier Hansson, a student in Copenhagen, Denmark, to develop their project management application. Rather than use the then-common tools such as Perl or PHP, Hansson was convinced that 37signals could develop the application far more quickly and completely by using Ruby. Previously a PHP coder, Hansson was beginning to feel the pain of using PHP for large Web application development and felt a new direction should be sought.

As development on the nascent application (entitled "Basecamp") progressed, the team members showed it to others in the industry and quickly realized from the responses they heard that they should release the application to the public rather than keep it for their own use.

With a successful public release of Basecamp in February 2004—only about four months after beginning the project—the development methodology adopted by 37signals and Hansson was proven, and 37signals began a rapid transition into an application development company, with Hansson eventually becoming a partner at the company.

Ruby proved to be the silver bullet that powered the rapid development of Basecamp. Hansson used Ruby's object orientation and reflection features to build a framework that made developing database-driven Web applications easier than ever before. This framework became known as Ruby on Rails, and was first released to the public in

July 2004. 37signals continued to develop new products quickly using the power of the new framework.

Like Ruby itself, the Ruby on Rails framework didn't immediately experience an explosion of popularity, but found a small number of ardent fans who began to realize its power and, in many cases, wished to replicate 37signals' success.

How the Web (2.0) Was Won

Ruby on Rails wasn't a wallflower for long. 2005 was an epic year for Ruby on Rails, and Ruby's popularity exploded alongside it. The initial fans of Ruby on Rails had began blogging feverishly about the technology and were winning over converts with an unintentional, but surprisingly potent, grassroots viral marketing campaign.

In January 2005, Slashdot, the world's most popular technology community Web site at the time, published its first post mentioning Ruby on Rails, and since then has run scores of stories on the technology, each encouraging existing PHP, Perl, and Python developers to give Ruby and Ruby on Rails a try.

In March 2005, Hansson announced the development of the first commercial Rails book, which came out in beta PDF form in May of that year. In September 2005, the print version of the book went on sale and immediately topped the Amazon.com chart for programming books.

In the space of a year, Rails books were under development and being released by a multitude of publishers; tens of thousands of blog posts had been made about the technology; hundreds of thousands of screencasts (watchable screenshot videos demonstrating how to use Rails) had been watched online; and David Heinemeier Hansson had won numerous awards, including Google and O'Reilly's "Best Hacker of the Year 2005." Tens of thousands of developers were suddenly flocking to Ruby on Rails and, therefore, Ruby.

The Ruby ecosystem was rapidly thrust into the limelight, especially on the back of the "Web 2.0" concept, a coined term that refers to a supposed second generation in Internet-based services, and is often used to refer to the culture of blogs, social networking, wikis, and other user-content–driven Web sites. As Ruby and Rails make these sites easy to develop, many developers have used these tools to their advantage to get ahead in the Web 2.0 field.

The Open Source Culture

When Ruby was initially developed, Matz didn't have a specific development culture in mind. He developed the language to be for his own use and to fit his own mindset. For the first couple years he kept the language mostly to himself. Most of today's culture relating to *how* to develop software with Ruby has evolved in the last few years and is partly shared with other programming languages.

A common element of the Ruby development culture that's crucial to understand is the *open source* movement.

■**Tip** Feel free to skip this section and move on to "Where and How to Get Help" if you're already familiar with the concepts surrounding open source.

What Is Open Source?

If you've used Linux or downloaded certain types of software, you might be familiar with the term "open source." Simply, open source means that the source code to an application or library is made available publicly for other people to look at and use. There might be restrictions on what people can do with the code (generally via a license), but it's publicly viewable. Much like Linux, Ruby, along with nearly all its libraries, is released under an open source license—in contrast to, say, Microsoft Windows, whose source code isn't readily available.

The terms of Ruby's license don't require that any applications you produce with Ruby also need to be made open source. You can develop proprietary "closed source" applications with Ruby and never let anyone else see the code. Choosing whether to release your code as open source or not can be a tough decision. (You can read the full text of Ruby's license in Appendix B.)

There are often shades of gray in the open source versus closed source decision. When 37signals developed the first Ruby on Rails–powered application, Basecamp, they didn't release the source openly, but they did extract the Ruby on Rails framework and release that as open source. The result is that their company has received a lot of publicity, and 37signals has hired some great coders who worked on Ruby on Rails for free, benefiting everybody. Software products such as the popular Apache Web server and the MySQL database system are also available under varying open source licenses and are routinely improved by unpaid coders.

The open source community is one of sharing knowledge freely and collaborating to improve the systems and services that most of us use. Although proprietary software will always have its place, open source is rapidly becoming the de facto way to develop programming languages, libraries, and other non-application types of software.

Understanding open source is an important key to understanding the Ruby community. Although many developers don't necessarily open source the code to their applications, they'll often release the tools and code tricks to the community so that they can benefit from the peer review and popularity that results.

Releasing your code as open source isn't necessarily a bad business decision. It could actually improve the quality of your code and tools, and make you much better known in the industry.

Where and How to Get Help

This book will help you learn all the essentials about Ruby and more besides, but it's often useful to get more timely or domain-specific assistance while coding. In this section, you'll look at a few ways that you can get assistance from the large community of Ruby developers. (There's also a more succinct and complete list of resources in Appendix C that you might prefer for future reference.)

Mailing Lists

Mailing lists have always been popular havens for discussion about programming languages. Favored by the more technical members of any programming language's culture, they're a good place to ask questions about the internals or future of the language, along with esoteric queries that only a true language uber-geek could answer. They are not, however, suited for basic queries.

Ruby has three official mailing lists for English speakers to which you can subscribe as follows:

- `ruby-talk`: Deals with general topics and questions about Ruby

- `ruby-core`: Discussion of core Ruby issues, specifically about the development of the language

- `ruby-doc`: Discussion of the documentation standards and tools for Ruby (rarely used)

Further information about these lists is available at `http://www.ruby-lang.org/en/20020104.html`, and a Web forum-style view of the `ruby-talk` mailing list is available at `http://www.nabble.com/ruby-talk-f13890.html`.

Lists are also available in Japanese, French, and Portuguese, and these are similarly listed on the first page in the preceding paragraph. The Japanese mailing lists, being comprised of some of the most experienced Ruby developers, are often read by English speakers using translation software. Information about this is also available at the aforementioned Web page.

Usenet Newsgroups

Until about 2002, the newsgroup system (Usenet) was a common way for large groups of people with a common interest to share and discuss their knowledge.

The advent of Google Groups allows easy access to the newsgroups, and often you can get good answers from the other people using them. The newsgroups are better suited to asking minor questions than the mailing lists, but if your question is considered to be a "frequently asked question," prepare to be warned.

Ruby's primary newsgroup is `comp.lang.ruby`, and if you have no newsgroup software installed, you can read it on the Web at `http://groups.google.com/group/comp.lang.ruby`. As of 2006, the group still gets about 20 new posts a day and is actively used by a large group of Ruby developers.

Internet Relay Chat (IRC)

Internet Relay Chat is a real-time Internet chat system that allows potentially thousands of people to congregate into "channels" to discuss various topics. The immediacy of real-time chat makes IRC suitable for quick questions, although participants are often surprisingly willing to help users with deeper problems (see Figure 5-3 for an example of an IRC channel in operation). The only downside is that you might get no response at all and be left reading a conversation already in progress.

IRC has proven popular with Ruby developers, and there are two particularly notable channels where almost–24-hour support for Ruby and Ruby on Rails is available as follows:

- *For Ruby language discussion*: #ruby-lang on the `irc.freenode.net` server

- *For Ruby on Rails discussion*: #rubyonrails on the `irc.freenode.net` server

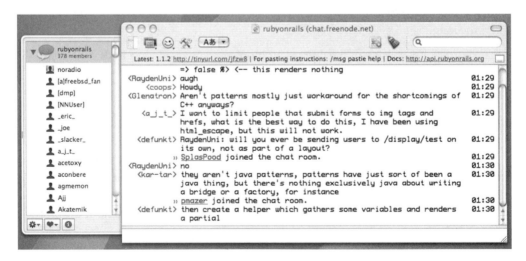

Figure 5-3. *A sample conversation in the Ruby on Rails IRC channel*

To use IRC, it's necessary to download and install an IRC "client" onto your computer that allows you to get onto the real-time IRC channels. Although the installation of this software is beyond the scope of this book, I'd recommend these clients for Windows, Linux, and OS X:

- *Windows*: mIRC (`http://www.mirc.com`)

- *Mac OS X*: Colloquy (`http://colloquy.info/`)

- *Linux/Unix*: XChat (`http://www.xchat.org/`)

Be sure to respect that other users in the channel are not solely there to answer your questions; otherwise you might be deemed a "help vampire" and be ignored! However, with care, you can easily talk to some of the biggest names in the Ruby world on these channels.

Note To learn more about IRC see `http://en.wikipedia.org/wiki/Internet_Relay_Chat`.

Documentation

There's a significant amount of documentation available on the Web for Ruby developers. The best documentation is the official reference documentation at `http://www.ruby doc.org/` that provides full, though often basic, coverage of the standard Ruby classes and the most popular Ruby libraries and add-ins.

The API documentation for the current stable release of Ruby is available at `http://www.ruby-doc.org/core/`. Produced automatically from the Ruby source code with Ruby's in-built documentation tool rdoc, the structure of the documentation isn't immediately obvious. Usually you can choose between viewing documentation for certain files that make up Ruby, documentation for each different base class, or documentation for certain methods. You don't get a logical order to follow and there are no deep tutorials. This sort of documentation is for reference purposes only.

Most Ruby libraries and applications use a similar scheme for their documentation, and the links to this are made available on their official sites. For example, Ruby on Rails' API documentation is available at `http://api.rubyonrails.com/`.

Forums

Forums make up some of the most popular Web sites on the Internet. Unlike newsgroups or mailing lists, which tend to be the domain of more technical people, forums provide extremely easy access to a non–real-time discussion on the Web. Forums are a particularly good place to ask more basic questions and to get general advice.

Several Ruby forums are available to try:

- *Ruby-Forum.com* (http://www.ruby-forum.com/): Ruby-Forum.com provides a forum-style view onto some of the popular Ruby mailing lists. This means it isn't a true forum in the strictest sense, but people used to forums will appreciate the structure.

- *Ruby Forums* (http://www.rubyforums.com/forumdisplay.php?f=1): Ruby Forums is a set of about 15 smaller forums that cover Ruby topics, from general discussion and installation queries through to editors and Ruby on Rails.

- *SitePoint Ruby Forums* (http://www.sitepoint.com/forums/forumdisplay.php?f=227): SitePoint is a popular Web development site that provides forums on multiple topics and that launched a Ruby forum in October 2005. The forum is well populated and friendly.

- *Rails Forum* (http://railsforum.com/): Rails Forum is a forum focused on Ruby on Rails that began in May 2006 but that's proven consistently popular. It's particularly friendly to beginners.

Joining the Community

One of the reasons for programming communities is so that people can get help from others who are experienced with the language, but also to share knowledge and to develop useful tools and documentation together. Solely "taking" from the community is natural at the start of a developer's experience with a new language, but it's essential to give something back once you've developed some knowledge of your own. Ruby developers are proud that their community is one of the friendliest and easiest to get involved with, and there are a number of ways to make a mark.

Give Help to Others

In the previous section we looked at the ways that you can get help from other Ruby developers, but once you've gained a certain amount of Ruby knowledge you'll be able to start helping people yourself. You can participate on the IRC chatrooms, forums, and mailing lists, and begin to answer some of the questions for those with lesser knowledge than yourself.

Helping others isn't always the selfless, time-consuming act it might seem at first. Often, questions are asked that relate to your knowledge but require you to work out something new or to identify a new solution to a problem you've already solved. My personal experience with helping people in the IRC chatrooms has been that my mind has been constantly stretched. Although sometimes I might have the best answer, other times I might give an inaccurate or confusing answer that's then corrected by someone else, helping me to gain a new insight.

Don't be afraid to dive in and try to help others. If you feel your answer is right, even if it's not, it's likely that several people will try to help, and the Ruby community is generally forgiving of such errors. In the Ruby community, effort is often prized above prowess.

Contribute Code

Once you begin to develop your own Ruby applications, you might find features missing in the applications or libraries you wish to use, and you'll either develop your own or work on upgrading those that already exist. If a project is open source, you should be able to supply your changes and upgrades back to the project, meaning that you improve the quality of the software for the entire community. Other than benefiting others, this also means your code is likely to be extended and improved itself, and you'll be able to reap even more benefit than if you kept your code to yourself.

All open source Ruby libraries and applications have someone who is in charge of maintaining them, and if no guidance is provided on the project's Web site, simply contact the maintainer and see whether you can contribute your code.

Alternatively, if you don't feel confident enough to supply code, but see large gaps in the documentation for a project—perhaps even in Ruby itself—maintainers are often ecstatic if you'll supply documentation. You can learn more about how to document Ruby programs in Chapter 7. Many coders aren't good at documentation or don't have the time to complete it, so if you have a skill for it, contributing documentation to a project could make you very popular indeed!

Weblogs

In the last few years it has become common for developers to maintain *weblogs* (also known as *blogs*), Web sites that act somewhat like informal online diaries full of observations. Originally the conserve of diarists and philosophers, developer weblogs are now extremely popular, and have proven instrumental in Ruby's success.

It isn't uncommon for Ruby developers to post newly found knowledge or useful code snippets to their weblogs, and by subscribing to these weblogs you could extend your Ruby knowledge every day. Seeing how hundreds of other programmers code and

solve problems helps extend your mindset, and often the ideal code snippet or Ruby trick
will appear on someone's weblog at just the right time.

Hundreds of weblogs are maintained by Ruby developers, but the following are some
of the most popular or Ruby specific:

- *Ruby Inside* (`http://www.rubyinside.com/`): The semi-official site for this book. Ruby
  Inside is a blog posting daily links to interesting Ruby news, code, and tutorials
  found all around the Web. Ideally suited for beginners and experts alike.

- *RedHanded* (`http://redhanded.hobix.com/`): A blog maintained by the charismatic
  Ruby developer *whytheluckystiff*. The blog tends to focus on clever Ruby tricks and
  cutting-edge Ruby news, and is a favorite among advanced Ruby developers.

- *Yukihiro Matsumoto's Blog* (`http://www.rubyist.net/~matz/`): Because he's the main
  developer of Ruby, many users like to check out Matz's blog. It's in Japanese
  though, but there are often interesting snippets of code or presentations to look at.

- *Planet Ruby On Rails* (`http://www.planetrubyonrails.com/`): If you don't have time to
  read many different blogs, Planet Ruby On Rails aggregates most of the best Ruby
  blogs into a single page. Despite the name, its Ruby coverage is strong, although it
  tries to focus on Rails.

By visiting these weblogs you'll quickly learn about hundreds of other Ruby
resources, tricks, and sources of documentation. If you comment on these sites and
begin to update a weblog yourself with your experiences of Ruby, you'll quickly become
established in the Ruby community.

Summary

In this chapter we've taken a break from coding to focus on the culture, community, and
"ecosystem" surrounding the Ruby language. Understanding the larger world around the
Ruby language is extremely useful, as it's from this community that most developers will
get assistance, advice, code, and even paying work.

Being able to get help and give help in return benefits the community, helps the
cause of Ruby to progress, and ultimately helps with your own programming skills.

The Ruby community is important and friendly to new Ruby developers, making it
ideal to get involved as soon as possible when you begin to learn Ruby. Make sure you
use the resources the community provides to the fullest as you learn Ruby and begin to
develop applications. A single book cannot turn anyone into a Ruby expert, but a collection of valuable resources and participation in the community can.

Refer to Appendix C for a large collection of URLs and links to other Ruby resources
that are available online.

PART 2

■■■

The Core of Ruby

This part of the book walks you through the remaining essential elements of Ruby and goes into more detail about some previously seen aspects of the language. By the end of Part 2, you'll be able to develop Ruby applications complete with complex class and object arrangements of your own; know how to test, document, and deploy them; and use databases and external data sources to feed your applications.

CHAPTER 6

■■■

Classes, Objects, and Modules

In Chapter 2 we dove straight into the principles of object orientation, the method of representing concepts in Ruby by using *classes* and *objects*. Since then we've looked at Ruby's standard classes, such as String and Array; worked with them; and then branched off to look at Ruby's logic and other core features.

In this chapter the focus is back onto object orientation, but rather than looking at the concepts from afar, we'll be getting into the details. We'll look at why classes and objects behave the way they do, why object orientation is a viable development tool, how you can implement classes to match your own requirements, and how to *override* and *extend* the classes Ruby provides by default. Finally, you'll implement a basic "dungeon" in text adventure form to demonstrate how myriad real-life concepts can combine into an easily maintainable set of interconnected classes.

Why Use Object Orientation?

Object orientation is not the only development style with which to develop software. The *procedural* style of programming predates it, and continues to be used in languages such as C. Whereas object orientation dictates that you define concepts and processes as classes from which you can create objects, programming procedurally means you focus on the steps required to complete a task instead, without paying particular attention to how the data is managed.

Imagine two developers within a single software development company who are vying to be respected as the most knowledgeable programmer in the company. Capitalizing on the rivalry, their boss issues both of them the same tasks and uses the best code in each case. There's only one difference between the two programmers. One follows the principles of object-oriented development, and the other is a procedural programmer coding without using classes and objects.

For a forthcoming project, the boss demands some code that can work out the perimeter and area of various shapes. He says the shapes required are squares and triangles.

The procedural programmer rushes away and quickly comes up with four obvious routines:

```
def perimeter_of_square(side_length)
  side_length * 4
end

def area_of_square(side_length)
  side_length * side_length
end

def perimeter_of_triangle(side1, side2, side3)
  side1 + side2 + side3
end

def area_of_triangle(base_width, height)
  base_width * height / 2
end
```

■**Note** Remember, it's not necessary to use `return` to return values from methods in Ruby. The last expression within the method is used as the return value by default.

Finishing first, the procedural programmer is sure his code will be chosen.

The object-oriented programmer takes longer. He recognizes that the specifications might change in future, and that it would be useful to define a Shape class and then create classes that would inherit from Shape. This would mean that if extra features needed to be added to shapes in general, the code would be ready. He submits his initial solution:

```
class Shape
end

class Square < Shape
  def initialize(side_length)
    @side_length = side_length
  end

  def area
    @side_length * @side_length
  end
```

```
  def perimeter
    @side_length * 4
  end
end

class Triangle < Shape
  def initialize(base_width, height, side1, side2, side3)
    @base_width = base_width
    @height = height
    @side1 = side1
    @side2 = side2
    @side3 = side3
  end

  def area
    @base_width * @height / 2
  end

  def perimeter
    @side1 + @side2 + @side3
  end
end
```

Note This code might seem complex and alien at this time, but we'll be covering the techniques used here later in this chapter. For now, simply recognize the structure of laying down classes and methods, as covered in Chapter 2.

The procedural programmer scoffs at the object-oriented solution. "Why all the pointless assignments of data?" he mocks. "That object-oriented code is 90% structure and 10% logic!"

The boss is impressed by the shortness of the procedural code, but decides to try them out for himself. He quickly spots a big difference:

```
puts area_of_triangle(6,6)
puts perimeter_of_square(5)
```

18
20

```
my_square = Square.new(5)
my_triangle = Triangle.new(6, 6, 7.81, 7.81, 7.81)
puts my_square.area
puts my_square.perimeter
puts my_triangle.area
puts my_triangle.perimeter
```

```
25
20
18
23.43
```

The boss notices that with the object-oriented code, he can create as many shapes as he wants in a logical way, whereas the procedural code expects him to have a mental note of the shapes he wants to work with. He isn't without his concerns, though.

"More lines of code means more time required," he says. "Is it worth taking the object-oriented route if it means more lines of code, more time, and more hassles?"

The object-oriented developer has heard this complaint before, and immediately springs into action. "Try dealing with a large number of random shapes," he says.

The boss isn't entirely up to date with modern development trends, but when he discovers that many new types of shapes can be produced easily by copying and pasting the existing classes with some minor tweaks, he begins to be won over. He also realizes that if a shape could be stored as an object referenced by a single variable, and that if each shape class accepted the same methods, the type of shape presented wouldn't matter. He could call the perimeter or area method on *any* shape without worry. The procedural code, on the other hand, is just a jumble of different routines, and the developer would be forced to keep track of the different types of shapes to know which procedures to run. The Shape class also provides a way to give general functionality to all the different types of shapes if it's necessary in future. The boss knows which code to choose!

"Object-oriented code requires a little more setup, but when it comes to scaling that code to fit real-life requirements, there's no contest!" he says.

The basic advantage with object-oriented programming is that even if there's more structure involved in setting up your code, it's easy for a nonexpert to understand how classes and objects relate, and it's easier to maintain and update the code to deal with real-life situations.

Object Orientation Basics

Let's recap our basic knowledge of classes and objects that we learned over the past few chapters:

A *class* is a blueprint for objects. You only have one class called Shape, but with it you can create multiple *instances* of shapes (shape *objects*), all of which have the methods and attributes defined by the Shape class.

An *object* is an *instance* of a class. If Shape is the class, then x = Shape.new creates a new Shape instance and assigns the object to the variable x. You would then say x is a Shape object, or an object of class Shape.

Local, Global, Object, and Class Variables

In Chapter 2 you created some classes and added methods to them. To recap, here's a simple demonstration of a class with two methods, and how to use it. First, here's the class itself:

```
class Square
  def initialize(side_length)
    @side_length = side_length
  end

  def area
    @side_length * @side_length
  end
end
```

Next, let's create some square objects and use their area methods:

```
a = Square.new(10)
b = Square.new(5)
puts a.area
puts b.area
```

```
100
25
```

The first method—and when I say "first," I mean the first method in our example; the actual order of methods in code is irrelevant—in the Square class is initialize. initialize is a special method that's called when a new object based on that class is created. When you call Square.new(10), the Square class creates a new object instance of itself, and then calls initialize upon that object.

In this case, initialize accepts side_length as an argument, as passed through from Square.new(10), and assigns the number 10 to a variable called @side_length. The @ symbol before the variable name is important in this case. But why? To understand why some variables are prefixed with certain symbols requires understanding that there are multiple types of variables, such as local, global, object, and class variables.

Local Variables

In previous examples you've created variables simply, like so:

```
x = 10
puts x
```

```
10
```

In Ruby, this sort of basic variable is called a *local variable*. It can only be used in the same place as where it is defined. If you jump to using an object's methods or a separate method of your own, the variable x doesn't come with you. It's considered to be local in *scope*. That is, it's only present within the local area of code. Here's an example that demonstrates this:

```
def basic_method
  puts x
end

x = 10
basic_method
```

This example defines x to equal 10, and then jumps to a local method called basic_method. If you ran this code through irb, you would get an error like this:

```
NameError: undefined local variable or method `x' for main:Object
        from (irb):2:in `basic_method'
```

What's happening is that when you jump to basic_method, you're no longer in the same *scope* as the variable x that you created. Because x is a local variable, it only exists where it was defined. To avoid this problem, it's important to remember to use only local variables where they're being directly used, as this is what they're really for.

Here's an example where you have two local variables with the same name but in different scopes:

```
def basic_method
  x = 50
  puts x
end

x = 10
basic_method
puts x
```

```
50
10
```

This demonstrates that local variables live entirely in their original scope. You set x to 10 in the main code, and set x to 50 inside the method, but x is still 10 when you return to the original scope. *The x variable inside basic_method is not the same x variable that's outside of the method.* They're separate variables, distinct within their own scopes.

Global Variables

In direct opposition to local variables, Ruby can also use *global variables*. Much as their name suggests, global variables are available from everywhere within an application, including inside classes or objects.

Global variables can be useful, but aren't commonly used in Ruby. They don't mesh well with the ideals of object-oriented programming, as once you start using global variables across an application, your code is likely to become dependent on them. Because the ability to separate blocks of logic from one another is a useful aspect of object-oriented programming, global variables are not favored. However, I'll touch on global variables again later in this book, so it's useful to know how they're constructed.

You define global variables by putting a dollar sign ($) in front of the variable name, like so:

```
def basic_method
  puts $x
end
```

```
$x = 10
basic_method
```

```
10
```

$x is defined as a global variable, and you can use it anywhere in your application.

Instance Variables

Where local variables are specific to the local scope, and global variables have global scope, *object variables* are so named because they have scope within, and are associated to, the current object. A demonstration of this concept was shown at the start of this section with the Square class:

```
class Square
  def initialize(side_length)
    @side_length = side_length
  end

  def area
    @side_length * @side_length
  end
end
```

Object variables are prefixed with an @ symbol. In the Square class, you assign the side_length provided to the class to @side_length. @side_length, as an object variable, is then accessible from any other method inside that object. That's how the area method can then use @side_length to calculate the area of the square represented by the object:

```
a = Square.new(10)
b = Square.new(5)
puts a.area
puts b.area
```

```
100
25
```

The results are different, even though the code to work out the area in both cases is @side_length * @side_length. This is because @side_length is an object variable associated only with the current object or instance.

Tip If you didn't fully understand the Shape/Square/Triangle example at the start of this chapter, now would be a good time to look back at it, as it used several object variables to develop its functionality.

Class Variables

The last major type of variable is the *class variable*. The scope of a class variable is within the current class, as opposed to within specific objects of that class. Class variables start with two @ symbols (@@) as opposed to the single @ symbol of object variables.

Class variables are particularly useful for storing information relevant to all objects of a certain class. For example, you could store the number of objects created so far in a certain class using a class variable like so:

```
class Square
  def initialize
    if defined?(@@number_of_squares)
      @@number_of_squares += 1
    else
      @@number_of_squares = 1
    end
  end
end
```

Because @@number_of_squares is a class variable, it's already defined each time you create a new object (except for the first time, but that's why you check to see if it's defined, and if not, give it an initial value of 1).

Note In Chapter 3 you learned about the ternary operator, and that can be used to simplify the above method down to @@number_of_squares = defined?(@@number_of_squares) ? @@number_of_squares + 1 : 1

Class Methods vs. Object Methods

In your Square class you defined two methods: initialize and area. Both are object methods, as they relate to, and operate directly upon, an object. Here's the code again:

```
class Square
  def initialize(side_length)
    @side_length = side_length
  end

  def area
    @side_length * @side_length
  end
end
```

Once you've created a square with s = Square.new(10), you can use s.area to get back the area of the square represented by s. The area method is made available in all objects of class Square, so it's considered to be an *object method*.

However, methods are not just useful to have available on object instances. It can be useful to have methods that work directly upon the class itself. In the previous section you used a class variable to keep a count of how many square objects had been created, and it would be useful to access the @@number_of_squares class variable in some way other than through Square objects.

Here's a simple demonstration of a class method:

```
class Square
  def self.test_method
    puts "Hello from the Square class!"
  end

  def test_method
    puts "Hello from an instance of class Square!"
  end
end

Square.test_method
Square.new.test_method
```

```
Hello from the Square class!
Hello from an instance of class Square!
```

This class has two methods. The first is a class method, and the second is an instance method, although both have the same name of test_method. The difference is that the class method is denoted with self., where self represents the current class, so def self.test_method defines the method as being specific to the class. However, with no prefix, methods are automatically instance methods.

Alternatively, you could define the method like so:

```ruby
class Square
  def Square.test_method
    puts "Hello from the Square class!"
  end
end
```

The style you use (ClassName.method_name versus self.method_name) comes down to personal preference. Using self.method_name (as in self.test_method) doesn't require you to restate the class name over and over, but ClassName.method_name (as in Square.test_method) is a closer match to what you'll be using to call that method later on.

■**Note** Throughout the rest of this book, I'll use the ClassName.method_name style, but you can use whichever style you like in your own code.

Class methods give you the mechanism to properly implement the "object counter" hinted at earlier:

```ruby
class Square
  def initialize
    if defined?(@@number_of_squares)
      @@number_of_squares += 1
    else
      @@number_of_squares = 1
    end
  end

  def Square.count
    @@number_of_squares
  end
end
```

Let's give it a try:

```ruby
a = Square.new
puts Square.count
b = Square.new
```

```
puts Square.count
c = Square.new
puts Square.count
```

```
1
2
3
```

Notice you don't refer to a, b, or c at all to get the count. You just use the Square.count class method directly. Consider it as if you're "asking the class" to do something that's relevant to the class as a whole, rather than asking the objects.

Inheritance

One of the most interesting object-oriented programming concepts is *inheritance*, as it allows you to generate a taxonomy of classes and objects. If you consider all living things as a class called LivingThing (see Figure 6-1), under that class you could have (and let's keep this simple, biologists!) Plant and Animal classes. Under Animal you'd have Mammal, Fish, Amphibian, and so forth. Digging into Mammal, you could work through Primate and Human. A Human is a living thing, a Human is an Animal, a Human is a Mammal, and so forth, but each level down is more specific and targeted than that above it. This is class inheritance in action! The same system applied to the Shape example where Triangle and Square inherited directly from Shape.

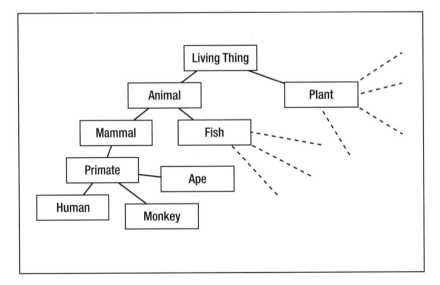

Figure 6-1. *An example of a hierarchy of "living things"*

The benefit of inheritance is that classes lower down the hierarchy get the features of those higher up, but can also add specific features of their own. The basic "all living things" class is so generic that the only functionality you could give to it is a basic "living or dead" method. However, at the animal level, you could add methods such as eat, excrete, or breathe. At the human level you'd inherit all this functionality but be able to add human methods and qualities such as sing, dance, and love.

Ruby's inheritance features are similarly simple. Any class can inherit the features and functionality of another class, but a class can only inherit from a *single* other class. Some other languages support *multiple inheritance*, a feature that allows classes to inherit features from multiple classes, but Ruby doesn't support this. Multiple inheritance can cause some confusing situations—for instance, classes could inherit from one another in an endless loop—and the efficacy of multiple inheritance is debatable.

Let's look at how inheritance works in code form:

```ruby
class ParentClass
  def method1
    puts "Hello from method1 in the parent class"
  end

  def method2
    puts "Hello from method2 in the parent class"
  end
end

class ChildClass < ParentClass
  def method2
    puts "Hello from method2 in the child class"
  end
end

my_object = ChildClass.new
my_object.method1
```

```
Hello from method1 in the parent class
```

```ruby
my_object.method2
```

```
Hello from method2 in the child class
```

First you create the ParentClass with two methods, method1 and method2. Then you create ChildClass and make it inherit from ParentClass using the ChildClass < ParentClass notation. Last, you create an object instance of ChildClass and call its method1 and method2 methods.

The first result demonstrates inheritance perfectly. ChildClass has no method1 of its own, but because it has inherited from ParentClass, and ParentClass has a method1, it uses it.

However, in the second case, ChildClass already has a method2 method, so the method2 method supplied by the parent class is ignored. In many cases, this is ideal behavior, as it allows your more specific classes to override behavior provided by more general classes. However, in some situations you might want a child method to call an inherited method and do something with the result.

Consider some basic classes that represent different types of people:

```
class Person
  def initialize(name)
    @name = name
  end

  def name
    return @name
  end
end

class Doctor < Person
  def name
    "Dr. " + super
  end
end
```

In this case you have a Person class that implements the basic functionality of storing and returning a person's name. The Doctor class inherits from Person and overrides the name method. Within the name method for doctors, it returns a string starting with Dr., appended with the name as usual. This occurs by using super, which looks up the inheritance chain and calls the method of the same name on the next highest class. In this example, you only have two tiers, so using super within the name method in Doctor then uses the name method in Person.

The benefit of using inheritance in this way is that you can implement generic functionality in generic classes, and then only implement the specific functionality that more specific child classes require. This saves a lot of repetition and means that if you make changes to the parent classes, child classes will inherit these changes too. A good example of this might be if you changed Person to take two arguments, firstname and lastname.

The Doctor class wouldn't need to be changed at all to support this change. With one child class this doesn't seem too important, but when you have hundreds of different classes in an application, it pays to cut down on repetition!

Note The concept of cutting down on repetition is commonly called *DRY*, meaning Don't Repeat Yourself. If you can code something once and reuse it from multiple places, that's usually the best way to be DRY.

Overriding Existing Methods

Because it's a dynamic language, one clever thing you can do with Ruby is override existing classes and methods. For example, consider Ruby's String class. As covered in Chapter 3, if you create a string, you end up with an object of class String; for example:

```
x = "This is a test"
puts x.class
```

```
String
```

You can call a number of different methods upon the String object stored in x:

```
puts x.length
puts x.upcase
```

```
14
THIS IS A TEST
```

Let's stir things up a bit by overriding the length method:

```
class String
  def length
    20
  end
end
```

Many newcomers to Ruby, even experienced developers, initially fail to believe this will work, but the results are exactly as the code dictates:

```
puts "This is a test".length
puts "a".length
puts "A really long line of text".length
```

```
20
20
20
```

Some libraries and extensions (add-ons) to Ruby override the methods supplied by the core classes to extend the functionality of Ruby in general. However, this demonstration shows why it's always necessary to tread with caution and be aware of what's going on in your application. If you were relying on being able to measure the length of strings, and the length method gets overridden, you're going to have a hard time!

You should also note that you can override your own methods. In fact, you've probably been doing it a lot already by following these examples in irb:

```
class Dog
  def talk
    puts "Woof!"
  end
end

my_dog = Dog.new
my_dog.talk
```

```
Woof!
```

```
class Dog
  def talk
    puts "Howl!"
  end
end

my_dog.talk
```

```
Howl!
```

In this example, you created a basic class with a simple method, then reopened that class and redefined a method on the fly. The results of the redefinition were made effective immediately, and my_dog began to howl as a result.

This ability to reopen classes and add and redefine methods is relatively unique among object-oriented languages. Although it allows you to perform a number of interesting tricks (some of which you'll see in action later), it can also cause the same sections of code to act in different ways depending on whether certain classes upon which you depend were changed in the application, as demonstrated by your redefinition of String's length method previously.

■**Note** You might have noticed this class-reopening technique in action in some of our earlier examples where you created methods in one example, only to add new methods in a later example. If running under irb or within the same program, reopening a class lets you add new methods or change old ones without losing anything.

Reflection and Discovering an Object's Methods

Reflection is the name of the process by which a computer program can inspect, analyze, and modify itself while it's running and being used. Ruby takes reflection to an extreme, and allows you to change the functionality of great swathes of the language itself while running your own code.

It's possible to query almost any object within Ruby for the methods that are defined within it. This is another part of reflection.

```
a = "This is a test"
puts a.methods.join(' ')
```

```
methods instance_eval % rindex map << split any? dup sort strip size
instance_variables downcase min gsub! count include? succ! instance_of? extend
downcase! intern squeeze! eql? * next find_all each rstrip! each_line + id sub
slice! hash singleton_methods tr replace inject reverse taint unpack sort_by
lstrip frozen? instance_variable_get capitalize max chop! method kind_of?
capitalize! scan select to_a display each_byte type casecmp gsub protected_methods
empty? to_str partition tr_s tr! match grep rstrip to_sym instance_variable_set
next! swapcase chomp! is_a? swapcase! ljust respond_to? between? reject to_supto
```

```
hex sum class object_id reverse! chop <=> insert < tainted? private_methods ==
delete dump === __id__ member? tr_s! > concat nil? untaint succ find strip!
each_with_index >= to_i rjust <= send index collect inspect slice oct all? clone
length entries chomp =~ public_methods upcase sub! squeeze __send__ upcase!crypt
delete! equal? freeze detect zip [] lstrip! center []= to_f
```

The methods method on any object (unless it has been overridden, of course!) returns an array of methods made available by that object. Due to Ruby's heavily object-oriented structure, that's usually a significantly larger number of methods than those you have specifically defined yourself!

The results reveal some other reflective methods too. For example, protected_methods, private_methods, and public_methods all reveal methods encapsulated in different ways (more on this in the next section).

Another interesting method is instance_variables. It returns the names of any instance variables associated with an instance (as opposed to class variables):

```
class Person
  attr_accessor :name, :age
end

p = Person.new
p.name = "Fred"
p.age = 20
puts p.instance_variables.inspect
```

```
["@age", "@name"]
```

At this stage you might not see the value in these reflective methods, but as you progress toward becoming a Ruby guru, they'll become more important. This book doesn't go deeply into the arts of metaprogramming and advanced reflective techniques, as although they're interesting topics, they aren't widely used until you reach a significant level of competence, and are therefore beyond the scope of a beginner's book.

Encapsulation

Encapsulation is the ability for an object to have certain methods and attributes available for use publicly (from any section of code), but for others to be visible only *within* the class itself or by other objects of the same class.

■**Note** At a more technical level, encapsulation refers to the ability of objects to hide their constituent data behind an abstracted interface, and this ability is implicitly considered here.

The rationale for encapsulation is that you should make as few methods available from your classes as possible, so that even if you choose to rewrite the internals of your classes, you can maintain a few methods that interface between other elements of your system and your classes and objects. Encapsulation helps you keep a lot of functionality within your classes, but gives you the security of only having a few ways for the outside world to manipulate your object's data. This can allow you to extend and change your classes without the worry that other elements of your application will break.

Here's an example class that represents a person:

```ruby
class Person
  def initialize(name)
    set_name(name)
  end

  def name
    @first_name + ' ' + @last_name
  end

  def set_name(name)
    first_name, last_name = name.split(/\s+/)
    set_first_name(first_name)
    set_last_name(last_name)
  end

  def set_first_name(name)
    @first_name = name
  end

  def set_last_name(name)
    @last_name = name
  end
end
```

In previous examples, you would have written this with a single attr_accessor :name and simply assigned the name to an object variable. Unfortunately, though, real-life constraints often require a different approach.

In this case, the first name and last name are stored separately within each `Person` object, in object variables called `@first_name` and `@last_name`. When a `Person` object is created, the name is split into two halves and each is assigned to the correct object variable by `set_first_name` and `set_last_name`, respectively. One possible reason for such a construction could be that although you want to work with complete names in your application, the database design might demand you have first names and last names in separate columns. Therefore, you need to hide this difference by handling it in the class code, as in the preceding code.

Note A side benefit of this approach is also that you can perform checks on the data before assigning it to the object variables. For example, in the `set_first_name` and `set_last_name` methods, you could check that the names contain enough characters to be considered valid names. If not, you can then raise an error.

The code appears to work fine:

```
p = Person.new("Fred Bloggs")
puts p.name
```

```
Fred Bloggs
```

However, it appears you still have some problems:

```
p = Person.new("Fred Bloggs")
p.set_last_name("Smith")
puts p.name
```

```
Fred Smith
```

Uh-oh! You wanted to abstract the first name/last name requirement and only allow full names to be set or retrieved. However, the `set_first_name` and `set_last_name` are still public and you can use them directly from any code where you have `Person` objects. Luckily, encapsulation lets you solve the problem:

```
class Person
  def initialize(name)
    set_name(name)
  end
```

```ruby
  def name
    @first_name + ' ' + @last_name
  end

  private

  def set_name(name)
    first_name, last_name = name.split(/\s+/)
    set_first_name(first_name)
    set_last_name(last_name)
  end

  def set_first_name(name)
    @first_name = name
  end

  def set_last_name(name)
    @last_name = name
  end
end
```

The only difference to the Person class from the first time you created it is that the keyword private has been added. What private does is tell Ruby that any methods declared in this class from there on should be kept "private." This means that only code within the object's methods can access those private methods, whereas code outside of the class cannot. For example, this code no longer works:

```ruby
p = Person.new("Fred Bloggs")
p.set_last_name("Smith")
```

```
NoMethodError: private method 'set_last_name' called for #<Person:0x337b68
@last_name="Bloggs", @first_name="Fred">
```

The opposite of the private keyword is public. You could put private before one method, but then revert back to public methods again afterwards using public, like so:

```ruby
class Person
  def anyone_can_access_this
    ...
  end
```

```
  private
  def this_is_private

    ...

  end

  public
  def another_public_method

    ...

  end
end
```

You can also use `private` as a command by passing in symbols representing the methods you want to keep private, like so:

```
class Person
  def anyone_can_access_this; ...; end

  def this_is_private; ...; end

  def this_is_also_private; ...; end

  def another_public_method; ...; end

  private :this_is_private, :this_is_also_private
end
```

■**Note** Ruby supports ending lines with semicolons (;) and allows you to put multiple lines of code onto a single line (for example, `x = 10; x += 1; puts x`). In this case, it's been done to save on lines of code in the example, although it's not considered good style in production-quality Ruby code.

The command tells Ruby that `this_is_private` and `this_is_also_private` are to be made into `private` methods. Whether you choose to use `private` as a directive before methods, or as a command specifying the method names directly, is up to you, and is another of many technically unimportant stylistic decisions you'll make as a Ruby programmer. However, it's important to note that in the preceding example the `private` declaration has to come after the methods are defined.

Ruby supports a third form of encapsulation (other than `public` and `private`) called `protected` that makes a method private, but within the scope of a class rather than within a single object. For example, you were unable to directly call a private method outside the scope of that object and its methods. However, you can call a `protected` method from the scope of the methods of any object that's a member of the same class:

```
class Person
  def initialize(age)
    @age = age
  end

  def age
    @age
  end

  def age_difference_with(other_person)
    (self.age - other_person.age).abs
  end

  protected :age
end

fred = Person.new(34)
chris = Person.new(25)
puts chris.age_difference_with(fred)
puts chris.age
```

```
9
:20: protected method `age' called for #<Person:0x1e5f28 @age=25>
(NoMethodError)
```

The preceding example uses a `protected` method so that the age method cannot be used directly, except within any method belonging to an object of the Person class. However, if age were made `private`, the preceding example would fail because other_person.age would be invalid. That's because `private` makes methods accessible only by methods of a specific object.

Note that when you use age directly, on the last line, Ruby throws an exception.

Polymorphism

Polymorphism is the concept of writing code that can work with objects of multiple types and classes at once. For example, the + method works for adding numbers, joining strings, and adding arrays together. What + does depends entirely on *what* type of things you're adding together.

Here's a Ruby interpretation of a common demonstration of polymorphism:

```ruby
class Animal
  attr_accessor :name

  def initialize(name)
    @name = name
  end
end

class Cat < Animal
  def talk
    "Meaow!"
  end
end

class Dog < Animal
  def talk
    "Woof!"
  end
end

animals = [Cat.new("Flossie"), Dog.new("Fido"), Cat.new("Tinkle")]
animals.each do |animal|
  puts animal.talk
end
```

```
Meaow!
Woof!
Meaow!
```

In this example, you define three classes: an Animal class, and Dog and Cat classes that inherit from Animal. In the code at the bottom, you create an array of various animal objects: two Cat objects and a Dog object (whose names are all processed by the generic initialize method from the Animal class).

Next, you iterate over each of the animals, and on each loop you place the animal object into the local variable, animal. Last, you run puts animal.talk for each animal in turn. As the `talk` method is defined on both the `Cat` and `Dog` class, but with different output, you get the correct output of two "Meaow!"s and two "Woof!"s.

This demonstration shows how you can loop over and work upon objects of different classes, but get the expected results in each case if each class implements the same methods.

If you were to create new classes under the `Cat` or `Dog` classes with inheritance (for example, `class Labrador < Dog`), then `Labrador.new.talk` would still return "Woof!" thanks to inheritance.

Some of Ruby's built-in standard classes (such as `Array`, `Hash`, `String`, and so on) have polymorphic methods of their own. For example, you can call the `to_s` method on many built-in classes to return the contents of the object as a string:

```
puts 1000.to_s
puts [1,2,3].to_s
puts ({ :name => 'Fred', :age => 10 }).to_s
```

```
1000
123
age10nameFred
```

The output isn't particularly useful in this case, but being able to rely on most objects to return a string with `to_s` comes in particularly useful in many situations.

Nested Classes

In Ruby, it's possible to place classes within other classes. These are called *nested* classes. Nested classes are useful when a class depends on other classes, but those classes aren't necessarily useful anywhere else. They can also be useful when you want to separate classes into groups of classes rather than keep them all distinct. Here's an example:

```
class Drawing
  class Line
  end

  class Circle
  end
end
```

Nested classes are defined in the same way as usual. However, they're used differently.

From within Drawing, you can access the Line and Circle classes directly, but from outside the Drawing class, you can only access Line and Circle as Drawing::Line and Drawing::Circle. For example:

```
class Drawing
  def Drawing.give_me_a_circle
    Circle.new
  end

  class Line
  end

  class Circle
    def what_am_i
      "This is a circle"
    end
  end
end

a = Drawing.give_me_a_circle
puts a.what_am_i
a = Drawing::Circle.new
puts a.what_am_i
a = Circle.new
puts a.what_am_i
```

```
This is a circle
This is a circle
NameError: uninitialized constant Circle
```

a = Drawing.give_me_a_circle calls the give_me_a_circle class method, which returns a new instance of Drawing::Circle. Next, a = Drawing::Circle.new gets a new instance of Drawing::Circle directly, which also works. The third attempt, a = Circle.new, does not work, however, because Circle doesn't exist. That's because as a nested class under Drawing, it's known as Drawing::Circle instead.

You're going to use nested classes in a project at the end of this chapter, where you'll see how they work in the scope of an entire program.

The Scope of Constants

In Chapter 3 you looked at constants: special variables whose value(s) are unchanging and permanent throughout an application, such as Pi = 3.141592. Here's an example:

```
def circumference_of_circle(radius)
  2 * Pi * radius
end

Pi = 3.141592
puts circumference_of_circle(10)
```

```
31.41592
```

In this sense, a constant appears to work like a global variable, but it's not. Constants are defined within the scope of the current class and are made available to all child classes, unless they're overridden. For example:

```
Pi = 3.141592

class OtherPlanet
  Pi = 4.5

  def OtherPlanet.circumference_of_circle(radius)
    radius * 2 * Pi
  end
end

puts OtherPlanet.circumference_of_circle(10)
```

```
90.0
```

```
puts OtherPlanet::Pi
```

```
4.5
```

```
puts Pi
```

```
3.141592
```

This example demonstrates that constants have scope within the context of classes. The OtherPlanet class has its own definition of Pi. However, if you hadn't redefined it there, the original Pi would have been available to OtherPlanet, as the OtherPlanet class is defined within the global scope.

The second section of the preceding example also demonstrates that you can interrogate constants within other classes directly. OtherPlanet::Pi refers directly to the Pi constant within OtherPlanet.

Modules, Namespaces, and Mix-Ins

Modules provide a structure to collect Ruby classes, methods, and constants into a single, separately named and defined unit. This is useful so you can avoid clashes with existing classes, methods, and constants, and also so that you can add (mix in) the functionality of modules into your classes. First, we'll look at how to use modules to create *namespaces* to avoid name-related clashes.

Namespaces

One common feature used in Ruby is the ability to include code situated in other files into the current program (this is covered in depth in the next chapter). When including other files, you can quickly run into conflicts, particularly if files or libraries you're including then include multiple files of their own. You cannot guarantee that no file that's included (or one that's included in a long chain of includes) will clash with code you've already written or processed.

Take this example:

```
def random
  rand(1000000)
end
```

```
puts random
```

The random method returns a random number between 0 and 999,999. This method could be in a remote file where it's easily forgotten, which would cause problems if you had another file you included using require that implemented a method like so:

```
def random
  (rand(26) + 65).chr
end
```

This random method returns a random capital letter.

■Note (rand(26) + 65).chr generates a random number between 0 and 25 and adds 65 to it, giving a number in the range of 65 to 90. The chr method then converts a number into a character using the ASCII standard where 65 is A, through to 90, which is Z. You can learn more about the ASCII character set at http://en.wikipedia.org/wiki/ASCII, or refer to Chapter 3 where this topic was covered in more detail.

Now you have two methods called random. If the first random method is in a file called number_stuff.rb and the second random method is in a file called letter_stuff.rb, you're going to hit problems:

```
require 'number_stuff'
require 'letter_stuff'

puts random
```

Which version of the random method is called?

■Note require is the Ruby statement used to load in code contained within another file. This is covered in detail in the next chapter.

As the last file loaded, it turns out to be the latter version of random, and a random letter should appear onscreen. Unfortunately, however, it means your other random method has been lost.

This situation is known as a *name conflict*, and it can happen in even more gruesome situations than the simplistic example shown in the preceding code. For example, class names can clash similarly, and you could end up with two classes mixed into one by accident. If a class called Song is defined in one external file, and then defined in a second external file, the class Song available in your program will be a dirty mix of the two. Sometimes this might be the intended behavior, but in other cases this can cause significant problems.

Modules help to solve these conflicts by providing *namespaces* that can contain any number of classes, methods, and constants, and allow you to address them directly. For example:

```
module NumberStuff
  def NumberStuff.random
    rand(1000000)
  end
end
```

```ruby
module LetterStuff
  def LetterStuff.random
    (rand(26) + 65).chr
  end
end

puts NumberStuff.random
puts LetterStuff.random
```

```
184783
X
```

Note Due to the randomness introduced by using `rand`, the preceding results will vary every time you run the program.

In this demonstration it's clear which version of `random` you're trying to use in the two last lines. The modules defined in the preceding code look a little like classes, except they're defined with the word `module` instead of `class`. However, in reality, you cannot define instances of a module, as they're not actually classes, nor can they inherit from anything. Modules simply provide ways to organize methods, classes, and constants into separate namespaces.

A more complex example could involve demonstrating two classes with the same name, but in different modules:

```ruby
module ToolBox
  class Ruler
    attr_accessor :length
  end
end

module Country
  class Ruler
    attr_accessor :name
  end
end
```

```
a = ToolBox::Ruler.new
a.length = 50
b = Country::Ruler.new
b.name = "Ghengis Khan from Moskau"
```

Rather than having the Ruler classes fighting it out for supremacy, or ending up with a mutant Ruler class with both name and length attributes (how many measuring rulers have names?), the Ruler classes are kept separately in the ToolBox and Country namespaces.

You'll be looking at why namespaces are even more useful than this later, but first you have to look at the second reason why modules are so useful.

Mix-Ins

Earlier you studied inheritance: the feature of object orientation that allows classes (and their instance objects) to inherit methods from other classes. You discovered that Ruby doesn't support *multiple inheritance*, the ability to inherit from multiple classes at the same time. Instead, Ruby's inheritance functionality only lets you create simple trees of classes, avoiding the confusion inherent with multiple inheritance systems.

However, in some cases, it can be useful to share functionality between disparate classes. In this sense, modules act like a sort of "super" class and can be *included* into other classes, extending that class with the methods the module offers. For example:

```
module UsefulFeatures
  def class_name
    self.class.to_s
  end
end

class Person
  include UsefulFeatures
end

x = Person.new
puts x.class_name
```

```
Person
```

In this code, UsefulFeatures looks almost like a class, and it almost is. However, modules are organizational tools rather than classes themselves. The class_name method exists within the module, and is then *included* into the Person class. Here's another example:

```
module AnotherModule
  def do_stuff
    puts "This is a test"
  end
end

include AnotherModule
do_stuff
```

```
This is a test
```

As you can see, you can include module methods into the current scope, even if you're not directly within a class. Somewhat like a class, though, you can use the methods directly:

```
AnotherModule.do_stuff
```

Therefore, include takes a module and includes its contents into the current scope.

Ruby comes with several modules by standard that you can use. For example, the Kernel module contains all the "standard" commands you use in Ruby without getting involved with objects or classes, such as load, require, exit, puts, and eval. None of those methods are taking place directly in the scope of an object (as with the methods in your own programs), but they're special methods that get included into all classes (including the main scope), by default, through the Kernel module.

However, of more interest to us are the modules Ruby provides that you can include into your own classes to gain more functionality immediately. Two such modules are Enumerable and Comparable.

Enumerable

In previous chapters you've performed the process of *iteration*, like so:

```
[1,2,3,4,5].each { |number| puts number }
```

In this case, you create a temporary array containing the numbers one through five and use the each iterator to pass each value into the code block, assigning each value to number that you then print to the screen with puts.

The each iterator gives you a lot of power, as it allows you to go through all the elements of an array or a hash and use the data you retrieve to work out, for example, the mean average of an array of numbers, or the length of the longest string in an array, like so:

```
my_array = %w{this is a test of the longest word check}
longest_word = ''
my_array.each do |word|
  longest_word = word if longest_word.length < word.length
end
puts longest_word
```

```
longest
```

In this case, you loop through my_array, and if the currently stored longest word is shorter than the length of word, you assign it to longest_word. When the loop finishes, the longest word is in longest_word.

The same code could be tweaked to find the largest (or smallest) number in a set of numbers:

```
my_array = %w{10 56 92 3 49 588 18}
highest_number = 0
my_array.each do |number|
  number = number.to_i
  highest_number = number if number > highest_number
end
puts highest_number
```

```
588
```

However, the Array class (for one) has preincluded the methods provided by the Enumerable module, a module that supplies about 20 useful counting- and iteration-related methods, including collect, detect, find, find_all, include?, max, min, select, sort, and to_a. All of these use Array's each method to do their jobs, and if your class can implement an each method, you can include Enumerable, and get all those methods for free in your own class!

■**Note** The main methods provided by Enumerable are referenced in Appendix B.

First, some examples of the methods provided by Enumerable:

```
[1,2,3,4].collect { |i| i.to_s + "x" }
```

```
=> ["1x", "2x", "3x", "4x"]
```

```
[1,2,3,4].detect { |i| i.between?(2,3) }
```

```
=> 2
```

```
[1,2,3,4].select { |i| i.between?(2,3) }
```

```
=> [2,3]
```

```
[4,1,3,2].sort
```

```
=> [1,2,3,4]
```

```
[1,2,3,4].max
```

```
=> 4
```

```
[1,2,3,4].min
```

```
=> 1
```

You can make your own class, implement an each method, and get these methods for "free":

```
class AllVowels
  @@vowels = %w{a e i o u}
  def each
    @@vowels.each { |v| yield v }
  end
end
```

This is a class that, in reality, doesn't need to provide multiple objects, as it only provides an enumeration of vowels. However, to keep the demonstration simple, it is ideal. Here's how it works:

```
x = AllVowels.new
x.each { |v| puts v }
```

```
a
e
i
o
u
```

Your AllVowels class contains a class array containing the vowels, and the instance-level each method iterates through the class array @@vowels and yields to the code block supplied to each, passing in each vowel, using yield v. Let's get Enumerable involved:

```
class AllVowels
  include Enumerable

  @@vowels = %w{a e i o u}
  def each
    @@vowels.each { |v| yield v }
  end
end
```

■Note yield and its relationship to code blocks was covered near the end of Chapter 3, if you need a refresher.

Now let's try to use those methods provided by Enumerable again. First let's get an AllVowels object:

```
x = AllVowels.new
```

Now you can call the methods upon x:

```
x.collect { |i| i + "x" }
```

```
=> ["ax", "ex", "ix", "ox", "ux"]
```

```
x.detect { |i| i > "j" }
```

```
=> "o"
```

```
x.select { |i| i > "j" }
```

```
=> ["o", "u"]
```

```
x.sort
```

```
=> ["a", "e", "i", "o", "u"]
```

```
x.max
```

```
=> "u"
```

```
x.min
```

```
=> "a"
```

Comparable

The Comparable module provides methods that give other classes comparison operators such as < (less than), <= (less than or equal to), == (is equal to), >= (greater than or equal to), and > (greater than), as well as the between? method that returns true if the value is between (inclusively) the two parameters supplied (for example, 4.between?(3,10) == true).

To provide these methods, the Comparable module uses the <=> operator on the class that includes it. <=> returns -1 if the supplied parameter is higher than the object's value, 0 if they are equal, or 1 if the object's value is higher than the parameter. For example:

```
1 <=> 2
```

```
-1
```

```
1 <=> 1
```

```
0
```

```
2 <=> 1
```

```
1
```

With this simple method, the Comparable module can provide the other basic comparison operators and between?. Create your own class to try it out:

```
class Song
  include Comparable

  attr_accessor :length
  def <=>(other)
    @length <=> other.length
  end

  def initialize(song_name, length)
    @song_name = song_name
```

```
    @length = length
  end

end

a = Song.new('Rock around the clock', 143)
b = Song.new('Bohemian Rhapsody', 544)
c = Song.new('Minute Waltz', 60)
```

Here are the results of including the Comparable module:

```
a < b
```

```
=> true
```

```
b >= c
```

```
=> true
```

```
c > a
```

```
=> false
```

```
a.between?(b,c)
```

```
=> true
```

You can compare the songs as if you're comparing numbers. Technically, you are. By implementing the <=> method on the Song class, individual song objects can be compared directly, and you use their lengths to do so. You could have implemented <=> to compare by the length of the song title, or any other attribute, if you wished.

Modules give you the same ability to implement similar generic sets of functionality that you can then apply to arbitrary classes. For example, you could create a module that implements longest and shortest methods that could be included into Array, Hash, or other classes, and returns the longest or shortest string in a list.

Using Mix-Ins with Namespaces and Classes

In a previous example, I demonstrated how you can use modules to define namespaces using the following code:

```
module ToolBox
  class Ruler
    attr_accessor :length
  end
end

module Country
  class Ruler
    attr_accessor :name
  end
end

a = ToolBox::Ruler.new
a.length = 50
b = Country::Ruler.new
b.name = "Ghengis Khan of Moskau"
```

In this case, the Ruler classes were accessed by directly addressing them via their respective modules (as ToolBox::Ruler and Country::Ruler).

However, what if you wanted to assume temporarily that Ruler (with no module name prefixed) was Country::Ruler, and that if you wanted to access any other Ruler class, you'd refer to it directly? include makes it possible.

In the previous sections, you've used include to include the methods of a module into the current class and scope, but it also includes the classes present within a module (if any) and makes them locally accessible too. Say, after the prior code, you did this:

```
include Country
c = Ruler.new
c.name = "King Henry VIII"
```

Success! The Country module's contents (in this case, just the Ruler class) are brought into the current scope, and you can use Ruler as if it's a local class. If you want to use the Ruler class located under ToolBox, you can still refer to it directly as ToolBox::Ruler.

Building a Dungeon Text Adventure with Objects

So far in this chapter you've looked at object-oriented concepts in depth, mostly in a technical sense. At this point, it would be useful to extend that knowledge by applying it in a real-world scenario.

In this section, you're going to implement a mini text adventure/virtual dungeon. Text adventures were popular in the 1980s, but have fallen out of favor with modern gamers seeking graphical thrills. They're perfect playgrounds for experimenting with classes and objects, though, as replicating the real world in a virtual form requires a complete understanding of mapping real-world concepts into classes.

Dungeon Concepts

Before you can develop your classes, you have to figure out what you're trying to model. Your dungeon isn't going to be complex at all, but you'll design it to cope with at least the following concepts:

- *Dungeon*: You need a general class that encapsulates the entire concept of the dungeon game.

- *Player*: The player provides the link between the dungeon and you. All experience of the dungeon comes through the player. The player can move between rooms in the dungeon.

- *Rooms*: The rooms of the dungeon are the locations that the player can navigate between. These will be linked together in multiple ways (doors to the north, west, east, and south, for example) and have descriptions.

A complete adventure would also have concepts representing items, enemies, other characters, waypoints, spells, and triggers for various puzzles and outcomes. You could easily extend what you'll develop into a more complete game later on if you wished to.

Creating the Initial Classes

Our first concept to develop is that of the dungeon and the game itself. Within this framework come the other concepts, such as the player and rooms.

Using nested classes you can lay down the initial code like so:

```
class Dungeon
  attr_accessor :player
```

```
  def initialize(player_name)
    @player = Player.new(player_name)
    @rooms = []
  end

  class Player
    attr_accessor :name, :location

    def initialize(player_name)
      @name = player_name
    end
  end

  class Room
    attr_accessor :reference, :name, :description, :connections

    def initialize(reference, name, description, connections)
      @reference = reference
      @name = name
      @description = description
      @connections = connections
    end
  end
end
```

This code lays down the framework for your entire dungeon. As the central concept that ties everything together, the Dungeon class wraps all the other classes, because the Player and Room classes are useless, in this case, without a Dungeon to hold them. This is not to say that any class that's dependent on other classes should be nested, but simply that in this situation, it makes sense to structure the classes in this way.

Your dungeon currently has instance variables to store the player and the list of rooms (@rooms = [] creates an empty Array; it's equivalent to @rooms = Array.new).

The Player class lets the player object keep track of his or her name and current location. The Room class lets room objects store their name, description (for example, "Torture Chamber" and "This is a dark, foreboding room."), and connections to other rooms, as well as a reference (to be used by other rooms for their connections).

When you create a dungeon with Dungeon.new, it expects to receive the name of the player, whereupon it creates that player and assigns it to the dungeon's instance variable @player. This is because the player and the dungeon need to be linked together, so storing the player object within the dungeon object makes sense. You can easily access the player because the `player` variable has been made into an accessor with `attr_accessor`. For example:

```
my_dungeon = Dungeon.new("Fred Bloggs")
puts my_dungeon.player.name
```

```
Fred Bloggs
```

You can access the player functionality directly by going *through* the dungeon object. As `@player` contains the `player` object, and as `@player` has been made publicly accessible with `attr_accessor :player`, you get complete access.

Structs: Quick and Easy Data Classes

One thing should stand out about the main code listing so far. It's repetitive. The `Room` and `Player` classes are merely acting as basic placeholders for data rather than as true classes with logic and functionality. There's an easier way to create this sort of special data-holding class in Ruby with a single line of a class called a `Struct`.

A struct is a special class whose only job is to have attributes and to hold data. Here's a demonstration:

```
Person = Struct.new(:name, :gender, :age)
fred = Person.new("Fred", "male", 50)
chris = Person.new("Chris", "male", 25)
puts fred.age + chris.age
```

```
75
```

Simply, the `Struct` class builds classes to store data. On the first line you create a new class called `Person` that has built-in name, gender, and age attributes. On the second line you create a new object instance of `Person` and set the attributes on the fly. The first line is equivalent to this longhand method:

```
class Person
  attr_accessor :name, :gender, :age
```

```
  def initialize(name, gender, age)
    @name = name
    @gender = gender
    @age = age
  end
end
```

Note In actuality, this code is not *exactly* equivalent to the struct code, because parameters are optional when initializing a Struct class, whereas the preceding Person class code requires the three parameters (name, gender, and age) be present.

This code creates a Person class the long way. If all you want to do is store some data, then the struct technique is quicker to type and easier to read, although if you ultimately want to add more functionality to the class, creating a class the long way is worth the effort. However, the good thing is that you can start out with a struct and recode it into a full class when you're ready. This is what you're going to do with your dungeon. Let's rewrite it from scratch:

```
class Dungeon
  attr_accessor :player

  def initialize(player_name)
    @player = Player.new(player_name)
    @rooms = []
  end

  Player = Struct.new(:name, :location)
  Room = Struct.new(:reference, :name, :description, :connections)
end
```

It's certainly shorter, and because parameters are optional when creating instances of Struct classes, you can still use Player.new(player_name), and the location attribute is merely set to nil. If you ever need to add methods to Player or Room, you can rewrite them as classes and add the attributes back with attr_accessor.

ATTR_ACCESSOR

Throughout the code in this chapter, as well as that in Chapter 2, you have used `attr_accessor` within classes to provide attributes for your objects. `attr_accessor` allows you to do this:

```ruby
class Person
  attr_accessor :name, :age
end


x = Person.new
x.name = "Fred"
x.age = 10
puts x.name, x.age
```

However, in reality, `attr_accessor` isn't doing anything magical. It's simply writing some code for you. This code is equivalent to the single `attr_accessor :name, :age` line in the preceding Person class:

```ruby
class Person
  def name
    @name
  end

  def name=(name)
    @name = name
  end

  def age
    @age
  end

  def age=(age)
    @age = age
  end
end
```

This code defines the `name` and `age` methods that return the current object variables for those attributes, so that `x.name` and `x.age` (as in the prior code) work. It also defines two "setter" methods that assign the values to the @name and @age object variables.

If you pay attention to the names of the setter methods, you'll see they're the same as the methods that return values but suffixed with an equal sign (=). This means they're the methods that are run for code such as `x.name = "Fred"` and `x.age = 10`. In Ruby, assignments are just calls to regular methods! Indeed, `x.name = "Fred"` is merely shorthand for writing `x.name=("Fred")`.

Creating Rooms

Your dungeon now has the basic classes in place, but there's still no way to create rooms, so let's add a method to the Dungeon class:

```
class Dungeon
  def add_room(reference, name, description, connections)
    @rooms << Room.new(reference, name, description, connections)
  end
end
```

You want to add rooms to the dungeon, so adding a method to dungeon objects makes the most sense. Now you can create rooms like so (if my_dungeon is still defined, of course):

```
my_dungeon.add_room(:largecave, "Large Cave", "a large cavernous cave", { ➥
:west => :smallcave })


my_dungeon.add_room(:smallcave, "Small Cave", "a small, claustrophobic cave", { ➥
:east => :largecave })
```

add_room accepts the reference, name, description, and connections arguments and creates a new Room object with them before pushing that object onto the end of the @rooms array.

The reference, name, and descriptions arguments should seem obvious, but the connections argument is designed to accept a hash that represents the connections that a particular room has with other rooms. For example, { :west => :smallcave } ties two symbols (:west and :smallcave) together. Your dungeon logic uses this link to connect the rooms. A connections hash of { :west => :smallcave, :south => :another_room } creates two connections (one to the west, and one to the south).

Making the Dungeon Work

You have all the rooms loaded for your basic dungeon (and can add more whenever you like with the add_room method), but you have no way of navigating the dungeon itself.

The first step is to create a method within Dungeon that "starts" everything off by placing the user into the dungeon and giving you the description of the initial location:

```
class Dungeon
  def start(location)
    @player.location = location
    show_current_description
  end
```

```ruby
  def show_current_description
    puts find_room_in_dungeon(@player.location).full_description
  end

  def find_room_in_dungeon(reference)
    @rooms.detect { |room| room.reference == reference }
  end

  class Room
    def full_description
      @name + "\n\nYou are in " + @description
    end
  end
end
```

You define a start method within the dungeon that sets the player's location attribute. It then calls the dungeon's show_current_description method, which finds the room based on the player's location, and then prints the full description of that location to the screen. full_description does the work of taking the location's name and description and turning it into a full, useful description. find_room_in_dungeon, on the other hand, iterates through the @rooms array and picks out the room whose reference matches that of the current location.

However, the problem with the preceding code is that Room is a struct, rather than a full class, so it becomes necessary to turn it into a full class once again (as hinted at earlier). This change requires a few key changes, so to keep things simple, here's the complete code so far, along with the change of Room to a regular class and some additional methods to aid navigation of the dungeon:

```ruby
class Dungeon
  attr_accessor :player

  def initialize(player_name)
    @player = Player.new(player_name)
    @rooms = []
  end

  def add_room(reference, name, description, connections)
    @rooms << Room.new(reference, name, description, connections)
  end
```

```ruby
def start(location)
  @player.location = location
  show_current_description
end

def show_current_description
  puts find_room_in_dungeon(@player.location).full_description
end

def find_room_in_dungeon(reference)
  @rooms.detect { |room| room.reference == reference }
end

def find_room_in_direction(direction)
  find_room_in_dungeon(@player.location).connections[direction]
end

def go(direction)
  puts "You go " + direction.to_s
  @player.location = find_room_in_direction(direction)
  show_current_description
end

class Player
  attr_accessor :name, :location

  def initialize(name)
    @name = name
  end
end

class Room
  attr_accessor :reference, :name, :description, :connections

  def initialize(reference, name, description, connections)
    @reference = reference
    @name = name
    @description = description
    @connections = connections
  end
```

```
    def full_description
      @name + "\n\nYou are in " + @description
    end
  end

end


# Create the main dungeon object
my_dungeon = Dungeon.new("Fred Bloggs")

# Add rooms to the dungeon
my_dungeon.add_room(:largecave, "Large Cave", "a large cavernous cave", { ➥
:west => :smallcave })
my_dungeon.add_room(:smallcave, "Small Cave", "a small, claustrophobic cave", { ➥
:east => :largecave })

# Start the dungeon by placing the player in the large cave
my_dungeon.start(:largecave)
```

```
Large Cave

You are in a large cavernous cave
```

It's a long piece of source code, but most of it should make sense. You've changed Room and Player into true classes once more, and implemented the basics of the dungeon. Two particularly interesting methods have been added to the Dungeon class:

```
def find_room_in_direction(direction)
  find_room_in_dungeon(@player.location).connections[direction]
end

def go(direction)
  puts "You go " + direction.to_s
  @player.location = find_room_in_direction(direction)
  show_current_description
end
```

The go method is what makes navigating the dungeon possible. It takes a single argument—the direction to travel in—and uses that to change the player's location to the room that's in that direction. It does this by calling find_room_in_direction, a method that takes the reference related to the relevant direction's connection on the current room, and returns the reference of the destination room. Remember that you define a room like so:

```
my_dungeon.add_room(:largecave, "Large Cave", "a large cavernous cave", { ➡
:west => :smallcave })
```

If :largecave is the current room, then find_room_in_direction(:west) will use the connections on that room to return :smallcave, and this is then assigned to @player. location to define that as the new current location.

To test the navigation of the dungeon, you can simply type go commands if you're using irb, or if you're working with a source file in an editor, you'll need to add the go commands to the end of your source code and re-run it. Here's what happens:

```
my_dungeon.show_current_description
```

```
Large Cave

You are in a large cavernous cave
```

```
my_dungeon.go(:west)
```

```
You go west
Small Cave

You are in a small, claustrophobic cave
```

```
my_dungeon.go(:east)
```

```
You go east
Large Cave

You are in a large cavernous cave
```

The code has no error checking (try going to a nonexistent room with my_dungeon.go(:south)), and lacks items, an inventory, and other basic text adventure features, but you now have an operational group of objects that represents a dungeon, and that can be navigated in a basic fashion.

This code is ripe for extension and manipulation. With another class and several more methods you could easily add support for items within the game that you can place at different locations, pick up, and then drop at other locations.

In Chapter 9 you'll look at how to interact with files and read data from the keyboard. At that point, you could extend the dungeon game to be properly interactive and accept input from the user, validate that it represents a valid direction, and then call the go method if so. With these additions and the addition of several more rooms, you're most of the way to a viable text adventure!

Summary

In this chapter, we've covered the essentials of object orientation and the features Ruby provides to make object-oriented code a reality. You've looked at the concepts that apply to object orientation in most languages, such as inheritance, encapsulation, class methods, instance methods, and the various types of variables that you can use. Lastly, you developed a basic set of classes to produce a simple dungeon.

Let's reflect on some of the concepts we covered in this chapter:

- *Classes*: A class is a collection of methods and data that are used as a blueprint to create multiple objects relating to that class.

- *Objects*: An object is a single instance of a class. An object of class Person is a single person. An object of class Dog is a single dog. If you think of objects as real-life objects, a class is the classification, whereas an object is the actual object or "thing" itself.

- *Local variable*: A variable that can only be accessed and used from the current scope.

- *Instance/object variable*: A variable that can be accessed and used from the scope of a single object. An object's methods can all access that object's instance variables.

- *Global variable*: A variable that can be accessed and used from anywhere within the current program.

- *Class variable*: A variable that can be accessed and used within the scope of a class and all of its child objects.

- *Encapsulation*: The concept of allowing methods to have differing degrees of visibility outside of their class or associated object.

- *Polymorphism*: The concept of methods being able to deal with different classes of data and offering a more generic implementation (as with the `area` and `perimeter` methods offered by your `Square` and `Triangle` classes).

- *Module*: An organizational element that collects together any number of classes, methods, and constants into a single namespace.

- *Namespace*: A named element of organization that keeps classes, methods, and constants from clashing.

- *Mix-in*: A module that can mix its methods in to a class to extend that class's functionality.

- `Enumerable`: A mix-in module provided as standard with Ruby that implements iterators and list-related methods for other classes such as `collect`, `map`, `min`, and `max`. Ruby uses this module by default with the `Array` and `Hash` classes.

- `Comparable`: A mix-in module provided as standard with Ruby that implements comparison operators (such as `<`, `>`, and `==`) on classes that implement the generic comparison operator `<=>`.

Throughout the next several chapters, I'll assume you have a knowledge of how classes and objects work, and how the different scopes of variables (including local, global, object, and class variables) work.

CHAPTER 7

■ ■ ■

Projects and Libraries

In previous chapters we've looked at and worked with Ruby from a low-level perspective by working directly with classes, objects, and functions. Each line of code we've used in the small projects so far has been written specifically for that project from scratch. In this chapter, we'll look at how to build larger projects with Ruby, and how to reuse code written previously. Finally, we'll look at how to use code already written and prepared by other developers within your own applications, so that you don't need to reinvent the wheel every time you create a new program.

This chapter is about the bigger picture: dealing with projects and libraries.

Projects and Using Code from Other Files

As you become more familiar with Ruby and find more uses for it, it's likely that you'll want to move from writing single small programs (with fewer than 100 or so lines) to more complex applications and systems made up of multiple parts. Larger applications and systems therefore often become known as *projects*, and are managed in a different way than simple one-file scripts.

The most common way to separate functionality in Ruby is to put different classes in different files. This gives you the ability to write classes that could be used in multiple projects simply by copying the file into your other project.

Basic File Inclusion

Consider this code:

```
puts "This is a test".vowels.join('-')
```

If you try to execute this code, you'll get an error complaining that the `vowels` method is not available for the `"This is a test"` object of class `String`. This is true because Ruby doesn't provide that method. Let's write an extension to the `String` class to provide it:

```
class String
  def vowels
    self.scan(/[aeiou]/i)
  end
end
```

If this definition were included in the same file as the prior `puts` code, the result would be as follows:

```
i-i-a-e
```

In this case, you've extended `String` with a `vowels` method that uses `scan` to return an array of all the vowels (the `i` option on the end makes the regular expression case-insensitive).

However, you might want to write a number of methods to add to `String` that you'd like to use in multiple programs. Rather than copy and paste the code each time, you can copy it out to a separate file and use the `require` command to load the external file into the current program. For example, put this code in a file called `string_extensions.rb`:

```
class String
  def vowels
    self.scan(/[aeiou]/i)
  end
end
```

And put this code in a file called `vowel_test.rb`:

```
require 'string_extensions'
puts "This is a test".vowels.join('-')
```

If you run `vowel_test.rb`, the expected result would appear onscreen. The first line, `require 'string_extensions'`, simply loads in the `string_extensions.rb` file and processes it as if the code were local. This means that, in this case, the `vowels` method is available, all with a single line.

As well as `require`, you can also use `load` to load external source code files into your program. For example, this code would seem identical to the preceding:

```
load 'string_extensions'
puts "This is a test".vowels.join('-')
```

It performs in the same way, but let's try a different example. Put this in a.rb:

```
puts "Hello from a.rb"
```

And put this in a file called b.rb:

```
require 'a'
puts "Hello from b.rb"
require 'a'
puts "Hello again from b.rb"
```

Run with ruby b.rb to get the result:

```
Hello from a.rb
Hello from b.rb
Hello again from b.rb
```

In this example, the a.rb file is included only once. It's included on line 1, and "Hello from a.rb" gets printed to the screen, but then when it's included again on line 3 of b.rb, nothing occurs. In contrast:

```
load 'a'
puts "Hello from b.rb"
load 'a'
puts "Hello again from b.rb"
```

```
Hello from a.rb
Hello from b.rb
Hello from a.rb
Hello again from b.rb
```

With load, the code is loaded and reprocessed anew each time you use the load method. require, on the other hand, only processes external code once.

Note Ruby programmers generally use require rather than load. The effects of load are only useful if the code in the external file has changed or if it contains active code that will be executed immediately. However, a good programmer will avoid the latter situation, and external files will only contain classes and *modules* that will, generally, rarely change.

Inclusions from Other Directories

Both load and require can take local or absolute filenames. For example, require 'a' first looks for a.rb in the current directory, and then iterates through a multitude of other directories on your hard drive looking for a.rb. By default, these other directories are the various directories where Ruby stores its own files and libraries, although you can override this, if necessary.

Ruby stores the list of directories to search for included files in a special variable called $:. You can see what $: contains by default, using irb:

```
$:.each { |d| puts d }
```

```
/usr/local/lib/ruby/site_ruby/1.8
/usr/local/lib/ruby/site_ruby/1.8/i686-darwin8.8.1
/usr/local/lib/ruby/site_ruby
/usr/local/lib/ruby/1.8
/usr/local/lib/ruby/1.8/i686-darwin8.8.1
.
```

Note This result is what appears on my machine, running Mac OS X. The list of directories will probably differ significantly on your machine, particularly if you're using Windows, where the path layout will be entirely different, with the drive letter at the start and backslashes instead of forward slashes.

If you want to add extra directories to this, it's simple:

```
$:.push '/your/directory/here'
require 'yourfile'
```

$: is an array, so you can push extra items to it, or use unshift to add an element to the start of the list (if you want your directory to be searched before the default Ruby ones—useful if you want to override Ruby's standard libraries).

Note Ruby keeps track of the files include has processed by using the name used to access them. If you have two paths pointing to the same file, and include the same file but by using two unique, full filenames, Ruby will duly load the same file twice.

Logic and Including Code

require and load both act like normal code in Ruby programs. You can put them at any point in your Ruby code and they'll behave as if they were processed at that point. For example:

```
$debug_mode = 0
require $debug_mode == 0 ? "normal-classes" : "debug-classes"
```

It's an obscure example, but what it does is check if the global variable $debug_mode is set to 0. If it is, it requires normal-classes.rb, and if not, debug-classes.rb. This gives you the power to include a different source file dependent on the value of a variable, ideal for situations where your application has "regular" and "debug" modes. You could even write an application that works perfectly, but then use a different require to include a whole different set of files that have new or experimental functionality.

A commonly used shortcut uses arrays to quickly load a collection of libraries at once. For example:

```
%w{file1 file2 file3 file4 file5}.each { |l| require l }
```

This loads five different external files or libraries with just two lines of code. However, some coders are not keen on this style, as it can make the code harder to read, even if it's more efficient.

Nested Inclusions

Code from files that are included into others with require and load has the same freedom as if the code were pasted directly into the original file. This means files that you include can call load and require themselves. For example, assume a.rb contains the following:

```
require 'b'
```

And b.rb contains the following:

```
require 'c'
```

And c.rb contains the following:

```
def example
  puts "Hello!"
end
```

And `d.rb` contains the following:

```
require 'a'
example
```

```
Hello!
```

`d.rb` includes `a.rb` with `require`, `a.rb` includes `b.rb`, and `b.rb` includes `c.rb`, meaning the example method is available to `d.rb`.

This functionality makes it easy to put together large projects with interdependent parts, as the structure can be as deep as you like.

Libraries

In computer programming, a *library* is a collection of routines that can be called by separate programs, but that exist independently of those programs. For example, you could create a library to load and process a data file, and then use the routines in that library from any number of other programs.

Earlier in this chapter, we looked at using the `require` command to load external files into your Ruby programs, and then we looked at how modules can be used to separate elements of functionality into separate namespaces. You can use both of these concepts, jointly, to make libraries in Ruby.

At the start of this chapter you developed an extremely simple library called `string_extensions.rb`, like so:

```
class String
  def vowels
    self.scan(/[aeiou]/i)
  end
end
```

And you used this library with the following code:

```
require 'string_extensions'
puts "This is a test".vowels.join('-')
```

```
i-i-a-e
```

Nearly all libraries are more complex than this, but nonetheless, this is a basic demonstration of how a library works.

Next we're going to look at the libraries that come with Ruby as standard, and look at a way to download and use libraries that other developers have made available on the Internet.

The Standard Libraries

Ruby comes with more than 100 standard libraries, as standard. They provide Ruby with a wide selection of functionality "out of the box," from Web serving and networking tools through to encryption, benchmarking, and testing routines.

■**Note** Collectively the "standard libraries" are often called "the Standard Library." When you see this term (it's used particularly often in Chapter 16), it's important to remember it most likely refers to the collection rather than one library in particular.

In this section we're going to look at how you can use just two random standard libraries (net/http and OpenStruct), so that you're prepared for using and working with other libraries in later chapters, where you'll be using many other standard libraries in a similar way.

A list of all the standard libraries, including documentation, is available at http:// www.ruby-doc.org/stdlib/, although a sizable number of them are covered in more detail in Chapter 16 of this book.

■**Note** Some users might discover that the number of standard libraries might have been trimmed down, particularly if using a preinstalled version of Ruby. However, if you installed Ruby from source, all the demonstrations in this section should work.

---

net/http

HTTP stands for HyperText Transfer Protocol, and it's the main protocol that makes the World Wide Web work, as it provides the mechanism by which Web pages, files, and other media can be sent between Web servers and clients.

Ruby provides basic support for HTTP via the net/http library. For example, it's trivial to write a Ruby script that can download and print out the contents of a particular Web page:

```
require 'net/http'
Net::HTTP.get_print('www.rubyinside.com', '/')
```

If you ran this code, after a few seconds many pages of HTML code should fly past on your screen. The first line loads the net/http library into the current program, and the second line calls a class method on the Net::HTTP class (where Net is a module defining the Net namespace, and HTTP is a subclass) that gets and prints (hence get_print) the Web page at http://www.rubyinside.com/.

It's just as easy to put the contents of any Web page into a string, for further manipulation by your program:

```
require 'net/http'
url = URI.parse('http://www.rubyinside.com/')
response = Net::HTTP.start(url.host, url.port) do |http|
  http.get(url.path)
end
content = response.body
```

In this example, you use the URI library (another standard library, and one that's loaded automatically by net/http) to decipher a URL such as http://www.rubyinside.com/ into its constituent parts for the net/http library to use to make its request. Once the URL has been parsed, an HTTP connection is "started," and within the scope of that connection a GET request is made with the get method (if this doesn't make sense, don't worry; it's part of how the HTTP protocol works). Finally, you retrieve the content from response.body, a string containing the contents of the Web page at http://www.rubyinside.com/.

■**Note** The net/http library is only a basic library, and it requires its input to be sanitized in advance, as in the preceding examples. The URI library is ideally suited to this task.

In Chapter 14, we'll look at net/http and some of its sister libraries, such as net/pop and net/smtp, in more detail.

OpenStruct

In Chapter 6 you worked with a special type of data structure called `Struct`. `Struct` allowed you to create small data-handling classes on the fly, like so:

```
Person = Struct.new(:name, :age)
me = Person.new("Fred Bloggs", 25)
me.age += 1
```

`Struct` gives you the luxury of being able to create simple classes without having to define a class in the long-handed way.

The `OpenStruct` class provided by the ostruct library makes it even easier. It allows you to create data objects without specifying the attributes, and allows you to create attributes on the fly:

```
require 'ostruct'
person = OpenStruct.new
person.name = "Fred Bloggs"
person.age = 25
```

`person` is a variable pointing to an object of class `OpenStruct`, and `OpenStruct` allows you to call attributes whatever you like, on the fly. It's similar to how a hash works, but using the object notation.

As the name implies, `OpenStruct` is more flexible than `Struct`, but this comes at the cost of harder-to-read code. There's nowhere to determine exactly, at a glance, which attributes have been used. However, with traditional structs, you can see the attribute names at the same place the struct is created.

As you can see, using libraries is pretty easy. In most cases you just use `require` to load the relevant classes and methods, and then you can start using them right away. However, for more complex scenarios, read on!

RubyGems

RubyGems is a packaging system for Ruby programs and libraries. It enables developers to package their Ruby libraries in a form that's easy for users to maintain and install. RubyGems makes it easy to manage different versions of the same libraries on your machine, and gives you the ability to install them with a single line at the command prompt.

Each individually packaged Ruby library (or application) is known simply as a *gem* or *RubyGem*. Gems have names, version numbers, and descriptions. You can manage your computer's local installations of gems using the `gem` command, available from the command line.

Installing RubyGems

Before you can use RubyGems, it's necessary to install it (or make sure it's already installed), as it's not part of Ruby, officially. However, it is the de facto packaging system for Ruby libraries, and installation is easy.

Windows

If you installed Ruby using the "one-click installer" as described in Chapter 1, you'll already have RubyGems installed and can skip down to the "Finding Gems" section.

    However, if you're running a different version of Ruby on Windows that doesn't have RubyGems installed, refer to the following OS X and Linux instructions, as they're quite generic.

Mac OS X, Linux, and Other Unix

Developed in pure Ruby, RubyGems installs in a similar manner on all platforms. These instructions are tailored toward OS X and Linux, but could be used on all platforms:

1. Go to the RubyGems project site at `http://rubyforge.org/projects/rubygems/`.

2. Find the "Download" link (presently at the right after "Latest File Releases") and go to the download page.

3. Download the latest .tar.gz or ZIP file available. The latest release should be highlighted.

4. Uncompress the .tar.gz or ZIP file. On OS X or Linux this can be done with `tar xzvf rubygems-0.9.0.tgz`, where the filename should be replaced with the filename of the file you just downloaded.

5. Go to the folder created by uncompressing the RubyGems file with `cd rubygems-0.9.0` (or similar).

6. Run `ruby setup.rb` as a superuser (that is, root) or by using sudo: `sudo ruby setup.rb`, and entering your password (on OS X) or the root password (on other systems) at the prompt.

7. RubyGems installs itself and reports success (in case of error, refer to the messages raised).

■Note For Linux users: If you get errors during installation that say certain libraries are missing (such as YAML or Zlib), you're probably using a preinstalled version of Ruby that came with your Linux distribution. If you don't want to install a fresh version of Ruby from source (which is usually the best idea, and is covered in Chapter 1), your distribution might let you install these missing libraries using its package management system. For example, on Ubuntu or Debian, `apt-get libyaml-ruby` and `apt-get libzlib-ruby` can commonly resolve the problem.

After installation, the main RubyGems application, gem, should be in a directory that's included in your path (such as `/usr/bin/` or `/usr/local/bin/`), and so should run immediately from the command line by typing **gem** and pressing Enter. If it does not, it will be necessary to find where gem is installed and add its directory to your path. Alternately, you could use gem in future by prefixing it with its full location (for example, `/usr/bin/gem`).

■Note It's possible to install RubyGems in a local, user directory if you don't have permission to install it system wide. To learn more about this, refer to the RubyGems documentation at `http://docs.rubygems.org/`.

Finding Gems

One of the things it's useful to do is to get a list of the gems that are installed on your machine, as well as get a list of the gems available for download and installation. To do this, you use gem's `list` command. If you run `gem list` from your command line, you'll get a result similar to this:

```
*** LOCAL GEMS ***

sources (0.0.1)
    This package provides download sources for remote gem installation
```

It's not much, but it's a start. This list shows that you have the "sources" gem installed (version 0.0.1) and a basic description of the gem.

You can query the remote gem server (currently hosted by RubyForge) like so:

```
gem list --remote
```

```
*** REMOTE GEMS ***

abstract (1.0.0)
    a library which enables you to define abstract method in Ruby

ackbar (0.1.1, 0.1.0)
    ActiveRecord KirbyBase Adapter

action_profiler (1.0.0)
    A profiler for Rails controllers

actionmailer (1.2.3, 1.2.2, 1.2.1, 1.2.0, 1.1.5, 1.1.4, 1.1.3, 1.1.2, 1.1.1, 1.0.1,
1.0.0, 0.9.1, 0.9.0, 0.8.1, 0.8.0, 0.7.1, 0.7.0, 0.6.1, 0.6.0, 0.5.0, 0.4.0,
0.3.0)
    Service layer for easy email delivery and testing.
```

[..1,000s of lines about other gems removed for brevity..]

Within a minute or so, many hundreds of gems and descriptions should go flying past (do allow a couple minutes though, as RubyForge can often be extremely busy).

Wading through such a list is impractical for most purposes, but generally you'll be aware of which gem you want to install before you get to this stage. People on the Internet will recommend gems, or you'll be asked to install a particular gem by this book or another tutorial.

However, if you wish to "browse," the best way to do so is to visit `http://rubyforge.org/`, the home for the RubyGems repository. RubyForge features search tools and more information about each gem in the repository.

Alternatively, you can use the search features offered by the gem program directly, like so:

```
gem query --remote --name-matches class
```

```
*** REMOTE GEMS ***

calibre-classinherit (2.1.0)
    Provides class-level inheritance for mixin modules.

calibre-classmethods (2.0.0, 1.0.0)
    Provides class-level inheritance for included modules.
```

```
calibre-nackclass (0.5.1)
    Nack, which stands for Not-ACKnowledged, is a more efficient tool
    for deferable errors.

calibre-nullclass (1.0.0)
    Null is a alternate to Nil that's doesn't raise NoMethodError.

classifier (1.3.0, 1.2.0, 1.1.1, 1.1, 1.0)
    A general classifier module to allow Bayesian and other types of
    classifications.

classroom (0.0.2, 0.0.1)
    ClassRoom is a 'class server' based on DRb
```

In this case, you asked the repository for all gems with names including the word "class."

■**Note** In Chapter 16, we're going to look at a large collection of RubyGems and other libraries and see how each works and can be used in your own projects.

Installing a Simple Gem

Once you've found the name of a gem you wish to install, you can install it with a single command at the command line (where `feedtools` would be replaced with the name of the gem you wish to install, although fccdtools is a fine gem to test with):

```
gem install feedtools
```

■**Caution** On Unix-related platforms (including OS X and Linux), you're likely to receive an error shortly thereafter, complaining that you don't have permission to install the gem. The reason for this is that Ruby is usually installed as a system application, and your current user doesn't have the privileges to install new libraries at the system level. To resolve this, you can either switch to the root user and re-run the `gem install` command, or use sudo: `sudo gem install feedtools`.

If all goes well, you'll get output like this:

```
Attempting local installation of 'feedtools'
Local gem file not found: feedtools*.gem
Attempting remote installation of 'feedtools'
Updating Gem source index for: http://gems.rubyforge.org
Successfully installed feedtools-0.2.26
Installing RDoc documentation for feedtools-0.2.26...
```

First, RubyGems looks to see if the gem exists in the current directory (you can keep your own store of gems locally, if you like), and if not, it heads off to RubyForge to download the gem and install it from afar. Last, it builds the documentation for the library using rdoc (covered in Chapter 8), and installation is complete. This process is the same for nearly all gems.

Note In many cases, installing one gem requires other gems to be installed too. That is, the gem you're trying to install might have other gems it needs to operate. If this is the case, gem will tell you, and will install the required gems in each case if you agree.

If you run gem list again at this point, your local list of gems will include the newly installed gem (in this case, feedtools).

Using Gems

As the RubyGems system isn't an integrated part of Ruby, it's necessary to tell your programs that you want to use and load gems.

To demonstrate how gems can be used, you'll install the redcloth gem, a library that can convert specially formatted text into HTML, ready to be used on a Web page. Use gem install redcloth (or sudo gem install redcloth, if you aren't running as root or a superuser), as demonstrated earlier, to install the gem.

Once the gem is installed, run irb or create a new Ruby source file, and use the redcloth gem like so:

```
require 'rubygems'
require 'RedCloth'
r = RedCloth.new("this is a *test* of _using RedCloth_")
puts r.to_html
```

```
<p>this is a <strong>test</strong> of <em>using RedCloth</em></p>
```

In this example, you first load up the RubyGems library, and then load up the Red-Cloth library with `require`. When RubyGems is loaded on the first line, the RubyGems library overrides the `require` method and enables it to be used to load gems as if they were normal, local libraries.

After that point, you can use the RedCloth library, create an object, and call a method on that object. If you get the HTML as output, everything was a success. You've used your first gem.

Note The "one-click installer" used by Windows users to install Ruby and RubyGems makes it so that RubyGems is loaded by default with all Ruby programs run on that machine, so `require 'rubygems'` isn't required, although it does no harm either way.

Installing a More Complex Gem

Let's look at a second example of installing a gem to see the realities of installing more complex gems.

Hpricot is an HTML/Web page processing library for Ruby that uses a parser written in C for speed. This requires the C code to be compiled, and although C compilers are commonly available on Unix/Linux and Mac OS X machines, they're less common on Windows machines. This demands that two versions of each release of the Hpricot gem are made available: one for machines that can compile the C code, and one for Windows machines with a precompiled version.

Note You'll use Hpricot in Chapter 14 to process Web page content, so installing Hpricot now is advised if you're working through this book in order.

You can start by installing the Hpricot gem in the usual fashion:

```
gem install hpricot
```

```
Attempting local installation of 'hpricot'
Local gem file not found: hpricot*.gem
Attempting remote installation of 'hpricot'
Updating Gem source index for: http://gems.rubyforge.org
Select which gem to install for your platform (i686-darwin8.8.1)
 1. hpricot 0.4 (ruby)
 2. hpricot 0.4 (mswin32)
 3. Cancel installation
>
```

Rather than just going ahead and installing the gem, the gem client notifies you that there are two different types of gems available of the Hpricot 0.4 gem. One version is marked "ruby" and the other "mswin32." The "ruby" gem is a generic gem that's designed to be installed on any machine that has a Unix-like environment and a C compiler available (this can include Cygwin, a Unix line environment for Windows). The "mswin32" version is specifically designed for users using Ruby under a pure Windows environment, and includes a precompiled binary version of the HTML parser for use on a 32-bit x86 Windows environment.

You select your choice by typing the number required and pressing Enter.

Once Hpricot is installed, it's easy to check if everything went okay:

```
require 'rubygems'
require 'hpricot'
puts "Hpricot installed successfully" if Hpricot
```

If you want to try out some more-complex code examples with Hpricot, refer to Chapter 14, where you use Hpricot to process Web page content.

As well as having generic and Windows builds of each version of the Hpricot gem, Hpricot is also available in a special developers' version that's kept up to date with the latest changes made by the developer. Although it's still common practice to release libraries in fixed versions from time to time, the advent of test-driven development has made it practical and reasonably safe to use more up-to-date versions of libraries that the developer is actively working on. Therefore, you can choose to install the finished, fixed versions of the Hpricot gem from the default gem servers, or you can choose to install the "up to the minute" source version from the developer's own gem server.

Hpricot's developers' build is not stored on the default gem servers, but on a gem server maintained by the Hpricot developer himself. To access it, you only need to adjust the gem install command slightly:

```
gem install hpricot --source code.whytheluckystiff.net
```

This command instructs gem to not look at the default gem servers but to use code.whytheluckystiff.net specifically. Many projects have their own developer gem servers, so if you want to install experimental, cutting-edge versions of gems and libraries, refer to the project's Web site for information on installing the edge/source/experimental versions (all the prior terms can be used to describe the cutting-edge versions).

Running the prior command gives you a lot more options than installing from the default gem servers.

```
Select which gem to install for your platform (i686-darwin8.8.1):
 1. hpricot 0.4.52 (ruby)
 2. hpricot 0.4.52 (mswin32)
 3. hpricot 0.4.47 (ruby)
 4. hpricot 0.4.43 (mswin32)
 5. hpricot 0.4.43 (ruby)
 6. hpricot 0.4 (mswin32)
 7. hpricot 0.4 (ruby)
 8. hpricot 0.3.32 (mswin32)
 9. hpricot 0.3.32 (ruby)
10. hpricot 0.3.0 (mswin32)
11. hpricot 0.3 (ruby)
12. hpricot 0.2 (ruby)
13. hpricot 0.1 (ruby)
14. Cancel installation
>
```

As gem version numbers are incremental, running in significance from left to right, the best build available here is 0.4.52, options 1 and 2 for the generic and Windows builds respectively.

■**Note** Ruby on Rails also makes an "edge" build available, as opposed to the fixed versions. Many developers choose to use the edge versions, as they offer significantly more features than the latest official release. However, rather than use version numbers like Hpricot, the Rails team uses a single revision number such as 5098 or 5200, where the higher the number, the more up-to-date the build. This is covered in more detail in Chapter 13.

Upgrading and Uninstalling Gems

One of the main features of RubyGems is that gems can be updated easily. You can update all of your currently installed gems with a single line:

```
gem update
```

This makes gem go to the remote gem repository, look for new versions of all the gems you currently have installed, and if there are new versions, installs them. If you only want to upgrade a specific gem, suffix the preceding command line with the name of the gem in question.

Uninstalling gems is the simplest task of all. Use the `uninstall` command (where `feedtools` is replaced by the name of the gem you wish to uninstall):

```
gem uninstall feedtools
```

If there are multiple versions of the same gem on the machine, gem will ask you which version you want to uninstall first (or you can tell it to uninstall all versions at once), as in this example:

```
$ gem uninstall rubyforge
```

```
Select RubyGem to uninstall:
 1. rubyforge-0.3.0
 2. rubyforge-0.3.1
 3. All versions
```

Creating Your Own Gems

Naturally, it's possible to create gems from your own libraries and applications. This entire process is covered in Chapter 10, along with the other ways you can deploy your applications to users (or the world!).

Summary

In this chapter we've looked at some of the methods Ruby provides to make it possible to handle larger projects, as well as access the vast universe of prewritten code libraries to make development easier.

As well as being able to include code from other files, we've looked at using modules (and their namespaces) to separate potentially clashing classes, methods, and constants into distinct groups. Modules also provide a way to mix in functionality to other classes without using inheritance.

Ruby provides a wealth of useful libraries within the main distribution, but using tools such as RubyGems allows you to get access to code written by thousands of other Ruby developers, allowing you to implement more-complex programs more quickly than would otherwise be possible.

Let's reflect on the main concepts covered in this chapter:

- *Project*: Any collection of multiple files and subdirectories that form a single instance of a Ruby application or library.

- `require`: A method that loads and processes the Ruby code from a separate file, including whatever classes, modules, methods, and constants are in that file into the current scope. `load` is similar, but rather than performing the inclusion operation once, it reprocesses the code every time `load` is called.

- *Library*: A collection of routines, classes, methods, and/or modules that provides a set of features that many other applications can use.

- *RubyGems*: Packaging system for Ruby libraries and/or applications that makes them easier to install and maintain by developers.

- *Edge/source/development builds*: Special versions of libraries and applications that aren't official releases, but reflect the latest work performed by the developers of the library or application. However, with the popularity of test-driven development, many of these cutting-edge libraries are still reliable to use, though their most recently added features might not be fully documented or tested.

- *Gem*: A single library (or application) packaged up using the RubyGems system. Can also be called a "RubyGem."

In many of the chapters from here on, we'll be using the power of libraries, and combining multiple libraries to make single applications. One such example is the Ruby on Rails framework we'll be covering in Chapter 13, which is, in essence, a giant library made up of several libraries itself!

In Chapter 16, we'll come back to RubyGems and look at some of the most useful gems available, their functions, and how to use them.

■ ■ ■

## CHAPTER 8

Documentation, Error Handling, Debugging, and Testing

In this chapter we're going to look at the finer details of developing reliable programs: documentation, error handling, debugging, and testing. These tasks aren't what most people think of as development, but are as important to the overall process as general coding tasks. Without documenting, debugging, and testing your code, it's unlikely that anyone but you could work on the code with much success, and you run the risk of releasing faulty scripts and applications.

This chapter demonstrates how to produce documentation, handle errors in your programs, test the efficiency of your code, and make sure that your code is (mostly) bug free, all using tools that come with Ruby.

Documentation

Even if you're the only person to use and work on your Ruby code, it's inevitable that over time you'll forget the nuances of how it was put together and how it works. To guard against code amnesia, you should document your code as you develop it.

Traditionally, documentation would often be completed by a third party rather than the developer, or would be written after the majority of the development had been completed. Although developers have always been expected to leave comments in their code, true documentation of a quality such that other developers and users can understand it without seeing the source code has had less importance.

Compared to the documentation features of other languages, Ruby makes it extremely easy to document your code as you create it, using a utility called *RDoc* (standing for "Ruby Documentation").

Generating Documentation with RDoc

RDoc calls itself a "Document Generator for Ruby Source." It's a tool that reads through your Ruby source code files and creates structured HTML documentation. It comes with the standard Ruby distribution, so it's easy to find and use. If for some reason RDoc does not appear to come with your installation of Ruby, you can download it from the official RDoc site at `http://rdoc.sourceforge.net/`.

RDoc understands a lot of Ruby syntax and can create documentation for classes, methods, modules, and numerous other Ruby constructs without much prompting.

The way you document your code in a way that RDoc can use is to leave comments prior to the definition of the class, method, or module you want to document. For example:

```ruby
# This class stores information about people.
class Person
  attr_accessor :name, :age, :gender

  # Create the person object and store their name
  def initialize(name)
    @name = name
  end

  # Print this person's name to the screen
  def print_name
    puts "Person called #{@name}"
  end
end
```

This is a simple class that's been documented using comments. It's quite readable already, but RDoc can turn it into a pretty set of HTML documentation in seconds.

To use RDoc, simply run it from the command line using `rdoc <name of source file>.rb`, like so:

```
rdoc person.rb
```

■Note On Linux and OS X this should simply work (as long as the directory containing RDoc—usually `/usr/bin` or `/usr/local/bin`—is in the path). On Windows it might be necessary to prefix `rdoc` with its full location.

This command tells RDoc to process `person.rb` and produce the HTML documentation. By default, it does this by creating a directory called `doc` from the current directory and placing its HTML and CSS files in there. Once RDoc has completed, you can open index.html, located within doc, and you should see some basic documentation, as in Figure 8-1.

Files	Classes	Methods
person.rb	Person	new (Person)
		print_name (Person)

Class Person

In: person.rb
Parent: Object

This class stores information about people.

Methods
  new   print_name

Attributes
  age   [RW]
  gender [RW]
  name [RW]

Public Class methods

  new(name)

  Create the person object and store their name

Public Instance methods

  print_name()

  Print this person's name to the screen

[Validate]

Figure 8-1. *Basic RDoc HTML output as seen from a Web browser*

The HTML documentation is shown with three frames across the top containing links to the documented files, classes, and methods, respectively, and a main frame at the bottom containing the documentation being viewed at present. The top three frames let you jump between the various classes and methods with a single click. In a large set of documentation, this quickly becomes useful.

When viewing the documentation for the Person class, the documentation shows what methods it contains, the documentation for those methods, along with the attributes the class provides for its objects. RDoc works this out entirely from the source code and your comments directly.

RDoc Techniques

In the prior section, you got RDoc to generate documentation from a few simple comments in your source file. However, RDoc is rarely useful on such a small example, and its real power comes into play when you're working on larger projects and using its advanced functions. This section will cover some of these functions so you can comment the code on your larger projects correctly.

Note The following sections only give a basic overview of some of RDoc's features. To read the full documentation for RDoc and learn about features that are beyond the scope of this book, visit the official RDoc site at http://rdoc.sourceforge.net/doc/.

Producing Documentation for an Entire Project

Previously you used rdoc along with a filename to produce documentation for a single file. However, in the case of a large project, you could have many hundreds of files that you want processed. If you run rdoc with no filenames supplied, RDoc will process all the Ruby files found in the current directory and all other directories under that. The full documentation is placed into the doc directory, as before, and the entire set of documentation is available from index.html.

Basic Formatting

Formatting your documentation for RDoc is easy. RDoc automatically recognizes paragraphs within your comments, and can even use spacing to recognize structure. Here's an example of some of the formatting RDoc recognizes:

```
#= RDoc Example
#
#== This is a heading
#
#* First item in an outer list
#   * First item in an inner list
#   * Second item in an inner list
#* Second item in an outer list
#   * Only item in this inner list
#
#== This is a second heading
#
#Visit www.rubyinside.com
#
#== Test of text formatting features
#
```

```
#Want to see *bold* or _italic_ text? You can even embed
#+text that looks like code+ by surrounding it with plus
#symbols. Indented code will be automatically formatted:
#
#   class MyClass
#     def method_name
#       puts "test"
#     end
#   end
```

If you process this with RDoc, you'll get a result that looks like that in Figure 8-2. To learn more about RDoc's general formatting features, the best method is to look at existing code that is extensively prepared for RDoc, such as the source code to the Ruby on Rails framework, or refer to the official RDoc documentation at http://rdoc. sourceforge.net/doc/.

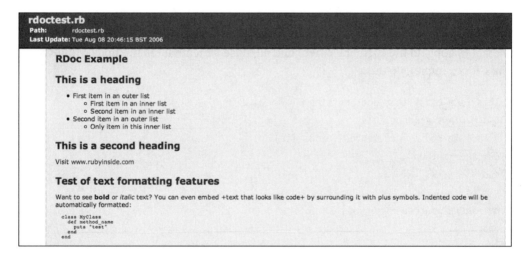

Figure 8-2. *How RDoc renders the formatting feature test file*

Modifiers and Options

RDoc can work without the developer knowing much about it, but to get the most from RDoc it's necessary to know how several of its features work and how they can be customized. RDoc supports a number of modifiers within comments, along with a plethora of command line options.

:nodoc: Modifier

By default, RDoc will attempt to use anything it considers relevant to build up its documentation. Sometimes, however, you'd rather RDoc ignore certain modules, classes, or methods, particularly if you haven't documented them yet. To do this, simply follow the module, class, or method definition with a comment of :nodoc:, like so:

```
# This is a class that does nothing
class MyClass
  # This method is documented
  def some_method
  end

  def secret_method #:nodoc:
  end
end
```

In this instance, RDoc will ignore secret_method.

:nodoc: only operates directly upon the elements upon which it is placed. If you want :nodoc: to apply to the current element and all those beneath it (all methods within a class, for example), do this:

```
# This is a class that does nothing
class MyClass #:nodoc: all
  # This method is documented (or is it?)
  def some_method
  end

  def secret_method
  end
end
```

Now *none* of MyClass is documented by RDoc.

Turning RDoc Processing on and off

You can stop RDoc from processing comments temporarily using #++ and #--, like so:

```
# This section is documented and read by RDoc.
#--
# This section is hidden from RDoc and could contain developer
# notes, private messages between developers, etc.
#++
# RDoc begins processing again here after the ++.
```

This feature is particularly ideal in sections where you want to leave comments to yourself but that aren't for general consumption.

■**Note** RDoc doesn't process comments that are within methods, so your usual code comments are not used in the documentation produced.

Command Line Options

Like most command line applications, including Ruby itself, you can give RDoc a number of options as follows:

- `--all`: Usually RDoc only processes public methods, but `--all` forces RDoc to document *all* methods within the source files.

- `--fmt <format name>`: Produce documentation in a certain format (default is `html`, but `xml`, `yaml`, `chm`, and `pdf` are available under some configurations).

- `--help`: Get help with using RDoc's command line options and find out which output formatters are available.

- `--inline-source`: Usually, source code is shown using popups, but this option forces code to be shown inline with the documentation.

- `--main <name>`: Set the class, module, or file that appears as the main index page for the documentation to `<name>` (for example, `rdoc --main MyClass`).

- `--one-file`: Make RDoc place all the documentation into a single file.

- `--op <directory name>`: Set the output directory to `<directory name>` (default is `doc`).

After any command line options, `rdoc` is then suffixed with the filename(s) of the files you want to have RDoc document. Alternatively, if you specify nothing, RDoc will traverse the current directory and all subdirectories and generate documentation for your entire project.

■**Note** RDoc supports many more command line options than these, and they are all covered in RDoc's official documentation. Alternatively, run RDoc with `rdoc --help` at the command line to get a list of its options.

Debugging and Errors

Errors happen. It's unavoidable that programs you develop will contain bugs, and you won't immediately be able to see what the errors are. A misplaced character in a regular expression, or a typo with a mathematical symbol, can make the difference between a reliable program and one that constantly throws errors or generates undesirable output.

Exceptions and Error Handling

An exception is an event that occurs when an error arises within a program. An exception can cause the program to quit immediately with an error message, or can be handled by *error handling* routines within the program to recover from the error in a sensible way.

For example, a program might depend on a network connection (the Internet, for example), and if the network connection is unavailable, an error will arise when the program attempts to use the network. Rather than brusquely terminating with an obscure error message, the code can handle the exception and print a human-friendly error message to the screen first. Alternatively, the program might have a mechanism by which it can work offline, and you can use the exception raised by trying to access an inaccessible network or server to enter that mode of operation instead.

Raising Exceptions

In Ruby, exceptions are packaged into objects of class Exception or one of Exception's many subclasses. Ruby has about 30 main predefined exception classes that deal with different types of errors, such as NoMemoryError, RuntimeError, SecurityError, ZeroDivisionError, and NoMethodError. You might have already seen some of these in error messages while working in irb. (A table of all of Ruby's standard exception classes is provided in Appendix B.)

When an exception is *raised* (exceptions are said to be *raised* when they occur within the execution of a program), Ruby immediately looks back up the tree of routines that called the current one (known as the *stack*) and looks for a routine that can handle that particular exception. If it can't find any error handling routines, it quits the program with the raw error message. For example:

```
irb(main):001:0> puts 10 / 0
```

```
ZeroDivisionError: divided by 0
        from (irb):1:in `/'
        from (irb):1
```

This error message shows that an exception of type ZeroDivisionError has been *raised*, because you attempted to divide ten by zero.

Ruby can raise exceptions automatically when you perform incorrect functions, and you can raise exceptions from your own code too. You do this with the raise method and by using an existing exception class, or by creating one of your own that inherits from the Exception class.

One of the standard exception classes is ArgumentError, which is used when the arguments provided to a method are fatally flawed. You can use this class as an exception if bad data is supplied to a method of your own:

```
class Person
  def initialize(name)
    raise ArgumentError, "No name present" if name.empty?
  end
end
```

If you create a new object from Person and supply a blank name, an exception will be raised:

```
fred = Person.new('')
```

```
ArgumentError: No name present
```

Note You can call raise with no arguments at all, and a generic RuntimeError exception will be raised. This is not good practice though, as the exception will have no message or meaning along with it. Always provide a message and a class with raise, if possible.

However, you could create your own type of exception if you wanted to. For example:

```
class BadDataException < RuntimeError
end
```

```
class Person
  def initialize(name)
    raise BadDataException, "No name present" if name.empty?
  end
end
```

This time you've created a `BadDataException` class inheriting from Ruby's standard `RuntimeError` exception class.

At this point, it might seem meaningless as to why raising different types of exceptions is useful. The reason is so that you can handle different exceptions in different ways with your error handling code, as you'll do next.

Handling Exceptions

In the previous section we looked at how exceptions work. When raised, exceptions halt the execution of the program and trace their way back up the stack to find some code that can handle them. If no handler for the exception is found, the program ceases execution and dies with an error message with information about the exception.

However, in most situations, stopping a program because of a single error isn't necessary. The error might only be minor, or there might be an alternative option to try. Therefore, it's possible to *handle* exceptions. In Ruby, the `rescue` clause is used, along with `begin` and `end`, to define blocks of code to handle exceptions. For example:

```
begin
  puts 10 / 0
rescue
  puts "You caused an error!"
end
```

```
You caused an error!
```

In this case, `begin` and `end` define a section of code to be run, where if an exception arises, it's handled with the code inside the `rescue` block. First, you try to work out ten divided by zero, which raises an exception of class `ZeroDivisionError`. However, being inside a block containing a `rescue` section means that the exception is handled by the code inside that `rescue` section. Rather than dying with a `ZeroDivisionError`, the text "You caused an error!" is instead printed to the screen.

This can become important in programs that rely on external sources of data. Consider this pseudo-code:

```
data = ""
begin
  <.. code to retrieve the contents of a Web page..>
  data = <..content of Web page..>
rescue
  puts "The Web page could not be loaded! Using default data instead."
```

```
  data = <..load data from local file..>
end
puts data
```

This code demonstrates why handling exceptions is extremely useful. If retrieving the contents of a Web page fails (if you're not connected to the Internet, for example), then the error handling routine rescues the exception, alerts the user of an error, and then loads up some data from a local file instead. Certainly better than exiting the program immediately!

In the previous section we looked at how to create your own exception classes, and the motivation for doing this is that it's possible to rescue different types of exceptions in a different way. For example, you might want to react differently if there's a fatal flaw in the code, versus a simple error such as a lack of network connectivity. There might also be errors you want to ignore, and only specific exceptions you wish to handle.

rescue's syntax makes handling different exceptions in different ways easy:

```
begin
  ... code here ...
rescue ZeroDivisionError
  ... code to rescue the zero division exception here ...
rescue YourOwnException
  ... code to rescue a different type of exception here ...
rescue
  ... code that rescues all other types of exception here ...
end
```

This code contains multiple rescue blocks, each of which is caused depending on the type of exception raised. If a ZeroDivisionError is raised within the code between begin and the rescue blocks, the rescue ZeroDivisionError code is executed to handle the exception.

Handling Passed Exceptions

As well as handling different types of exceptions using different code blocks, it's possible to *receive* exceptions and use them. This is achieved with a little extra syntax on the rescue block:

```
begin
  puts 10 / 0
rescue => e
  puts e.class
end
```

```
ZeroDivisionError
```

Rather than merely performing some code when an exception is raised, the exception object itself is assigned to the variable e, whereupon you can use that variable however you wish. This is particularly useful if the exception class contains extra functionality or attributes that you want to access.

Catch and Throw

Although creating your own exceptions and exception handlers is useful for resolving error situations, sometimes you want to be able to break out of a thread of execution (say, a loop) during normal operation in a similar way to an exception, but without actually generating an error. Ruby provides two methods, catch and throw, for this purpose.

catch and throw work in a way a little reminiscent of raise and rescue, but catch and throw work with symbols rather than exceptions. They're designed to be used in situations where no error has occurred, but being able to escape quickly from a nested loop, method call, or similar, is necessary.

```
catch(:finish) do
  1000.times do
    x = rand(1000)
    throw :finish if x == 123
  end

  puts "Generated 1000 random numbers without generating 123!"
end
```

The preceding example creates a block using catch. The catch block with symbol :finish as an argument will immediately terminate (and move on to any code after that block) if throw is called with the :finish symbol.

Within the catch block you generate 1,000 random numbers, and if the random number is ever 123, you immediately escape out of the block using throw :finish. However, if you manage to generate 1,000 random numbers without generating the number 123, the loop and the block completes, and you see the message.

catch and throw don't have to be directly in the same scope. throw works from methods called from within a catch block:

```
def generate_random_number_except_123
  x = rand(1000)
  throw :finish if x == 123
end
```

```
catch(:finish) do
  1000.times { generate_random_number_except_123 }
  puts "Generated 1000 random numbers without generating 123!"
end
```

This code operates in an identical way to the first. When `throw` can't find a code block using `:finish` in its current scope, it jumps back up the stack until it can.

The Ruby Debugger

Debugging is the process of fixing the bugs in a piece of code. This process can be as simple as changing a small section of your program, running it, monitoring the output, and then looping through this process again and again until the output is correct and the program behaves as expected.

However, constantly editing and rerunning your program gives you no insight into what's actually happening deep within your code. Sometimes you want to know what each variable contains at a certain point within your program's execution, or you might want to force a variable to contain a certain value. You can use `puts` to show what variables contain at certain points in your program, but you can soon make your code messy by interspersing it with debugging tricks.

Ruby provides a debugging tool you can use to *step* through your code line by line (if you wish), set *breakpoints* (places where execution will stop for you to check things out), and debug your code. It's a little like irb, except you don't need to type out a whole program. You can specify your program's filename and you'll be acting as if you are within that program.

For example, create a basic Ruby script called `debugtest.rb`:

```
i = 1
j = 0
until i > 1000000
  i *= 2
  j += 1
end
puts "i = #{i}, j = #{j}"
```

If you run this code with `ruby debugtest.rb`, you'll get the following result:

```
i = 1048576, j = 20
```

But say you run it with the Ruby debugger like this:

```
ruby -r debug debugtest.rb
```

You'll see something like this appear:

```
Debug.rb
Emacs support available

debugtest.rb:1:i = 1
(rdb:1)
```

This means the debugger has loaded. The third line shows you the current line of code ready to be executed (the first line, in this case), and the fourth line is a prompt that you can type on.

The function of the debugger is similar to irb, and you can type expressions and statements directly onto the prompt here. However, its main strength is that you can use special commands to run debugtest.rb line by line, or set breakpoints and "watches" (breakpoints that rely on a certain condition becoming true—for example, to stop execution when x is larger than 10).

Here are the most useful commands to use at the debugger prompt:

- list: Lists the lines of the program currently being worked upon. You can follow list by a range of line numbers to show. For example, list 2-4 shows code lines 2 through 4. Without any arguments, list shows a local portion of the program to the current execution point.

- step: Runs the next line of the program. step literally steps through the program line by line, executing a single line at a time. After each step, you can check variables, change values, and so on. This allows you to trace the exact point that bugs occur. Follow step by the number of lines you wish to execute if it's higher than 1, such as step 2 to execute two lines.

- cont: Runs the program without stepping. Execution will continue until the program ends, reaches a breakpoint, or a watch condition becomes true.

- break: Sets a breakpoint at a particular line number, such as with break 3 to set a breakpoint at line 3. This means that if you continue execution with cont, execution will run until line 3 and then stop again. This is useful for stopping execution at a place where you want to see what's going on.

- watch: Sets a condition breakpoint. Rather than choosing a certain line upon which to stop, you specify a condition that causes execution to stop. For example, if you want the program to stop when x is larger than 10, use watch x > 10. This is perfect for discovering the exact point where a bug occurs if it results in a certain condition becoming true.

- quit: Exits the debugger.

A simple debugging session with your debugtest.rb code might look like this:

```
# ruby -r debug debugtest.rb
Debug.rb
Emacs support available.

debugtest.rb:1:i = 1
(rdb:1) list
[-4, 5] in debugtest.rb
=> 1  i = 1
   2  j = 0
   3  until i > 1000000
   4    i *= 2
   5    j += 1
(rdb:1) step
debugtest.rb:2:j = 0
(rdb:1) i
1
(rdb:1) i = 100
100
(rdb:1) step
debugtest.rb:3:until i > 1000000
(rdb:1) step
debugtest.rb:4: i *= 2
(rdb:1) step
debugtest.rb:5: j += 1
(rdb:1) i
200
(rdb:1) watch i > 10000
Set watchpoint 1:i > 10000
(rdb:1) cont
Watchpoint 1, toplevel at debugtest.rb:5
debugtest.rb:5: j += 1
(rdb:1) i
```

```
12800
(rdb:1) j
6
(rdb:1) quit
Really quit? (y/n) y
```

This debugging session demonstrates stepping through the code, inspecting variables, changing variables in situ, and setting watch points. These are the tools you'll use 99 percent of the time while debugging, and with practice the debugging environment can become a powerful tool, much like irb.

However, many Ruby developers don't use the debugger particularly often, as its style of debugging and its workflow can seem a little out of date compared to modern techniques such as *test-driven development* and *unit testing*, which we'll look at next. If the debugger seems like it could be useful, testing will make you drool.

Testing

Testing is an essential part of modern software development, and helps you resolve many development snafus. Without a proper testing system in place, you can never be confident that your system is bug free. With a good testing system in place, you might only be 99 percent bug free, but it's a significant improvement.

Previously, we've looked at how to handle explicit errors, but sometimes your programs might perform oddly in certain situations. For example, certain data might cause an algorithm to return an incorrect result, or invalid data might be produced that, although invalid, does not result in an explicit error.

One way to resolve these problems is to debug your code, as you've seen, but debugging only solves one problem at a time. It's possible to debug your code to solve one problem, but create many others! Therefore, debugging alone has become viewed as a poor method of resolving bugs, and testing the overall functionality of code has become important.

In the past, users and developers might have performed testing manually by performing certain actions and seeing what happens. If an error occurs, the bug in question is fixed and testing continues. Indeed, there was a time when it was it commonplace solely to use user feedback as a testing mechanism!

However, things have changed quickly with the rapidly growing popularity of test-driven development (also often known as test-first development), a new philosophy that turns software development practices on their head. Ruby developers have been at the forefront of promoting and encouraging this technique.

The Philosophy of Test-Driven Development

Test-driven development is a technique where developers create a set of tests for a system to pass before coding the system itself, and then rigidly use these tests to maintain the integrity of the code. In a lighter form, however, it can also refer to the technique of implementing tests for any code, even if you don't necessarily create the tests before the code you're testing.

Note This section provides only a basic overview of test-driven development. The topic is vast, and many books and resources are available on the topic if you wish to learn more.

For example, you might add a simple method to String that's designed to capitalize text into titles:

```
class String
  def titleize
    self.capitalize
  end
end
```

Your intention is to create a method that can turn "this is a test" into "This Is A Test"; that is, a method that makes strings look as if they're titles. titleize, therefore, "capitalizes" the current string with the capitalize method. If you're in a rush or not bothering to test your code, disaster will soon strike when the code is released into the wild. capitalize only capitalizes the first letter of a string, not the whole string!

```
puts "this is a test".titleize
```

```
"This is a test"
```

That's not the intended behavior! However, with test-driven development, you could have avoided the pain of releasing broken code by first writing some tests to demonstrate the outcome you expect:

```
raise "Fail 1" unless "this is a test".titleize == "This Is A Test"
raise "Fail 2" unless "another test 1234".titleize == "Another Test 1234"
raise "Fail 3" unless "We're testing titleize".titleize == "We're Testing Titleize"
```

These three lines of code raise exceptions unless the output of titleize is what you expect it to be.

■Note These tests are also known as *assertions*, as they're *asserting* that a certain condition is true.

If titleize passes these three tests, you can expect the functionality to be okay for other examples.

■Note A set of tests or assertions that test a single component or a certain set of functionality is known as a *test case*.

Your current code fails on the first test of this test case, so let's write the code to make it work:

```
class String
  def titleize
    self.gsub(/\b\w/) { |letter| letter.upcase }
  end
end
```

This code takes the current string, finds all word boundaries (with \b), passes in the first letter of each word (as obtained with \w), and converts it to upper case. Job done? Run the three tests again.

```
RuntimeError: Failed test 3
```

Why does test 3 fail?

```
puts "We're testing titleize".titleize
```

```
We'Re Testing Titleize
```

\b isn't smart enough to detect true word boundaries. It merely uses whitespace, or "non-word" characters to discriminate words from non-words. Therefore, in "We're," both the W and the R get capitalized. You need to tweak your code:

```
class String
  def titleize
    self.gsub(/\s\w/) { |letter| letter.upcase }
  end
end
```

If you make sure the character before the letter to capitalize is whitespace, you're guaranteed to be in a true, new word.

Re-run the tests:

```
RuntimeError: Failed test 1
```

You're back to square one.

One thing you failed to take into account is that looking for whitespace before a word doesn't allow the *first* word of each string to be capitalized, because those strings *start with a letter, and not whitespace.* It sounds trivial, but it's a great demonstration of how complex simple functions can become, and why testing is so vital to eradicate bugs. However, the ultimate solution is simple:

```
class String
  def titleize
    self.gsub(/(\A|\s)\w/){ |letter| letter.upcase }
  end
end
```

If you run the tests again now, you'll notice they pass straight through. Success!

This basic example provides a sharp demonstration of why testing is important. Small changes can lead to significant changes in functionality, but with a set of trusted tests in place, you can focus on solving problems rather than worrying if your existing code has bugs.

Rather than writing code and waiting for bugs to appear, you can proactively determine what your code should do and then act as soon as the results don't match up with the expectations.

Unit Testing

In the previous section you created some basic tests using `raise`, `unless`, and `==`, and compared the results of a method call with the expected results. It's possible to test a lot in this way, but with more than a few tests, it soon becomes messy, as there's no logical place for the tests to go (and you certainly don't want to include tests with your actual, functional code).

Luckily, Ruby comes with a library, Test::Unit, that makes testing easy and organizes test cases into a clean structure. *Unit testing* is the primary component of test-driven development, and means that you're testing each individual unit of functionality within a program or system. Test::Unit is Ruby's official library for performing unit tests.

One of the benefits of Test::Unit is that it gives you a standardized framework for writing and performing tests. Rather than writing assertions in an inconsistent number of ways, Test::Unit gives you a core set of assertions to use.

Let's take the titleize method from before to use as a demonstration of Test::Unit's features and create a new file called test_titleize.rb:

```ruby
class String
  def titleize
    self.gsub(/\s(\w)/) { |letter| letter.upcase }.gsub(/^\w/) do |letter|
      letter.upcase
    end
  end
end


require 'test/unit'

class TestTitleize < Test::Unit::TestCase
  def test_basic
    assert_equal("This Is A Test", "this is a test".titleize)
    assert_equal("Another Test 1234", "another test 1234".titleize)
    assert_equal("We're Testing", "We're testing".titleize)
  end
end
```

First you include the titleize extension to String (this could be done using require if it's in a separate file). Next you load the Test::Unit class using require. Finally you create a test case by inheriting from Test::Unit::TestCase. Within this class you have a single method (though you can have as many as you like to separate your tests logically) that contains three assertions, similar to the assertions made in the previous section.

If you run this script, you'll see the tests in action:

```
Loaded suite test_titleize
Started
.
Finished in 0.000363 seconds.

1 tests, 3 assertions, 0 failures, 0 errors
```

This output shows that the tests are started, a single test method is run (test_basic, in this case), and that a single test method with three assertions passed successfully.

Say you add an assertion to test_basic that's certainly going to fail, like so:

```
assert_equal("Let's make a test fail!", "foo".titleize)
```

And re-run the tests:

```
Loaded suite test_titleize
Started
F
Finished in 0.239156 seconds.

  1) Failure:
test_basic(TestTitleize) [blah.rb:14]:
<"Let's make a test fail!"> expected but was
<"Foo">.

1 tests, 4 assertions, 1 failures, 0 errors
```

You've added an assertion that was bound to fail, and it has. However, Test::Unit has given you a full explanation of what happened. Using this information, you can go back and either fix the assertion or fix the code that caused the test to fail. In this case, you forced it to fail, but if your assertions are created normally, a failure such as this would demonstrate a bug in your code.

More Test::Unit Assertions

In the previous section you used a single type of assertion, assert_equal. assert_equal asserts that the first and second arguments are equal (whether they're numbers, strings, arrays, or objects of any other kind). The first argument is assumed to be the *expected* outcome and the second argument is assumed to be the generated output, as with your prior assertion:

```
assert_equal("This Is A Test", "this is a test".titleize)
```

■**Note** assert_equal can also accept an optional third argument as a message to be displayed if the assertion fails. A message might, in some cases, prove more useful than the default assertion failure message.

You're likely to find several other types of assertions useful as follows:

- `assert(<boolean expression>)`: Only passes if the boolean expression isn't `false` or `nil` (for example, `assert 2 == 1` will always fail).

- `assert_equal(expected, actual)`: Only passes if the *expected* and *actual* values are equal (as compared with the `==` operator). `assert_equal('A', 'a'.upcase)` will pass.

- `assert_not_equal(expected, actual)`: The opposite of `assert_equal`. This test will fail if the *expected* and *actual* values are equal.

- `assert_raise(exception_type, ..) { <code block> }`: Only passes if the code block following the assertion raises an exception of the type(s) passed as arguments. `assert_raise (ZeroDivisionError) { 2 / 0 }` will pass.

- `assert_nothing_raised(exception_type, ..) { }`: The opposite of `assert_raise`. Only passes if none of the exceptions listed are raised.

- `assert_instance_of(class_expected, object)`: Only passes if `object` is of class `class_expected`.

- `flunk`: `flunk` is a special type of assertion in that it will *always* fail. It's useful to use if you haven't quite finished writing your tests and you want to add a strong reminder that your test case isn't complete!

Note All the preceding assertions, including `flunk`, can take an optional message argument as the last argument, as with `assert_equal`.

You'll use assertions and unit testing more in Chapter 12, where you'll develop a set of tests for a library you'll build.

Benchmarking and Profiling

Once your code is bug free and working properly, it's natural to think it's ready for release. In the real world, however, code can often be inefficient or run more slowly than it needs to. As of version 1.8, the Ruby interpreter is not particularly fast, although Ruby 1.9 and onward (including 2.0), with their entirely new implementation, are significantly faster. However, it's always important to *benchmark* your code to make sure it's running as efficiently as possible.

Benchmarking is the process in which you get your code or application to perform a function (often many hundreds of times in succession to average out discrepancies), and the time it takes to execute is measured. You can then refer to these times as you optimize your code. If future benchmarks run faster than previous ones, you're heading in the right direction. Luckily, Ruby provides a number of tools to help you benchmark your code.

Simple Benchmarking

Ruby's standard library includes a module called Benchmark. Benchmark provides several methods that measure the speed it takes to complete the code you provide. For example:

```
require 'benchmark'
puts Benchmark.measure { 10000.times { print "." } }
```

This code measures how long it takes to print 10,000 periods to the screen. Ignoring the periods produced, the output (on my machine; yours might vary) is as follows:

```
0.050000   0.040000   0.090000 (   0.455168)
```

The columns, in order, represent the amount of user CPU time, system CPU time, total CPU, and "real" time taken. In this case, although it took nine-hundredths of a second of CPU time to send 10,000 periods to the screen or terminal, it took almost half a second for them to finish being printed to the screen among all the other things the computer was doing.

Because measure accepts code blocks, you can make it as elaborate as you wish:

```
require 'benchmark'
iterations = 1000000

b = Benchmark.measure do
  for i in 1..iterations do
    x = i
  end
end

c = Benchmark.measure do
  iterations.times do |i|
    x = i
  end
end
```

```
puts b
puts c
```

In this example, you benchmark two different ways of counting from one to one million. The results might look like this:

```
0.800000   0.010000   0.810000 (  0.949338)
0.890000   0.010000   0.900000 (  1.033589)
```

These results show little difference, except that slightly more user CPU time is used when using the `times` method rather than using `for`. You can use this same technique to test different ways of calculating the same answers in your code, and optimize your code to use the fastest methods.

Benchmark also includes a way to make completing multiple tests more convenient. You can rewrite the preceding benchmarking scenario like this:

```
require 'benchmark'
iterations = 1000000

Benchmark.bm do |bm|
  bm.report("for:") do
    for i in 1..iterations do
      x = i
    end
  end
  bm.report("times:") do
    iterations.times do |i|
      x = i
    end
  end
end
```

The primary difference with using the `bm` method is that it allows you to collect a group of benchmark tests together and display the results in a prettier way. Example output for the preceding code is as follows:

```
        user       system     total        real
for:    0.850000   0.000000   0.850000 (  0.967980)
times:  0.970000   0.010000   0.980000 (  1.301703)
```

bm makes the results even easier to read and provides headings for each column.

Another method, bmbm, repeats the benchmark set twice, using the first as a "rehearsal" and the second for the true results, as in some situations CPU caching, memory caching, and other factors can taint the results. Therefore, repeating the test can lead to more accurate figures. Replacing the bm method with bmbm in the preceding example gives results like these:

```
Rehearsal ----------------------------------------
for:   0.780000    0.000001    0.780001 (  0.958378)
times: 0.100000    0.010000    0.110000 (  1.342837)
------------------------------ total: 0.890001sec

        user      system     total       real
for:   0.850000    0.000000    0.850000 (  0.967980)
times: 0.970000    0.010000    0.980000 (  1.301703)
```

bmbm runs the tests twice and gives both sets of results, where the latter set should be the most accurate.

Profiling

Where benchmarking is the process of measuring the total time it takes to achieve something and comparing those results between different versions of code, profiling tells you *what code* is taking *what amount of time*. For example, you might have a single line in your code that's causing the program to run slowly, so by profiling your code you can immediately see where you should focus your optimization efforts.

■**Note** Some people consider profiling to be the holy grail of optimization. Rather than thinking of efficient ways to write your application ahead of time, some developers suggest writing your application, profiling it, and then fixing the slowest areas. This is to prevent premature optimization. After all, you might prematurely optimize something that didn't actually warrant it, but miss out on an area of code that could do with significant optimization.

Ruby comes with a code profiler built in, and all you have to do to have your code profiled automatically is to add require "profile" to the start of your code, or run it with ruby --r profile before your source file name.

Here's a basic example:

```ruby
require 'profile'
class Calculator
  def self.count_to_large_number
    x = 0
    100000.times { x += 1 }
  end

  def self.count_to_small_number
    x = 0
    1000.times { x += 1 }
  end
end


Calculator.count_to_large_number
Calculator.count_to_small_number
```

% time	cumulative seconds	self seconds	calls	self ms/call	total ms/call	name
70.76	7.38	7.38	2	3690.00	5215.00	Integer#times
29.24	10.43	3.05	101000	0.03	0.03	Fixnum#+
0.00	10.43	0.00	2	0.00	0.00	Kernel.singleton_method_added
0.00	10.43	0.00	1	0.00	110.00	Calculator#count_to_small_nu..
0.00	10.43	0.00	1	0.00	10320.00	Calculator#count_to_large_nu..
0.00	10.43	0.00	1	0.00	0.00	Class#inherited
0.00	10.43	0.00	1	0.00	10430.00	#toplevel

There's a lot of information given, but it's easy to read. The code itself is simple. Two class methods are defined that both count up to different numbers. `Calculator.count_to_large_number` contains a loop that repeats 100,000 times, and `Calculator.count_to_small_number` contains a loop that repeats 1,000 times.

> ■**Note** The reason larger numbers, such as the 1,000,000 loops in the benchmarking tests, weren't used is because profiling adds a severe overhead to the operating speed of a program, unlike benchmarking. Although the program will run slower, this slowness is consistent, so the accuracy of the profiling results is ensured regardless.

The result contains a number of columns. The first is the percentage of time spent within the method named in the far right column. In the preceding example, the profiler shows that 70.76 percent of the total execution time was spent in the `times` method in the `Integer` class. The second column shows the amount of time in seconds rather than as a percentage.

The `calls` column specifies how many times that method was called. In our case, `times` was only called twice. This is true, even though the code block passed to `times` was run 101,000 times. This is reflected in the number of calls for `Fixnum`'s addition (+) method, with 101,000 total calls shown there.

You can use the profiler's results to discover the "sticky" points in your program and help you work around using inefficient methods that suck up CPU time. It's not worth spending time optimizing routines that barely consume any time already, so use the profile to find those routines using the lion's share of the CPU and focus on optimizing those.

> ■**Tip** You can use a library called `profiler` (which `profile` actually uses to do its work) to profile a *specific section* of your program rather than the entire thing. To do this, use `require 'profiler'` and the commands `Profiler__::start_profile`, `Profiler__::stop_profile`, and `Profiler__::print_ profile($stdout)` in the relevant locations.

Summary

In this chapter we've looked at the process behind, and the tools Ruby supplies for, documentation, error handling, testing, benchmarking, and profiling.

The quality of the documentation, error handling, and tests associated with a program or section of code demonstrates the professionalism of the developer and the program. Small, quickly developed scripts might not require any of these elements, but if you're developing a system that's designed to be used by other people or that's mission critical, it's essential to understand the basics of error handling and testing to avoid the embarrassment of your code causing problems and behaving erroneously.

Furthermore, it's important to benchmark and profile your code so that your code has the ability to scale over time. You might only expect your code to perform a certain small set of functions—for example, processing small files—but in the future you might need to process significantly larger amounts of data with the same code and add extra, unanticipated features. The small amount of time taken to benchmark, profile, and optimize your code can pay dividends with reduced execution times later.

Let's reflect on the main concepts covered in this chapter:

- *RDoc*: A tool that comes with Ruby that builds HTML documentation using the structure and comments in your source code.

- *Debugging*: The process of resolving errors in source code, often by stepping through and inspecting the state of a program in situ.

- *Test-driven development/test-first development*: The development process of first writing tests that enforce certain expectations, then writing the code to produce the correct results.

- *Test case*: A group of tests to test and check the functionality of a section of your program (for example, a class or module).

- *Assertion*: A single test to see whether a certain condition or result is met, which checks that a certain piece of code is working properly.

- *Unit testing*: The process of testing code by making assertions on all of its various pieces of functionality to make sure the entire system operates as expected.

- *Optimization*: The process of improving the efficiency of your code by reworking algorithms and finding new ways of solving problems.

- *Benchmarking*: A process involving testing the speed of your code to see how quick it is under certain conditions, or using certain methods and algorithms. You can use the benchmark results to compare different versions of code, or compare coding techniques.

- *Profiling*: A process that shows you which methods and routines are taking up the most execution time in your programs.

Most of these concepts are not used directly in the code samples in this book, as they're principally relevant to longer-term projects or code being prepared for release. This doesn't mean they're unimportant concepts, but as in-depth parts of a longer development process they aren't within the scope of the code examples used in other chapters.

We'll look briefly at testing methodologies again in Chapter 12 where we develop some simple tests while developing a library.

## CHAPTER 9

Files and Databases

In this chapter we're going to look at how to store, process, and interact with external sources of data from our Ruby programs. In Chapter 4 we briefly looked at how to load files to get data into an application, but this chapter will extend upon that greatly and allow you to create files from scratch from your Ruby programs.

Later in this chapter we'll look at databases—specialized organizations of data—and how to interact with them, along with some notes on interacting with popular database systems such as SQLite, MySQL, PostgreSQL, Oracle, and Microsoft SQL Server. You can use databases for simple tasks such as storing information about a small set of items or as an address book, but databases are also used in the world's busiest data processing environments. By the end of this chapter, you'll be able to use databases the same way as, or at least in a similar way to, those used by professional developers around the world.

Input and Output

Interaction, in computer terms, relates to the input and output of data, or *I/O* for short. Most programming languages have built-in support for I/O, and Ruby's is particularly well designed.

I/O streams are the basis for all input and output in Ruby. An *I/O stream* is a conduit or channel for input and output operations between one resource and another. Usually this will be between your Ruby program and the keyboard, or between your Ruby program and a file. Along this stream, input and output operations can take place. In some cases, such as when using the keyboard, only input can be retrieved, as you can't send data *to* a keyboard, and data can only be sent *to*, and not from, the screen.

In this section we're going to look at using the keyboard, using files, and other forms of I/O in Ruby and how they can be used.

Keyboard Input

The simplest way to get external data into a program is to use the keyboard. For example:

```
a = gets
puts a
```

gets accepts a single line of data from the *standard input*—the keyboard in this case—and assigns it to a. You then print it, using puts, to the standard output—the screen in this case.

STANDARD INPUT AND OUTPUT

The *standard input* is a default stream supplied by many operating systems that relates to the standard way to accept input from the user. In our case, the standard input is the keyboard, but if, for example, you were to redirect data to a Ruby application from a Unix-like operating system, such as Linux or Mac OS X, the standard input would be the data piped to it. For example:

```
ruby test.rb < somedata.txt
```

The output provided this time would be the first line of somedata.txt, as gets would retrieve a single line from the standard input that, in this case, would be the contents of the file somedata.txt.

Conversely, *standard output* is usually referring to the screen or display, but if the results of your Ruby script are being redirected to a file or another program, that destination file or program becomes the target for the standard output.

Alternatively, you can read multiple lines in one go by using readlines:

```
lines = readlines
```

readlines accepts line after line of input until a terminator, most commonly known as EOF (End Of File), is found. You can create EOF on most platforms by pressing Ctrl+D. When the terminating line is found, all the lines of input given are put into an array that's assigned to lines. This is particularly ideal for programs that accept piped or redirected input on standard input. For example, say you have a script called linecount.rb containing this single line:

```
puts readlines.length
```

And you pass in a text file containing ten lines:

```
ruby linecount.rb < textfile.txt
```

You get this result:

```
10
```

In reality, however, this mechanism is rarely used, unless writing shell scripts for use at a Unix prompt. In most cases you'll be writing to and from files directly, and you'll require only minimal keyboard input that you can get with `gets`.

File I/O

In Chapter 4 you used the `File` class to open a text file so you could read in the contents for your program to process. The `File` class is used as an abstraction to access and handle file objects that can be accessed from a Ruby program. The `File` class lets you write to both plain text and binary files and offers a collection of methods to make handling files easy.

Opening and Reading Files

The most common file-related procedure is reading a file's data for use within a program. As you saw in Chapter 4, this is easily done:

```
File.open("text.txt").each { |line| puts line }
```

The `File` class's `open` method is used to open the text file, `text.txt`, and upon that `File` object the `each` method returns each line one by one. You can also do it this way:

```
File.new("text.txt", "r").each { |line| puts line }
```

This method clarifies the process involved. By opening a file, you're creating a new `File` object that you can then use. The second parameter `"r"` defines that you're opening the file for reading. This is the default mode, but when using `File.new` it can help to clarify what you want to do with the file. This becomes important later when you write to files or create new ones from scratch.

For opening and reading files, `File.new` and `File.open` appear identical, but they have different uses. `File.open` can accept a code block, and once the block is finished, the file will be closed automatically. However, `File.new` only returns a `File` object referring to the file. To close the file, you have to use its `close` method. Let's compare the two methods. First, look at `File.open`:

```
File.open("text.txt") do |f|
  puts f.gets
end
```

This code opens `text.txt` and then passes the file handle into the code block as `f`. `puts f.gets` takes a line of data from the file and prints it to the screen. Now, have a look at the `File.new` approach:

```
f = File.new("text.txt", "r")
puts f.gets
f.close
```

In this example, a file handle/object is assigned to `f` directly. You close the file handle manually with the `close` method at the end.

Both the code block and file handle techniques have their uses. Using a code block is a clean way to open a single file quickly and perform operations in a single location. However, assigning the `File` object with `File.new` makes the file reference available throughout the entire current scope without needing to contain file manipulation code within a single block.

■**Note** You might need to specify the location of files directly, as `text.txt` might not appear to be in the current directory. Simply replace `f = File.new("text.txt", "r")` with `f = File.new("c:\full\path\here\text.txt", "r")`, including the full path as necessary. Alternatively, use the result of `Dir::pwd` to see what the current working directory is and put `text.txt` there.

You could also choose to assign the file handle to a class or instance variable:

```
class MyFile
  attr_reader :handle

  def initialize(filename)
    @handle = File.new(filename, "r")
  end

  def finished
    @handle.close
  end
end

f = MyFile.new("text.txt")
puts f.handle.gets
f.finished
```

This is only a proof of the concept, but it demonstrates how `File.new` can be more useful in certain situations.

More File-Reading Techniques

In the previous section you used a `File` object's `each` method to read each line one by one within a code block. However, you can do a lot more than that. Let's assume your `text.txt` file contains this dummy data:

```
Fred Bloggs,Manager,Male,45
Laura Smith,Cook,Female,23
Debbie Watts,Professor,Female,38
```

Next we'll look at some of the different techniques you can use to read the file, along with their outputs. First, you can read an I/O stream line by line using `each`:

```
File.open("text.txt").each { |line| puts line }
```

```
Fred Bloggs,Manager,Male,45
Laura Smith,Cook,Female,23
Debbie Watts,Professor,Female,38
```

Note `each` technically reads from the file delimiter by delimiter, where the standard delimiter is a "newline" character. You can change this delimiter. See Appendix B's "Special Variables" section for details.

You can read an I/O stream with `each` using a custom delimiter of your choosing:

```
File.open("text.txt").each(',') { |line| puts line }
```

```
Fred Bloggs,
Manager,
Male,
45
Laura Smith,
Cook,
Female,
23
Debbie Watts,
Professor,
Female,
38
```

In this case, you passed an optional argument to each that specified a different delimiter from the default "newline" delimiter. Commas delimit the input.

Tip You can override the default delimiter by setting the special variable $/ to any delimiter you choose.

You can read an I/O stream byte by byte with each_byte:

```
File.open("text.txt").each_byte { |byte| puts byte }
```

```
70
114
101
100
...many lines skipped for brevity...
51
56
10
```

Note When reading byte by byte you get the single byte values of each character rather than the characters themselves, much like when you do something like puts "test"[0]. To convert into text characters, you can use the chr method.

Here's how to read an I/O stream line by line using gets:

```
File.open("text.txt") do |f|
  2.times { puts f.gets }
end
```

```
Fred Bloggs,Manager,Male,45
Laura Smith,Cook,Female,23
```

gets isn't an iterator like each or each_byte. Therefore, you have to call it multiple times to get multiple lines. In this example it was used twice, and pulled out the first two lines of the example file. Like each, however, gets can accept an optional delimiter:

```
File.open("text.txt") do |f|
  2.times { puts f.gets(',') }
end
```

```
Fred Bloggs,
Manager,
```

There's also a noniterative version of each_byte called getc:

```
File.open("text.txt") do |f|
  2.times { puts f.getc }
end
```

```
70
114
```

You can also read an entire file into an array, split by lines, using readlines:

```
puts File.open("text.txt").readlines.join("--")
```

```
Fred Bloggs,Manager,Male,45
--Laura Smith,Cook,Female,23
--Debbie Watts,Professor,Female,38
```

Last but not least, you can choose to read an arbitrary number of bytes from a file into a single variable using read:

```
File.open("text.txt") do |f|
  puts f.read(6)
end
```

```
Fred B
```

■Note You can use all these methods on any file, such as binary files (images, executables, and so on), not just text files. However, on Windows, you might need to open the file in binary mode. This is covered in the section "Writing to Files."

The File class makes some convenience methods available so that you don't need to do things like File.open(filename).read to be able to read a file into a string. Instead, you can do this:

```
data = File.read(filename)
```

This acts as a shorthand for opening the file, using the standard read method, and then closing the file again.

You can also do this:

```
array_of_lines = File.readlines(filename)
```

Simple!

Generally, you should try to use these shortcut methods wherever possible, as they result in shorter, easier-to-read code, and you don't have to worry about closing the files. Everything is taken care of for you in one step. Of course, if reading a file line by line is necessary (perhaps if you're working with extremely large files), then you can use the techniques demonstrated earlier in this chapter for reading line by line.

Your Position Within a File

When reading a file, it can be useful to know where you are within that file. The pos method gives you access to this information:

```
f = File.open("text.txt")
puts f.pos
puts f.gets
puts f.pos
```

```
0
Fred Bloggs,Manager,Male,45
28
```

Before you begin to read any text from the file, the position is shown as 0. Once you've read a line of text, the position is shown as 28. This is because pos returns the position of the file pointer (that is, the current location within the file that you're reading from) in the number of bytes from the start of the file.

However, pos can work both ways, as it has a sister method, pos=:

```
f = File.open("text.txt")
f.pos = 8
puts f.gets
puts f.pos
```

```
ggs,Manager,Male,45
28
```

In this instance the file pointer was placed 8 bytes into the file before reading anything. This meant that "Fred Blo" was skipped, and only the rest of the line was retrieved.

Writing to Files

The ability to jump easily around files, read lines based on delimiters, and handle data byte by byte makes Ruby ideal for manipulating data, but I haven't yet covered how to write new information to files or how to make changes to existing files.

Generally, you can mirror most of the techniques used to read files when writing to files. For example:

```
File.open("text.txt", "w") do |f|
  f.puts "This is a test"
end
```

This code creates a new file (or overwrites an existing file) called text.txt and puts a single line of text within it. Previously you've used puts on its own to output data to the screen, but when used with a File object it writes the data to the file instead. Simple!

The "w" passed as the second argument to File.open tells Ruby to open the file for writing only, and to create a new file or overwrite what is already in the file. This is in contrast with the "r" mode used earlier when opening a file for reading only.

However, you can use several different file modes, as covered in Table 9-1.

Table 9-1. *File Modes Usable with* File.new

File Mode	Properties of the I/O Stream
r	Read-only. The file pointer is placed at the start of the file.
r+	Both reading and writing are allowed. The file pointer is placed at the start of the file.
w	Write-only. A new file is created (or an old one overwritten as if new).
w+	Both reading and writing are allowed, but File.new creates a new file from scratch (or overwrites an old one as if new).
a	Write (in append mode). The file pointer is placed at the end of the file and writes will make the file longer.
a+	Both reading and writing are allowed (in append mode). The file pointer is placed at the end of the file and writes will make the file longer.
b	Binary file mode (only required on Windows). You can use it in conjunction with any of the other modes listed.

Using the append mode described in Table 9-1, it's trivial to create a program that appends a line of text to a file each time it's run:

```
f = File.new("logfile.txt", "a")
f.puts Time.now
f.close
```

If you run this code multiple times, logfile.txt will contain several dates and times, one after the other. Append mode is particularly ideal for log file situations where new information has to be added at different times.

The read and write modes work in a simple manner. If you want to open a file in a mode where it can be read from and written to at the same time, you can do just that:

```
f = File.open("text.txt", "r+")
puts f.gets
f.puts "This is a test"
puts f.gets
f.close
```

The second line of this code reads the first line of text from the file, meaning the file pointer is waiting at the start of the second line of data. However, the following f.puts statement then *inserts* a new line of text into the file at that position, pushing your previous second line to the third line of the file. Next, you read the next line of text, which is now the third line of text.

Whereas `puts` outputs lines of text, you can perform the writing equivalents of `getc` and `read` with `putc` and `write`:

```
f = File.open("text.txt", "r+")
f.putc "X"
f.close
```

This example opens `text.txt` for reading and writing, and changes the first character of the first line to X. Similarly:

```
f = File.open("text.txt", "r+")
f.write "123456"
f.close
```

This example overwrites the first six characters of the first line with 123456.

Note It's worth noticing that `putc` and `write` overwrite existing content in the file rather than *inserting* it.

Renaming and Deleting Files

If you want to change the name of a file, you *could* create a new file with the new name and read into that file all the data from the original file. However, this isn't necessary, and you can simply use `File.rename` like so:

```
File.rename("file1.txt", "file2.txt")
```

Deleting a file is just as simple. You can delete either one file at a time or many at once:

```
File.delete("file1.txt")
File.delete("file2.txt", "file3.txt", "file4.txt")
File.unlink("file1.txt")
```

Note `File.unlink` does exactly the same thing as `File.delete`.

File Operations

The File class offers you more than just the ability to read and write files. You can also perform a number of checks and operations upon files.

Checking for Identical Files

Checking whether two files are identical is easy:

```
puts "They're identical!" if File.identical?("file1.txt", "file2.txt")
```

Creating Filenames Platform-Independently

Windows and Unix-related operating systems have different ways of denoting filenames. Windows filenames look like c:\directory\filename.ext, whereas Unix-style filenames look like /directory/filename.ext. If your Ruby scripts work with filenames and need to operate under both systems, the File class provides the join method.

　　Under both systems, filenames (and complete paths) are built up from directory names and local filenames. For example, in the preceding examples, the directory is called directory, but on Windows backslashes are used as opposed to forward slashes.

■**Note** In recent versions of Ruby, it's possible to use Unix-style pathnames using forward slashes as directory separators, rather than having to format filenames in a Windows style with backslashes. However, this section is included for completeness, or for instances where you need to work with libraries that don't respect Unix-style pathnames on other operating systems.

　　On Windows, you can use File.join to put together a filename using directory names and a final filename:

```
File.join('full', 'path', 'here', 'filename.txt')
```

```
full\path\here\filename.txt
```

■**Note** Depending on how your system is set up, you might even see a forward-slash version of the preceding code on Windows, although that is technically a Unix-style path.

On Unix-related operating systems, such as Linux, the code is the same:

```
File.join('full', 'path', 'here', 'filename.txt')
```

```
full/path/here/filename.txt
```

The `File.join` method is simple to use, and it allows you to write the same code to run on both systems rather than choosing between backslashes and forward slashes in your code.

The separator itself is stored in a constant called `File::SEPARATOR`, so you can easily turn a filename into an absolute filename (with an absolute path) by appending the directory separator to the start, like so:

```
File.join(File::SEPARATOR , 'full', 'path', 'here', 'filename.txt')
```

```
/full/path/here/filename.txt
```

Similarly, you can use `File.expand_path` to turn basic filenames into complete paths. For example:

```
File.expand_path("text.txt")
```

```
/Users/peter/text.txt
```

■Note The result of `File.expand_path` will vary according to the operating system the code is run under. As `text.txt` is a relative filename, it converts it to an absolute filename and references the current working directory.

Seeking

In a previous example you changed the position of the file pointer using `pos=`. However, this only allows you to specify the exact position of the file pointer. If you want to move the pointer forward by a certain offset or move the pointer to a certain position backwards from the *end* of the file, you need to use seek.

seek has three modes of operation:

- IO::SEEK_CUR   Seeks a certain number of bytes ahead of the current position.

- IO::SEEK_END   Seeks to a position based on the end of the file. This means to seek to a certain position from the end of the file you'll probably need to use a negative value.

- IO::SEEK_SET   Seeks to an absolute position in the file. Identical to pos=.

Therefore, to position the file pointer 5 bytes from the end of the file and change the character to an X, you would use seek as follows:

```
f = File.new("test.txt", "r+")
f.seek(-5, IO::SEEK_END)
f.putc "X"
f.close
```

Note Notice that because you're writing to the file, you use the r+ file mode to enable writing as well as reading.

Or you could do this to print every fifth character in a file:

```
f = File.new("test.txt", "r")
while a = f.getc
  puts a.chr
  f.seek(5, IO::SEEK_CUR)
end
```

Finding Out When a File was Last Modified

To establish when a file was last modified, use File.mtime:

```
puts File.mtime("text.txt")
```

```
Fri Jan 11 18:25:42 2007
```

The time is returned as a `Time` object, so you can get more information directly:

```
t = File.mtime("text.txt")
puts t.hour
puts t.min
puts t.sec
```

```
18
25
42
```

Note You can learn more about the `Time` class and its methods in Chapter 3.

Checking If a File Exists

It's useful to check whether a file actually exists, particularly if your program relies on that file or if a user supplied the filename. If the file doesn't exist, you can raise a user-friendly error or exception. Invoke the `File.exist?` method to check for the existence of a file:

```
puts "It exists!" if File.exist?("file1.txt")
```

`File.exist?` returns `true` if the named file exists. You could edit the `MyFile` class created in a previous example to check for the existence of a file before opening it to avoid a potential exception being thrown, like so:

```
class MyFile
  attr_reader :handle

  def initialize(filename)
    if File.exist?(filename)
      @handle = File.new(filename, "r")
    else
      return false
    end
  end
end
```

Getting the Size of a File

`File.size` returns the size of a file in bytes. If the file doesn't exist, an exception is thrown, so it would make sense to check its existence with `File.exist?` first.

```
puts File.size("text.txt")
```

How to Know When You're at the End of a File

In previous examples you've either used iterators to give you all the lines or bytes in a file, or you've pulled only a few lines from a file here and there. However, it would be useful to have a foolproof way to know when the file pointer is at, or has gone past, the end of the file. The `eof?` method provides this feature:

```
f = File.new("test.txt", "r")
catch(:end_of_file) do
  loop do
    throw :end_of_file if f.eof?
    puts f.gets
  end
end
f.close
```

This example uses an "infinite" loop that you break out of by using `catch` and `throw` (as covered in Chapter 8). `throw` is only called if the file pointer is at, or past, the end of the file. This specific example is not particularly useful, as `f.each` could have performed a similar task, but in situations where you might be moving the file pointer around manually, or making large jumps through a file, checking for an "end of file" situation is useful.

Directories

All files are contained within various *directories*, and Ruby has no problem handling these too. Whereas the `File` class handles files, directories are handled with the `Dir` class.

Navigating Through Directories

To change directory within a Ruby program, use `Dir.chdir`:

```
Dir.chdir("/usr/bin")
```

This example changes the current directory to /usr/bin.

You can find out what the current directory is with `Dir.pwd`. For example, here's the result on my installation:

```
puts Dir.pwd
```

```
/Users/peter
```

```
Dir.chdir("/usr/bin")
puts Dir.pwd
```

```
/usr/bin
```

You can get a list of the files and directories within a specific directory using `Dir.entries`:

```
puts Dir.entries("/usr/bin").join(' ')
```

```
. .. a2p aclocal aclocal-1.6 addftinfo afmtodit alias amlint ant appleping
appletviewer apply apropos apt ar arch as asa at at_cho_prn atlookup atos
atprint...items removed for brevity... zless zmore znew zprint
```

`Dir.entries` returns an array with all the entries within the specified directory. `Dir.foreach` provides the same feature, but as an iterator:

```
Dir.foreach("/usr/bin") do |entry|
  puts entry
end
```

An even more concise way of getting directory listings is by using `Dir`'s class array method:

```
Dir["/usr/bin/*"]
```

```
["/usr/bin/a2p", "/usr/bin/aclocal", "/usr/bin/aclocal-1.6",
"/usr/bin/addftinfo",
 "/usr/bin/afmtodit", "/usr/bin/alias", "/usr/bin/amlint", "/usr/bin/ant",
...items
 removed for brevity...]
```

In this case, each entry is returned as an absolute filename, making it easy to use the File class's methods to perform checks upon each entry if you wished.

You could take this process a step further and be a little more platform independent:

```
Dir[File.join(File::SEPARATOR, 'usr', 'bin', '*')]
```

■**Note** Of course, only Unix systems have /usr/bin directories, so this technique is moot in this instance, but it might be useful in your own programs.

Creating a Directory

You use Dir.mkdir to create directories, like so:

```
Dir.mkdir("mynewdir")
```

Once the directory has been created you can navigate to it with Dir.chdir.

You can also specify absolute paths to create directories under other specific directories:

```
Dir.mkdir("/mynewdir")
Dir.mkdir("c:\test")
```

However, you cannot create directories under directories that don't yet exist themselves. If you want to create an entire structure of directories you must create them one by one from the top down.

■**Note** On Unix-related operating systems, Dir.mkdir accepts a second optional argument: an integer, specifying the permissions for the directory. You can specify this in octal, as with 0666 or 0777, representing modes 666 and 777 respectively.

Deleting a Directory

Deleting a directory is similar to deleting a file:

```
Dir.delete("testdir")
```

Note `Dir.unlink` and `Dir.rmdir` perform exactly the same function and are provided for convenience.

As with `Dir.mkdir`, you can use absolute pathnames.

One thing you need to consider when deleting directories is whether they're empty. If a directory isn't empty, you cannot delete it with a single call to `Dir.delete`. You need to iterate through each of the subdirectories and files and remove them all first. You can do that iteration with `Dir.foreach`, looping recursively through the file tree by pushing new directories and files to remove onto an array.

Creating Files in the Temporary Directory

Most operating systems have the concept of a "temporary" directory where temporary files can be stored. Temporary files are those that might be created briefly during a program's execution but aren't a permanent store of information.

`Dir.tmpdir` provides the path to the temporary directory on the current system, although the method is not available by default. To make `Dir.tmpdir` available it's necessary to use `require 'tmpdir'`:

```
require 'tmpdir'
puts Dir.tmpdir
```

```
/tmp
```

You can use `Dir.tmpdir` with `File.join` to create a platform-independent way of creating a temporary file:

```
require 'tmpdir'
tempfilename = File.join(Dir.tmpdir, "myapp.dat")
tempfile = File.new(tempfilename, "w")
tempfile.puts "This is only temporary"
tempfile.close
File.delete(tempfilename)
```

This code creates a temporary file, writes data to it, and deletes it.

Ruby's standard library also includes a library called `Tempfile` that can create temporary files for you:

```
require 'tempfile'
f = Tempfile.new('myapp')
f.puts "Hello"
puts f.path
f.close
```

```
/tmp/myfile1842.0
```

Unlike creating and managing your own temporary files, `Tempfile` automatically deletes the files it creates after they have been used. This is an important consideration when choosing between the two techniques. (There's more information about temporary files and the `tempfile` library in Chapter 16.)

Basic Databases

Many applications need to store, access, or manipulate data. In some cases this is by loading files, making changes to them, and outputting data to the screen or back to a file. In many situations, however, a database is required.

A database is a system for organizing data on a computer in a systematic way. A database can be as simple as a text file containing data that can be manipulated programmatically by a computer program, or as complex as many gigabytes of data spread across hundreds of dedicated database servers. You can use Ruby in these scenarios and for those in between.

First, we're going to look at how to use simple text files as a form of organized data.

Text File Databases

One simple type of database can be stored in a text file in a format commonly known as CSV. CSV stands for Comma-Separated Values, and means that for each item of data you're storing, you can have multiple attributes separated with commas. The dummy data in your `text.txt` file in the previous section used CSV data. To recap, `text.txt` initially contained this code:

```
Fred Bloggs,Manager,Male,45
Laura Smith,Cook,Female,23
Debbie Watts,Professor,Female,38
```

Each line represents a different person, and commas separate the attributes relating to each person. The commas allow you to access (and change) each attribute separately.

Ruby's standard library includes a library called csv that allows you to use text files containing CSV data as simple databases that are easy to read, create, and manipulate.

Reading and Searching CSV Data

The CSV class provided by csv manages the manipulation of the data for you:

```
require 'csv'
CSV.open('text.txt', 'r') do |person|
  puts person.inspect
end
```

```
["Fred Bloggs", "Manager", "Male", "45"]
["Laura Smith", "Cook", "Female", "23"]
["Debbie Watts", "Professor", "Female", "38"]
```

You open the text.txt file by using CSV.open, and each line (that is, each individual "person" in the file) is passed into the block one by one. The inspect method demonstrates that each entry is now represented in array form. This makes it easier to read the data than when it was in its plain text form.

You can also use CSV alongside the File class:

```
require 'csv'
people = CSV.parse(File.read('text.txt'))
puts people[0][0]
puts people[1][0]
puts people[2][0]
```

```
Fred Bloggs
Laura Smith
Debbie Watts
```

This example uses the File class to open and read in the contents of a file, and CSV.parse immediately uses these to convert the data into an array of arrays. The elements in the main array represent each line in the file, and each element in those elements represents a different attribute (or field) of that line. Therefore, by printing out the first element of each entry, you get the people's names only.

An even more succinct way of loading the data from a CSV-formatted file into an array is with `CSV.read`:

```
puts CSV.read('text.txt').inspect
```

```
[["Fred Bloggs", "Manager", "Male", "45"], ["Laura Smith", "Cook", "Female",
"23"],
["Debbie Watts", "Professor", "Female", "38"]]
```

The `find` and `find_all` methods provided by the `Enumerable` module to `Array` make it easy for you to perform searches upon the data available in the array. For example, you'd use this code if you wanted to pick out the first person in the data called Laura:

```
require 'csv'
people = CSV.read('text.txt')
laura = people.find { |person| person[0] =~ /Laura/ }
puts laura.inspect
```

```
["Laura Smith", "Cook", "Female", "23"]
```

Using the `find` method with a code block that looks for the first matching line where the name contains "Laura" gives you back the data you were looking for.

Where `find` returns the first matching element of an array or hash, `find_all` returns *all* valid matches. Let's say you want to find the people in your database whose ages are between 20 and 40:

```
young_people = people.find_all do |p|
  p[3].to_i.between?(20, 40)
end
puts young_people.inspect
```

```
[["Laura Smith", "Cook", "Female", "23"], ["Debbie Watts", "Professor",
"Female", "38"]]
```

This operation provides you with the two matching people contained within an array that you can iterate through.

Saving Data Back to the CSV File

Once you can read and query data, the next step is being able to change it, delete it, and rewrite your CSV file with a new version of the data for future use. Luckily, this is as simple as reopening the file with write access and "pushing" the data back to the file. The CSV module handles all of the conversion.

```
require 'csv'
people = CSV.read('text.txt')
laura = people.find { |person| person[0] =~ /Laura/ }
laura[0] = "Lauren Smith"

CSV.open('text.txt', 'w') do |csv|
  people.each do |person|
    csv << person
  end
end
```

You load in the data, find a person to change, change her name, and then open up the CSV file and rewrite the data back to it. Notice, however, that you have to write the data person by person. Once complete, `text.txt` is updated with the name change. This is how to write back CSV data to file. (There's more information about CSV, along with information about FasterCSV, a faster CSV implementation that's available as a library, in Chapter 16.)

Storing Objects and Data Structures

Working with CSV is easy, but it doesn't feel very smooth. You're always dealing with arrays, so rather than getting nice names such as `name`, `age`, or `job` for the different attributes, you have to remember in which element and at which position each attribute is located.

You're also forced to store simple arrays for each separate entry. There's no nesting, no way to relate one thing to another, no relationship to object orientation, and the data is flat. This is ideal for basic data, but what if you simply want to take data that already exists in Ruby data structures such as arrays and hashes and save that data to disk for later use?

PStore

PStore is a core Ruby library that allows you to use Ruby objects and data structures as you normally would, and then store them in a file. Later on, you can reload the objects back into memory from the disk file. This technique is known as *object persistence*, and relies on a technique called *marshalling*, where standard data structures are turned into a form of flat data that can be stored to disk or transmitted over a network for later reconstruction.

Let's create a class to represent the structure of the data you were using in the CSV examples:

```
class Person
  attr_accessor :name, :job, :gender, :age
end
```

You can re-create your data like so:

```
fred = Person.new
fred.name = "Fred Bloggs"
fred.age = 45

laura = Person.new
laura.name = "Laura Smith"
laura.age = 23
```

■**Note** For brevity, you'll only work with these two objects in this example.

Rather than have your data in arrays, you now have your data available in a fully object-oriented fashion. You could create methods within the Person class to help you manipulate your objects and so forth. This style of storing and manipulating data is true to the Ruby way of things and is entirely object-oriented. However, until now, your objects have only lasted until the end of a program, but with PStore it's easy to write them to a file:

```
require 'pstore'
store = PStore.new("storagefile")
store.transaction do
  store[:people] ||= Array.new
  store[:people] << fred
  store[:people] << laura
end
```

In this example you create a new PStore in a file called storagefile. You then start a transaction (data within a PStore file can only be read or updated while inside a "transaction" to prevent data corruption), and within the transaction you make sure the :people element of the store contains something or gets assigned to be an array. Next, you push the fred and laura objects to the :people element of the store, and then end the transaction.

The reason for the hash syntax is because a PStore is, effectively, a disk-based hash. You can then store whatever objects you like *within* that hash. In this example, you've created an array within store[:people] and pushed your two Person objects to it.

Later on, you can retrieve the data from the PStore database:

```
require 'pstore'
store = PStore.new("storagefile")
people = []
store.transaction do
  people = store[:people]
end

# At this point the Person objects inside people can be treated
# as totally local objects.
people.each do |person|
  puts person.name
end
```

```
Fred Bloggs
Laura Smith
```

With only a simple storage and retrieval process, PStore makes it easy to add storage facilities to existing Ruby programs by allowing you to store existing objects into a PStore database. Object persistence is not ideal for many types of data storage, but if your program is heavily dependent on objects, and you want to store those objects to disk for later use, PStore provides a simple method to use.

YAML

YAML (standing for YAML Ain't Markup Language) is a special text-based markup language that was designed as a data serialization format that's readable by humans. You can use it in a similar way to PStore to serialize data structures, but unlike PStore's data, humans can easily read YAML data, and even directly edit it with a text editor and a basic knowledge of YAML syntax.

The YAML library comes as part of Ruby's standard library, so it's easy to use. Unlike PStore, though, the YAML library converts data structures to and from YAML and doesn't provide a hash to use, so the technique is a little different. This example writes an array of objects to disk:

```ruby
require 'yaml'

class Person
  attr_accessor :name, :age
end

fred = Person.new
fred.name = "Fred Bloggs"
fred.age = 45

laura = Person.new
laura.name = "Laura Smith"
laura.age = 23

test_data = [ fred, laura ]

puts YAML::dump(test_data)
```

```
---
- !ruby/object:Person
  age: 45
  name: Fred Bloggs
- !ruby/object:Person
  age: 23
  name: Laura Smith
```

You use YAML::dump to convert your Person object array into YAML data, which, as you should agree, is extremely readable! YAML::load performs the operation in the other direction, turning YAML code into working Ruby objects. For example, let's modify the YAML data a little and see if it translates back into working objects:

```ruby
require 'yaml'

class Person
  attr_accessor :name, :age
end

yaml_string = <<END_OF_DATA
```

```
---
- !ruby/object:Person
  age: 45
  name: Jimmy
- !ruby/object:Person
  age: 23
  name: Laura Smith
END_OF_DATA

test_data = YAML::load(yaml_string)
puts test_data[0].name
puts test_data[1].name
```

```
Jimmy
Laura Smith
```

Here YAML::load converts the YAML data back into the test_data array of Person objects successfully.

You can use YAML to convert between most types of Ruby objects (including basic types such as Array and Hash) and YAML and back. This makes it an ideal intermediary format for storing data (such as configuration files) your applications need to access.

■**Note** When dealing with serialized objects, you must still have the classes used by those objects defined within the program somewhere, otherwise they won't be usable.

As plain text, you can safely transmit YAML via e-mail, store it in normal text files, and move it around more easily than the binary data created by libraries such as PStore.

To learn more about YAML formatting, read its Wikipedia entry at http://en.wikipedia.org/wiki/YAML, or refer to the official YAML Web site at http://www.yaml.org/.

Relational Databases and SQL

In the previous section you created some extremely simplistic databases using text files and object persistence. Text files, of course, have their limitations. They're not reliable if many processes are using them at the same time. and they're slow. Loading a CSV file into memory is fine when the dataset is small, but when it grows, the process of working directly with files can soon become sluggish.

When developing more-robust systems, you pass database filing and management off to a separate application or system, and applications simply connect to a database system to pass data back and forth. In the previous section you were working with database files and the data within them quite directly, and that's unacceptable when performance and reliability are necessary.

Relational Database Concepts

One major benefit of using a dedicated database system is getting support for *relational databases*. A relational database is a database that's comprised of data grouped into one or more *tables* that can be linked together. A table stores information about one type of thing. For example, an address book database might be made up of a people table, an addresses table, and a phonenumbers table. Each table stores information about people, addresses, and phone numbers, respectively.

The people table would likely have a number of attributes (known as *columns*, in database land) such as name, age, and gender. Each row of the table—that is, an individual person—would then have information in each column. Figure 9-1 shows an example.

Columns

ID	Name	Job	Age	Gender
1	Fred Bloggs	Manager	45	Male
2	Laura Smith	Cook	23	Female
3	Debbie Watts	Professor	38	Female

Figure 9-1. *A basic* people *table containing three rows*

Figure 9-1's example also includes a column called id. In relational databases it's standard procedure to have an id column on most tables to identify each row uniquely. Although you could look up and retrieve data based on other columns, such as name, numeric IDs are useful when you're creating *relationships* between tables.

■Note In Figure 9-1, the table headings are written in a typical style, as you'd expect in a normal address book or spreadsheet. However, when dealing with relational databases at a lower level, it's reasonably common to use all lowercase names for column and table names. This explains why the text, and later code examples, in this chapter, will refer to table and column names in lowercase only.

One benefit of relational databases is the way rows in different tables can be related to one another. For example, your `people` table could have an `address_id` column that stores the ID of the address associated with this user. If you want to find out the address of a particular person, you can look up his or her `address_id`, and then look up the relevant row of the `addresses` table.

The reason for this sort of relationship is that many people in your `people` database might share the same address, and rather than store the address separately for each person, it's more efficient to store a reference instead. This also means that if you update the address in the future, it updates for all the relevant users at the same time.

Relationships also make it possible to do *many-to-many* relationships. You could create a separate table called `related_people` that has two columns, `first_person_id` and `second_person_id`. This table could store pairs of ID numbers that signify two people are related to each other. To work out to whom a person is related, you can simply look for any rows mentioning his or her ID number and you'd get back the ID numbers of that person's related people. This sort of relationship is used in most databases and is what makes relational databases so useful.

The Big Four: MySQL, PostgreSQL, Oracle, and SQLite

Four well-known relational database systems available today that work on both Windows and Unix operating systems are MySQL, PostgreSQL, Oracle, and SQLite. Each has significantly different features from the others, and therefore has different uses.

■**Note** Microsoft SQL Server is also popular, though on Microsoft platforms only.

Most Web developers will be familiar with MySQL, as it comes with most Web hosting packages and servers. Therefore, MySQL is the most commonly used database engine on the Internet. It's also the default engine used by the Ruby on Rails framework (to be covered in Chapter 13), so it's likely you'll be using it at some point.

PostgreSQL and Oracle also have their own niches, with Oracle being a well-known enterprise-level database that can cost quite a lot of money to license. However, it's used by a lot of larger companies.

For our purposes in the next few sections of this chapter, we'll be using a system called SQLite. Unlike MySQL, PostgreSQL, and Oracle, SQLite doesn't run as a "server," so it doesn't require any special resources. Whereas MySQL, PostgreSQL, and Oracle all run as permanent server applications, SQLite is "on-demand" and works entirely on your local machine. Despite this, it's still fast and reliable, and is ideal for local database purposes. You can easily carry much of the knowledge you learn with SQLite across to other systems.

Nonetheless, toward the end of this chapter we'll look at how you can connect to databases using these other architectures, so that you can get direct access to your existing databases from your Ruby applications.

Installing SQLite

The first step to getting a database system up and running quickly is to install SQLite3—the latest version of SQLite. SQLite's download page at `http://www.sqlite.org/` `download.html` contains binary downloads of the SQLite3 libraries for Windows (DLL) and Linux (shared library), as well as the source code for compilation on other systems.

Mac OS X DarwinPorts users can install SQLite3 by typing **sudo port install sqlite3** at the command prompt. Users of certain Linux distributions may be able to install SQLite3 using the respective package manager.

■**Note** For Windows users there's a video screencast of the SQLite 3 installation process at `http://` `blip.tv/file/48664`.

Once the SQLite3 libraries are installed, you can install the Ruby library that gives Ruby access to SQLite3 databases as a gem. The gem is called sqlite-ruby and can be installed on all systems with `gem install sqlite3-ruby` or `sudo gem install sqlite3-ruby` on Unix-related operating systems if you aren't running as a super-user. (For information about installing Ruby gems, refer to Chapter 7.)

You can check that everything was installed okay with this code:

```
require 'rubygems'
require 'sqlite3'
puts "It's all okay!" if defined?(SQLite3::Database)
```

```
It's all okay!
```

If the installation didn't progress smoothly, links to SQLite resources are available in Appendix C.

A Crash Course in Basic Database Actions and SQL

To manage databases with any of the various database systems at a basic level, knowledge of several SQL commands is required. In this section we're going to look at how to create tables, add data to them, retrieve data, delete data, and change data.

Throughout this section, think entirely in terms of databases separately from Ruby. A demonstration of how Ruby can use SQL to manipulate a database is covered in detail in the later section "Using SQLite with Ruby."

■**Note** If you're already familiar with SQL, you can skip the next few sections and jump straight to the section "Using SQLite with Ruby" to see SQL in action alongside Ruby.

What Is SQL?

Structured Query Language (SQL) is a special language, often known as a *query language*, used to interact with database systems. You can use SQL to create, retrieve, update, and delete data, as well as create and manipulate structures that hold those data. Its basic purpose is to support the interaction between a client and a database system. In this section I'm going to give you a primer on SQL's syntax and how you can use it from Ruby.

Be aware that this section is only a very basic introduction to SQL, as a full and deep explanation of SQL is beyond the scope of this book. If you wish to learn SQL in more depth, please refer to the resources mentioned in Appendix C.

Note that the way different database systems use and implement SQL can vary wildly, which is why the following sections will only cover that which is reasonably standard and enables you to perform basic data operations.

CREATE TABLE

Before you can add data into a database, it's necessary to create one or many tables to hold it. To create a table, you need to know what you want to store in it, what you want to call it, and what attributes you want to store.

For your table `people`, you want to have `name`, `job`, `gender`, and `age` columns, as well as a unique `id` column for possible relationships with other tables. To create a table, you use a syntax like so:

```
CREATE TABLE table_name (
column_name data_type options,
column_name data_type options,
...,
...
)
```

Therefore, for your `people` table, you'd use this syntax:

```
CREATE TABLE people (
id integer primary key,
name varchar(50),
job varchar(50),
gender varchar(6),
age integer)
```

This SQL command creates a `people` table and gives it five columns. The data types for the `name`, `job`, and `gender` columns are all VARCHARs, meaning they're variable-length character fields. In basic terms, it means they can contain strings. The number in brackets refers to the maximum length of that string, so the `name` column can hold a maximum of 50 characters.

The `id` column has the words `primary key` as its options. This means that the `id` column is the primary reference to each row and that the `id` must be unique for each row. In SQLite, this means SQLite will automatically assign a unique `id` to each row, so you don't need to specify one yourself each time you add a new row.

INSERT INTO

You use the INSERT command to add rows to tables:

```
INSERT INTO people (name, age, gender, job) VALUES ("Chris Scott", 25, "Male",➥
  "Technician")
```

First, you specify the table you want to add a row to, then list the columns you wish to fill out, before passing in the values with which to fill the row.

You can omit the list of columns if the data passed after VALUES is in the correct order:

```
INSERT INTO people VALUES ("Chris Scott", 25, "Male", "Technician")
```

■**Caution** This particular INSERT would cause an error on your people table! It's missing the id column.

However, it's safer and more convenient if you specify the columns beforehand, as in the first example. The second example clearly demonstrates why this is the case, as it's hard to tell which item of data relates to which column.

Columns that don't have any data specified for them will be filled in automatically with the defaults specified in the CREATE TABLE statement for that table. In the case of the people table, the id column will automatically receive a unique ID number for each row added.

SELECT

You use the SELECT command to retrieve data from tables. You specify which columns you want to retrieve (or use * as a wildcard to retrieve them all), the table you want to retrieve data from, and optionally include a condition upon which to base the retrieval. For example, you might only want to choose a particular row, or rows that match certain criteria.

This SQL statement retrieves the data from all columns for all rows in the people table:

```
SELECT * FROM people
```

This SQL retrieves all the values from just the name column of rows in the people table (for example, "Fred Bloggs," "Chris Scott," "Laura Smith"):

```
SELECT name FROM people
```

This SQL retrieves rows with an id column equal to 2 from the people table (usually, because id is a column containing unique values, only one row would be returned for such a query):

```
SELECT * FROM people WHERE id = 2
```

This SQL retrieves any rows that have a name column equal to "Chris Scott":

```
SELECT * FROM people WHERE name = "Chris Scott"
```

This SQL retrieves all rows of people whose ages are between 20 and 40 inclusive:

```
SELECT * FROM people WHERE age >= 20 AND age <= 40
```

The conditions used in SQL are somewhat similar to those used in Ruby and other programming languages, except that logical operators such as AND and OR are written as plain English. Also, as in Ruby, you can use parentheses to group expressions and build up more complex requests.

It's also possible to have the results returned in a certain order by appending an ORDER BY clause such as ORDER column_name to the SQL query. You can further append ASC to the column name to sort in an ascending fashion, or DESC to sort in a descending fashion. For example, this SQL returns all rows from the people table ordered by the name column in descending order (so names starting with Z come before those beginning with A):

```
SELECT * FROM people ORDER BY name DESC
```

This SQL returns all rows of those people between the ages of 20 and 40 in order of age, youngest first:

```
SELECT * FROM people WHERE age >= 20 AND age <= 40 ORDER BY age ASC
```

Another useful addition to a SELECT command is LIMIT. LIMIT allows you to place a limit on the amount of rows returned on a single query:

```
SELECT * FROM people ORDER BY name DESC LIMIT 5
```

In conjunction with ORDER, you can use LIMIT to find extremes in the data. For example, finding the oldest person is easy:

```
SELECT * FROM people ORDER BY age DESC LIMIT 1
```

This sorts the rows in descending order by age and returns the first result, the highest. To get the youngest person, you could use ASC instead of DESC on the ordering.

▪**Note** Database engines sort columns automatically by their data type. Strings of text are formatted alphanumerically, whereas integer and other number columns are sorted by their value.

DELETE

The DELETE SQL command deletes rows from tables. You can delete rows based upon an SQL condition. For example:

```
DELETE FROM people WHERE name="Chris"
DELETE FROM people WHERE age > 100
DELETE FROM people WHERE gender = "Male" AND age < 50
```

As with SELECT, you can place limits upon the number of deletions:

```
DELETE FROM people WHERE age > 100 LIMIT 10
```

In this case, only 10 rows with an age over 100 would be deleted.

Think of the DELETE command to be like SELECT, but instead of returning the rows, it erases them. The format is otherwise reasonably similar.

UPDATE

UPDATE provides the ability to update and amend information within the database. As with DELETE, the syntax for UPDATE is similar to that of SELECT. Consider this:

```
SELECT * FROM people WHERE name = "Chris"
UPDATE people SET name = "Christopher" WHERE name = "Chris"
```

UPDATE first accepts the name of a table whose row(s) might be updated, then accepts the column(s) to be changed along with the new data, and finally an optional condition for the change. Some examples follow.

This SQL changes the name column to "Christopher" on all rows where the name column is currently equal to "Chris":

```
UPDATE people SET name = "Christopher" WHERE name = "Chris"
```

This SQL changes the name column to "Christopher" and the age column to 44 where the name column is currently equal to "Chris":

```
UPDATE people SET name = "Christopher", age = 44 WHERE name = "Chris"
```

This SQL changes the name column to "Christopher" where the name column is "Chris" *and* the age column equals 25. Therefore, a row where the name is Chris and the age is 21 will *not* be updated by this example query:

```
UPDATE people SET name = "Christopher" WHERE name = "Chris" AND age = 25
```

This SQL changes the name column to "Christopher" on *every* row of the people table. This demonstrates why it pays to be careful when building SQL queries, as short statements can have big ramifications!

```
UPDATE people SET name = "Christopher"
```

Using SQLite with Ruby

Now that you've installed SQLite and we've covered the basics of how SQL works, let's put together a basic demonstration of how it all works in conjunction with Ruby. To do this you're going to write a program that allows you to manipulate a database based on the people table that we've talked about so far in this chapter.

The first step is to write the basic code that can load or create a database. The SQLite-Ruby gem makes this simple with the SQLite3::Database.new method. For example:

```
require 'rubygems'
require 'sqlite3'
$db = SQLite3::Database.new("dbfile")
$db.results_as_hash = true
```

From this point you can use $db in a similar way to the file handles you used earlier in this chapter. For example, $db.close will similarly close the database file, just as you closed regular files.

The $db.results_as_hash = true line forces SQLite to return data in a hash format rather than as an array of attributes (as with CSV). This makes the results easier to access.

■**Note** The database handle has been assigned to a global variable, $db, so that you can split your program into multiple methods without creating a class. You can therefore access the database handle, $db, from anywhere you wish.

To cope with the closing situation, you'll create a method specifically for disconnecting the database and ending the program:

```
def disconnect_and_quit
  $db.close
  puts "Bye!"
  exit
end
```

■**Note** Remember that you must define methods before you use them, so put these separate methods at the top of your source file.

Now let's create a method that will use the CREATE TABLE SQL statement to create the table where you'll store your data:

```
def create_table
  puts "Creating people table"
  $db.execute %q{
    CREATE TABLE people (
    id integer primary key,
    name varchar(50),
    job varchar(50),
    gender varchar(6),
    age integer)
  }
end
```

A database handle will allow you to execute arbitrary SQL with the execute method. All you need to do is pass the SQL as an argument, and SQLite will execute the SQL upon the database.

Next, let's create a method that asks for input from the user to add a new person to the database:

```
def add_person
  puts "Enter name:"
  name = gets.chomp
  puts "Enter job:"
  job = gets.chomp
  puts "Enter gender:"
  gender = gets.chomp
  puts "Enter age:"
  age = gets.chomp
  $db.execute("INSERT INTO people (name, job, gender, age) VALUES (?, ?, ?, ?)",➥
    name, job, gender, age)
end
```

■**Note** The chomp method added to gets removes the newline characters that appear at the end of keyboard output retrieved with gets.

The start of the add_person method is mundane. You ask for each of the person's attributes in turn and assign them to variables. However, the $db.execute is more intriguing this time. In the previous section, the INSERT SQL was shown with the data in the main statement, but in this method you're using question marks (?) as placeholders for the data.

Ruby performs an automatic substitution from the other parameters passed to execute into the placeholders. This acts as a way of securing your database. The reason is that if you interpolated the user's input directly into the SQL, the user might type some SQL that could break your query. However, when you use the placeholder method, the SQLite-Ruby library will clean up the supplied data for you and make sure it's safe to put into the database.

Now you need a way to be able to access the data entered. Time for another method! This code example shows how to retrieve person data for a given name and ID:

```ruby
def find_person
  puts "Enter name or ID of person to find:"
  id = gets.chomp

  person = $db.execute("SELECT * FROM people WHERE name = ? OR ➡
    id = ?", id, id.to_i).first

  unless person
    puts "No result found"
    return
  end

  puts %Q{Name: #{person['name']}
Job: #{person['job']}
Gender: #{person['gender']}
Age: #{person['age']}}
end
```

The find_person method asks the user to enter either the name or the ID of the person he or she is looking for. The $db.execute line cleverly checks both the name and id columns at the same time. Therefore, a match on either the id or name will work. If no match is found, the user will be told, and the method will end early. If there's a match, the information for that user will be extracted and printed onscreen.

You can tie it up with a main routine that acts as a menu system for the four methods described earlier. You already have the database connection code in place, so creating a menu is simple:

```
loop do
  puts %q{Please select an option:

    1. Create people table
    2. Add a person
    3. Look for a person
    4. Quit}

  case gets.chomp
    when '1'
      create_table
    when '2'
      add_person
    when '3'
      find_person
    when '4'
      disconnect_and_quit
  end
end
```

If the code is put together properly and then run, a typical first session could go like this:

```
Please select an option:

1. Create people table
2. Add a person
3. Look for a person
4. Quit
1
Creating people table
Please select an option:
```

```
1. Create people table
2. Add a person
3. Look for a person
4. Quit
2
Enter name:
Fred Bloggs
Enter job:
Manager
Enter gender:
Male
Enter age:
48
Please select an option:

1. Create people table
2. Add a person
3. Look for a person
4. Quit
3
Enter name or ID of person to find:
1
Name: Fred Bloggs
Job: Manager
Gender: Male
Age: 48

Please select an option:

1. Create people table
2. Add a person
3. Look for a person
4. Quit
3
Enter name or ID of person to find:
Jane Smith
No result
```

Your quick and basic application provides a way to add data and retrieve data from a remote data source in only a handful of lines!

Connecting to Other Database Systems

In the previous section we looked at SQL and how to use it with the SQLite library, a library that provides a basic database system on the local machine. More commonly, however, you might want to connect to more mainstream database servers, such as those running on MySQL, PostgreSQL, MS SQL Server, or Oracle. In this section we'll look quickly at how to connect to each of these types of databases.

■**Note** A library called DBI is available that provides a database-agnostic interface between Ruby and database systems. In theory you can write a program that talks with any database, and easily switch between different types of databases as long as you use DBI. In practice this isn't always possible, but learning how to use DBI can give you access to using MySQL, PostgreSQL, and Oracle in the future. Links to a number of resources about DBI are supplied in Appendix C.

MySQL

MySQL is the most common database system available from Web hosting providers. This is because MySQL comes in an open source variety that's free to download and use. MySQL also has a reputation as being simple to use, and a large ecosystem has built up around it.

MySQL support is given to Ruby with the MySQL library that's available as a RubyGem in generic Unix and Windows varieties. To install, use this code:

```
gem install mysql
```

■**Note** On OS X, installing the mysql gem can be easier said than done. A number of problems can arise, as covered at http://www.caboo.se/articles/2005/08/04/installing-ruby-mysql-bindings-2-6-on-tiger-troubleshooting and http://bugs.mysql.com/bug.php?id=23201. If at first you don't succeed, look around the Web, as there's always a solution!

The mysql gem provides a class and a number of methods to Ruby so that you can connect to a preinstalled MySQL server. It does not include the MySQL server itself! If you don't have a MySQL server to connect to, you'll need to ask for details from your Web hosting provider or install a version of MySQL on your local machine.

Once the mysql gem is installed, connecting to and using a MySQL server from Ruby is almost as simple as using a SQLite database:

```ruby
require 'rubygems'
require 'mysql'

# Connect to a MySQL database 'test' on the local machine
# using username of 'root' with no password.
db = Mysql.connect('localhost', 'root', '', 'test')

# Perform an arbitrary SQL query
db.query("INSERT INTO people (name, age) VALUES('Chris', 25)")

# Perform a query that returns data
begin
  query = db.query('SELECT * FROM people')

  puts "There were #{query.num_rows} rows returned"

  query.each_hash do |h|
    puts h.inspect
  end
rescue
  puts db.errno
  puts db.error
end

# Close the connection cleanly
db.close
```

This code demonstrates a basic, arbitrary SQL query, as well as a query that results in data being returned (in a row-by-row hash format). It also features basic error reporting by catching exceptions with a `rescue` block and using the error-retrieval methods provided by the MySQL library.

■**Note** You can also access MySQL databases using the database-agnostic DBI library, covered later in this chapter.

PostgreSQL

Like MySQL, PostgreSQL (pronounced post-gres-Q-L) is a free relational database server that's available under an open source license, allowing you to download and use it for free.

Although PostgreSQL offers many of the same features as MySQL, it's quite different. PostgreSQL users claim it's faster and more stable and offers more features. It is also often claimed that PostgreSQL follows SQL standards more correctly, whereas MySQL is more pragmatic (in the sense that it's more willing to break away from established standards) and extends the SQL language for its own benefits.

As with MySQL, PostgreSQL access is achieved in Ruby with a library, also available as a RubyGem. To install, use this code:

```
gem install postgres
```

On some setups it might be necessary to specify where PostgreSQL is installed, like so:

```
gem install postgres -- --with-pgsql-dir=/var/pgsql
```

The interface for the Postgres library is totally different from that for MySQL or SQLite, and it's documented in full at `http://ruby.scripting.ca/postgres/rdoc/`. (You can also access PostgreSQL databases using the database-agnostic DBI library, covered in the later section "DBI: A Generic Database Connectivity Library.")

Oracle

Oracle Corp. is a company that provides database tools, services, and software, and is primarily known for the development of the Oracle RDBMS, a relational database management system. The Oracle database system is not open source and is not, in its full version, available for free to use commercially. However, it's reasonably popular in enterprise situations, so you might need to know how to connect to it.

■Note Oracle does offer versions of its database systems for free, but they are only to be used for development purposes.

As with the other database systems, access to Oracle databases is provided through a library, in this case called OCI8.

Oracle has provided a great tutorial on its Web site that's specific to getting Ruby connected to Oracle databases, and that should be suitable for anyone familiar with Oracle databases. For more information see `http://www.oracle.com/technology/pub/articles/ haefel-oracle-ruby.html`.

You can use the OCI8 library through the database-agnostic DBI system, as covered in a following section.

MS SQL Server

Microsoft SQL Server (sometimes known as MS SQL Server) is Microsoft's relational database management system software, and is the primary database server used on Microsoft platforms (although most of the other systems covered in the past few sections work on Windows too).

The way you connect to a Microsoft SQL Server can vary depending on what operating system your script is running under. For example, at the time of writing, on Windows, you can use ActiveX Data Objects (ADO) with WIN32OLE to connect directly to the server. On OS X, you can use iODBC. On Linux and other Unix-related platforms, you can use unixODBC. However, connecting to MS SQL Server from Ruby is an uncommon task, and the drivers are changing on a regular basis, so the best references are tutorials and blog posts found online. Use your favorite search engine to search for "ruby ms sql" or "ruby microsoft sql server" and you'll find several useful resources.

At the time of writing, these pages provide the best instructions for approaching MS SQL Server from Ruby:

```
http://wiki.rubyonrails.org/rails/pages/
HowtoConnectToMicrosoftSQLServer
```

```
http://wiki.rubyonrails.org/rails/pages/
HowtoConnectToMicrosoftSQLServerFromRailsOnOSX
```

```
http://wiki.rubyonrails.org/rails/pages/
HowtoConnectToMicrosoftSQLServerFromRailsOnLinux
```

If you decide to take the DBI route, read the following section for information on how to use Ruby's DBI library.

DBI: A Generic Database Connectivity Library

The DataBase Interface (DBI) library is a database-agnostic library that uses database drivers and provides a generic interface to them. This allows you to write your code without a specific database in mind, and lets you use the same methods on nearly all databases. This means you lose the ability to access some of the more-advanced features offered by database drivers, but DBI can give you a little more simplicity and cross-database operability.

Unfortunately, at the time of writing, the DBI library is not available as a RubyGem (although this might change, so you might want to perform a quick search, as it'll make the installation a lot easier!). Therefore, to install, you need to refer to the instructions and files available at `http://ruby-dbi.rubyforge.org/`. These instructions and files are updated regularly, so I won't repeat them here for fear of being out of date by the time you're reading this.

■**Note** If you're a Perl programmer, DBI will be instantly familiar to you, as it follows many of the same conventions as the Perl version.

Once you have Ruby DBI installed, along with any database drivers you require, DBI makes it easy to use a database supported by your drivers, as demonstrated in this example:

```ruby
require 'dbi'

# Connect to a database
db = DBI.connect('DBI:Mysql:db_name', 'username', 'password')

# Perform raw SQL statements with 'do', supports interpolation
db.do("INSERT INTO people (name, age) VALUES (?, ?)", name, age)

# Construct and execute a query that will return data in
# the traditional way..
query = db.prepare('SELECT * FROM people')
query.execute

while row = query.fetch do
  puts row.inspect
end

query.finish
```

```
# Pull data direct from the database in a single sweep
# This technique is cleaner than the previous
db.select_all('SELECT * FROM people') do |row|
  puts row.inspect
end

db.disconnect
```

In this example you connect to a MySQL database using the Mysql driver, but if you had the Oracle driver installed for use by DBI, you could just as easily connect to an Oracle database using a DSN such as DBI:OCI8:db_name. For more up-to-date information about this functionality, and how to get other drivers, refer to http://ruby-dbi. rubyforge.org/.

ActiveRecord: A Sneak Peek

So far in this chapter you've worked directly with databases using a whole new language: SQL. Working with a database in this way is more efficient and reliable than putting data into text files, as you did earlier, but ActiveRecord makes it easier still. ActiveRecord is a product of the Ruby on Rails framework, which we'll be covering in Chapter 13, but can be used entirely independently of it. ActiveRecord will be covered in more depth in that chapter, but deserves a brief summary here.

ActiveRecord abstracts away all the details of SQL and database design and makes it possible to relate to items within databases in an object-oriented fashion, as you did with PStore. ActiveRecord gives you objects that correspond to rows and classes that correspond to tables, and you can work with the data using Ruby syntax, like so:

```
person = Person.find(:first, :conditions => ["name = ?", "Chris"])
person.age = 50
person.save
```

This code looks through the people table for a row whose name column matches "Chris," and puts an object relating to that row into person. ActiveRecord makes attributes available for all that row's columns, so changing the age column is as easy as assigning to the object's attribute. However, once the object's value has been changed, you issue the save method to save the changes back to the database.

■**Note** The pluralization from a Person class to a people table is an automatic part of ActiveRecord's functionality.

The previous code could replace SQL such as this:

```
SELECT * FROM people WHERE name = "Chris"
UPDATE people SET age = 50 WHERE name = "Chris"
```

Even SQL gurus familiar with Ruby tend to find Ruby's syntax more natural, particularly in the scope of a Ruby program. There's no need to mix two different languages in one program if both sets of features can be provided in Ruby alone.

ActiveRecord will be covered in detail in Chapter 13.

■**Note** ActiveRecord is not the only library to offer features that relate objects to database tables. Og and Lafcadio (`http://lafcadio.rubyforge.org/`) are two alternatives, though they're far less popular than ActiveRecord.

Summary

In this chapter we've looked at how data can flow into and out of your Ruby programs. Initially we looked at the low-level concept of I/O streams before quickly moving on to the pragmatism of databases. Databases provide a way to work with data in a more abstracted fashion without worrying about the underlying structure of the data on the computer's filesystem. Indeed, databases can be located within memory or on totally different machines, and our code could remain the same.

Let's reflect on the main concepts covered in this chapter:

- *I/O*: Input/Output. The concept of receiving input and sending output by various means on a computer, often via I/O streams.

- *I/O stream*: A channel along which data can be sent and/or received.

- *Standard input (stdin)*: A stream that relates to the default way of accepting data into the application, usually the keyboard.

- *Standard output (stdout)*: A stream that relates to the default way of outputting data from the application, usually to the screen.

- *File pointer*: An abstract reference to the current "location" within a file.

- *Database*: An organized collection of data structured in a way that makes it easy to be accessed programmatically.

- *CSV*: Comma-Separated Values. A way of structuring data with attributes separated with commas. CSV can be stored in plain text files.

- *Marshalling*: The process of converting a live data structure or object into a flat set of data that can be stored on disk, sent across a network, and then can be used to reconstruct the original data structure or object elsewhere or at some other time.

- *Table*: A collection of data organized into rows, with multiple columns, where each column represents a different attribute of each row. There are usually multiple tables within a database, containing different types of data.

- *SQLite*: An open source, public-domain relational database API and library that works on a single-user basis on a local machine. It supports SQL as its querying language.

- *MySQL*: An open source relational database system available in both community and professional editions. It is maintained by MySQL AB. Web hosting companies commonly offer MySQL database support.

- *PostgreSQL*: A free, open source relational database system licensed under the BSD license, making it possible to repackage and sell within commercial products. PostgreSQL is often considered to be of higher performance and have better conformity to SQL standards than MySQL, although it's less commonly used.

- *Oracle*: A commercial relational database system developed by Oracle Corp. It's generally used by large businesses for managing extremely large datasets.

- *Primary key*: A column (or multiple columns) on a table whose data uniquely identifies each row.

- *DBI*: DataBase Interface. A database-agnostic library that makes it easy to communicate between Ruby and database systems.

- *SQL*: Structured Query Language. A language specifically designed to create, amend, retrieve, and otherwise manipulate data in relational database systems.

- *ActiveRecord*: A library that abstracts databases, rows, columns, and SQL into standard Ruby syntax using classes and objects. It's a major part of the Ruby on Rails framework, which is covered in detail in Chapter 13.

With the ability to load, manipulate, and store data, the amount of useful Ruby applications you can develop increases significantly. Few applications depend entirely on data typed in every time, and having access to files and databases makes it easy to build powerful systems that can be used over time to manage data.

Please note that this is not the last of this book's coverage of Ruby's database features. In Chapter 12 we're going to use more of these database features at a deeper level to create a larger application.

Next, in Chapter 10, we're going to look at how you can release your applications and libraries to the world.

CHAPTER 10

■ ■ ■

Deploying Ruby Applications and Libraries

In this chapter we're going to look at how to deploy and distribute the programs you create with Ruby.

Developing Ruby applications is so simple that you'll soon want to release them to the world. As covered in Chapter 5, Ruby has a proud history of community and sharing, and nearly every Ruby developer will release code or completed applications at some point. Indeed, as Ruby is an interpreted language, the source code has to be distributed whenever you deploy your Ruby applications. If this isn't desired, there are some workarounds, and we'll look at those in this chapter too.

In essence, this chapter will walk you through the considerations and processes of deploying Ruby applications, libraries, and remotely accessible services (with HTTP daemons and as CGI scripts).

Distributing Basic Ruby Programs

Ruby is an interpreted language, so to distribute Ruby programs you can simply distribute the source code files you've written. Anyone else who has Ruby installed can then run the files in the same way that you do.

This process of distributing the actual source code for a program is typically how most programs developed using a scripting language, such as Ruby, are shared, but more traditionally software has been distributed without the source code included. Popular desktop application development languages such as C and C++ are *compiled* languages whose source code is converted directly into *machine code* that runs on a certain platform. This software can be distributed by copying the resulting compiled machine code files, rather than the source, from machine to machine. However, this technique is not possible with Ruby, as there is currently no Ruby compiler available, so you have to distribute your source code in one sense or another for other people to be able to run your programs.

■Note Later in this chapter we'll look at making the functionality of your Ruby programs available across a network. This technique does not require you to make your source code available, although it does require you to maintain a running copy of your program on a machine that's network accessible.

To see how you can distribute Ruby source code, let's take an example Ruby file and call it test.rb:

```
puts "Your program works!"
```

If you copy test.rb to another computer that has the Ruby interpreter installed on it, you can run the program directly with the Ruby interpreter as you would normally:

```
ruby test.rb
```

```
Your program works!
```

This technique works well if you're passing programs between your own machines or servers, or if you're distributing your programs to other developers. As long as the other users and machines have the same Ruby libraries or gems that your program uses, your program should run fine. This is one benefit of interpreted languages over compiled languages. If the same version of the Ruby interpreter is available on a different platform, it should run the same programs that your Ruby interpreter does. With compiled code (code that is specifically compiled down to machine code for a specific platform), it is not the case that it will run identically on all platforms; in fact, it usually won't!

What if you want to distribute your Ruby program to people who aren't *au fait* with the Ruby interpreter? Depending on the target operating system (that is, the operating system the user is running), there are several ways to make deploying Ruby applications simpler.

The Shebang Line

On Unix-related operating systems (Linux, OS X, BSD, and so on) you can engineer your program to run more simply by using a *shebang line*.

■Note In certain situations, such as when using the Apache HTTP server, shebang lines can work in Windows. You can use shebang lines such as #!ruby and #!c:\ruby\bin\ruby.exe to make Ruby CGI scripts work under Apache on Windows.

For example, say your script were to look like this:

```
#!/usr/bin/ruby

puts "Your program works!"
```

Unix-related operating systems support putting the name of the interpreter of a file on the first line of the file with a shebang line, where the "shebang" is simply the pound (#) sign and the exclamation mark (!).

■**Note** The shebang line only needs to be in the file that's initially run. It doesn't need to be in library or support files used by the main program.

In this case, `/usr/bin/ruby`, the Ruby interpreter, is used to interpret the rest of the file. One problem you might run into, though, is that your Ruby interpreter might be located in `/usr/bin/local/ruby` or have a different name entirely. However, there's a reasonably portable way to work around this problem. Many Unix-related operating systems (including most Linuxes and OS X) have a tool called env that stores the location of certain applications and settings. You can use this to load up Ruby without knowing its exact location. For example:

```
#!/usr/bin/env ruby

puts "Your program works!"
```

You could copy this example to many different Linux or OS X machines, for example, and it would work on the majority (env is not universal).

If this script were called `test.rb` and located in the current working directory, you could simply run it from a command line, like so:

```
./test.rb
```

■**Note** On most Unix-like operating systems, as well as adding a shebang line, it's necessary to make the Ruby script "executable" by using `chmod` for the preceding example to work, as in `chmod +x test.rb`.

Naturally, if you copied the script elsewhere (/usr/bin, for example), you could access it directly:

```
/usr/bin/test.rb
```

Or if the script's location is in the path, it's even easier:

```
test.rb
```

Associated File Types in Windows

Whereas shebang lines are used on Unix-like operating systems, Windows users are more familiar with file extensions (such as DOC, EXE, JPG, MP3, or TXT) dictating how a file is processed.

If you use My Computer or Windows Explorer to find a folder containing a Ruby file, the file might or might not already be associated with the Ruby interpreter (depending on which Ruby package you installed). Alternatively, Ruby files might be associated with your text editor. In any case, if you want to be able to double-click Ruby files in Windows and have them run directly as regular Ruby programs, you can do this by changing the default action for files with an extension of RB (or any other arbitrary extension you wish to use).

The easiest way to set an association is to right-click the icon representing a Ruby file and choose the "Open With" (or "Open," if it's currently not associated with any program) option from the menu. Associate the program with the ruby.exe Ruby interpreter on your computer, and check the "Always use the selected program to open this kind of file" option. This will cause Ruby files to be executed directly by the Ruby interpreter in future.

■Note Microsoft provides more information about this technique at http://support.microsoft. com/kb/307859.

"Compiling" Ruby

The shebang line and associated file type options involve collecting all the Ruby source code associated with an application and passing it on to a user, who then either has to run it from a command line or create a file association.

For nontechnical users, these options can prove confusing, and compared to deploying a typical application for Linux, OS X, or Windows they make Ruby look unprofessional. This is the nature of deploying code written in an interpreted language, because Ruby cannot be compiled down to a single, tidy executable file that can be used like any other executable file.

However, some clever developers have come up with a couple different systems to work around this problem and give the impression of creating a single, compiled executable file. One trick is to embed a Ruby interpreter and the source code into a single file and then use these components to make the application work transparently.

RubyScript2Exe

RubyScript2Exe is a program that can convert Ruby source code into executable files that can be used primarily on Windows and Linux. It collects your source code, along with all the files used to make your application work (including Ruby and its libraries), and packages them up into a single file that works like a typical application.

As of the time of writing, RubyScript2Exe has been tested on several Linux distributions with varying versions of Ruby, and on Windows 95, 98, 2000, and XP. There is also experimental support for OS X (although for OS X users, another tool, Platypus, is covered next).

To download and learn about RubyScript2Exe, visit the official site at `http://www.erikveen.dds.nl/rubyscript2exe/`. Once you've created a simple executable file for the platform(s) of your choice, it becomes easy to deploy applications, as you no longer need to worry whether your target users have Ruby preinstalled or not.

Platypus

Platypus is a generic development tool for Mac OS X that can create native, integrated applications from Ruby scripts, as well as scripts written in other interpreted languages (such as Perl, Python, and PHP).

It has more features than RubyScript2Exe, although it works in a slightly different way that's specific to Mac OS X. You can get Platypus to encrypt its output files so that your source code isn't directly visible (although no encryption is foolproof), and you can get drag-and-drop features, embed non-Ruby files into your application (such as images, SQLite database files, or sounds), and use OS X's security framework to allow your script to have unfettered access to the machine it's running on.

Platypus is free (although donations are requested by the author) and can be obtained at `http://www.sveinbjorn.org/platypus`. Platypus (shown in Figure 10-1) is an excellent tool, and has been used by a multitude of interpreted programs that have become regular applications.

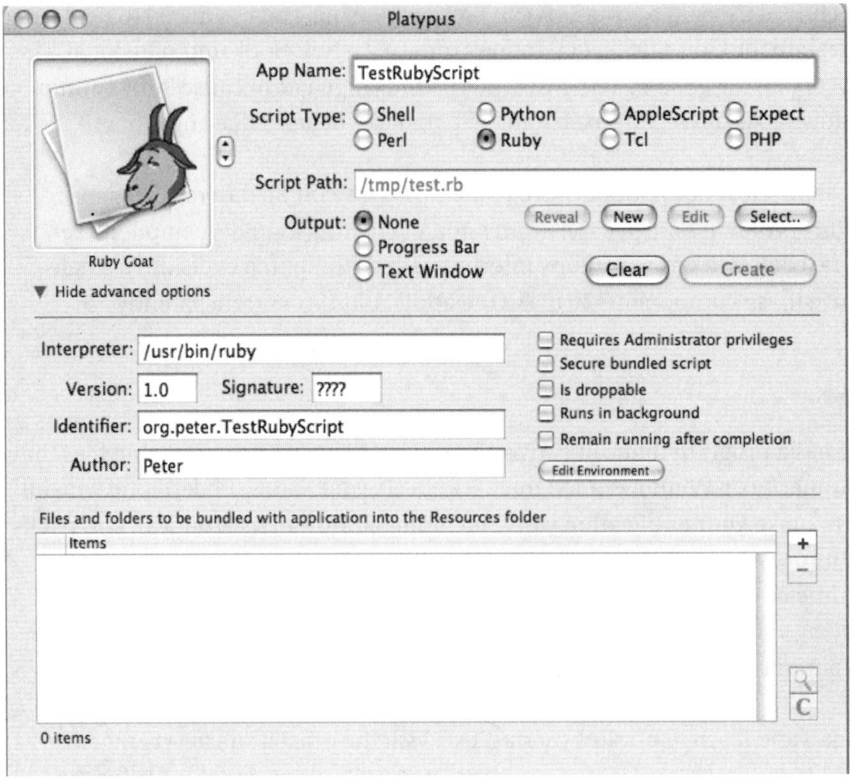

Figure 10-1. *A view of the main Platypus screen, where an executable package is put together.*

Detecting Ruby's Runtime Environment

Deploying Ruby programs can be made easier with the tools covered in the previous section, but you can use a number of techniques directly within Ruby to make Ruby's interactions with its surrounding environment even better.

For example, it's possible to detect information about the machine upon which a Ruby script is running and then change the way the program operates on the fly. You can also retrieve parameters passed to the program via the command line.

Detecting the runtime environment while the program is running can be useful to restrict access to users on specific platforms if your program isn't relevant to other users, or to tailor internal settings in your program so that your program will work better on the user's operating system. It can also be a useful way to get system-specific information (rather than operating-system–specific information) that's relevant directly to the machine the program is running on, as it could affect the operation of your program.

A common example of this is retrieving the current user's *path*: a string of various directory names on the system that can be searched as default locations for files. There are also environment variables dictating where to store temporary files, and so forth.

Easy OS Detection with RUBY_PLATFORM

Among the myriad special variables Ruby makes accessible, a variable called RUBY_PLATFORM contains the name of the current environment (operating system) you're running under. You can easily query this variable to detect what operating system your program is running under. This can be useful if you want to use a certain filesystem notation or features that are implemented differently under different operating systems.

On my Windows machine, RUBY_PLATFORM contains "i386-mswin32," on my OS X machine it contains "powerpc-darwin8.6.0," and on my Linux machine it contains "i686-linux." This gives you the immediate power to segregate features and settings by operating system.

```
if RUBY_PLATFORM =~ /win32/
  puts "We're in Windows!"
elsif RUBY_PLATFORM =~ /linux/
  puts "We're in Linux!"
elsif RUBY_PLATFORM =~ /darwin/
  puts "We're in Mac OS X!"
elsif RUBY_PLATFORM =~ /freebsd/
  puts "We're in FreeBSD!"
else
  puts "We're running under an unknown operating system."
end
```

Environment Variables

Whenever a program is run on a computer, it's contained with a certain *environment*, whether that's the command line or a GUI. The operating system sets a number of special variables called *environment variables* that contain information about the environment. They vary by operating system, but can be a good way of detecting things that could be useful in your programs.

You can quickly and easily inspect the environment variables (as supplied by your operating system) on your current machine with irb by using the special ENV hash:

```
irb(main):001:0> ENV.each {|e| puts e.join(': ') }
```

```
TERM_PROGRAM: iTerm.app
TERM: vt100
SHELL: /bin/bash
USER: peter
PATH:
/bin:/sbin:/usr/bin:/usr/sbin:/usr/local/bin:/opt/local/bin:/usr/local/sbin
PWD: /Users/peter
SHLVL: 1
HOME: /Users/peter
LOGNAME: peter
SECURITYSESSIONID: 51bbd0
_: /usr/bin/irb
LINES: 32
COLUMNS: 120
```

Specifically, these are the results from my machine, and yours will probably be quite different. For example, when I try the same code on a Windows machine, I get results such as these:

```
ALLUSERSPROFILE: F:\Documents and Settings\All Users
APPDATA: F:\Documents and Settings\Peter\Application Data
CLIENTNAME: Console
HOMEDRIVE: F:
HOMEPATH: \Documents and Settings\Peter
LOGONSERVER: \\PSHUTTLE
NUMBER_OF_PROCESSORS: 2
OS: Windows_NT
Path: F:\ruby\bin;F:\WINDOWS\system32;F:\WINDOWS
PATHEXT: .COM;.EXE;.BAT;.CMD;.VBS;.VBE;.JS;.JSE;.WSF;.WSH;.RB;.RBW
ProgramFiles: F:\Program Files
SystemDrive: F:
SystemRoot: F:\WINDOWS
TEMP: F:\DOCUME~1\Peter\LOCALS~1\Temp
TMP: F:\DOCUME~1\Peter\LOCALS~1\Temp
USERDOMAIN: PSHUTTLE
USERNAME: Peter
USERPROFILE: F:\Documents and Settings\Peter
windir: F:\WINDOWS
```

You can use these environment variables to decide where to store temporary files, or to find out what sort of features your operating system offers, in real time, much as you did with RUBY_PLATFORM:

```
tmp_dir = '/tmp'
if ENV['OS'] =~ /Windows_NT/
  puts "This program is running under Windows NT/2000/XP!"
  tmp_dir = ENV['TMP']
elsif ENV['PATH'] =~ /\/usr/
  puts "This program has access to a UNIX-style file system!"
else
  puts "I cannot figure out what environment I'm running in!"
  exit
end

[.. do something here ..]
```

■**Note** You can also set environment variables with ENV['variable_name'] = value, but only do this if you have a valid reason to use them. However, setting environment variables from within a program only applies to the local process and any child processes, meaning that the variables' application is extremely limited.

Although ENV acts like a hash, it's technically a special object, but you can convert it to a true hash using its .to_hash method, as in ENV.to_hash.

Accessing Command Line Arguments

In Chapter 4 you used a special array called ARGV. ARGV is an array automatically created by the Ruby interpreter that contains the parameters passed to the Ruby program (whether on the command line or by other means). For example, say you created a script called argvtest.rb:

```
puts ARGV.join('-')
```

You could run it like so:

```
ruby argvtest.rb these are command line parameters
```

```
these-are-command-line-parameters
```

The parameters are passed into the program and become present in the ARGV array, where they can be processed as you wish. Use of ARGV is ideal for command-line tools where filenames and options are passed in this way.

Using ARGV also works if you call a script directly. On Unix operating systems, you could adjust argvtest.rb to be like this:

```
#!/usr/bin/env ruby
puts ARGV.join('-')
```

And you could call it in this way:

```
./argvtest.rb these are command line parameters
```

```
these-are-command-line-parameters
```

You generally use command line arguments to pass options, settings, and data fragments that might change between executions of a program. For example, a common utility found on most operating systems is *copy* or *cp*, which is used to copy files. It's used like so:

```
cp /directory1/from_filename /directory2/destination_filename
```

This would copy a file from one place to another (and rename it along the way) within the filesystem. The two filenames are both command line arguments, and a Ruby script could receive data in the same way, like so:

```
#!/usr/bin/env ruby
from_filename = ARGV[0]
destination_filename = ARGV[1]
```

Distributing and Releasing Ruby Libraries As Gems

Over time it's likely you'll develop your own libraries to solve various problems with Ruby so that you don't need to write the same code over and over in different programs, but can call on the library for support.

Usually you'll want to make these libraries available to use on other machines, on servers upon which you deploy applications, or to other developers. You might even open-source your libraries to get community input and a larger developer base.

If you've read Chapter 5, you'll have a good feel for Ruby's commitment to open source and how open source is important to Ruby developers. This section looks at how to release your code and libraries in such a way that other developers can find them useful.

Luckily, deploying libraries is generally less problematic than deploying entire applications, as the target audience is made up of other developers who are usually familiar with installing libraries.

In Chapter 7 we looked at RubyGems, a library installation and management system for Ruby. We looked at how RubyGems makes it easy to install libraries, but RubyGems also makes it easy to create "gems" of your own from your own code.

Creating a Gem

Let's first create a simple library that extends the String class and puts it in a file called string_extend.rb:

```
class String
  def vowels
    scan(/[aeiou]/i)
  end
end
```

This code adds a vowels method to the String class, which returns an array of all the vowels in a string:

```
"This is a test".vowels
```

```
["i", "i", "a", "e"]
```

As a local library within the scope of a larger application, it could be loaded with require:

```
require 'string_extend'
```

However, you want to turn it into a gem that you can use anywhere. Building a gem involves three steps. The first is to organize your code and other files into a structure that can be turned into a gem. The second is to create a *specification file* that lists information about the gem. The third is to use the *gem* program to build the gem from the source files and the specification.

■**Note** This section assumes that RubyGems is fully installed, as covered in Chapter 7.

Structuring Your Files

Before you can build a gem, it's necessary to collect all the files you want to make up the gem. This is usually done using a standard structure. So far you have your `string_extend.rb` file, and this is the only file you want within your gem.

First, it's necessary to create a folder to contain all the gem's folders, so you create a folder called `string_extend`. Under this folder you create several other folders as follows:

- `lib`: This directory will contain the Ruby code related to the library.

- `pkg`: This is a temporary directory where the gem will be generated.

- `test`: This directory will contain any unit tests or other testing scripts related to the library.

- `doc`: This is an optional directory that could contain documentation about the library, particularly documentation created with or by rdoc.

- `bin`: This is another optional directory that can contain system tools and command line scripts that are related to the library. For example, RubyGems itself installs the gem command line tool; such a tool would be placed into `bin`.

At a minimum, you should end up with `string_extend/lib`, `string_extend/pkg`, and `string_extend/test`.

In this example, you should place `string_extend.rb` within the `string_extend/lib` directory. If you have tests, documentation, or command line scripts, place them into the respective directories.

■**Note** The preceding directory names are written in a Unix style, but on Windows would be represented similarly to this: `c:\gems\string_extend`, `c:\gems\string_extend\lib`, and so on. Take this into account throughout this entire section.

Creating a Specification File

Once your files are organized, it's time to create a specification file that describes the gem and provides RubyGems with enough information to create the final gem. Create a text file called `string_extend.gemspec` (or a filename that matches your own project name) in the main `string_extend` folder, and fill it out like so:

```
require 'rubygems'

spec = Gem::Specification.new do |s|
  s.name = 'string_extend'
  s.version = '0.0.1'
  s.summary = "StringExtend adds useful features to the String class"
  s.files = Dir.glob("**/**/**")
  s.test_files = Dir.glob("test/*_test.rb")
  s.autorequire = 'string_extend'
  s.author = "Your Name"
  s.email = "your-email-address@email.com"
  s.has_rdoc = false
  s.required_ruby_version = '>= 1.8.2'
end
```

This is a basic specification file. The specification file is effectively a simple Ruby script that passes information through to `Gem::Specification`. The information it provides is mostly simple, but let's look at a few key areas.

First you define the name of the gem, setting it to `'string_extend'`:

```
s.name = 'string_extend'
```

Next, you define the version number. Typically, version numbers for Ruby projects (and for Ruby itself) contain three parts in order of significance. Early versions of software, before an official release, perhaps, often begin with 0, as in `0.0.1` here:

```
s.version = '0.0.1'
```

The summary line is displayed by `gem list`, and can be useful to people prior to installing the gem. Simply put together a short description of your library/gem here:

```
s.summary = "StringExtend adds useful features to the String class"
```

The `files` attribute accepts an array of all the files to include within the gem. In this case you use `Dir.glob` to get an array of all the files under the current directory:

```
s.files = Dir.glob("**/**/**")
```

However, you could explicitly reference every file in an array in the preceding line.

The `test_files` attribute, like the `files` attribute, accepts an array of files, in this case associated with tests. You can leave this line intact even if you have no `test` folder, as `Dir.glob` will just return an empty array. For example:

```
s.test_files = Dir.glob("test/*_test.rb")
```

The `autorequire` parameter specifies a file to be loaded automatically with `require` when the gem is loaded. This parameter isn't particularly important, because users will generally use `require 'string_extend'` in their code anyway, but if your gem contains multiple Ruby files that need to be loaded, it could come in handy:

```
s.autorequire = 'string_extend'
```

Last, sometimes libraries rely on features in certain versions of Ruby. You can specify the required version of Ruby with the `require_ruby_version` parameter. If there's no required version, you can simply omit this line:

```
s.required_ruby_version = '>= 1.8.2'
```

■**Note** A full list of the parameters you can use in a RubyGems specification file is available at
`http://www.rubygems.org/read/chapter/20`.

Building the Gem

Once the specifications file is complete, building the final .gem file is as simple as:

```
gem build <spec file>
```

In your case:

```
gem build string_extend.gemspec
```

This makes gem create the final gem file, `string_extend-0.0.1.gem`.

■**Note** In future, once you change and update your library, simply update the version numbers, rebuild, and you have a new gem ready to go that can be installed to upgrade the existing installed gem.

Easier Gem Creation

At the time of writing, a new tool called *newgem* has been developed and released by
Dr. Nic Williams that makes it a one-step process to create the structure and default files
for generating a gem. Use the following code to install newgem:

```
gem install newgem
```

Once it's installed, you can create gem directory structures and default files with a
single stroke:

```
newgem your_library_name
```

```
creating: your_library_name
creating: your_library_name/CHANGELOG
creating: your_library_name/README
creating: your_library_name/lib
creating: your_library_name/lib/your_library_name
creating: your_library_name/lib/your_library_name.rb
creating: your_library_name/lib/your_library_name/version.rb
creating: your_library_name/Rakefile
creating: your_library_name/test
creating: your_library_name/test/all_tests.rb
creating: your_library_name/test/test_helper.rb
creating: your_library_name/test/your_library_name_test.rb
creating: your_library_name/examples
creating: your_library_name/bin
```

newgem is likely to become more popular in future, as it radically simplifies the
process of creating gems. However, it's important to understand the previous few sections so that you have an idea of what goes into a gem, even if you choose to automate
the process later on.

The official RubyForge site for newgem is at http://rubyforge.org/projects/newgem/,
and a useful blog post by the author about the tool is available at http://drnicwilliams.
com/2006/10/11/generating-new-gems/.

Distributing a Gem

Distributing a gem is easy. You can upload it to a Web site or transfer it in any way you
would normally transfer a file. You can then install the gem with gem install by referring
to the local file.

However, distributing a gem in a fashion where the gem client can download it automatically is a little harder. The RubyGems system comes with a script called `gem_server` that runs a special server on your local machine (or any machine you choose to run it on) that can serve gems. To install a gem from a specific server you can use the `--source` option:

```
gem install gem_name --source http://server-name-here/
```

■**Note** In a similar fashion, you can also use a normal Web server or Web hosting package to host your gems, and you can install them using `--source`. To do this, you have to create a folder on your Web site called `/gems` and use RubyGems' `generate_yaml_index.rb` script to generate the metafiles required to make it work.

The best way to distribute gems, however, is in a form where they can be installed over the Internet without specifying a source. For example:

```
gem install gem_name
```

This command installs the gem `gem_name` by looking for it on the Internet and downloading it to the local machine. But how does gem know where to download gems from? By default, RubyGems searches a Ruby project repository called RubyForge for gems if no source is specified. We'll look at how to make gems available in the default database using RubyForge next.

RubyForge

RubyForge (`http://rubyforge.org/`) is the largest community repository for Ruby projects and libraries, and is maintained by Richard Kilmer and Tom Copeland. It contains thousands of projects and acts as a centralized location for the hosting of Ruby projects. Nearly all the major Ruby libraries are available from or hosted there, including Ruby on Rails.

As well as basic hosting, RubyForge lets project maintainers create simple Web sites hosted under subdomains of RubyForge (as with `http://mongrel.rubyforge.org/`), and it provides source management servers (CVS and SVN) for those who require them.

Importantly, however, RubyForge acts as the default source for gems. When a user runs `gem install rails` or `gem install mongrel`, gem looks for the gem files at RubyForge. Therefore, if you want your gem to be installed easily by users, hosting it at RubyForge is key. Hosting with RubyForge is also free, and with RubyForge's status in the community, hosting your project at RubyForge makes it look more legitimate.

To host a project with RubyForge, create a new account using the link from the front page at `http://rubyforge.org/`, and once you're set up, you can apply to create a new project. You have to enter several pieces of information about your project, but within a couple of days you should be approved and will be able to upload files. Gems associated with any project hosted in RubyForge become available to install with RubyGems within a few hours.

Deploying Ruby Applications As Remote Services

An alternative to giving people your source or packaging it up to be run locally on a user's machine is making a program's functionality available as a remote service over a network. This only works for a small subset of functionality, but providing functionality remotely gives you more control over your code and how it is used.

Ruby's networking and Web features will be covered in more depth in Chapters 14 and 15, but in this section we'll look at how to put together basic services with Ruby that allow users to access a program's functionality over a network.

CGI Scripts

A common way to make scripts available online is to upload them to Web hosting providers as CGI scripts. Common Gateway Interface (CGI) is a standard that allows Web server software (such as Apache or Microsoft IIS) to launch programs and send data back and forth between them and the Web client.

Many people associate the term CGI with the Perl language, as Perl has been the most common language with which to write CGI scripts. However, CGI is language agnostic, and you can just as easily write CGI scripts with Ruby (more easily, in fact!).

A Basic CGI Script

The most basic Ruby CGI script looks like this:

```
#!/usr/bin/ruby

puts "Content-type: text/html\n\n"
puts "<html><body>This is a test</body></html>"
```

If you called this script `test.cgi` and uploaded it to a Unix-based Web hosting provider (the most common type) with the right permissions, you could use it as a CGI script. For example, if you have the Web site `http://www.example.com/` hosted with a Linux Web hosting provider and you upload `test.cgi` to the main directory and give it execute permissions, then visiting `http://www.example.com/test.cgi` should return an HTML page saying "This is a test."

■**Note** Although `/usr/bin/ruby` is referenced in the previous example, for many users or Web hosting providers Ruby might be located at `/usr/local/bin/ruby`. Make sure to check, or try using `usr/bin/env ruby`.

When `test.cgi` is requested from a Web browser, the Web server looks for `test.cgi` on the Web site, and then executes it using the Ruby interpreter (due to the shebang line—as covered earlier in this chapter). The Ruby script returns a basic HTTP header (specifying the content type as HTML) and then returns a basic HTML document.

■**Note** There's more information about generating HTML documents in Chapter 14.

Ruby comes with a special library called *cgi* that enables more sophisticated interactions than those with the preceding CGI script. Let's create a basic CGI script that uses cgi:

```
#!/usr/bin/ruby

require 'cgi'

cgi = CGI.new

puts cgi.header
puts "<html><body>This is a test</body></html>"
```

In this example, you created a `CGI` object and used it to print the header line for you. This is easier than remembering what header to output, and it can be tailored. However, the real benefit of using the cgi library is so that you can do things such as accept data coming from a Web browser (or an HTML form) and return more complex data to the user.

Accepting CGI Variables

A benefit of CGI scripts is that they can process information passed to them from a form on an HTML page or merely specified within the URL. For example, if you had a Web form with an `<input>` element with a name of "text" that posted to `test.cgi`, you can access the data passed to it like this:

```ruby
#!/usr/bin/ruby

require 'cgi'
cgi = CGI.new

text = cgi['text']

puts cgi.header
puts "<html><body>#{text.reverse}</body></html>"
```

In this case, the user would see the text he or she entered on the form reversed. You could also test this CGI script by passing the text directly within the URL, such as with *http://www.example.com/test.cgi?text=this+is+a+test*.

Here's a more complete example:

```ruby
#!/usr/bin/ruby

require 'cgi'
cgi = CGI.new

from = cgi['from'].to_i
to = cgi['to'].to_i

number = rand(to-from+1) + from

puts cgi.header
puts "<html><body>#{number}</body></html>"
```

This CGI script responds with a random number that's between the number supplied in the `from` CGI variable and the `to` CGI variable. An associated, but basic, form that could send the correct data would have HTML code like so:

```html
<form method="POST" action="http://www.example.com/test.cgi">
For a number between <input type="text" name="from" value="" /> and
<input type="text" name="to" value="" /> <input type="submit"
value="Click here!" /></form>
```

In Chapter 16, the CGI library is covered in more depth, along with information about using HTTP cookies and sessions, so if this mode of deployment is of interest to you, please refer there for extended information and longer examples.

In general, however, CGI execution is becoming unpopular due to its lack of speed and the need for a Ruby interpreter to be executed on every request. This makes CGI unsuitable for high-use or heavy load situations.

Generic HTTP Servers

HTTP is the communications protocol of the World Wide Web. Even though it's commonly used to shuttle Web pages from one place to another, it can also be used on an internal network or even to communicate between services on a single machine.

Creating an HTTP server from your Ruby program can provide a way for users (or even other programs) to make requests to your Ruby program, meaning you don't need to distribute the source code, but can instead make your program's functionality available over a network (such as the Internet).

This section won't directly look at the applications of this functionality, as this is covered in Chapter 14, but will instead look at the practicalities of creating basic Web/HTTP servers with Ruby.

WEBrick

WEBrick is a Ruby library that makes it easy to build an HTTP server with Ruby. It comes with most installations of Ruby by default (it's part of the standard library), so you can usually create a basic Web/HTTP server with only several lines of code:

```
require 'webrick'

server = WEBrick::GenericServer.new( :Port => 1234 )

trap("INT"){ server.shutdown }

server.start do |socket|
  socket.puts Time.now
end
```

This code creates a generic WEBrick server on the local machine on port 1234, shuts the server down if the process is interrupted (often done with Ctrl+C), and for each new connection prints the current date and time. If you run this code, you could try to view the results in your Web browser by visiting http://127.0.0.1:1234/ or http://localhost:1234/.

■**Caution** Because your test program doesn't output valid HTTP, it's likely to fail with many Web browsers, particularly on Windows. However, if you understand how to use the *telnet* program, you can use `telnet 127.0.0.1 1234` to see the result. Otherwise, continue to the next example, where valid HTTP is returned for Web browsers to view.

However, a more powerful technique is when you create *servlets* that exist in their own class and have more control over the requests and responses made to them:

```ruby
require 'webrick'

class MyServlet < WEBrick::HTTPServlet::AbstractServlet
  def do_GET(request, response)
    response.status = 200
    response.content_type = "text/plain"
    response.body = "Hello, world!"
  end
end

server = WEBrick::HTTPServer.new( :Port => 1234 )
server.mount "/", MyServlet
trap("INT"){ server.shutdown }
server.start
```

This code is more elaborate, but you now have access to `request` and `response` objects that represent both the incoming request and the outgoing response.

For example, you can now find out what URL the user tried to access in his or her browser, with such a line:

```ruby
response.body = "You are trying to load #{request.path}"
```

`request.path` contains the path within the URL (for example, */abcd* from *http://127.0.0.1:1234/abcd*), meaning you can interpret what the user was trying to request, call a different method, and provide the correct output.

Here's a more elaborate example:

```ruby
require 'webrick'

class MyNormalClass
  def MyNormalClass.add(a, b)
    a.to_i + b.to_i
  end
```

```ruby
  def MyNormalClass.subtract(a,b)
    a.to_i - b.to_i
  end
end

class MyServlet < WEBrick::HTTPServlet::AbstractServlet
  def do_GET(request, response)
    if request.query['a'] && request.query['b']
      a = request.query['a']
      b = request.query['b']
      response.status = 200
      response.content_type = 'text/plain'
      result = nil

      case request.path
        when '/add'
          result = MyNormalClass.add(a,b)
        when '/subtract'
          result = MyNormalClass.subtract(a,b)
        else
          result = "No such method"
      end

      response.body = result.to_s + "\n"
    else
      response.status = 400
      response.body = "You did not provide the correct parameters"
    end
  end
end

server = WEBrick::HTTPServer.new(:Port => 1234)
server.mount '/', MyServlet
trap('INT'){ server.shutdown }
server.start
```

In this example you have a regular, basic Ruby class called `MyNormalClass` that implements two basic arithmetic methods. The WEBrick servlet uses the `request` object to retrieve parameters from the URL, as well as get the Ruby method requested from `request.path`. If the parameters aren't passed an HTTP error is returned.

To use the preceding script, you'd use URLs such as these:

```
http://127.0.0.1:1234/add?a=10&b=20
```

```
30
```

```
http://127.0.0.1:1234/subtract?a=100&b=10
```

```
90
```

```
http://127.0.0.1:1234/subtract
```

```
You did not provide the correct parameters.
```

```
http://127.0.0.1:1234/abcd?a=10&b=20
```

```
No such method.
```

■**Note** You can learn more about WEBrick from Gnome's Guide to WEBrick at `http://microjet.ath.cx/WebWiki/WEBrick.html`, or refer to Appendix C of this book.

Mongrel

Mongrel is a fast HTTP server and library for Ruby intended for hosting Ruby applications and services. It's similar to WEBrick, but is significantly faster, although the downside is that it doesn't come with Ruby by default. Many high-profile Ruby on Rails Web sites use Mongrel for their deployment because of its speed, stability, and reliability.

You can install Mongrel with RubyGem:

```
gem install --include-dependencies mongrel
```

■**Note** As always, remember to prefix these commands with `sudo`, if your operating system requires it.

As with WEBrick, you can tie Mongrel into an existing Ruby application easily. By associating a handler class with Mongrel, requests can be passed into and handled by your own code. The code could call functions in your application and the results can be passed back to the clients.

Here's a basic example of a Mongrel server that will return a simple HTML page when `http://localhost:1234` is loaded:

```
require 'rubygems'
require 'mongrel'

class BasicServer < Mongrel::HttpHandler
  def process(request, response)
    response.start(200) do |headers, output|
      headers["Content-Type"] = 'text/html'
      output.write('<html><body><h1>Hello!</h1></body></html>')
    end
  end
end

s = Mongrel::HttpServer.new("0.0.0.0", "1234")
s.register("/", BasicServer.new)
s.run.join
```

`Mongrel::HttpServer.new` can also take an optional third argument that specifies the number of threads to open to handle requests. For example:

```
s = Mongrel::HttpServer.new("0.0.0.0", "1234", 20)
```

The preceding line creates 20 processor threads that handle requests.

As you can see, Mongrel is reasonably similar to WEBrick, but with some extra benefits. You can learn more about it at the official Mongrel site at `http://mongrel.rubyforge.org/`.

Remote Procedure Calls

A common way to make program functionality available to remote programs is with Remote Procedure Calls (RPCs). In contrast to allowing control via a Web browser, RPC is designed for situations where one *program* gets to use the methods and procedures made available by another. When used correctly, using the methods and procedures made available by remotely located programs can feel almost as easy as using local methods and procedures.

Ruby has built-in support for two of the most popular RPC protocols, XML-RPC and SOAP, as well as a special system of its own called DRb.

XML-RPC

XML-RPC is a well-known RPC protocol that uses XML for its messaging and HTTP for its transport. One of the benefits of RPC is that you can create multiple programs in different languages, but still talk between them in a way that every language understands. It makes it possible to write a system in, say, PHP or Python, but call the methods made available by that program with Ruby.

▪**Note** SOAP is another popular RPC protocol, but is more complex. However, it's supported natively by Ruby, although you're only likely to use it if the systems you want to use support nothing else. Other systems, particularly those that are a lot simpler—such as REST—are becoming more popular. However, if you want to use SOAP, Ruby comes with a SOAP library as standard.

Calling an XML-RPC–Enabled Method

Calling a method made available over XML-RPC is incredibly simple:

```
require 'xmlrpc/client'

server = XMLRPC::Client.new2("http://xmlrpc-c.sourceforge.net/api/sample.php")
puts server.call("sample.sumAndDifference", 5, 3).inspect
```

```
{"difference"=>2, "sum"=>8}
```

■**Note** This program requires your computer to have access to the Internet. Also, if the XML-RPC sample server is unavailable, you might get an error message. Try a few times if you fail to get a result as this sample file is often under heavy use.

This example uses a remote application (written in PHP) that makes available a method called `sample.sumAndDifference`. First you create a handle that refers to the remote program using `XMLRPC::Client.new2`, then you call the method with two parameters. The results (the sum and the difference of your two arguments) come back in a hash.

Because dealing with remote programs can lead to errors (bad connections, remote service is unavailable, and so on), it makes sense to process errors that come back from RPC calls. XML-RPC offers a `call2` method that makes this easy:

```
require 'xmlrpc/client'

server = XMLRPC::Client.new2("http://xmlrpc-c.sourceforge.net/api/sample.php")
ok, results = server.call2("sample.sumAndDifference", 5, 3)

if ok
  puts results.inspect
else
  puts results.faultCode
  puts results.faultString
end
```

`call2` returns an array containing a "success" flag and the results. You can check to see if the first element of the array (the "success" flag) is `true`, but if not, you can investigate the error.

Making an XML-RPC–Enabled Program

Calling XML-RPC–enabled programs is easy, but so is XML-RPC–enabling your own:

```
require 'xmlrpc/server'

server = XMLRPC::Server.new(1234)
server.add_handler("sample.sumAndDifference") do |a,b|
  { "sum" => a.to_i + b.to_i,
    "difference" => a.to_i - b.to_i }
end
```

```
trap("INT") { server.shutdown }
server.serve
```

This program runs an XML-RPC server (based on WEBrick) on your local machine on port 1234, and operates in the same way as the sample.php used in the client in the previous section. The following client could use the sample.sumAndDifference method made available by the preceding server:

```
require 'xmlrpc/client'

server = XMLRPC::Client.new2("http://127.0.0.1:1234/")
puts server.call("sample.sumAndDifference", 5, 3).inspect
```

On the server side, just add more add_handler blocks that process the requests. You can use require to load classes associated with your program and then have a simple XML-RPC server in place to make your program's functionality available remotely. For example:

```
require 'xmlrpc/server'
require 'string_extend'

server = XMLRPC::Server.new(1234)

server.add_handler("sample.vowel_count") do |string|
  string.vowels
end

trap("INT") { server.shutdown }
server.serve
```

This XML-RPC server makes the functionality of your string_extend library available remotely. You can use it like so:

```
require 'xmlrpc/client'

server = XMLRPC::Client.new2("http://127.0.0.1:1234/")
puts server.call("sample.vowel_count", "This is a test").inspect
```

```
["i", "i", "a", "e"]
```

As with WEBrick and Mongrel, the XML-RPC server can also use other classes directly, as with WEBrick's servlets. For example:

```
class OurClass
  def some_method
    "Some test text"
  end
end

require 'xmlrpc/server'

server = XMLRPC::Server.new(1234)
server.add_handler(XMLRPC::iPIMethods('sample'), OurClass.new)

trap("INT") { server.shutdown }
server.serve
```

With this server, the methods are associated automatically with the XML-RPC server. A call to `sample.some_method` from an XML-RPC client would automatically be routed through to the instance method `some_method` made available from `OurClass`.

DRb

DRb stands for "Distributed Ruby," and is a Ruby-only RPC library. On the surface, DRb doesn't appear to be too different from XML-RPC, but if you only need to talk between Ruby programs, it's a lot more powerful. Unlike XML-RPC, DRb is object-oriented, and connecting to a DRb server gives the client an instance of a class located on the DRb server. You can then use the methods made available by that class as if they're local methods.

A DRb client can be as simple as this:

```
require 'drb'

remote_object = DRbObject.new nil, 'druby://:51755'
puts remote_object.some_method
```

Only one line is required to retrieve an instance of a class from a remote DRb server. Whereas with XML-RPC you first create a handle to the server, with DRb you create a handle to a class instance. After you use `DRbObject.new`, `remote_object` is a handle to the object served by a specific DRb server (in this case, a local server).

Let's look at the server associated with this client:

```
require 'drb'

class OurClass
  def some_method
    "Some test text"
  end
end

DRb.start_service nil, OurClass.new
puts "DRb server running at #{DRb.uri}"
trap("INT") { DRb.stop_service }
DRb.thread.join
```

It couldn't be simpler. `DRb.start_service` associates an instance of `OurClass` with the DRb server, it prints the URL to the DRb server to the screen, and then starts the DRb server and awaits client connections.

Note You need to change the `druby://` URL in the client example to match the URL given in output by the server example.

With DRb, data structures work almost seamlessly across the connection. If your remote classes want to return complex hashes, they can, and they'll be represented perfectly on the client. To an extent, using an object over a DRb connection is transparent, and the object will act as if it were local.

This is only a simple overview of the basics of DRb. However, in terms of DRb's basic RPC features, this simple server-and-client example demonstrates the core of DRb's feature set, and you can extend it to almost any complexity. If your code is already written using classes, you might be able to drop DRb in within minutes and immediately get your functionality working from afar.

Tip For another basic DRb tutorial, refer to `http://www.chadfowler.com/ruby/drb.html` or to the most recent documentation at `http://www.ruby-doc.org/stdlib/libdoc/drb/rdoc/index.html`.

Summary

In this chapter we've looked at how to deploy Ruby programs and libraries, as well as how to make their functions available to Web browsers and to other applications over a network. We've also interrogated the environment so we can pursue different techniques on a per–operating-system basis if we choose.

Let's reflect on the main concepts covered in this chapter:

- *Shebang line*: A special line at the start of a source code file that determines which interpreter is used to process the file. Used primarily on Unix-based operating systems, shebang lines can also work on Windows when used with the Apache Web server.

- RUBY_PLATFORM: A special variable preset by Ruby that contains the name of the current platform (environment).

- *Environment variables*: Special variables set by the operating system or other processes that contain information relevant to the current execution environment and information about the operating system.

- *RubyForge*: A centralized repository and Web site dedicated to hosting and distributing Ruby projects and libraries. You can find it at http://rubyforge.org/.

- *CGI*: Common Gateway Interface. A standard that enables Web servers to execute scripts and provide an interface between Web users and scripts located on that server.

- *WEBrick*: A simple and easy HTTP server library for Ruby that comes with Ruby as standard.

- *Mongrel*: A more powerful HTTP server library for Ruby by Zed Shaw that improves significantly upon WEBrick's speed, stability, and overall performance.

- *RPC*: Remote Procedure Call. A way to call methods in a different program using a network (either local or the Internet), a transport protocol (such as HTTP), and a messaging protocol (such as XML).

- *XML-RPC*: An RPC protocol that uses HTTP and XML for its transport and messaging.

- *SOAP*: Simple Object Access Protocol. Another RPC protocol that uses HTTP and XML for its transport and messaging.

- *DRb*: Distributed Ruby. A Ruby-only mechanism for implementing RPCs and object handling between separate Ruby scripts.

In Chapter 15 we're going to return to looking at network servers, albeit in a different fashion, but first, in Chapter 11, we're going to take a look at some more advanced Ruby topics to flesh out the ideas we've covered so far.

Advanced Ruby Features

In this chapter we're going to look at some advanced Ruby techniques that have not been covered in prior chapters. This chapter is the last instructional chapter in the second part of the book, and although we'll be covering useful libraries, frameworks, and Ruby-related technologies in Part 3, this chapter rounds off the mandatory knowledge that any proficient Ruby programmer should have. This means that although this chapter will jump between several different topics, each is essential to becoming a professional Ruby developer.

The myriad topics covered in this chapter include how to create Ruby code dynamically on the fly, methods to make your Ruby code safe, how to issue commands to the operating system, how to integrate with Microsoft Windows, and how to create libraries for Ruby using other programming languages. Essentially, this chapter is designed to cover a range of discrete, important topics that you might find you need to use, but that fall outside the immediate scope of other chapters.

Dynamic Code Execution

As a dynamic, interpreted language, Ruby is able to execute code created *dynamically*. The way to do this is with the `eval` method. For example:

```
eval "puts 2 + 2"
```

4

Note that while 4 is displayed, 4 is not returned as the result of the whole `eval` expression. `puts` always returns `nil`. To return 4 from `eval`, you can do this:

```
puts eval("2 + 2")
```

4

Here's a more complex example that uses strings and interpolation:

```
my_number = 15
my_code = %Q{#{my_number} * 2}
puts eval(my_code)
```

```
30
```

The `eval` method simply executes (or *evaluates*) the code passed to it and returns the result. The first example made `eval` execute `puts 2 + 2`, whereas the second used string interpolation to build a expression of 15 * 2, which was then evaluated and printed to the screen using `puts`.

Bindings

In Ruby, a *binding* is a reference to a context, scope, or state of execution. A binding includes things such as the current value of variables and other details of the execution environment.

It's possible to pass a binding to `eval` and to have `eval` execute the supplied code under that binding rather than the current one. In this way, you can keep things that happen with `eval` separate from the main execution context of your code.

Here's an example:

```
def binding_elsewhere
  x = 20
  return binding
end

remote_binding = binding_elsewhere

x = 10
eval("puts x")
eval("puts x", remote_binding)
```

```
10
20
```

This code demonstrates that eval accepts an optional second parameter, a binding, which in this case is returned from the binding_elsewhere method. The variable remote_binding contains a reference to the execution context within the binding_elsewhere method rather than in the main code. Therefore, when you print x, 20 is shown, as x is defined as equal to 20 in binding_elsewhere!

■Note You can obtain the binding of the current scope at any point with the Kernel module's binding method.

The previous example is easily extended:

```
eval("x = 10")
eval("x = 50", remote_binding)
eval("puts x")
eval("puts x", remote_binding)
```

```
10
50
```

In this example, two bindings are in play: the default binding, and the remote_binding (from the binding_elsewhere method).

Therefore, even though you set x first to 10, and then to 50, you're not dealing with the *same* x in each case. One x is a local variable in the current context, and the other x is a variable in the context of binding_elsewhere.

Other Forms of eval

Although eval executes code within the current context (or the context supplied with a binding), class_eval, module_eval, and instance_eval can evaluate code within the context of classes, modules, and object instances, respectively.

class_eval is ideal for adding methods to a class dynamically:

```
class Person
end
```

```
def add_accessor_to_person(accessor_name)
  Person.class_eval %Q{
    attr_accessor :#{accessor_name}
  }
end

person = Person.new
add_accessor_to_person :name
add_accessor_to_person :gender
person.name = "Peter Cooper"
person.gender = "male"
puts "#{person.name} is #{person.gender}"
```

```
Peter Cooper is male
```

In this example you use the add_accessor_to_person method to add accessors dynam-ically to the Person class. Prior to using the add_accessor_to_person method, neither the name nor gender accessors exist within Person.

Note that the key part of the code, the class_eval method, operates by using string interpolation to create the desired code for Person:

```
Person.class_eval %Q{
  attr_accessor :#{accessor_name}
}
```

String interpolation makes the eval methods powerful tools for generating different features on the fly. This ability is a power unseen in the majority of programming lan-guages, and is one that's used to great effect in systems such as Ruby on Rails (covered in Chapter 13).

It's possible to take the previous example a lot further and add an add_accessor method to every class by putting your class_eval cleverness in a new method, defined within the Class class (from which all other classes descend):

```
class Class
  def add_accessor(accessor_name)
    self.class_eval %Q{
      attr_accessor :#{accessor_name}
    }
  end
end
```

```
class Person
end

person = Person.new
Person.add_accessor :name
Person.add_accessor :gender
person.name = "Peter Cooper"
person.gender = "male"
puts "#{person.name} is #{person.gender}"
```

In this example, you add the add_accessor method to the Class class, thereby adding it to every other class defined within your program. This makes it possible to add accessors to any class dynamically, by calling add_accessor. (If the logic of this approach isn't clear, make sure to try this code yourself, step through each process, and establish what is occurring at each step of execution.)

The technique used in the previous example also lets you define classes like this:

```
class SomethingElse
  add_accessor :whatever
end
```

Because add_accessor is being used within a class, the method call will work its way up to the add_accessor method defined in class Class.

Moving back to simpler techniques, using instance_eval is somewhat like using regular eval, but within the context of an object (rather than a method). In this example you use instance_eval to execute code within the scope of an object:

```
class MyClass
  def initialize
    @my_variable = 'Hello, world!'
  end
end

obj = MyClass.new
obj.instance_eval { puts @my_variable }
```

```
Hello, world!
```

Creating Your Own Version of attr_accessor

So far you've used the attr_accessor method within your classes to generate accessor functions for instance variables quickly. For example, in longhand you might have this code:

```
class Person
  def name
    @name
  end

  def name=(name)
    @name = name
  end
end
```

This allows you to do things such as puts person.name and person.name = 'Fred'. Alternatively, however, you can use attr_accessor:

```
class Person
  attr_accessor :name
end
```

This version of the class is more concise and has exactly the same functionality as the longhand version. Now it's time to ask the question: how does attr_accessor work?

It turns out that attr_accessor isn't as magical as it looks, and it's extremely easy to implement your own version using eval. Consider this code:

```
class Class
  def add_accessor(accessor_name)
    self.class_eval %Q{
      def #{accessor_name}
        @#{accessor_name}
      end

      def #{accessor_name}=(value)
        @#{accessor_name} = value
      end
    }
  end
end
```

At first, this code looks complex, but it's very similar to the `add_accessor` code you created in the previous section. You use `class_eval` to define getter and setter methods dynamically for the attribute within the current class.

If `accessor_name` is equal to "name," then the code that `class_eval` is executing is equivalent to this code:

```
def name
  @name
end

def name=(value)
  @name = value
end
```

Thus, you have duplicated the functionality of `attr_accessor`.

You can use this technique to create a multitude of different "code generators" and methods that can act as a "macro" language to perform things in Ruby that are otherwise lengthy to type out.

Running Other Programs from Ruby

Often it's useful to be able to run other programs on the system from your own programs. In this way you can reduce the amount of features your program needs to implement, as you can pass off work to other programs that are already written. It can also be useful to hook up several of your own programs so that functionality is spread among them. Rather than using the Remote Procedure Call systems covered in the previous chapter, you can simply run other programs from your own with one of a few different methods made available by Ruby.

Getting Results from Other Programs

There are three simple ways to run another program from within Ruby: the `system` method (defined in the `Kernel` module), *backtick* syntax (` `` `), and *delimited input literals* (`%x{}`). Using `system` is ideal when you want to run another program and aren't concerned with its output, whereas you should use backticks when you want the output of the remote program returned.

These lines demonstrate two ways of running the system's `date` program:

```
x = system("date")
x = `date`
```

For the first line, x equals `true`, whereas on the second line x contains the output of the `date` command. Which method you use depends on what you're trying to achieve. If you don't want the output of the other program to show on the same screen as that of your Ruby script, then use backticks (or a literal, `%x{}`).

■**Note** `%x{}` is functionally equivalent to using backticks; for example, `%x{date}`.

Transferring Execution to Another Program

Sometimes it's desirable to jump immediately to another program and cease execution of the current program. This is useful if you have a multistep process and have written an application for each. To end the current program and invoke another, simply use the `exec` method in place of `system`. For example:

```
exec "ruby another_script.rb"
puts "This will never be displayed"
```

In this example, execution is transferred to a different program, and the current program ceases immediately—the second line is never executed.

Running Two Programs at the Same Time

Forking is where an instance of a program (a *process*) duplicates itself, resulting in two processes of that program running *concurrently*. You can run other programs from this second process by using `exec`, and the first (parent) process will continue running the original program.

`fork` is a method provided by the `Kernel` module that creates a fork of the current process. It returns the child process's *process ID* in the parent, but `nil` in the child process—you can use this to determine which process a script is in. The following example forks the current process into two processes, and only executes the `exec` command within the child process (the process generated by the fork):

```
if fork.nil?
  exec "ruby some_other_file.rb"
end

puts "This Ruby script now runs alongside some_other_file.rb"
```

If the other program (being run by exec) is expected to finish at some point, and you want to wait for it to finish executing before doing something in the parent program, you can use Process.wait to wait for all child processes to finish before continuing. Here's an example:

```
child = fork do
  sleep 3
  puts "Child says 'hi'!"
end

puts "Waiting for the child process..."
Process.wait child
puts "All done!"
```

```
Waiting for the child process...
<3 second delay>
Child says 'hi'!
All done!
```

■Note Forking is not possible with the Windows version of Ruby, as POSIX-style forking is not natively supported on that platform. However, threads, covered later in this chapter, provide a good alternative.

Interacting with Another Program

The previous methods are fine for simple situations where you just want to get basic results from a remote program and don't need to interact directly with it in any way while it's running. However, sometimes you might want to pass data back and forth between two separate programs.

Ruby's IO module has a popen method that allows you to run another program and have an I/O stream between it and the current program. The I/O stream between programs works like the other types of I/O streams we looked at in Chapter 9, but instead of reading and writing to a file, you're reading and writing to another program. Obviously, this technique only works successfully with programs that accept direct input and produce direct output at a command-prompt level (so not GUI applications).

Here's a simple read-only example:

```
ls = IO.popen("ls", "r")
while line = ls.gets
  puts line
end
ls.close
```

In this example, you open up an I/O stream with `ls` (the Unix command to list the contents of the current directory—try it with `dir` if you're using Microsoft Windows). You read the lines one by one, as with other forms of I/O streams, and close the stream when you're done.

Similarly, you can also open a program with a read/write I/O stream and handle data in both directions:

```
handle = IO.popen("other_program", "r+")
handle.puts "send input to other program"
handle.close_write
while line = handle.gets
  puts line
end
```

■**Note** The reason for the `handle.close_write` is to close the I/O stream's writing stream, thereby sending any data waiting to be written out to the remote program. `IO` also has a `flush` method that can be used if the write stream needs to remain open.

Safely Handling Data and Dangerous Methods

It's common for Ruby applications to be used in situations where the operation of a program relies on data from an outside source. This data cannot always be trusted, and it can be useful to protect your machines and environments from unfortunate situations caused by bad data or code. Ruby can be made safer both by considering external data to be *tainted* and by setting a *safe level* under which the Ruby interpreter restricts what features are made available to the code it executes.

Tainted Data and Objects

In Ruby, data is generally considered to be *tainted* if it comes from an external source, or if Ruby otherwise has no way of establishing whether it is safe. For example, data collected from the command line could be unsafe, so it's considered tainted. Data read from external files or over a network connection is also tainted. However, data that is hard coded into the program, such as string literals, is considered to be *untainted*.

Consider a simple program that illustrates why checking for tainted data can be crucial:

```
while x = gets
  puts "=> #{eval(x)}"
end
```

This code acts like a miniature version of irb. It accepts line after line of input from the user and immediately executes it:

```
10+2
=> 12
"hello".length
=> 5
```

However, what would happen if someone wanted to cause trouble and typed in `rm -rf /*`? It would run!

■**Caution** Do not type the preceding code into the program! On a Unix-related operating system under the right circumstances, running `rm -rf /*` is an effective way to wipe clean much of your hard drive!

Clearly there are situations where you need to check whether data has, potentially, been tainted by the outside world.

You can check if an object is considered tainted by using the `tainted?` method:

```
x = "Hello, world!"
puts x.tainted?

y = [x, x, x]
puts y.tainted?
```

```
z = 20 + 50
puts z.tainted?

a = File.open("somefile").readlines.first
puts a.tainted?

b = ENV["PATH"]
puts b.tainted?

c = [a, b]
puts c.tainted?
```

```
false
false
false
true
true
false
```

■**Note** One of the preceding examples depends on `somefile` being a file that actually exists in the local directory.

The first three examples are all operating upon data that is already defined within the program (*literal* data), so are not considered tainted. The last three examples all involve data from external sources (a contains the first line of a file, and b contains information from the operating system's environment). So, why is the last example considered untainted?

c is considered untainted because c is merely an array containing references to a and b. Although a and b are both tainted, an array containing them is not. Therefore, it's necessary to check whether each piece of data you use is tainted, rather than checking an overall data structure.

■**Note** An alternative to having to do any checks is to set the "safe level" of the Ruby interpreter, and any potentially dangerous operations will be disabled for you. This is covered in the following section.

It's possible to force an object to be seen as untainted by calling the `untaint` method on the object. For example, here's an extremely safe version of your Ruby interpreter:

```
while x = gets
  next if x.tainted?
  puts "=> #{eval(x)}"
end
```

However, it's incredibly useless, because all data accepted from the user is considered tainted, so nothing is ever run. Safety by inactivity! Let's assume, however, that you've come up with a method that can tell if a certain operation is safe:

```
def code_is_safe?(code)
  code =~ /[`;*-]/ ? false : true
end

while x = gets
  x.untaint if code_is_safe?(x)
  next if x.tainted?
  puts "=> #{eval(x)}"
end
```

■**Caution** `code_is_safe?` merely checks if the line of code contains a backtick, semicolon, asterisk, or hyphen, and deems the code unsafe if it does. This is *not* a valid way to check for safe code, and is solely provided as an illustration.

In this example you explicitly untaint the data if you deem it to be safe, so `eval` will execute any "safe" code.

■**Note** Similarly, you can explicitly taint an object by calling its `taint` method.

Safe Levels

Although it's possible to check whether data is tainted and perform preventative actions to clean it up, a stronger form of protection comes with Ruby's "safe levels." Safe levels allow you to specify what features Ruby makes available and how it should deal with tainted data.

The current safe level is represented by the variable $SAFE. By default, $SAFE is set to 0, providing the lowest level of safety and the highest level of freedom, but four other safe modes are available, as shown in Table 11-1.

Table 11-1. *Ruby's Safe Levels, As Represented by* $SAFE

Value of $SAFE	Description
0	No restrictions. This is the default safe level.
1	Potentially unsafe methods can't use tainted data. Also, the current directory is not added to Ruby's search path for loading libraries.
2	The restrictions of safe level 1, plus Ruby won't load any external program files from globally writable locations in the filesystem. This is to prevent attacks where hackers upload malicious code and manipulate existing programs to load them. Some potentially dangerous methods are also deactivated, such as File#chmod, Kernel#fork, and Process::setpriority.
3	The restrictions of level 2, plus newly created objects within the program are considered tainted automatically. You also cannot untaint objects.
4	The restrictions of level 3, plus nontainted objects created prior to the safe level being set cannot be modified. You can use this to set up an execution environment in a lower safe mode, and then provide a way to continue execution while protecting the original objects and environment.

To change the safe level, simply set $SAFE to whichever safe level you want to use. Do note, however, that once you set the safe level, you can only increase the safe level and not decrease it. The reason for this is that allowing the safe level to be reduced would make it possible for eval-ed code to merely turn down the safety level and cause havoc!

Working with Microsoft Windows

So far in this book the examples have been reasonably generic, with a little bias toward Unix-based operating systems. Ruby is a relative latecomer to the world of Microsoft Windows, but it now includes some libraries that make working directly with Windows' APIs easy.

This section looks at the basics of using the Windows API and Windows' OLE capabilities from Ruby, although you'll need in-depth knowledge of these topics if you wish to put together more-advanced code.

Using the Windows API

Microsoft Windows provides an Application Programming Interface (API) that acts as a library of core Windows-related functions for access to the Windows kernel, graphics interface, control library, networking services, and user interface. Ruby's Win32API library (included in the standard library) gives developers raw access to the Windows API's features.

■**Note** No code in this section will work under any operating system other than Microsoft Windows, and is unlikely to work on any version of Windows prior to Windows 98.

It's reasonably trivial to open a dialog box:

```
require 'Win32API'

title = "My Application"
text = "Hello, world!"

Win32API.new('user32', 'MessageBox', %w{L P P L}, 'I').call(0, text, title, 0)
```

First, you load the Win32API library into the program, and then you set up some variables with the desired title and contents of the dialog box. Next, you create a reference to the MessageBox function provided by the Windows API, before calling it with your text and title. The result is shown in Figure 11-1.

Figure 11-1. *Your basic dialog box*

The parameters to Win32API.new represent the following:

1. The name of the system DLL containing the function you want to access

2. The name of the function you wish to use

3. An array describing the format of each parameter to be passed to the function

4. A character representing the type of data to be returned by the function

In this case, you specify that you want to call the MessageBox function provided by user32.dll, that you'll be supplying four parameters (a number, two strings, and another number—L represents numbers, P represents strings), and that you expect an integer to be returned (I representing *integer*).

Once you have the reference to the function, you use the call method to invoke it with the four parameters. In MessageBox's case, the four parameters represent the following:

1. The reference to a parent window (none in this case)

2. The text to display within the message box

3. The title to use on the message box

4. The type of message box to show (0 being a basic OK button dialog box)

The call method returns an integer that you don't use in this example, but that will be set to a number representing which button on the dialog box was pressed.

You can, of course, create something more elaborate:

```
require 'Win32API'

title = "My Application"
text = "Hello, world!"

dialog = Win32API.new('user32', 'MessageBox', 'LPPL', 'I')
result = dialog.call(0, text, title, 1)

case result
  when 1:
    puts "Clicked OK"
  when 2:
    puts "Clicked Cancel"
  else
    puts "Clicked something else!"
end
```

This example keeps the result from the MessageBox function, and uses it to work out which button was pressed. In this case, you call the MessageBox function with a fourth parameter of 1, representing a dialog box containing both an OK and a Cancel button.

Figure 11-2. *The OK/Cancel dialog box*

If the OK button is clicked, dialog.call returns 1, whereas if Cancel is clicked, 2 is returned.

■**Note** You can create many different types of dialog boxes with the MessageBox function alone. To learn more, refer to Microsoft's documentation on the MessageBox function.

The Windows API provides many hundreds of functions that can do everything from printing, to changing the desktop wallpaper, to creating elaborate windows. In theory, you could even put together an entire Windows program using the raw Windows API functions, although this would be a major undertaking. For more information about the Windows API, a good place is to start is the Wikipedia entry for it at http://en.wikipedia.org/wiki/Windows_API.

Controlling Windows Programs

Although the Windows API allows you to access low-level functions of the Microsoft Windows operating system, it can also be useful to access functions made available by programs available on the system. The technology that makes this possible is called Windows Automation. Windows Automation provides a way for programs to trigger one another's features and to automate certain functions among themselves.

Access to Windows Automation is provided by Ruby's WIN32OLE (also included in the standard library). If you're already familiar with Windows Automation, COM, or OLE technologies, Ruby's interface will feel instantly familiar. Even if you're not, this code should be immediately understood:

```
require 'win32ole'

web_browser = WIN32OLE.new('InternetExplorer.Application')
web_browser.visible = true
web_browser.navigate('http://www.rubyinside.com/')
```

This code loads the WIN32OLE library and creates a variable, web_browser, that references an OLE automation server called 'InternetExplorer.Application'. This server is provided by the Internet Explorer Web browser that comes with Windows, and the OLE automation server allows you to control the browser's functions remotely. In this example, you make the Web browser visible before instructing it to load up a certain Web page.

WIN32OLE does not implement the visible and navigate methods itself. These dynamic methods are handled on the fly by method_missing (a special method that is run within a class whenever no predefined method is found) and passed to the OLE Automation server. Therefore, you can use any methods made available by any OLE Automation server directly from Ruby!

You can extend this example to take advantage of further methods made available by Internet Explorer:

```
require 'win32ole'

web_browser = WIN32OLE.new('InternetExplorer.Application')
web_browser.visible = true
web_browser.navigate('http://www.rubyinside.com/')

while web_browser.ReadyState != 4
  sleep 1
end

puts "Page is loaded"
```

This example uses the ReadyState property to determine when Internet Explorer has successfully finished loading the page. If the page is not yet loaded, Ruby sleeps for a second and checks again. This allows you to wait until a remote operation is complete before continuing.

Once the page loading is complete, Internet Explorer makes available the document property that allows you to get full access to the Document Object Model (DOM) of the Web page that it has loaded, much in the same fashion as from JavaScript. For example:

```
puts web_browser.document.getElementById('header').innerHtml.length
```

1056

Note Many Windows applications implement OLE Automation and can be remotely controlled and used from Ruby in this manner, but it's beyond the scope of this book to provide an advanced guide to Windows development. The Win32Utils project provides further Windows-related Ruby libraries at `http://rubyforge.org/projects/win32utils/`.

This section was designed to demonstrate that although Ruby's origins are in Unix-related operating systems, Ruby's Windows support is significant. You can access Windows' APIs, use OLE and OLE Automation, and access DLL files. Many Windows-related features are advanced and beyond the scope of this book, but I hope this section whetted your appetite to research further if this area of development interests you.

Threads

Thread is short for *thread of execution*. You use threads to split the execution of a program into multiple parts that can be run concurrently. For example, a program designed to e-mail thousands of people at once might split the task between 20 different threads that all send e-mail at once. Such parallelism is faster than processing one item after another, especially on systems with more than one CPU, because different threads of execution can be run on different processors. It can also be faster, because rather than wasting time waiting for a response from a remote machine, you can continue with other operations.

Ruby doesn't currently support threads in the traditional sense. Typically, threading capabilities are provided by the operating system and vary from one system to another. However, the Ruby interpreter provides Ruby's threading capabilities directly. This means that they work well on every platform that Ruby works upon, but they also lack some of the power of traditional system-level threads.

One of the major disadvantages of Ruby threads not being "true" operating system–level threads is that if a thread needs to do something that calls the operating system and waits for a response, the entire Ruby threading scheduler is paused. However, for general operations Ruby's threading system is fine.

Note It's likely that future versions of Ruby will implement system-level threads.

Basic Ruby Threads in Action

Here's a basic demonstration of Ruby threading in action:

```
threads = []

10.times do
  thread = Thread.new do
    10.times { |i| print i; $stdout.flush; sleep rand(2) }
  end

  threads << thread
end

threads.each { |thread| thread.join }
```

You create an array to hold your Thread objects, so that you can easily keep track of them. Then you create ten threads, sending the block of code to be executed in each thread to Thread.new, and add each generated thread to the array.

Note When you create a thread, it can access any variables that are within scope at that point. However, any local variables that are then created within the thread are entirely local to that thread. This is similar to the behavior of other types of code blocks.

Once you've created the threads, you wait for all of them to complete before the program finishes. You wait by looping through all the thread objects in threads and calling each thread's join method. The join method makes the main program wait until a thread's execution is complete before continuing. In this way you make sure all the threads are complete before exiting.

The preceding program results in output similar to the following (the variation is due to the randomness of the sleeping):

```
001012000100101012123121242325123234532343366345443655467445487765578866689756765
67979789878889899999
```

The example has created ten Ruby threads whose sole job is to count and sleep randomly. This results in the preceding pseudo-random output.

Rather than sleeping, the threads could have been fetching Web pages, performing math operations, or sending e-mails. In fact, Ruby threads are ideal for almost every situation where concurrency within a single Ruby program is desired.

■**Note** In Chapter 15 you'll be using threads to create a server that creates new threads of execution for each client that connects to it, so that you can develop a simple chat system.

Advanced Thread Operations

As you've seen, creating and running basic threads is fairly simple, but threads also offer a number of advanced features. These are discussed in the following subsections.

Waiting for Threads to Finish Redux

When you waited for your threads to finish by using the `join` method, you could have specified a timeout value (in seconds) for which to wait. If the thread doesn't finish within that time, `join` returns `nil`. Here's an example where each thread is given only one second to execute:

```ruby
threads.each do |thread|
  puts "Thread #{thread.object_id} didn't finish within 1s" unless thread.join(1)
end
```

Getting a List of All Threads

It's possible to get a global list of all threads running within your program using `Thread.list`. In fact, if you didn't want to keep your own store of threads, you could rewrite the earlier example from the section "Basic Ruby Threads in Action" down to these two lines:

```
10.times { Thread.new { 10.times { |i| print i; $stdout.flush; sleep rand(2) } } }
Thread.list.each { |thread| thread.join }
```

However, keeping your own list of threads is essential if you're likely to have more than one group of threads working within an application, and you want to keep them separate from one another when it comes to using `join` or other features.

The list of threads also includes the *main* thread representing the main program's thread of execution. You can check to see which thread is main by comparing the thread object to `Thread.main`, like so:

```
Thread.list.each { |thread| thread.join unless thread == Thread.main }
```

Thread Operations from Within Threads Themselves

Threads aren't just tiny, dumb fragments of code. They have the ability to talk with the Ruby thread scheduler and provide updates on their status. For example, a thread can stop itself:

```
Thread.new do
  10.times do |i|
    print i
    $stdout.flush
    Thread.stop
  end
end
```

Every time the thread created in this example prints a number to the screen, it stops itself. It can then only be restarted or resumed by the parent program calling the `run` method on the thread, like so:

```
Thread.list.each { |thread| thread.run }
```

A thread can also tell the Ruby thread scheduler that it wants to pass execution over to another thread. The technique of voluntarily ceding control to another thread is often known as *cooperative multitasking*, because the thread or process itself is saying that it's okay to pass execution on to another thread or process. Used properly, cooperative multitasking can make threading even more efficient, as you can code in pass requests at ideal locations. Here's an example showing how to cede control from a thread:

```
2.times { Thread.new { 10.times { |i| print i; $stdout.flush; Thread.pass } } }
Thread.list.each { |thread| thread.join unless thread == Thread.main }
```

```
00112233445566778899
```

In this example, execution flip-flops between the two threads, causing the pattern shown in the results.

RubyInline

As a dynamic, object-oriented programming language, Ruby wasn't designed to be a high-performance language in the traditional sense. This is not of particular concern nowadays, as most tasks are not computationally intensive, but there are still situations where raw performance is required for a subset of functionality.

In situations where extremely high performance is desirable, it can be a good idea to write the computationally-intensive code in a more powerful but less expressive language, and then call that code from Ruby. Luckily there's a library for Ruby called *RubyInline*, created by Ryan Davis and Eric Hodel, that makes it possible to write code in other more powerful languages within your Ruby code. It's most often used to write high-performance code in the C or C++ languages, and we'll focus on this in this section.

Installing RubyInline on Unix-related platforms (such as Linux and OS X) is easy with RubyGems:

```
gem install RubyInline
```

If you don't have *gcc*—a C compiler—installed, RubyInline's C support will not work, and RubyInline itself might not install. Refer to your operating system's documentation on how to install gcc.

Note At the time of writing, RubyInline has been reported as working on Microsoft Windows, with some significant adjustments needed (although it runs perfectly under the Cygwin environment). However, these are only to be attempted by advanced users, although they might be incorporated in the library automatically by the time of publishing. If you're a Windows user who wishes to use RubyInline, either work under Cygwin, or check the official Web site at http://www.zenspider.com/ZSS/Products/RubyInline/.

Why Use C As an Inline Language?

C is a general purpose, procedural, compiled programming language developed in the 1970s by Dennis Ritchie. It's one of the most widely used programming languages in the world, and is the foundation of nearly every major operating system currently available. C (and its object-oriented sister language, C++) is still a popular language due to its raw speed and flexibility. Although languages such as Ruby have been designed to be easy to develop with, C offers a lot of low-level access to developers, along with blazing speed. This makes C perfect for writing performance-intensive libraries and functions that can be called from other programming languages, such as Ruby.

> ■**Note** This section is not a primer on the C language, as that would be an entire book in its own right, but to learn more about the C programming language itself, visit `http://en.wikipedia.org/wiki/C_programming_language`.

Creating a Basic Method or Function

An ideal demonstration of RubyInline and C's power is to create a basic method (a *function* in C) to compute factorials. The factorial of a number is the product of all integers from itself down to 1. So, for example, the factorial of 8 is 8 * 7 * 6 * 5 * 4 * 3 * 2 * 1, or 40,320.

Calculating a factorial in Ruby is easy:

```ruby
class Fixnum
  def factorial
    (1..self).inject { |a, b| a * b }
  end
end

puts 8.factorial
```

```
40320
```

You can use your knowledge of benchmarking (from Chapter 8) to test how fast this method is:

```
require 'benchmark'

Benchmark.bm do |bm|
  bm.report('ruby:') do
    100000.times do
      8.factorial
    end
  end
end
```

	user	system	total	real
ruby:	0.930000	0.010000	0.940000 (	1.537101)

The results show that it takes about 1.5 seconds to run 100,000 iterations of your routine to compute the factorial of 8—approximately 66,666 iterations per second.

Let's write a factorial method in C using RubyInline:

```
class CFactorial
  class << self
    inline do |builder|
      builder.c %q{
        long factorial(int value) {
          long result = 1, i = 1;
          for (i = 1; i <= value; i++) {
            result *= i;
          }
          return result;
        }
      }
    end
  end
end
```

First you create a CFactorial class to house your new method. Then inline do |builder| starts the RubyInline environment, and builder.c is used to process the C code within the multiline string between %q{ and }. The reason for this level of depth is that RubyInline can work with multiple languages at the same time, so you need to enter the RubyInline environment first and then explicitly specify code to be associated with a particular language.

The actual C code in the preceding example begins following the builder.c line. Let's focus on it for a moment:

```
long factorial(int value) {
  long result = 1, i = 1;
  for (i = 1; i <= value; i++) {
    result *= i;
  }
  return result;
}
```

This code defines a C function called factorial that accepts a single integer parameter and returns a single integer value. The internal logic counts from 1 to the supplied value, and multiplies each number to obtain the factorial.

Benchmarking C vs. Ruby

Now that you have your C-based factorial routine written, let's benchmark it and compare it to the Ruby-based solution. Here's a complete program to benchmark the two different routines (C and Ruby):

```
require 'rubygems'
require 'inline'
require 'benchmark'

class CFactorial
  class << self
    inline do |builder|
      builder.c %q{
        long factorial(int value) {
          long result = 1, i = 1;
          for (i = 1; i <= value; i++) {
            result *= i;
          }
          return result;
        }
      }
    }
```

```ruby
      end
    end
end

class Fixnum
  def factorial
    (1..self).inject { |a, b| a * b }
  end
end

Benchmark.bm do |bm|
  bm.report('ruby:') do
    100000.times { 8.factorial }
  end

  bm.report('c:') do
    100000.times { CFactorial.factorial(8) }
  end
end
```

```
user     system     total          real
ruby:  0.930000  0.010000  3.110000  (  1.571207)
c:     0.020000  0.000000  0.120000  (  0.044347)
```

The C factorial function is so much faster as to barely leave a whisper on the bench-marking times! It's at least 30 times faster. There are certainly ways both implementations could be improved, but this benchmark demonstrates the radical difference between the performance of compiled and interpreted code, as well as the effect of Ruby's object-oriented overhead on performance.

Tip To learn more about RubyInline, refer to the official RubyInline Web site at `http://www.zenspider.com/ZSS/Products/RubyInline/`.

Unicode and UTF-8 Support

A common complaint about Ruby is that it doesn't support international character sets very well. The world is multilingual, and there are times when your Ruby code will need to reflect this.

Unicode is the industry-standard way of representing characters from every writing system in the world. It's the only viable way to be able to manage multiple different alphabets and character sets in a reasonably standard context.

When people complain about Ruby's international character support, they're usually complaining about its lack of Unicode support. In Ruby 1.8, this is certainly true, although there are workarounds that I'll cover in this section. However, in Ruby 1.9 and 2.0, the problems have been addressed and Ruby natively supports Unicode and multi-byte characters, so you might not need to read this section.

Note For a full rundown of Unicode and how it works and relates to software development, read `http://www.joelonsoftware.com/articles/Unicode.html`. The official Unicode site at `http://unicode.org/` also has specifications and further details.

The main problem is that Ruby 1.8, by default, treats characters in a string as 8-bit characters only. This works well with the Latin/English alphabet, as most texts can be represented with only eight bits per character. However, with languages such as Chinese or Japanese, the number of symbols is so large that characters may take up two, three, or even four bytes. However, Ruby only sees each byte as a character, rather than the larger group of bytes as each character. The problems this causes with Ruby 1.8 can be highlighted easily, as the following examples show.

Note The following examples should work with Ruby 2.0 as well as Ruby 1.8, although it has not been released at the time of writing. You can find more information about Ruby 2.0's multibyte character capabilities at `http://redhanded.hobix.com/inspect/futurismUnicodeInRuby.html`.

With English (or, more accurately, Latin alphabet characters), taking the first letter from a string is easy:

```
"test"[0].chr
```

```
t
```

With Japanese, however:

```
"権限の"[0].chr
```

<..nothing or a junk result..>

Because the Japanese characters are represented by more than one byte each, Ruby cannot work with them properly. Instead, it just picks off the first byte with [0] as opposed to the first *character* and tries to convert that meaningless byte's value back into a character.

One workaround provided by Ruby 1.8 is called *jcode*. This mechanism comes with Ruby and puts Ruby into a mode that has bare support for UTF-8 (or other character encodings, mostly related to Japanese, but we won't consider those here). UTF-8 is the most commonly used system of representing Unicode characters. By default, UTF-8 characters only take up one byte (for English alphabet characters, say), but, where necessary, will use more than one byte (for Japanese, Chinese, and so on).

Using jcode you can make regular expressions UTF-8 aware:

```
$KCODE = 'u'
require 'jcode'

"権限の".scan(/./) do |character|
  puts character
end
```

This result ensues:

```
権
限
の
```

Setting the $KCODE global variable to 'u' (for UTF-8) and loading jcode gives regular expressions awareness of UTF-8 characters, giving you each multibyte character correctly in the scan loop. Unfortunately this awareness spreads only to regular expressions, meaning that other Ruby methods such as length, first, last, and picking individual characters from strings using [ ] don't work properly on these strings.

There have been some noble projects to give strings methods that work in the same way as the default ones, but on UTF-8 strings. Most of these use regular expressions to get their results, and are therefore a lot slower than the built-in Ruby methods. For example:

```
$KCODE = 'u'
require 'jcode'
```

```
class String
  def reverse
    scan(/./).reverse.join
  end
end

puts "権限の".reverse
```

Here's the result:
権限の

In this example you override the `reverse` method in class `String` and implement your own using `scan`. This yields the correct result when working with the UTF-8 encoding.

■**Note** Further information about this technique is available at `http://redhanded.hobix.com/inspect/closingInOnUnicodeWithJcode.html`.

In mid-2006 a more permanent workaround was developed for Ruby 1.8 called *ActiveSupport::Multibyte*, now a standard part of the Ruby on Rails framework. (You can also download the library in a standalone form at `https://fngtps.com/projects/multibyte_for_rails`) ActiveSupport::Multibyte provides a basic proxy method called `chars` that gives access to the true characters within a string (rather than simply each block of 8 bits). It allows you to write examples like these:

```
puts "権限の".chars.reverse
```

With this result:
の限権

Or:

```
puts "権限の".chars[1..2]
```

Here's the result:
限の

There is a more full discussion of ActiveSupport::Multibyte at `http://www.ruby-forum.com/topic/81976`.

■**Note** Conversion between different character encodings is provided by the *iconv* library, covered in Chapter 16.

Summary

In this chapter we've looked at an array of advanced Ruby topics, from dynamic code execution to writing high-performance functions in the C programming language. This chapter is the last chapter that covers general Ruby-related knowledge that any intermediate Ruby programmer should be familiar with. In Chapter 12 we'll be taking a different approach and will develop an entire Ruby application, much as we did in Chapter 4.

Let's reflect on the main concepts covered in this chapter:

- *Binding*: A binding is a representation of a scope (execution) context as an object.

- *Forking*: When an instance of a program duplicates itself into two processes, one as a parent and one as a child, both continuing execution.

- *Tainted data*: Data whose source or origin cannot be entirely trusted or is unknown.

- *Safe levels*: Different safe levels result in the Ruby interpreter having different restrictions upon what code it will process and execute.

- *Win32API*: A Ruby library that gives you access to the Windows API: a set of libraries offering functions that provide access to the Windows kernel, graphics interface, control library, networking services, and user interface.

- *Windows Automation (also known as OLE Automation)*: A system that allows Windows applications to register servers for themselves that allow other applications to control them remotely. You can learn more at `http://en.wikipedia.org/wiki/OLE_Automation`.

- *Threads*: Separate "strands" of execution that run concurrently to each other. Ruby's threads are implemented entirely by the Ruby interpreter, but in general threads can also operate at the operating system level and are a commonly used tool in application development.

- *C*: A compiled, high-performance language developed in the 1970s that's used in most of the world's operating systems and low-level software. You can use C code within Ruby using the RubyInline library.

- *RubyInline*: A Ruby library by Ryan Davis that makes it easy to write C code *inline* with Ruby code, giving Ruby easy access to high-performance C functions.

- *Character encoding*: A system and code that pairs characters (whether they're Roman letters, Chinese symbols, Arabic letters, and so on) to a set of numbers that a computer can use to represent those characters.

- *UTF-8*: Unicode Transformation Format-8. A character encoding that can support any character in the Unicode standard. It supports variable-length characters, and is designed to support ASCII coding natively, while also providing the ability to use up to four bytes to represent characters from other character sets.

Now you can move on to Chapter 12, where we'll develop an entire Ruby application using the knowledge obtained in this book so far.

CHAPTER 12

■■■

Tying It Together: Developing a Larger Ruby Application

In this chapter we're going to step back from focusing on individual facets of Ruby and instead develop an entire program using the knowledge we've gained so far. We're going to focus on the structural concerns of application development and look at how a flexible program structure can benefit you and other developers in the long run.

The important thing to remember while working through this chapter is that the application itself is not as important as the concepts used while developing it. We'll be rapidly covering a number of areas relevant to most of application development, such as flowcharting, testing, and basic refactoring. These techniques are relevant to creating *any* application of a certain size.

Let's Build a Bot

Before we get to any code, we're going to look at what we're going to build, why we're going to build it, and how we're going to do it.

What Is a Bot?

In this chapter we're going to build a robot. Not a sci-fi type of robot, such as that in *Lost In Space,* but a computer program that can hold a conversation with us. These types of programs are commonly known as *bots* or *chatterbots*. Bots are present in a lot of different software and tools these days. AOL's popular Instant Messenger software comes with two bots added as default friends on your profile. You can ask them for gift ideas and movie times. In short, it's a little like talking to a customer service agent, except the agent is entirely automated.

You might be familiar with bots on your own computer. Microsoft Office comes with the "Clippy" bot turned on by default, and many Web sites have automated chat bots (IKEA's Web site provides an excellent example).

The history of bots goes back to the 1960s, when a computer scientist at MIT named Joseph Weizenbaum developed a bot called ELIZA. It eventually became so popular that most computer users throughout the 1980s and 1990s were exposed to it in one form or another through the many "talk to your computer"–type programs that became popular.

The conversations you can have with ELIZA-type bots aren't mind blowing, but can prove entertaining, as shown in Figure 12-1. The general mechanism ELIZA bots use is to take whatever you say and twist it around into a statement or question to you. For example, if you were to say "I am bored," ELIZA might respond, "How long have you been bored?" or "Why are you bored?" This form of bouncing back the user's input seems crude when described in this way, but people are often fooled into believing they're talking to something more intelligent simply because of its reflective nature (this is known as the *ELIZA effect*).

```
Eliza: Hi. I'm Eliza. Tell me your problems!
You  : I don't have any problems!
Eliza: We have to find the reason why you don't have any problems!
You  : How can there be a reason for that?
Eliza: Why do you ask?
You  : It was a rhetorical question.
Eliza: Perhaps you would like to talk about a problem?
You  : Okay, let's talk about my book.
Eliza: What does this mean for you, saying " Okay, let's talk about your book "?
You  : Huh?
Eliza: I understand!
You  : I'm glad about that.
Eliza: How long are you glad about that?
You  : Five seconds?
Eliza: I'm not sure wether I understand you!
You  : And you sure can't spell.
Eliza: Come on! Explain your thinkings!
```

Figure 12-1. *A demonstration of a session with an online ELIZA bot*

Our bot won't be exactly like ELIZA—that is, it won't be an ELIZA *clone*—but will share some of the same features and use some similar techniques. We'll also look at how to extend our bot with other features.

■**Note** If you want to learn about or play with some Internet-hosted versions of ELIZA, visit `http://en.wikipedia.org/wiki/ELIZA`.

Why a Bot?

The good thing about developing a bot is that it can be as simple or as complex as you like. Toward the end of this chapter we'll be looking at ways you can extend the bot, but the initial construction is quite simple.

You'll be using most of the techniques covered so far in this book to build your bot. You'll be doing a bit of testing and documentation, as well as using classes and complex data structures. You'll also be using files to store information the bot uses, and looking at how to make your bot available to the general public using HTTP servers and CGI scripts. This project also demands you use a lot of string and list-related functions, along with comparison logic. These are all things you're likely to use in a larger development project, and as Ruby is a particularly good language for text processing, this project is perfect for demonstrating Ruby's strengths.

A bot also allows you to have some fun and experiment. Working on a contact information management tool (for example) isn't that much fun, even though such a system would use similar techniques to your bot. You can still implement testing, documentation, classes, and storage systems, but end up with a fun result that can be extended and improved indefinitely.

How?

The primary focus of this chapter is to keep each fragment of functionality in your bot loosely coupled from the others. This is an important decision when developing certain types of applications if you plan to extend them in future. The plan for this bot is to make it as easy to extend, or change, as possible, allowing you to customize it, add features, and make it your own.

In terms of the general operation of the chatterbot, your bot will exist within a class, allowing you to replicate bots easily by creating new instances. When you create a bot, it will be "blank," except for the logic contained within the class, and you'll pass in a special data file to give it a set of knowledge and a set of responses it can use when conversing with users. User input will be via the keyboard, but the input mechanism will be kept flexible enough so that the bot could easily be used from a Web site or elsewhere.

Your bot will only have a few public methods to begin with. It needs to be able to load its data file into memory and accept input given by the user, then return its responses. Behind the scenes, the bot will need to parse what the users "say" and be able to build up a coherent reply. Therefore, the first step is to begin processing language and recognizing words.

Creating a Text Processing Tools Library

Several stages are required to accept input such as "I am bored" and turn it into a response such as "Why are you bored?" The first is to perform some *preprocessing*—tasks that make the text easier to parse—such as cleaning up the text, expanding terms such as "I'm" into "I am" and "you're" into "you are," and so forth. Next, you'll split up the input into sentences and words, choose the best sentence to respond to, and finally look up responses from your data files that match the input.

You can see these basic steps in the flowchart in Figure 12-2.

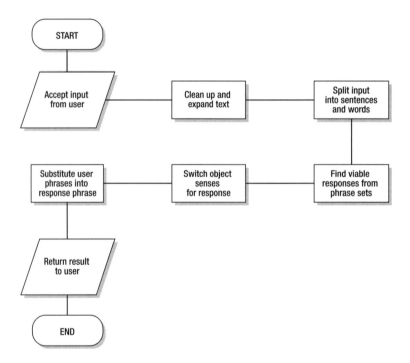

Figure 12-2. *Rudimentary flowchart for the basic operations of your bot's text processing system*

■**Note** A flowchart is a graphical representation of the steps involved in a system, such as within a computer program. Producing flowcharts such as the one in Figure 12-2 can help to define the steps within a process, making it easier to tie up your expectations for a program with the resulting code. You can learn more about flowcharts, the symbols they use, and how they work at http://en.wikipedia.org/wiki/Flowchart.

Some of these language tasks are generic enough that they could be useful in other applications, so you'll develop a basic library for them. This will make your bot code simpler, and give you a library to use in other applications if you need. Logic and methods that are specific to bots can go in the bot's source code, and generic methods that perform operations on text can go into the library.

This section covers the development of a simple library, including testing and documentation.

Building the WordPlay Library

You're going to call your text manipulation and processing library *WordPlay*, so create a file called wordplay.rb with a basic class:

```
class WordPlay
end
```

Now that you've got the library's main file set up, you'll move on to implementing some of the text manipulation and processing features you know your bot will require, but which are reasonably application agnostic. (I covered the construction of classes in depth in Chapter 6.)

Splitting Text into Sentences

Your bot, like most others, is only interested in single-sentence inputs. Therefore, it's important to accept only the first sentence of each line of input. However, rather than specifically tear out the first sentence, you'll split the input into sentences and then choose the first one. The reason for this approach is to have a generic sentence-splitting method, rather than to create a unique solution for each case.

You'll create a sentences method on Ruby's String class to keep the resulting code clean. You could create a class method within the WordPlay class, and use it like WordPlay.sentences(our_input), but it wouldn't feel as intuitive and as object-oriented as our_input.sentences, where sentences is a method of the String class.

```
class String
  def sentences
    gsub(/\n|\r/, ' ').split(/\.\s*/)
  end
end
```

You can test it easily:

```
%q{Hello. This is a test of
basic sentence splitting. It
even works over multiple lines.}.sentences
```

```
["Hello", "This is a test of basic sentence splitting", "It even works over
multiple lines"]
```

Splitting Sentences into Words

You also need your library to be able to split sentences into words. As with the sentences method, add a words method to the String class:

```ruby
class String
  def words
    scan(/\w[\w\'\-]*/)
  end
end


"This is a test of words' capabilities".words
```

```
["This", "is", "a", "test", "of", "words'", "capabilities"]
```

You can test words in conjunction with sentences:

```ruby
%q{Hello. This is a test of
basic sentence splitting. It
even works over multiple lines}.sentences[1].words[3]
```

```
test
```

This test picks out the second sentence with sentences[1] and then the fourth word with words[3]—remember, arrays are zero-based. (The splitting techniques covered in this section were also explained in Chapter 3.)

Word Matching

You can use the new methods, along with existing array methods, to extract sentences that match certain words, as in this example:

```
hot_words = %w{test ruby}
my_string = "This is a test. Dull sentence here. Ruby is great. So is cake."
my_string.sentences.find_all do |s|
  s.downcase.words.any? { |word| hot_words.include?(word) }
end
```

In this example you define two "hot" words that you want to find within sentences, and you look through the sentences in `my_string` for any that contain either of your hot words. The way you do this is by seeing if, for any of the words in the sentence, it's true that the `hot_words` array also contains that word.

Experienced readers will wonder if regular expressions could be used in this situation. They could, but the focus here is on clean list logic that's easy to extend and adjust. You also get the benefit, if you wish, to use the difference in lengths between the word array, and the word array with hot words removed, to rank sentences in the order of which match the most hot words. This could be useful if you decided to tweak your bot (or any other software using WordPlay) to pick out and process the *most important* sentence, rather than just the first one. For example:

```
def self.best_sentence(sentences, desired_words)
  ranked_sentences = sentences.sort_by do |s|
    s.words.length - (s.downcase.words - desired_words).length
  end

  ranked_sentences.last
end
```

This class method accepts an array of sentences and an array of "desired words" as arguments. Next it sorts the sentences by how many words difference each sentence has with the desired words list. If the difference is high, then there must be many desired words in that sentence. At the end of `best_sentence`, the sentence with the biggest number of matching words is returned.

Switching Subject and Object Pronouns

Switching pronouns is when you swap "you" and "I," "I" and "you," "my" and "your," and "your" and "my." This simple change makes sentences easy to use as a response. Consider what happens if you simply reflect back whatever the user says by switching the pronouns in his or her input. Some examples are shown in the following table:

Input	Response
My cat is sick.	Your cat is sick.
I hate my car.	You hate your car.
You are an awful bot.	I are an awful bot.

These aren't elaborate conversations, but the first two responses are valid English and are the sort of thing your bot can use. The third response highlights that you also need to pay attention to conjugating "am" to "are" and vice versa when using "I" and "you."

You'll add the basic pronoun-switching feature as a class method on the WordPlay class. As this feature won't be chained with other methods and doesn't need to be particularly concise, you can put it into the WordPlay class rather than continue to add more methods to the String class.

```ruby
def self.switch_pronouns(text)
  text.gsub(/\b(I am|You are|I|You|Your|My)\b/i) do |pronoun|
    case pronoun.downcase
      when "i"
        "you"
      when "you"
        "I"
      when "i am"
        "you are"
      when "you are"
        "i am"
      when "your"
        "my"
      when "my"
        "your"
    end
  end
end
```

This method accepts any text supplied as a string, and performs a substitution on each instance of "I am," "you are," "I," "you," "your," or "my." Next, a case construction is used to substitute each pronoun with its opposing pronoun. (You first used the case/when syntax in Chapter 3, where you can also find a deeper explanation of how it works.)

The reason for performing a substitution in this way is so that you only change each pronoun once. If you'd used four gsubs to change all "I's" to "you's," "you's" to "I's," and so on, changes made by the previous gsub would be overwritten by the next. Therefore, it's important to use one gsub that scans through the input pronoun by pronoun rather than making several blanket substitutions in succession.

Let's check the results:

```
WordPlay.switch_pronouns("Your cat is fighting with my cat")
```

```
my cat is fighting with your cat
```

```
WordPlay.switch_pronouns('You are my robot')
```

```
I am your robot
```

It's easy to find an exception to these results though:

```
WordPlay.switch_pronouns("I gave you life")
```

```
you gave I life
```

When the "you" or "I" is the *object* of the sentence, rather than the *subject*, "you" becomes "me" and "me" becomes "you," whereas "I" becomes "you" and "you" becomes "I" on the *subject* of the sentence.

Without descending into complex processing of sentences to establish which reference is the subject and which reference is the object, we'll assume that every reference to "you" that's not at the start of a sentence is an object and should become "me," and that if "you" is at the beginning of a sentence, you should assume it's the subject and use "I" instead. This new rule makes your method change slightly:

```
def self.switch_pronouns(text)
  text.gsub(/\b(I am|You are|I|You|Me|Your|My)\b/i) do |pronoun|
    case pronoun.downcase
      when "i"
        "you"
      when "you"
        "me"
```

```
      when "me"
        "you"
      when "i am"
        "you are"
      when "you are"
        "i am"
      when "your"
        "my"
      when "my"
        "your"
    end
  end.sub(/^me\b/i, 'i')
end
```

What you do in this case seems odd on the surface. You let switch_pronouns process the pronouns and then correct it when it changes "you" to "me" at the start of a sentence by changing the "me" to "I." This is done with the chained sub at the end.

Let's try it out:

```
WordPlay.switch_pronouns('Your cat is fighting with my cat')
```

```
my cat is fighting with your cat
```

```
WordPlay.switch_pronouns('My cat is fighting with you')
```

```
your cat is fighting with me
```

```
WordPlay.switch_pronouns('You are my robot')
```

```
i am your robot
```

```
WordPlay.switch_pronouns('I gave you hope')
```

```
you gave me hope
```

```
WordPlay.switch_pronouns('You gave me hope')
```

```
i gave you hope
```

Success!

If you were so cruelly inclined, you could create an extremely annoying bot with this method alone. Consider this basic example:

```
while input = gets
  puts '>> ' + WordPlay.switch_pronouns(input).chomp + '?'
end
```

```
I am ready to talk
>> you are ready to talk?
yes
>> yes?
You are a dumb computer
>> I am a dumb computer?
```

You clearly have work to do!

Testing the Library

When building a larger application, or libraries upon which other applications will depend, it's important to make sure everything is fully tested. In Chapter 8 we looked at using Ruby's unit testing features for simple testing. You can use the same methods here to test WordPlay.

You'll use the same process as in Chapter 8. Create a file called test_wordplay.rb in the same directory as wordplay.rb and implement the following basic structure:

```
require 'test/unit'
require 'wordplay'

class TestWordPlay < Test::Unit::TestCase
end
```

Running this script gives you an error, as no tests are defined, so let's write some.

Testing Sentence Separation

To add groups of test assertions to `test_wordplay.rb`, you can simply create methods with names starting with `test_`. Creating a simple test method for testing sentence separations is easy:

```
def test_sentences
  assert_equal(["a", "b", "c d", "e f g"], "a. b. c d. e f g.".sentences)

  test_text = %q{Hello. This is a test
of sentence separation. This is the end
of the test.}
  assert_equal("This is the end of the test", test_text.sentences[2])
end
```

The first assertion tests that the dummy sentence "a. b. c d. e f g." is successfully separated into the constituent "sentences." The second assertion uses a longer predefined text string and makes sure that the third sentence is correctly identified.

■**Note** Ideally, you'd extend this basic set of assertions with several more to test more-complex cases, such as sentences ending with multiple periods, commas, and other oddities. As these extra tests wouldn't demonstrate any further Ruby functionality, they're not covered here, but feel free to try some out!

Testing Word Separation

Testing that the `words` method works properly is even easier than testing `sentences`:

```
def test_words
  assert_equal(%w{this is a test}, "this is a test".words)
  assert_equal(%w{these are mostly words}, "these are, mostly, words".words)
end
```

These assertions are simple. You split sentences into words and compare them with predefined arrays of those words. The assertions pass.

This highlights one reason why test-first development can be a good idea. It's easy to see how you could develop these tests *first* and then use their passing or failure as an indicator that you've implemented `words` correctly. This is an advanced programming concept, but one worth keeping in mind if writing tests in this way "clicks" with you.

Testing Best Sentence Choice

You also need to test your WordPlay.best_sentence method, as your bot will use it to choose the sentence with the most interesting keywords from the user's input:

```ruby
def test_sentence_choice
  assert_equal('This is a great test',
               WordPlay.best_sentence(['This is a test',
                                       'This is another test',
                                       'This is a great test'],
                                      %w{test great this}))
  assert_equal('This is a great test',
               WordPlay.best_sentence(['This is a great test'],
                                      %w{still the best}))
end
```

This test method performs a simple assertion that the correct sentence is chosen from three options. Three sentences are provided to WordPlay.best_sentence, along with the desired keywords of "test," "great," and "this." Therefore, the third sentence should be the best match. The second assertion makes sure that WordPlay.best_sentence returns a sentence even if there are no matches, because in this case *any* sentence is a "best" match.

Testing Pronoun Switches

When you developed the switch_pronouns method, you used some vague grammatical rules, so testing is essential to make sure they stand up for at least basic sentences:

```ruby
def test_basic_pronouns
  assert_equal("i am a robot", WordPlay.switch_pronouns("you are a robot"))
  assert_equal("you are a person", WordPlay.switch_pronouns("i am a person"))
  assert_equal("i love you", WordPlay.switch_pronouns("you love me"))
end
```

These basic assertions prove that the "you are," "I am," "you," and "me" phrases are switched correctly.

You can also create a separate test method to perform some more-complex assertions:

```ruby
def test_mixed_pronouns
  assert_equal("you gave me life", WordPlay.switch_pronouns("i gave you life"))
  assert_equal("i am not what you are", WordPlay.switch_pronouns("you are not➡
what i am"))
  assert_equal("i annoy your dog", WordPlay.switch_pronouns("you annoy my dog"))
end
```

These examples are more complex but prove that switch_pronouns can handle a few more complex situations with multiple pronouns.

You can construct tests that cause switch_pronouns to fail:

```
def test_complex_pronouns
  assert_equal("yes, i rule", WordPlay.switch_pronouns("yes, you rule"))
  assert_equal("why do i cry", WordPlay.switch_pronouns("why do you cry"))
end
```

These tests both fail, because they circumvent the trick you used to make sure that "you" is translated to "me" and "I" in the right situations. In these situations, they should become "I," but because "I" isn't at the start of the sentence, they become "me" instead. It's important to notice that basic statements tend to work okay, whereas questions or more elaborate statements can fail. However, for your bot's purposes, the basic substitutions suffice.

If you were to focus solely on producing an accurate language processor, you could use tests such as these to guide your development, and you'll probably use this technique when developing libraries to deal with *edge cases* such as these in your own projects.

WordPlay's Source Code

Your nascent WordPlay library is complete, for now, and in a state that you can use its features to make your bot's source code simpler and easier to read. Next I'll present the source code for the library as is, as well as its associated unit test file. As an addition, the code also includes comments prior to each class and method definition, so that you can use RDoc to produce HTML documentation files, as covered in Chapter 8.

■**Note** Remember that source code for this book is available in the Source Code/Download area at http://www.apress.com, so it isn't necessary to type in code directly from the book.

---

wordplay.rb

Here's the code for the WordPlay library:

```
class String
  def sentences
    self.gsub(/\n|\r/, ' ').split(/\.\s*/)
  end
```

```ruby
  def words
    self.scan(/\w[\w\'\-]*/)
  end
end


class WordPlay
  def self.switch_pronouns(text)
    text.gsub(/\b(I am|You are|I|You|Me|Your|My)\b/i) do |pronoun|
      case pronoun.downcase
        when "i"
          "you"
        when "you"
          "me"
        when "me"
          "you"
        when "i am"
          "you are"
        when "you are"
          "i am"
        when "your"
          "my"
        when "my"
          "your"
      end
    end.sub(/^me\b/i, 'i')
  end

  def self.best_sentence(sentences, desired_words)
    ranked_sentences = sentences.sort_by do |s|
      s.words.length - (s.downcase.words - desired_words).length
    end

    ranked_sentences.last
  end
end
```

test_wordplay.rb

Here's the test suite associated with the WordPlay library:

```ruby
require 'test/unit'
require 'wordplay'

# Unit testing class for the WordPlay library
class TestWordPlay < Test::Unit::TestCase

  # Test that multiple sentence blocks are split up into individual
  # words correctly
  def test_sentences
    assert_equal(["a", "b", "c d", "e f g"], "a. b. c d. e f g.".sentences)

    test_text = %q{Hello. This is a test
of sentence separation. This is the end
of the test.}
    assert_equal("This is the end of the test", test_text.sentences[2])
  end

  # Test that sentences of words are split up into distinct words correctly
  def test_words
    assert_equal(%w{this is a test}, "this is a test".words)
    assert_equal(%w{these are mostly words}, "these are, mostly, words".words)
  end

  # Test that the correct sentence is chosen, given the input
  def test_sentence_choice
    assert_equal('This is a great test',
                 WordPlay.best_sentence(['This is a test',
                                         'This is another test',
                                         'This is a great test'],
                                        %w{test great this}))
    assert_equal('This is a great test',
                 WordPlay.best_sentence(['This is a great test'],
                                        %w{still the best}))
  end

  # Test that basic pronouns are switched by switch_pronouns
  def test_basic_pronouns
    assert_equal("i am a robot", WordPlay.switch_pronouns("you are a robot"))
    assert_equal("you are a person", WordPlay.switch_pronouns("i am a person"))
```

```
    assert_equal("i love you", WordPlay.switch_pronouns("you love me"))
  end

  # Test more complex sentence switches using switch_pronouns
  def test_mixed_pronouns
    assert_equal("you gave me life",
                 WordPlay.switch_pronouns("i gave you life"))

    assert_equal("i am not what you are",
                 WordPlay.switch_pronouns("you are not what i am"))
  end

end
```

Building the Bot's Core

In the previous section you put together the WordPlay library to provide some features
you knew that your bot would need, such as basic sentence and word separation. Now
you can get on with the task of fleshing out the logic of the bot itself.

You'll create the bot within a Bot class, allowing you to create multiple bot instances
and assign them different names and datasets, and work with them separately. This is the
cleanest structure, as it allows you to keep the bot's logic separated from the logic of
interacting with the bot. For example, if your finished Bot class exists in bot.rb, writing a
Ruby program to allow a user to converse with the bot using the keyboard could be as
simple as this:

```
require 'bot'

bot = Bot.new(:name => "Botty", :data_file => "botty.bot")

puts bot.greeting
while input = gets and input.chomp != 'goodbye'
  puts ">> " + bot.response_to(input)
end
puts bot.farewell
```

You'll use this barebones client program as a yardstick while creating the Bot class. In
the previous example, you created a bot object and passed in some parameters, which
enables you to use the bot's methods, along with keyboard input, to make the bot converse with the user.

In certain situations it's useful to write an example of the higher-level, more-abstracted code that you expect ultimately to write, and then write the lower-level code to satisfy it. This isn't the same as test-first development, although the principle is similar. You write the easiest, most abstract code first, and then work your way down to the details.

Next let's look at how you expect the bot to operate throughout a normal session and then begin to develop the required features one by one.

The Program's Life Cycle and Parts

In Figure 12-2 we looked at what happens when a bot is asked to respond to some user input. In Figure 12-3, however, we look at the more overall life cycle of a bot, and the client accessing it, that we'll develop.

Your entire application will be composed of four parts:

1. The Bot class, within bot.rb, containing all the bot's logic and any subclasses.

2. The WordPlay library, within wordplay.rb, containing the WordPlay class and extensions to String.

3. Basic "client" applications that create bots and allows users to interact with them. You'll first create a basic keyboard-entry client, but we'll look at some alternatives later in the chapter.

4. A helper program to generate the bot's data files easily.

Figure 12-3 demonstrates the basic life cycle of a sample client application and its associated bot object. The client program creates a bot instance, and then keeps requesting user input passing it to the bot. Responses are printed to the screen, and the loop continues until the user decides to quit.

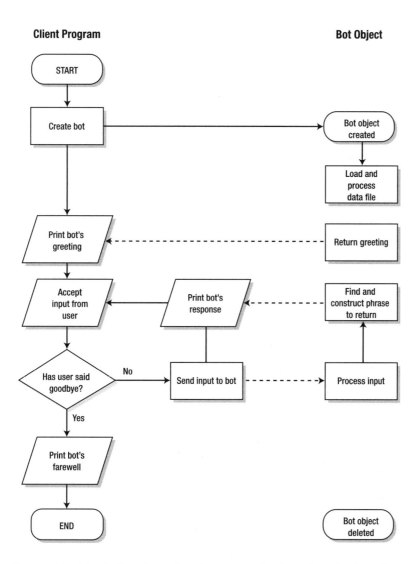

Figure 12-3. *A basic flowchart showing a sample life cycle of the bot client and bot object*

You'll begin putting together the Bot class and then look at how the bot will find and process its data.

Bot Data

One of your first concerns is where the bot will get its data. The bot's data includes information about word substitutions to perform during preprocessing, as well as myriad keywords and phrases that the bot can use in its responses.

The Data Structure

You'll keep the bot's data in a hash, somewhat like this:

```ruby
bot_data = {
  :presubs => [
    ["dont", "don't"],
    ["youre", "you're"],
    ["love", "like"]
  ],

  :responses => {
    :default   => [
                    "I don't understand.",
                    "What?",
                    "Huh?"
                  ],
    :greeting  => ["Hi. I'm [name]. Want to chat?"],
    :farewell  => ["Good bye!"],
    'hello'    => [
                    "How's it going?",
                    "How do you do?"
                  ],
    'i like *' => [
                    "Why do you like *?",
                    "Wow! I like * too!"
                  ]
  }
}
```

The main hash has two parent elements, :presubs and :responses. The :presubs element references an array of arrays that contain substitutions to be made to the user's input before the bot forms a response. In this instance, the bot will expand some contractions, and also change any reference of "love" to "like." The reason for this becomes clear when you look at :responses.

Note This data structure is deliberately lightly populated to save space for discussion of the practicalities. By the end of this chapter you'll have a more complete set of data to use with your bot. This style of data structure was also covered in Chapter 3.

`:responses` references another hash: one that has elements with the names `:default`, `:greeting`, `:farewell`, `'hello'`, and `'i like *'`. This hash contains all the different phrases the bot will use as responses, or templates used to create full phrases. The array assigned to `:default` contains some phrases to use at random when the bot cannot figure out what to say based on the input. Those associated with `:greeting` and `:farewell` contain generic greeting and farewell phrases.

More interesting are the arrays associated with `'hello'` and `'i like *'`. These phrases are used when the input matches the hash key for each array. For example, if a user says "hello computer," then a match with `'hello'` is made, and a response is chosen from the array at random. If a user says "i like computers," then `'i like *'` is matched and the asterisk is used to substitute the remainder of the user's input (after "i like") into the bot's output phrase. This could result in output such as "Wow! I like computers too," if the second phrase were to be used.

Storing the Data Externally

Using a hash makes data access easy (rather than relying on, say, a database) and fast when it comes to choosing sentences and performing matches. However, because your bot class needs to be able to deal with multiple datasets, it's necessary to store the hash of data for each bot within a file that can be chosen when a bot is started.

In Chapter 9 you learned about the concept of object persistence, where Ruby data structures can be "frozen" and stored. One library you used was called PStore, which stores Ruby data structures in a non-human-readable binary format, and the other was YAML, which is human-readable and represented as a specially formatted text file. For this project you'll use YAML, as you want to be able to make changes to the data files on the fly, to change things your bot will say, and to test out new phrases without constructing a whole new file each time.

It's possible to create your data files by hand and then let the Bot class load them in, but to make life easier, you'll create a small program that can create the initial data file for you, as you did in Chapter 9. An ideal name for it would be `bot_data_to_yaml.rb`:

```
require 'yaml'

bot_data = {
  :presubs => [
    ["dont", "don't"],
```

```
      ["youre", "you're"],
      ["love", "like"]
    ],

  :responses => {
    :default   => [
                    "I don't understand.",
                    "What?",
                    "Huh?"
                  ],
    :greeting  => ["Hi. I'm [name]. Want to chat?"],
    :farewell  => ["Good bye!"],
    'hello'    => [
                    "How's it going?",
                    "How do you do?"
                  ],
    'i like *' => [
                    "Why do you like *?",
                    "Wow! I like * too!"
                  ]
  }
}


# Show the user the YAML data for the bot structure
puts bot_data.to_yaml

# Write the YAML data to file
f = File.open(ARGV.first || 'bot_data', "w")
f.puts bot_data.to_yaml
f.close
```

This short program lets you define the bot data in the bot_data hash, and then shows the YAML representation on the screen before writing it to file. The filename is specified on the command line, or defaults to bot_data if none is supplied.

```
ruby bot_data_to_yaml.rb
```

```
---
:presubs:
- - dont
  - don't
```

```
- - youre
  - you're
- - love
  - like
:responses:
  i like *:
  - Why do you like *?
  - Wow! I like * too!
  :default:
  - I don't understand.
  - What?
  - Huh?
  hello:
  - How's it going?
  - How do you do?
  :greeting:
  - Hi. I'm [name]. Want to chat?
  :farewell:
  - Good bye!
```

Note that as the YAML data is plain text, you can edit it directly in the file, or just tweak the bot_data structure and re-run bot_data_to_yaml.rb. From here on out let's assume you've run this and generated the preceding YAML file as bot_data in the current directory.

Now that you have a basic data file, you need to construct the Bot class and get its initialize method to use it.

Constructing the Bot Class and Data Loader

Let's create bot.rb and the start of the Bot class:

```ruby
require 'yaml'
require 'wordplay'

class Bot
  attr_reader :name

  def initialize(options)
    @name = options[:name] || "Unnamed Bot"
    begin
      @data = YAML.load(File.read(options[:data_file]))
```

```
    rescue
      raise "Can't load bot data"
    end
  end
end
```

The `initialize` method sets up each newly created object and uses the `options` hash to populate two class variables, `@name` and `@data`. External access to `@name` is provided courtesy of `attr_reader`. `File.open`, along with the `read` method, opens the data file and reads in the full contents to be processed by the YAML library. `YAML.load` converts the YAML data into the original hash data structure and assigns it to the `@data` class variable. If the data file opening or YAML processing fails, an exception is raised, as the bot cannot function without data.

Now you can create the `greeting` and `farewell` methods that display a random greeting and farewell message from the bot's data set. These methods are used when people first start to use the bot or just before the bot client exits.

```
def greeting
  @data[:responses][:greeting][rand(@data[:responses][:greeting].length)]
end
```

```
def farewell
  @data[:responses][:farewell][rand(@data[:responses][:farewell].length)]
end
```

Ouch! This isn't nice at all. You have access to the greetings (and farewells) via `@data[:responses]`, but selecting a single random phrase gets ugly fast. This looks like an excellent opportunity to create a private method that retrieves a random phrase from a selected response group:

private

```
def random_response(key)
  random_index = rand(@data[:responses][key].length)
  @data[:responses][key][random_index].gsub(/\[name\]/, @name)
end
```

This method simplifies the routine of taking a random phrase from a particular phrase set in `@data`. The second line of `random_response` performs a substitution so that any responses that contain [name] have [name] substituted for the bot's name. For example, one of the demo greeting phrases is "Hi. I'm [name]. Want to chat?" However, if you created the bot object and specified a name of "Fred," the output would appear as "Hi. I'm Fred. Want to chat?"

> **Note** Remember that a private method is a method that cannot be called from outside the class itself. As `random_response` is only needed internally to the class, it's a perfect candidate to be a private method.

Let's update `greeting` and `farewell` to use `random_response`:

```
def greeting
  random_response :greeting
end

def farewell
  random_response :farewell
end
```

Isn't separating common functionality into distinct methods great? These methods now look a lot simpler and make immediate sense compared to the jumble they contained previously.

> **Note** This technique is also useful in situations where you have "ugly" or complex-looking code and you simply want to hide it inside a single method you can call from anywhere. Keep complex code in the background and make the rest of the code look as simple as possible.

The response_to Method

The core of the `Bot` class is the `response_to` method. It's used to pass user input to the bot and get the bot's response in return. However, the method itself should be simple and have one line per required operation to call private methods that perform each step.

   `respond_to` must perform several actions:

1. Accept the user's input.

2. Perform preprocessing substitutions, as described in the bot's data file.

3. Split the input into sentences and choose the most keyword-rich sentence.

4. Search for matches against the response phrase set keys.

5. Perform pronoun switching against the user input.

6. Pick a random phrase that matches (or a default phrase if there are no matches) and perform any substitutions of the user input into the result.

7. Return the completed output phrase.

Let's look at each action in turn.

Accepting Input and Performing Substitutions

First, you accept the input as a basic argument to the `response_to` method:

```
def response_to(input)
end
```

Then you move on to performing the preprocessing word and phrase substitutions as dictated by the `:presubs` array in the bot data file. You'll recall the `:presubs` array is an array of arrays that specifies words and phrases that should be changed to another word or phrase. The reason for this is so that you can deal with multiple terms with a single phrase. For example, if you substitute all instances of "yeah" for "yes," a relevant phrase will be shown whether the user says "yeah" or "yes," even though the phrase is only matching on "yes."

As you're focusing on keeping `response_to` simple, you'll use a single method call:

```
def response_to(input)
  prepared_input = preprocess(input).downcase
end
```

Now you can implement `preprocess` as a private method:

private

```
def preprocess(input)
  perform_substitutions input
end
```

Then you can implement the substitution method itself:

```
def perform_substitutions(input)
  @data[:presubs].each { |s| input.gsub!(s[0], s[1]) }
  input
end
```

This code loops through each substitution defined in the `:presubs` array and uses `gsub!` on the input.

At this point it's worth wondering why you have a string of methods just to get to the `perform_substitutions` method. Why not just call it directly from `response_to`?

The rationale in this case is that you're trying to keep logic separated from other logic within this program as much as possible. This is how larger applications work, as it allows you to extend them more easily. For example, if you wanted to perform more preprocessing tasks in future, you could simply create methods for them and call them from `preprocess` without having to make any changes to `response_to`. Although this looks inefficient, it actually results in code that's easy to extend and read in the long run. A little verbosity is the price for a lot of flexibility. You'll see a lot of similar techniques used in other Ruby programs, which is why it's demonstrated so forcefully here.

Choosing the Best Sentence

After you have the preprocessed input at your disposal, it's time to split it up into sentences and choose the best one. You can add another line to `response_to`:

```ruby
def response_to(input)
  prepared_input = preprocess(input.downcase)
  sentence = best_sentence(prepared_input)
end
```

Then you can implement `best_sentence` as a private method:

```ruby
def best_sentence(input)
  hot_words = @data[:responses].keys.select do |k|
    k.class == String && k =~ /^\w+$/
  end

  WordPlay.best_sentence(input.sentences, hot_words)
end
```

First, `best_sentence` collects an array of single words from the keys in the `:responses` hash. It looks for all keys that are strings (you don't want the `:default`, `:greeting`, or `:farewell` symbols getting mixed in) and only a single word. You then use this list with the `WordPlay.best_sentence` method you developed earlier in this chapter to choose the sentence from the user input that matches the most "hot words" (if any).

You could rewrite this method in any style you wish. If you only ever wanted to choose the *first* sentence in the user input, that's easy to do:

```ruby
def best_sentence(input)
  input.sentences.first
end
```

Or how about the longest sentence?

```ruby
def best_sentence(input)
  input.sentences.sort_by { |s| s.length }.last
end
```

Again, by having the tiny piece of logic of choosing the best sentence in a separate method, you can change the way the program works without meddling with larger methods.

Looking for Matching Phrases

Now you have the sentence you want to parse and the substitutions have been performed. The next step is to find the phrases that are suitable as responses to the chosen sentence and to pick one at random.

Let's extend response_to again:

```ruby
def response_to(input)
  prepared_input = preprocess(input.downcase)
  sentence = best_sentence(prepared_input)
  responses = possible_responses(sentence)
end
```

And implement possible_responses:

```ruby
def possible_responses(sentence)
  responses = []

  # Find all patterns to try to match against
  @data[:responses].keys.each do |pattern|
    next unless pattern.is_a?(String)

    # For each pattern, see if the supplied sentence contains
    # a match. Remove substitution symbols (*) before checking.
    # Push all responses to the responses array.
    if sentence.match('\b' + pattern.gsub(/\*/, '') + '\b')
      responses << @data[:responses][pattern]
    end
  end

  # If there were no matches, add the default ones
  responses << @data[:responses][:default] if responses.empty?
```

```
  # Flatten the blocks of responses to a flat array
  responses.flatten
end
```

possible_responses accepts a single sentence, then uses the string keys within the :responses hash to check for matches. Whenever the sentence has a match with a key from :responses, the various suitable responses are pushed onto the responses array. This array is flattened so a single array is returned.

If no specifically matched responses are found, the default ones (found in :responses with the :default key) are used.

Putting Together the Final Phrase

You now have all the pieces available in response_to to put together the final response. Let's choose a random phrase from responses to use:

```
def response_to(input)
  prepared_input = preprocess(input.downcase)
  sentence = best_sentence(prepared_input)
  responses = possible_responses(sentence)
  responses[rand(responses.length)]
end
```

If you weren't doing any substitutions against the pronoun-switched sentence, this version of response_to would be the final one. However, your bot has the capability to use some of the user's input in its responses. A section of your dummy bot data looked like this:

```
'i like *' => [
              "Why do you like *?",
              "Wow! I like * too!"
            ]
```

This rule matches when the user says "I like." The first possible response—"Why do you like *?"—contains an asterisk symbol that you'll use to substitute in part of the user's sentence in conjunction with the pronoun-switching method you developed in WordPlay earlier.

For example, a user might say, "I like to talk to you." If the pronouns were switched you'd get "You like to talk to me." If the segment following "You like" were substituted into the first possible response, you'd end up with "Why do you like to talk to me?" This is a great response that compels the user to continue typing and demonstrates the power of the pronoun-switching technique.

Therefore, if the chosen response contains an asterisk (the character you're using as a placeholder in response phrases), you'll need to substitute in the relevant part of the original sentence into the phrase and perform pronoun switching on that part.

Here's the new version of `possible_responses` with the changes in bold:

```ruby
def possible_responses(sentence)
  responses = []

# Find all patterns to try to match against
  @data[:responses].keys.each do |pattern|
    next unless pattern.is_a?(String)

    # For each pattern, see if the supplied sentence contains
    # a match. Remove substitution symbols (*) before checking.
    # Push all responses to the responses array.
    if sentence.match('\b' + pattern.gsub(/\*/, '') + '\b')
      # If the pattern contains substitution placeholders,
      # perform the substitutions
      if pattern.include?('*')
        responses << @data[:responses][pattern].collect do |phrase|
          # First, erase everything before the placeholder
          # leaving everything after it
          matching_section = sentence.sub(/^.*#{pattern}\s+/, '')

          # Then substitute the text after the placeholder, with
          # the pronouns switched
          phrase.sub('*', WordPlay.switch_pronouns(matching_section))
        end
      else
        # No placeholders? Just add the phrases to the array
        responses << @data[:responses][pattern]
      end
    end
  end

  # If there were no matches, add the default ones
  responses << @data[:responses][:default] if responses.empty?

  # Flatten the blocks of responses to a flat array
  responses.flatten
end
```

This new version of `possible_responses` checks to see if the pattern contains an asterisk, and if so, extracts the correct part of the source sentence to use into `matching_section`, switches the pronouns on that section, and then substitutes that into each relevant phrase.

Playing with the Bot

You have the basic methods implemented in the `Bot` class, so let's play with it as-is before looking at extending it any further. The first step is to prepare a better set of data for the bot to use so that your conversations can be more engaging than those with the dummy test data shown earlier in this chapter.

Fred: Your Bot's Personality

In this section you're going to tweak the `bot_data_to_yaml.rb` script you created earlier to generate a YAML file for your first bot to use. Its name will be Fred and you'll generate a bot data file called `fred.bot`. Here's `bot_data_to_yaml.rb` extended with a better set of phrases and substitutions:

```ruby
require 'yaml'

bot_data = {
  :presubs => [
    ["dont", "do not"],
    ["don't", "do not"],
    ["youre", "you're"],
    ["love", "like"],
    ["apologize", "are sorry"],
    ["dislike", "hate"],
    ["despise", "hate"],
    ["yeah", "yes"],
    ["mom", "family"]
  ],

  :responses => {
    :default    => [
                    "I don't understand.",
                    "What?",
                    "Huh?",
                    "Tell me about something else.",
                    "I'm tired of this. Change the subject."
                   ],
```

```ruby
  :greeting    => [
                    "Hi. I'm [name]. Want to chat?",
                    "What's on your mind today?",
                    "Hi. What would you like to talk about?"
                  ],
  :farewell    => ["Good bye!", "Au revoir!"],
  'hello'      => [
                    "How's it going?",
                    "How do you do?",
                    "Enough of the pleasantries!"
                  ],
  'sorry'      => ["There's no need to apologize."],
  'different'  => [
                    "How is it different?",
                    "What has changed?"
                  ],
  'everyone *' => ["You think everyone *?"],
  'do not know'=> ["Are you always so indecisive?"],
  'yes'        => [
                    "At least you're positive about something!",
                    "Great."
                  ],
  'family'     => ["Tell me about your family"],
  'you are *'  => [
                    "What makes you think I am *?",
                    "Are you so sure I am *?"
                  ],
  'i am *'     => [
                    "Is it normal for you to be *?",
                    "Do you like being *?"
                  ],
  'i do not *' => ["Why don't you *?"],
  'what'       => ["Why do you ask?", "Why?", "I don't know. Do you?"],
  'no'         => [
                    "Really?",
                    "Fair enough."
                  ],
  'why does *' => [
                    "I don't know why *",
                    "Do you already know the answer?"
                  ],
  'why can\'t i *' => ["Do you want to *?"],
```

```
        'why can\'t you *' => ["Do you want me to *?"],
        'hates *'     => [
                        "Why do you think they hate *?"
                        ],
        'hate *'      => [
                        "Why don't you like *?",
                        "Why the dislike of *?"
                        ],
        'i like *'    => [
                        "Why do you like *?",
                        "Wow! I like * too!"
                        ]
    }
}


# Show the user the YAML data for the bot structure
puts bot_data.to_yaml

# Write the YAML data to file
f = File.open(ARGV.first || 'bot_data', "w")
f.puts bot_data.to_yaml
f.close
```

If you run this with `ruby bot_data_to_yaml.rb fred.bot`, you'll end up with a bot data file called `fred.bot` that contains the necessary data to converse with a basic bot.

The First Real Conversation

Here's a basic program that can use the Bot class, which reads input from the keyboard and prints the bot's responses to the screen:

```
require 'bot'

bot = Bot.new(:name => 'Fred', :data_file => 'fred.bot')

puts bot.greeting

while input = gets and input.chomp != 'end'
  puts '>> ' + bot.response_to(input)
end

puts bot.farewell
```

It's almost the same as the script we thought of before implementing the Bot class. You used the method names dictated by that program and made it fit. (The completed source for the Bot class is provided in the next section if you want to refer to it.)

Without further ado, give it a try and see if you can have a conversation. Here's a demonstration run:

```
Hi. What would you like to talk about?
I don't know
>> Are you always so indecisive?
Yes, usually
>> Great.
I'm sorry!
>> There's no need to apologize.
So why can't you talk to me properly?
>> Do you want me to talk to you properly?
Yes
>> At least you're positive about something!
I don't know about that
>> Are you always so indecisive?
Woe is me, why can't I make decisions?
>> Do you want to make decisions?
Everyone does
>> You think everyone does?
```

Your bot works! The conversation might be a little stilted and manipulated to use some of the phrases and words covered by your data set, but with this basic mechanism, and a data set extended even further, significantly more complex conversations would be possible. Unfortunately, it's outside the scope of this book to provide a large data set.

In the next section the final code for the basic bot is presented, and then you'll see how you can extend the bot's functionality further.

Main Bot Code Listings

This section makes available the full source code to the Bot class, bot.rb, including extra documentation that RDoc can use. Also included is the source to a basic bot client that you can use to converse with a bot on a one-on-one basis using the keyboard from the command line.

As this code is commented, as opposed to the examples so far in this chapter, I recommend you at least browse through the following code to get a feel for how the entire program operates as a set of parts.

■**Note** You can also find these listings available to download in the Source Code/Download area of
http://www.apress.com/.

bot.rb

Here's the source code for the main Bot class:

```ruby
require 'yaml'
require 'wordplay'

# A basic implementation of a chatterbot
class Bot
  attr_reader :name

  # Initializes the bot object, loads in the external YAML data
  # file and sets the bot's name. Raises an exception if
  # the data loading process fails.
  def initialize(options)
    @name = options[:name] || "Unnamed Bot"
    begin
      @data = YAML.load(File.open(options[:data_file]).read)
    rescue
      raise "Can't load bot data"
    end
  end

  # Returns a random greeting as specified in the bot's data file
  def greeting
    random_response(:greeting)
  end

  # Returns a random farewell message as specified in the bot's
  # data file
  def farewell
    random_response(:farewell)
  end

  # Responds to input text as given by a user
  def response_to(input)
```

```ruby
    prepared_input = preprocess(input.downcase)
    sentence = best_sentence(prepared_input)
    reversed_sentence = WordPlay.switch_pronouns(sentence)
    responses = possible_responses(sentence)
    responses[rand(responses.length)]
  end


  private

  # Chooses a random response phrase from the :responses hash
  # and substitutes metadata into the phrase
  def random_response(key)
    random_index = rand(@data[:responses][key].length)
    @data[:responses][key][random_index].gsub(/\[name\]/, @name)
  end

  # Performs preprocessing tasks upon all input to the bot
  def preprocess(input)
    perform_substitutions(input)
  end

  # Substitutes words and phrases on supplied input as dictated by
  # the bot's :presubs data
  def perform_substitutions(input)
    @data[:presubs].each { |s| input.gsub!(s[0], s[1]) }
    input
  end

  # Using the single word keys from :responses, we search for the
  # sentence that uses the most of them, as it's likely to be the
  # 'best' sentence to parse
  def best_sentence(input)
    hot_words = @data[:responses].keys.select do |k|
      k.class == String && k =~ /^\w+$/
    end

    WordPlay.best_sentence(input.sentences, hot_words)
  end
```

```ruby
# Using a supplied sentence, go through the bot's :responses
# data set and collect together all phrases that could be
# used as responses
def possible_responses(sentence)
  responses = []

  # Find all patterns to try to match against
  @data[:responses].keys.each do |pattern|
    next unless pattern.is_a?(String)

    # For each pattern, see if the supplied sentence contains
    # a match. Remove substitution symbols (*) before checking.
    # Push all responses to the responses array.
    if sentence.match('\b' + pattern.gsub(/\*/, '') + '\b')
      # If the pattern contains substitution placeholders,
      # perform the substitutions
      if pattern.include?('*')
        responses << @data[:responses][pattern].collect do |phrase|
          # First, erase everything before the placeholder
          # leaving everything after it
          matching_section = sentence.sub(/^.*#{pattern}\s+/, '')

          # Then substitute the text after the placeholder, with
          # the pronouns switched
          phrase.sub('*', WordPlay.switch_pronouns(matching_section))
        end
      else
        # No placeholders? Just add the phrases to the array
        responses << @data[:responses][pattern]
      end
    end
  end

  # If there were no matches, add the default ones
  responses << @data[:responses][:default] if responses.empty?

  # Flatten the blocks of responses to a flat array
  responses.flatten
end

end
```

basic_client.rb

This basic client accepts input from the user via the keyboard and prints the bot's responses back to the screen. This is the simplest form of client possible.

```
require 'bot'

bot = Bot.new(:name => ARGV[0], :data_file => ARGV[1])

puts bot.greeting

while input = $stdin.gets and input.chomp != 'end'
  puts '>> ' + bot.response_to(input)
end

puts bot.farewell
```

Use the client like so:

```
ruby basic_client.rb <bot name> <data file>
```

■**Note** You can find listings for basic Web, bot-to-bot, and text file clients in the next section of this chapter, "Extending the Bot."

Extending the Bot

One significant benefit of keeping all your bot's functionality well separated within its own class and with multiple interoperating methods is that you can tweak and add functionality easily. In this section we're going to look at some ways we can easily extend the basic bot's functionality to handle other input sources than just the keyboard.

When you began to create the core Bot class, you looked at a sample client application that accepted input from the keyboard, passed it on to the bot, and printed the response. This simple structure demonstrated how abstracting separate sections of an application into loosely coupled classes makes applications easier to amend and extend. You can use this loose coupling to create clients that work with other forms of input.

■**Note** When designing larger applications, it's useful to keep in mind the usefulness of loosely coupling the different sections so that if the specifications or requirements change over time, it doesn't require a major rewrite of any code to achieve the desired result.

Using Text Files As a Source of Conversation

You could create an entire one-sided conversation in a text file and pass it in to a bot to test how different bots respond to the same conversation. Consider the following example:

```
require 'bot'

bot = Bot.new(:name => ARGV[0], :data_file => ARGV[1])
user_lines = File.readlines(ARGV[2], 'r')

puts "#{bot.name} says: " + bot.greeting

user_lines.each do |line|
  puts "You say: " + line
  puts "#{bot.name} says:" + bot.response_to(line)
end
```

This program accepts the bot's name, data filename, and conversation filename as command line arguments, reads in the user-side conversation into an array, and loops through the array, passing each line to the bot in turn.

Connecting the Bot to the Web

One common thing to do with many applications is to tie them up to the Web so that anyone can use them. This is a reasonably trivial process using the WEBrick library covered in Chapter 10.

```
require 'webrick'
require 'bot'

# Class that responds to HTTP/Web requests and interacts with the bot
class BotServlet < WEBrick::HTTPServlet::AbstractServlet
```

```ruby
  # A basic HTML template consisting of a basic page with a form
  # and text entry box for the user to converse with our bot. It uses
  # some placeholder text (%RESPONSE%) so the bot's responses can be
  # substituted in easily later.
  @@html = %q{
<html><body>
  <form method="get">
    <h1>Talk To A Bot</h1>
    %RESPONSE%
    <p>
      <b>You say:</b> <input type="text" name="line" size="40" />
      <input type="submit" />
    </p>
  </form>
</body></html>
  }

  def do_GET(request, response)
    # Mark the request as successful and set MIME type to support HTML
    response.status = 200
    response.content_type = "text/html"

    # If the user supplies some text, respond to it
    if request.query['line'] && request.query['line'].length > 1
      bot_text = $bot.response_to(request.query['line'].chomp)
    else
      bot_text = $bot.greeting
    end

    # Format the text and substitute into the HTML template
    bot_text = %Q{<p><b>I say:</b> #{bot_text}</p>}
    response.body = @@html.sub(/\%RESPONSE\%/, bot_text)
  end
end

# Create an HTTP server on port 1234 of the local machine
# accessible via http://localhost:1234/ or http://127.0.0.1:1234/
server = WEBrick::HTTPServer.new( :Port => 1234 )
$bot = Bot.new(:name => "Fred", :data_file => "fred.bot")
server.mount "/", BotServlet
trap("INT"){ server.shutdown }
server.start
```

Upon running this script, you can talk to the bot using your Web browser by visiting
`http://127.0.0.1:1234/` or `http://localhost:1234/`. An example of what this should look
like is shown in Figure 12-4.

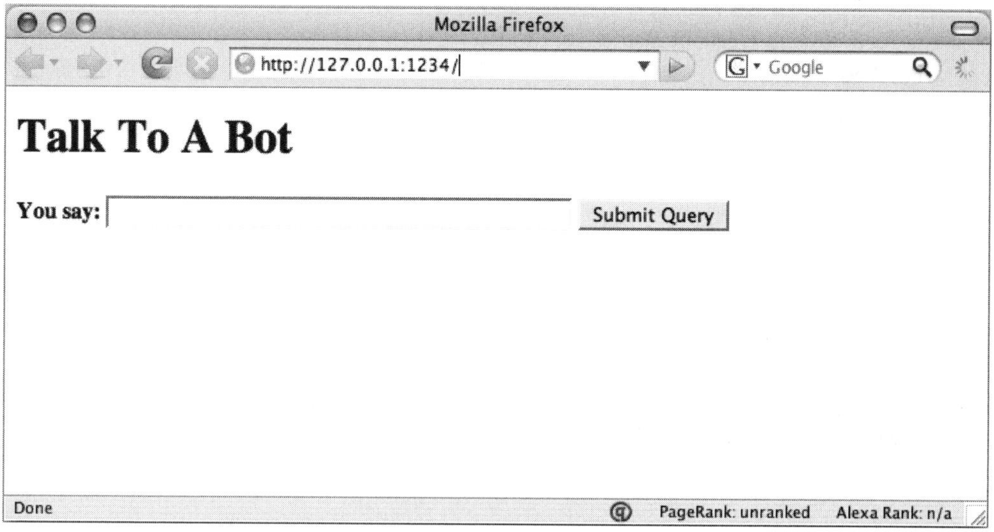

Figure 12-4. *Accessing the bot Web client with a Web browser*

Alternatively, you could create a CGI script (called `bot.cgi`, or similar) that could be
used with any Web hosting provider that provides Ruby as a supported language:

```ruby
#!/usr/bin/env ruby

require 'bot'
require 'cgi'

# A basic HTML template creating a basic page with a forum and text
# entry box for the user to converse with our bot. It uses some
# placeholder text (%RESPONSE%) so the bot's responses can be
# substituted in easily later
html = %q{
  <html><body>
    <form method="get">
      <h1>Talk To A Bot</h1>
      %RESPONSE%
      <p>
        <b>You say:</b> <input type="text" name="line" size="40" />
        <input type="submit" />
```

```
      </p>
    </form>
  </body></html>
}


# Set up the CGI environment and make the parameters easy to access
cgi = CGI.new
params = cgi.params
line = params['line'] && params['line'].first


bot = Bot.new(:name => "Fred", :data_file => "fred.bot")


# If the user supplies some text, respond to it
if line && line.length > 1
  bot_text = bot.response_to(line.chomp)
else
  bot_text = bot.greeting
end


# Format the text and substitute into the HTML template
# as well as sending the MIME header for HTML support
bot_text = %Q{<p><b>I say:</b> #{bot_text}</p>}
puts "Content-type: text/html\n\n"
puts html.sub(/\%RESPONSE\%/, bot_text)
```

■**Note** You also need to make sure you upload the `bot.rb`, `wordplay.rb`, and bot data file(s).

Bot-to-Bot Conversations

As well as letting users interact with the bot, you can let bots interact with *each other*!
Because it only takes a single method on the bot instance to elicit a response, you can
pipe responses back and forth between two bots with just a few lines of code:

```
require 'bot'

fred = Bot.new(:name => 'Fred', :data_file => 'fred.bot')
chris = Bot.new(:name => 'Chris', :data_file => 'fred.bot')
```

```
r = fred.greeting
10.times do
  puts "#{fred.name} said: " + r
  r = chris.response_to(r)
  puts "#{chris.name} said: " + r
  r = fred.response_to(r)
end
```

This could result in the following conversation (it will vary due to the randomness of some of the multiple responses available in the data files):

```
Fred said: Hi. What would you like to talk about?
Chris said: Why?
Fred said: What?
Chris said: I don't know. Do you?
Fred said: What?
Chris said: Why do you ask?
Fred said: I don't understand.
Chris said: Tell me about something else.
Fred said: Tell me about something else.
Chris said: Tell me about something else.
Fred said: I'm tired of this. Change the subject.
Chris said: What?
Fred said: Why?
Chris said: Tell me about something else.
Fred said: I don't understand.
Chris said: What?
Fred said: Why do you ask?
Chris said: What?
Fred said: Why?
Chris said: Huh?
```

It's not the greatest conversation ever seen, but it's certainly entertaining to see two ersatz therapists getting along with each other. Of course, if you manage to develop two bots that actually have an engrossing conversation, you'll be on the path to artificial-intelligence stardom!

The key problem with your bot's data is that none of the default data contains any keywords that can be picked up by other phrases, so both bots are locked in a loop of throwing default phrases at each other. That's why it's important to extend the basic set of data if you want to use the bot for anything that looks impressive!

Summary

In this chapter we looked at developing a simple chatterbot, and developed a library along the way, produced tests for the library, worked with storing our bot's vocabulary in an external file, and looked at a number of ways to extend our project with databases or by hooking it up to a Web site.

This chapter marks the end of the second part of this book, and you should now have enough Ruby knowledge to pass as a solid, intermediate Ruby developer. You should be able to understand the majority of Ruby documentation available online and be able to use Ruby productively either professionally or for fun.

Part 3 of this book digs a little deeper into Ruby's libraries and frameworks, from Ruby on Rails and the Web, to general networking and library use. Chapter 16, which looks at a plethora of different Ruby libraries and how to use them, will be particularly useful to rcfcr to as you develop your own programs, so that you don't reinvent the wheel too often!

PART 3

■ ■ ■

Ruby Online

This part of the book looks at Ruby's Internet and networking abilities. The knowledge covered in this part of the book is not essential for developing general Ruby applications, but as the Internet and the Web are becoming rapidly more important in the scope of modern software development, you're sure to find these chapters useful. This part of the book concludes with a reference-style chapter that covers a swathe of Ruby libraries and the features they offer.

CHAPTER 13

■■■

Ruby on Rails: Ruby's Killer App

In this chapter we're going to look at the *Ruby on Rails* framework, a cutting-edge Web application development framework. We'll walk through developing a basic Rails application and getting it running with a database, before looking at a few more-advanced Web development topics.

Although this book is a Ruby book, rather than a *Rails* (as Ruby on Rails is known in its shortened form) book, Rails has become such an important part of the Ruby world that it demands attention even in a beginner's guide such as this. However, Apress does have a selection of books specifically about Ruby on Rails and Web development available, if you wish to progress further down this line of development.

First Steps

Before you can begin to develop Web applications using Rails, it's essential first to know what it is and why it's used, as well as how to get it running, as its installation process is more involved than that of other Ruby libraries.

What Is Rails and Why Use It?

Ruby on Rails is an open source Web application development framework. It makes the development of Web applications simple. For some of the nontechnical history behind Rails, including the motivation for its development, refer to Chapter 5.

The goal of Rails is to make it possible to develop Web applications in an easy, straightforward manner, and with as few lines of code as necessary. By default, Rails makes a lot of assumptions and has a default configuration that works for most Web applications. Naturally, it's easy to override any defaults, but they are designed to keep initial application development simple.

Rails operates upon a *Model-View-Controller* (MVC) architectural pattern. This means that Rails applications are primarily split into three sections: models, views, and controllers. In Rails, these components have the following roles:

- *Models*: These are used to represent forms of data used by the application and contain the logic to manipulate and retrieve that data. In Rails, a model is represented as a class. You can think of models as abstracted, idealized interfaces between controller code and data.

- *Views*: These are the templates and HTML code that users of the Web application see. They turn data into a format that users can view. They can output data as HTML for Web browsers, XML, RSS, and other formats.

- *Controllers*: Controllers form the logic binding together models, data, and views. They process input and deliver data for output. Controllers call methods made available by models and deliver it to the views. Controllers contain methods known as *actions* that, generally, represent each action relevant to that controller, such as "show," "hide," "view," "delete," and so forth.

The basic relationship between these components is shown in Figure 13-1.

Note   You can learn more about the MVC paradigm at `http://en.wikipedia.org/wiki/Model-view-controller`.

The most common motivation to use Rails is that it removes a lot of the groundwork necessary to develop Web applications using other technologies. Features such as database access, dynamic page elements (using *Ajax*—Asynchronous JavaScript and XML), templating, and data validation are either preconfigured or take only a few lines of code to configure.

Rails also encourages good development practices. All Rails applications come with support for unit testing (among other forms of testing), and Rails' guiding principles are "Don't Repeat Yourself" (known as DRY) and "Convention Over Configuration."

User with Web Browser

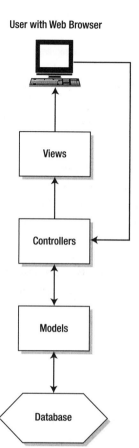

Figure 13-1. *The interactions between users, views, controllers, and models*

Installing Rails

The Rails framework is made up of several different libraries, but it's simple to install because all the parts are distributed as RubyGems. For completeness, though, the following is a list of Rails' constituent libraries:

- *Rails*: The core library of the Ruby on Rails framework that ties the other libraries together.

- *ActionMailer*: A library that makes it easy to send e-mail from Rails applications. A basic overview of ActionMailer, including how to use it to send mail separately from Rails, is given in Chapter 14.

- *ActionPack*: A library providing useful methods used in views and controllers to generate HTML and dynamic page elements, such as Ajax and JavaScript, or manage data objects.

- *ActionWebService*: Provides methods to make it easy to offer functionality from your Rails application as a Web service. This section of Rails is being removed as of Rails 1.2 in favor of alternative techniques, but it's mentioned here for completeness.

- *ActiveRecord*: An *object-relational mapper* (ORM) that ties database tables to classes. If you have an ActiveRecord object that references a row in a database table, you can work with that object as you would any other Ruby object (by using attributes and other methods), and changes will be stored in the relevant database table. A basic overview of ActiveRecord was given in Chapter 9.

- *ActiveSupport*: A library that collects a number of support and utility classes used by various Rails features. For example, ActiveSupport implements many useful methods for manipulating times, numbers, arrays, and hashes.

Generally you won't need to know or care about each of these elements as a discrete library because you can install them all at once using RubyGems, like so:

```
gem install rails
```

gem asks you if you want to install each of the libraries one by one (you can skip this by using `gem install --include-dependencies rails` instead), then gem installs each of them along with their documentation.

If you are confident about installing Ruby libraries by this point, these instructions might be enough for you to have a basic installation of the Rails framework in place. However, there are easier alternatives that can simplify the process in Windows or on Mac OS X.

Windows users can install *Instant Rails* (http://instantrails.rubyforge.org/), a one-stop Rails installation solution that includes Ruby, Rails, Apache, and MySQL, all preconfigured and ready to run "out of the box." These elements are kept separate from your usual installations, so you can begin developing Rails applications immediately. This system is ideal to tide you over if you have problems installing Rails and/or MySQL normally.

Mac users can install *Locomotive* (http://locomotive.raaum.org/), which provides the same features as Instant Rails, but on OS X. Locomotive will get your Mac running with Rails without breaking any existing configuration or tools you have installed.

Database Considerations

As Rails is used primarily to develop data-driven Web applications, it's necessary to have a database system available to use on your computer. Instant Rails and Locomotive users have MySQL installed automatically, but if you don't have a database system installed you'll need to obtain one.

Database engines are covered in Chapter 9, and you can use all those covered (MySQL, SQLite, PostgreSQL, Oracle, and Microsoft SQL Server) with Ruby on Rails. However, most developers use MySQL or PostgreSQL, as Rails supports these database engines best. You often have to make "hacks" and tweaks to have your Rails application work with other database engines, which are beyond the scope of this chapter.

This chapter assumes you have a MySQL server present on your local machine that Rails applications can use. If you don't, you can download and install the "community" edition of MySQL for free by visiting `http://dev.mysql.com/downloads/mysql/5.0.html`.

Building a Basic Rails Application

As explained in the previous section, Rails is popular because it makes developing Web applications easy. In this section I'll demonstrate that by showing you how to generate a basic Web application and looking through how it works.

Creating a Blank Rails Application

As you can use Rails to develop both small and large applications, different types of files are organized into different directories to keep elements separated for tidiness on large projects. A lot of pre-created files are also placed within a new, blank Rails project. The quickest way to look at these files and the overall directory structure is to leap right in and create a new Rails project.

Your project in this chapter will be to create a simplistic online diary system, similar to a blog (or weblog). The resulting application will let you view your diary, and add, delete, or edit specific entries. The basic features of being able to Create, Read, Update, and Delete items are known as CRUD features, and most types of Web applications feature CRUD mechanisms at one level or another. For example, a photo gallery site allows you to add, view, edit, and delete photos, which are all CRUD actions. Therefore, the mechanics of developing a basic diary tool are easily transferable to developing most other types of Web applications.

The rails Command Line Tool

When you installed Rails, a script called `rails` was also installed. You use the `rails` script to create new Rails projects, their default files, and their directory structure. To use it, navigate to a place in your filesystem where you would like to store Rails projects (possibly creating a `rails` directory in the process) and run `rails`, specifying an application name as the sole argument:

```
rails mydiary
```

```
      create
      create  app/controllers
      create  app/helpers
      create  app/models
      create  app/views/layouts
      create  config/environments
      create  components
      create  db
      create  doc
      create  lib
      create  lib/tasks
      create  log
      create  public/images
      create  public/javascripts
      create  public/stylesheets
      create  script/performance
      create  script/process
      create  test/fixtures
      create  test/functional
      create  test/integration
      create  test/mocks/development
      create  test/mocks/test
      create  test/unit
      create  vendor
      create  vendor/plugins
      create  tmp/sessions
      create  tmp/sockets
      create  tmp/cache
      create  Rakefile
      create  README
      create  app/controllers/application.rb
```

```
create  app/helpers/application_helper.rb
create  test/test_helper.rb
create  config/database.yml
create  config/routes.rb
create  public/.htaccess
create  config/boot.rb
create  config/environment.rb
create  config/environments/production.rb
create  config/environments/development.rb
create  config/environments/test.rb
create  script/about
create  script/breakpointer
create  script/console
create  script/destroy
create  script/generate
create  script/performance/benchmarker
create  script/performance/profiler
create  script/process/reaper
create  script/process/spawner
create  script/runner
create  script/server
create  script/plugin
create  public/dispatch.rb
create  public/dispatch.cgi
create  public/dispatch.fcgi
create  public/404.html
create  public/500.html
create  public/index.html
create  public/favicon.ico
create  public/robots.txt
create  public/images/rails.png
create  public/javascripts/prototype.js
create  public/javascripts/effects.js
create  public/javascripts/dragdrop.js
create  public/javascripts/controls.js
create  public/javascripts/application.js
create  doc/README_FOR_APP
create  log/server.log
create  log/production.log
create  log/development.log
create  log/test.log
```

A lot of files and directories are produced, but don't feel overwhelmed! You won't even use many of them in this chapter, as they are for more advanced uses that aren't relevant to basic Web application development. In most cases, Rails provides sane defaults anyway, so you don't need to change a lot of files unless you're doing something special. However, you'll explore what many of these directories are for in the following section.

■**Note** The exact file and directory structure might vary on your system depending on what version of Rails you're running. The preceding structure was generated by Rails 1.1.6, the official production release of Rails at the start of 2007.

Files and Directories Within a Rails Application

In this section we're going to go through the directories and files created by `rails` and look at what they're for. Don't become overwhelmed by this section. If there's something you don't understand, keep going, as most of the new terms and concepts mentioned here are explained as we use them throughout this chapter.

`rails` generates the following main folders:

- app: This folder contains most of the Ruby source code and output templates directly associated with the application. It contains several other folders that I'll cover next.

- app/controllers: Contains the controller files. In an empty project, only application.rb exists. application.rb is an application-wide controller where you can define methods that all other controllers inherit.

- app/helpers: Contains helper files—Ruby source code files that provide methods that you can use from views.

- app/models: Contains a file for each model in the application. In an empty project no models are yet defined, so this directory is empty.

- app/views: Contains the output templates (views) for the application. Typically each controller has its own folder under app/views, with templates located in those folders. There's also a layouts folder that Rails uses to store generic application-wide templates.

- components: Contains discrete MVC "component" applications. This feature isn't commonly used any more and is mostly there for historical reasons (indeed, this folder might not even be present in your Rails project depending on the version of Rails you're using). Plugins, covered at the end of this chapter, have largely replaced components.

- config: An important folder that contains configuration files for the application. database.yml is a YAML file with information about the database(s) that the application will use. environment.rb and boot.rb are prebuilt files that you usually won't need to edit, unless you want to tweak fine details of how your application is started. routes.rb is covered later in this chapter in the section "Routing."

- db: A folder to be used for database dumps, backups, and migrations.

- doc: Contains any RDoc documentation generated for the application. In an empty project it contains a basic text file called README_FOR_APP, which you can use as a plain-text documentation file, perhaps to contain instructions for others on how to install your app.

- lib: Contains third-party libraries and Rake tasks. You won't need to use this directory at all for most Rails application development. Plugins have largely superseded the features offered by libraries that were placed into lib.

- log: Contains log files relating to the operation of the application.

- public: Contains nondynamic files that are accessible under your application's URL scheme; for example, JavaScript libraries, images, and CSS stylesheets. This folder also includes several "dispatch" files and an .htaccess file that make it possible to set up your application to run under Web servers such as Apache and LightTPD.

- script: Contains scripts and command line tools that are used in constructing and deploying Rails applications. console is an irb-like tool that preloads your Rails application's environment before giving you a prompt. generate is a script that can generate certain types of Rails code for you from templates. server is used to run a basic WEBrick or LightTPD server you can use to access your application from a Web browser. The other scripts are not of any immediate use to you.

- test: Contains the test subsystems for a Rails application. This folder is covered in more detail later in this chapter in the "Testing" section.

- tmp: Temporary storage area for data created and used by your Rails application.

- vendor: This folder is used for storing versions of the Rails framework that your application is bound to, and for storing plugins (under the vendor/plugins directory).

I'll briefly mention many of these folders again throughout the rest of the chapter as you create files within them to get your basic application working.

Database Initialization

Earlier I said that Rails applications are generally database dependent. With this in mind, it's necessary to create a database for your application on your database server.

The technique you'll use to create a database for your application will vary with database type and how you have your database server installed. In this section I'll assume you have a MySQL server installed and have either downloaded a tool you can use to manage MySQL databases or have access to the standard MySQL command line client.

■**Note** If you're using a different type of database, you must refer to the documentation and programs associated with your database system and look up how to create a database and a log in to that database on your system.

From the command line MySQL client, it's quick and easy to create a database. Here's an example session showing you how to create a database and associate it with a username and password for future access:

```
~/rails/mydiary $ mysql -u root -p
Enter password:
Welcome to the MySQL monitor.  Commands end with ; or \g.
Your MySQL connection id is 10 to server version: 5.0.27-standard

Type 'help;' or '\h' for help. Type '\c' to clear the buffer.

mysql> CREATE DATABASE mydiary;
Query OK, 1 row affected (0.08 sec)

mysql> GRANT ALL PRIVILEGES ON mydiary.* TO mydiary@localhost➥
IDENTIFIED BY 'mypassword';
Query OK, 0 rows affected (0.30 sec)

mysql> QUIT
Bye
```

In this session you create a database called mydiary and then grant all the privileges to use that database to a user called mydiary with a password of mypassword. You can check that the database and the user was created successfully by using the MySQL command line client to access the mydiary database:

```
~/rails/mydiary $ mysql -u mydiary -p
Enter password: <type mypassword at this point>
Welcome to the MySQL monitor.  Commands end with ; or \g.
Your MySQL connection id is 12 to server version: 5.0.27-standard

Type 'help;' or '\h' for help. Type '\c' to clear the buffer.

mysql> QUIT
Bye
```

If MySQL gives no error, generally everything is okay. If you get an error saying that the username is invalid, then the granting of privileges in the prior section wasn't successful, so refer to any error messages that appeared at that point.

If you're using a GUI MySQL client or even a client for a totally different database system, make sure that you've created a database called mydiary and made it accessible to a user. Your client should allow you to test this easily.

Once the database has been created, you can tell your Rails application of its existence by editing the config/database.yml file. Here's what it contains by default for your empty application:

```
# MySQL (default setup).  Versions 4.1 and 5.0 are recommended.
#
# Install the MySQL driver:
#   gem install mysql
# On MacOS X:
#   gem install mysql -- --include=/usr/local/lib
# On Windows:
#   There is no gem for Windows.  Install mysql.so from RubyForApache.
#   http://rubyforge.org/projects/rubyforapache
#
# And be sure to use new-style password hashing:
#   http://dev.mysql.com/doc/refman/5.0/en/old-client.html
development:
  adapter: mysql
  database: mydiary_development
  username: root
  password:
  host: localhost

# Warning: The database defined as 'test' will be erased and
```

```
# regenerated from your development database when you run 'rake'.
# Do not set this db to the same as development or production.
test:
  adapter: mysql
  database: mydiary_test
  username: root
  password:
  host: localhost

production:
  adapter: mysql
  database: mydiary_production
  username: root
  password:
  host: localhost
```

Ignoring the comments, you'll notice three main sections in database.yml called "development," "test," and "production." These represent the three different *environments* your application can run under. For example, while developing, you want your application to return verbose error messages and automatically detect changes you make to the code. In production (better thought of as being a "deployment" environment) you want speed, caching, and nonverbose error messages. The test environment is provided so that testing can occur on a different database away from your regular data.

The section you're interested right now is the "development" section. You need to edit the details in this section to reflect those necessary to connect to the database you created previously. For example:

```
development:
  adapter: mysql
  database: mydiary
  username: mydiary
  password: mypassword
  host: localhost
```

Make the changes and save the file without changing anything else.

Creating a Model and Migrations

The last critical step before you can work on your application properly is to generate database tables to represent the models that your application will work upon. In this case we're going to keep it simple to start with and focus entirely on diary entries, so you'll call your database table entries.

In Rails, models and database tables generally have a direct relationship. If you have a database table called `entries`, then this will be directly related to a model class in your Rails application called `Entry`.

Note By default, table names are pluralized and model names are singular. Rails works out the conversion between singular and plural names automatically. However, it's possible to enforce table names manually to work under different situations (for example, using a table called `diary_entries` with a model class called `Entry`), but this is beyond the scope of this chapter.

You can create an `entries` table in your `mydiary` database in two ways at this point.

The first option is to use SQL through the MySQL command line client (or whatever alternative you're using) and generate a table by hand, like so:

```
CREATE TABLE entries (
  id int auto_increment,
  title varchar(255),
  content text,
  created_at datetime,
  PRIMARY KEY(id)
);
```

This SQL statement creates the `entries` table with four columns: an `id` column, a `title` column to store the title of the diary entry, a `content` column, and a `created_at` column that stores the date and time when the entry was created.

Creating tables with SQL or a GUI client works well, but a better alternative is to use a system Rails provides called *migrations*. Migrations provide a programmatic way to manage your database's schema and data. Migrations allow you to manage the evolution of your database's schema over time and give you the functionality to "roll back" your schema or create it all at once upon a new database.

Note Full information about migrations is available from `http://www.rubyonrails.org/api/classes/ActiveRecord/Migration.html`.

Let's create a migration that builds your `entries` table by using the `generate` script found in the `script` folder:

```
ruby script/generate migration AddEntriesTable
```

```
create  db/migrate
create  db/migrate/001_add_entries_table.rb
```

■**Note** On OS X and Linux, you might be able to use a shorter format to use scripts in the `script` folder, such as `./script/generate`. However, the preceding format is designed to work across platforms by referring to the Ruby interpreter explicitly.

generate has created the db/migrate folder for you (where all migrations are stored) and then created a Ruby file called 001_add_entries_table.rb where you can define what you want the database to do.

■**Note** Even though you used the name `AddEntriesTable` for this migration, it could, in effect, be almost anything. This was simply used because it's the common style for migration names.

Let's look at 001_add_entries_table.rb:

```
class AddEntriesTable < ActiveRecord::Migration
  def self.up
  end

  def self.down
  end
end
```

This is an empty migration featuring two methods, up and down. You use up to create things and perform operations necessary for the migration to work. You use down when "rolling back" from the state where a migration is finished back to how things were before the migration was run.

In the up method you'll use some methods Rails provides to generate the entries table, and in the down method you'll use a method to remove that table. The final 001_add_entries_table.rb looks like this:

```
class AddEntriesTable < ActiveRecord::Migration
  def self.up
    create_table :entries do |table|
      table.column :title, :string
```

```
      table.column :content, :text
      table.column :created_at, :datetime
    end
  end

  def self.down
    drop_table :entries
  end
end
```

In the up class method you use the `create_table` method to create the `entries` table, and within the code block you use the `column` method to create columns of varying types.

■**Note** You don't have to create the `id` column explicitly; this is done for you automatically.

To perform the migration (and therefore actually create the `entries` table using the migration), you use a *Rake task* (see the following "Rake Tasks" sidebar for more information about these) called `db:migrate`:

```
rake db:migrate
```

```
(in /Users/peter/rails/mydiary)
== AddEntriesTable: migrating ================================================
-- create_table(:entries)
   -> 0.3683s
== AddEntriesTable: migrated (0.3685s) =======================================
```

Each step of the migration is shown in the preceding results. The `AddEntriesTable` migration is run and the `entries` table created. No error messages are shown, and the `mydiary` database now contains an operational `entries` table.

RAKE TASKS

Rake tasks are administrative tasks associated with your application that are managed by the Rake tool. Rake, meaning "Ruby Make," is a tool that you can use to process and trigger actions to perform upon Ruby projects and code, and it's used commonly within Rails projects to do things such as start unit tests and perform migrations.

To perform a Rake task, you simply run `rake` followed by the name of a task:

```
rake <task name>
```

You can also get a list of all the Rake tasks available:

```
rake --tasks
```

With Rails 1.1.6, there are 41 tasks by default. To save space they aren't listed here, but it's worth looking through the list to get a feel for what tasks are available.

Migrations are generally preferred over performing SQL statements directly upon the database because they're mostly database independent (Rails outputs the correct SQL for the methods used within migrations for the database engine being used), and the database operations are stored in code rather than being ephemeral operations.

Migrations also make it easy to make changes to the database over time. For example, if you wanted to add another column to the `entries` table, you could simply create a new migration and use `add_column` and `remove_column` methods in the `up` and `down` methods of that new migration. For example:

```
ruby script/generate migration AddUpdatedAtColumnToEntries
```

```
exists  db/migrate
create  db/migrate/002_add_updated_at_column_to_entries.rb
```

Then you could write `002_add_updated_at_column_to_entries.rb` like so:

```ruby
class AddUpdatedAtColumnToEntries < ActiveRecord::Migration
  def self.up
    add_column :entries, :updated_at, :datetime
  end
```

```
  def self.down
    remove_column :entries, :updated_at
  end
end
```

Then put that migration into action:

```
rake db:migrate
```

```
(in /Users/peter/rails/mydiary)
== AddUpdatedAtColumnToEntries: migrating ======================================
-- add_column(:entries, :updated_at, :datetime)
   -> 0.2381s
== AddUpdatedAtColumnToEntries: migrated (0.2383s) =============================
```

The new migration adds an updated_at DATETIME column to the entries table.

If you wanted to, you could "roll back" this migration and go back to the state after the first migration by using this Rake task:

```
rake db:migrate VERSION=1
```

```
(in /Users/peter/rails/mydiary)
== AddUpdatedAtColumnToEntries: reverting ======================================
-- remove_column(:entries, :updated_at)
   -> 0.0535s
== AddUpdatedAtColumnToEntries: reverted (0.0536s) =============================
```

Note In some circumstances, migrations are created automatically and you simply need to fill them in. For example, if you use Rails' model generator, a migration is automatically created for creating the table associated with the newly generated model. In this chapter, however, we're working in the opposite direction. There's always more than one way to do it!

Scaffolding

In the last couple sections you've created a database and migrations to produce a working `entries` table. In this section you'll create enough code to make a basic Web application that can perform CRUD operations upon data in your `entries` table.

Rails provides a mechanism called *scaffolding* that generates default, generic code to provide CRUD operations for any of your models. You can then build your own views and controller methods off of this basic scaffolding. It's designed to give you a jump start without making you code everything from scratch (although you can code from scratch if you want to, particularly if your ambitions differ wildly from what the scaffolding provides).

To generate scaffolding for your `entries` table, use the `generate` script again:

```
ruby script/generate scaffold Entry
```

```
     exists  app/controllers/
     exists  app/helpers/
     create  app/views/entries
     exists  test/functional/
 dependency  model
     exists     app/models/
     exists     test/unit/
     exists     test/fixtures/
     create     app/models/entry.rb
     create     test/unit/entry_test.rb
     create     test/fixtures/entries.yml
     create  app/views/entries/_form.rhtml
     create  app/views/entries/list.rhtml
     create  app/views/entries/show.rhtml
     create  app/views/entries/new.rhtml
     create  app/views/entries/edit.rhtml
     create  app/controllers/entries_controller.rb
     create  test/functional/entries_controller_test.rb
     create  app/helpers/entries_helper.rb
     create  app/views/layouts/entries.rhtml
     create  public/stylesheets/scaffold.css
```

When creating scaffolding, Rails looks at the database table associated with the model you're building scaffolding for (the `entries` table for the `Entry` model, in this case) and generates a controller, views, and a model file reflecting the structure of the table. The generated files are shown in the preceding results listing.

■**Note** Scaffolding depends on the structure of the database table, so you must always create and run the table's migration before creating any scaffolding.

The scaffolding generator also creates a layout file, several test-related files, and a stylesheet used by the scaffolding layout. It also generates any missing directories needed.

That's all you have to do to get a working application! To try it out, you need to run the `server` script that provides a basic WEBrick Web server through which to access the application:

```
ruby script/server
```

```
=> Booting WEBrick...
=> Rails application started on http://0.0.0.0:3000
=> Ctrl-C to shutdown server; call with --help for options
[2007-03-19 19:37:48] INFO  WEBrick 1.3.1
[2007-03-19 19:37:48] INFO  ruby 1.8.5 (2006-08-32) [i686-darwin8.8.1]
[2007-03-19 19:37:48] INFO  WEBrick::HTTPServer#start: pid=10999 port=3000
```

At this point the application sits there doing nothing. This is because it's waiting for requests from Web browsers.

■**Note** If you have the Mongrel library installed, you can use that to serve the Rails application. Just run `mongrel_rails start` instead of `ruby script/server`.

Go to your Web browser of choice and access the application using the URL given by the WEBrick output (`http://0.0.0.0:3000/` in this case, but it might be `http://localhost:3000/` or `http://127.0.0.1:3000/` on your machine). You should see a page like the one in Figure 13-2.

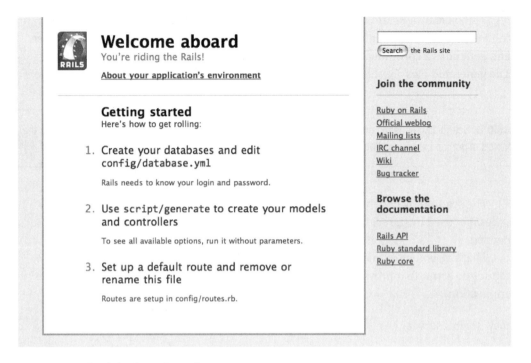

Figure 13-2. *The default Rails application* index.html *page*

The page you're seeing is the index.html file from the public folder. This is because if no action is found within a Rails application that associates with the URL you're loading from your Web browser, a Rails application should return a file from the public folder—if any file matches—or an error message. Because the default page to load on a Web server is usually index.html, public/index.html is returned.

When you generated the scaffolding for the Entry model, a controller called entries was created. By default, you access controller methods in a Rails application using a URL in the format of http://<hostname>/controller/action.

So, with your application, load http://localhost/entries (replace localhost with whatever hostname is used on your local machine). No action name is specified, but by default an action name of index is assumed, and the scaffolding has implemented this. If you're successful, you'll see a basic list of entries, as shown in Figure 13-3.

Listing entries

Title Content Created at

New entry

Figure 13-3. *The basic list or index view of the* entries *scaffolding*

The list of entries in Figure 13-3 is noticeably bare. This is because your entries table has no data contained within it. The column headings for your table are obvious, though (Title, Content, and Created at), and a "New entry" link is available.

Clicking "New entry" takes you to http://localhost/entries/new—the new method within the entries controller—and presents you with a page containing a form that allows you to fill out the data for a single entry. This view is demonstrated in Figure 13-4.

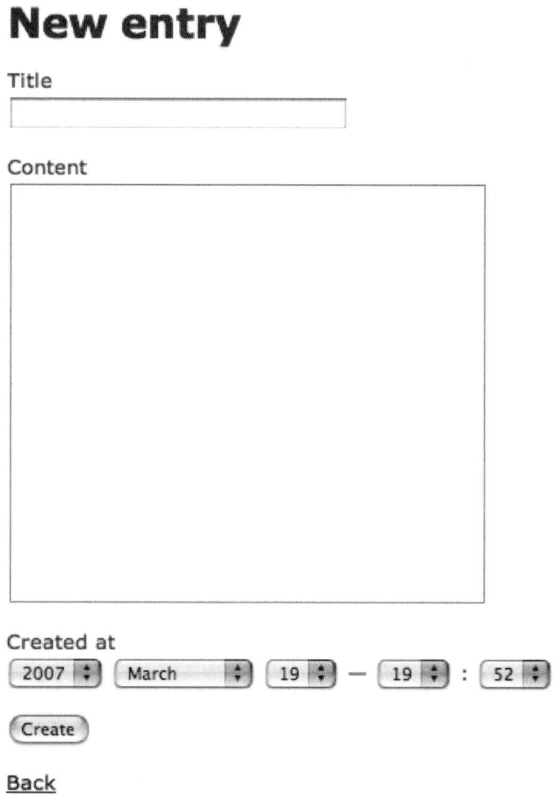

New entry

Title

Content

Created at
2007   March   19   —   19 : 52

Create

Back

Figure 13-4. *The* new *method of the* entries *controller, used to create new entries*

From this point you can create new entries, return to the list, edit those entries (the form looks similar to that in Figure 13-4) and delete entries. That covers all the CRUD functions!

With scaffolding you get a basic, but complete, data-driven Web application with just a single line typed at the command prompt. However, next you need to look at what the scaffolding generator actually generated, and learn how to customize the models, controllers, and views to create the application that you want.

Controllers and Views

In the last section you put together a basic Web application that allowed you to create, edit, list, and delete diary entries. You used scaffolding, which let you put a whole, working application together with no coding effort required. In this section, you're going to look at what the scaffolding generated, how it works, and how you can extend the application with your own methods and views.

Controller Actions

The first URL you accessed within your application was `http://localhost/entries/list`. This URL takes you to the `entries` controller's `list` method. Let's look in `app/controllers/entries_controller.rb` to find it:

```ruby
class EntriesController < ApplicationController
  def index
    list
    render :action => 'list'
  end

  # GETs should be safe (see http://www.w3.org/2001/tag/doc/whenToUseGet.html)
  verify :method => :post, :only => [ :destroy, :create, :update ],
         :redirect_to => { :action => :list }

  def list
    @entry_pages, @entries = paginate :entries, :per_page => 10
  end

  def show
    @entry = Entry.find(params[:id])
  end

  def new
    @entry = Entry.new
```

```
    end

    def create
      @entry = Entry.new(params[:entry])
      if @entry.save
        flash[:notice] = 'Entry was successfully created.'
        redirect_to :action => 'list'
      else
        render :action => 'new'
      end
    end

    def edit
      @entry = Entry.find(params[:id])
    end

    def update
      @entry = Entry.find(params[:id])
      if @entry.update_attributes(params[:entry])
        flash[:notice] = 'Entry was successfully updated.'
        redirect_to :action => 'show', :id => @entry
      else
        render :action => 'edit'
      end
    end

    def destroy
      Entry.find(params[:id]).destroy
      redirect_to :action => 'list'
    end
  end
end
```

This code shows that Ruby controllers are implemented as classes that inherit from ApplicationController (which is found in app/controllers/application.rb and in turn inherits from ActionController::Base), which in turn inherits from a core Rails class, ActionController::Base.

When a user tries to access the list method of the entries controller, control is delegated to the list method (or action) in the EntriesController class, shown on its own here:

```
def list
  @entry_pages, @entries = paginate :entries, :per_page => 10
end
```

This code is simple for what it does. It relies on a method provided by Rails called `paginate` that provides items from a particular model (in this case, entries) in groups of ten (in this instance). The reason for pagination is because if your system contained 1,000 entries, showing them all on one page would be cumbersome. However, the `paginate` method returns entries in groups of ten and recognizes a `page` variable passed from the Web browser (via the URL) so that the correct group of ten entries is shown.

However, you could rewrite the `list` method to load all the entries like so:

```
def list
  @entries = Entry.find(:all)
end
```

`Entry` is the model class, and models inherit from `ActiveRecord::Base`, which provides methods suitable to navigate and find data in the associated table for that model. Therefore, `Entry.find(:all)` returns all rows (as objects) from the `entries` table and places them as an array into `@entries`.

Views and Embedded Ruby

Now let's look at the equivalent view for the `list` controller action examined in the previous section. The view template is located in app/views/entries/list.rhtml:

```
<h1>Listing entries</h1>

<table>
  <tr>
  <% for column in Entry.content_columns %>
    <th><%= column.human_name %></th>
  <% end %>
  </tr>

<% for entry in @entries %>
  <tr>
  <% for column in Entry.content_columns %>
    <td><%=h entry.send(column.name) %></td>
  <% end %>
    <td><%= link_to 'Show', :action => 'show', :id => entry %></td>
    <td><%= link_to 'Edit', :action => 'edit', :id => entry %></td>
    <td><%= link_to 'Destroy', { :action => 'destroy', :id => entry },
                    :confirm => 'Are you sure?', :post => true %></td>
  </tr>
<% end %>
</table>
```

```
<%= link_to 'Previous page', { :page => @entry_pages.current.previous }
        if @entry_pages.current.previous %>
<%= link_to 'Next page', { :page => @entry_pages.current.next }
        if @entry_pages.current.next %>

<br />

<%= link_to 'New entry', :action => 'new' %>
```

If you're familiar with both Ruby and HTML, you'll note that this view is, basically, HTML with Ruby embedded in it (with the Ruby located between <% and %> tags).

■Note The file extension of HTML views that can have embedded Ruby is RHTML rather than HTML.

The first dynamic section of the preceding view looks like this:

```
<% for column in Entry.content_columns %>
  <th><%= column.human_name %></th>
<% end %>
```

This code works like a normal Ruby loop. The for loop iterates through the results of Entry.content_columns (an ActiveRecord method that returns each column as an object).

In your application's case, the column names are Title, Content, and Created at (*humanized* versions of the actual column names: title, content, and created_at), so the preceding loop, which uses each column's human_name method, results in the following HTML being generated and returned to the visiting Web browser:

```
<th>Title</th>
<th>Content</th>
<th>Created at</th>
```

The core part of the list view contains this code:

```
<% for entry in @entries %>
  <tr>
  <% for column in Entry.content_columns %>
    <td><%=h entry.send(column.name) %></td>
  <% end %>
    <td><%= link_to 'Show', :action => 'show', :id => entry %></td>
    <td><%= link_to 'Edit', :action => 'edit', :id => entry %></td>
    <td><%= link_to 'Destroy', { :action => 'destroy', :id => entry },
                    :confirm => 'Are you sure?', :post => true %></td>
  </tr>
<% end %>
```

This view code results in the primary part of the page being rendered: the actual list of entries. I won't go into this code line by line, but there a few key things to note. This whole section is a loop over each element of @entries (where for entry in @entries is an alternative way of saying @entries.each do |entry|). You should recall that your controller code placed Entry objects from the database into the @entries array, so the view code iterates over each element (or each entry). Next, within the main loop is another loop that iterates through each of the columns associated with each of these entries.

After the data for the entry has been shown, you reach this:

```
<td><%= link_to 'Show', :action => 'show', :id => entry %></td>
<td><%= link_to 'Edit', :action => 'edit', :id => entry %></td>
<td><%= link_to 'Destroy', { :action => 'destroy', :id => entry },
                      :confirm => 'Are you sure?', :post => true %></td>
```

The important parts to look at are the calls to the link_to method. link_to is a special method provided by Rails that generates an HTML link to another controller and/or action within the application. Let's look at the first line:

```
<td><%= link_to 'Show', :action => 'show', :id => entry %></td>
```

Whereas the general Ruby code in the view is located within <% and %> tags, Ruby code that results in something to be rendered in the document (that is, shown on the Web page) is included within <%= and %> tags. The link_to method accepts the text to use for the link, and then it accepts parameters, formatted as a hash, that represent where the eventual link is to point to. In this case, the link is created to point to the show method of the current controller (you could specify a different controller with an option such as :controller => 'controllername'), with an ID matching that of the current entry you're iterating over.

For example, let's assume entry refers to an Entry object with attributes and data, as such:

```
id: 3
title: Example Entry
content: This is an example entry.
```

At this point, entry.id is equal to 3, entry.title is equal to Example Entry, and entry.content is equal to This is an example entry.

Let's build up to the link_to example in a few steps showing some example view code and what it would render in this example:

```
<%= entry.id %>
```

```
<%= entry.content %>
```

```
This is an example entry.
```

```
<%= link_to 'Show', :action => 'show' %>
```

```
<a href="/entries/show">Show</a>
```

```
<%= link_to entry.title, :action => 'show', :id => entry.id %>
```

```
<a href="/entries/show/3">Example Entry</a>
```

```
<%= link_to 'Show', :action => 'show', :id => entry %>
```

```
<a href="/entries/show/3">Show</a>
```

It's important to understand how these examples work, as many elements of views rendered by Rails will contain patterns such as these, whether for generating links, including images, or creating forms to post data back to your application.

■Note The last example uses `:id => entry` rather than `:id => entry.id`. This is allowable, as `id` is considered to be the default column if no other is supplied in situations where links are being created.

Creating a New Action and View

Let's use the basic knowledge you've gathered so far to create your own controller action and view from scratch to show all your diary entries in full on a single page in a diary or blog-style layout.

Creating a new method is as easy as adding a method to the controller of your choice. Add the following method to app/controllers/entries_controller.rb:

```
def view_all
  @entries = Entry.find(:all, :order => 'created_at DESC')
end
```

This code defines a method (and therefore, a controller action) called view_all that contains a single line that retrieves all the entries from your database, ordered in chronologically descending order (like a blog). The order is defined by the optional :order parameter. ActiveRecord methods, such as find, have many useful optional parameters such as these to get the results you desire. You can learn all about them from the official Ruby on Rails documentation, as there are too many to cover here.

Now you have an action that will respond when you visit http://localhost/entries/view_all, but if you try to access that URL, you'll get the following error:

```
Template is missing
Missing template script/../config/../app/views/entries/view_all.rhtml
```

The error reminds you that even though you have an action, you don't have a view associated with that action. To create the associated view, you can just create a new file in app/views/entries called view_all.rhtml. Within view_all.rhtml, place this code:

```
<% @entries.each do |entry| %>
  <h1><%= entry.title %></h1>
  <p><%= entry.content %></p>
  <p><em>Posted at <%= entry.created_at %></em></p>
<% end %>

<%= link_to 'Add New entry', :controller => 'entries', :action => 'new' %>
```

Once this code is in place, you can access http://localhost/entries/view_all successfully, resulting in a page as shown in Figure 13-5.

Third entry

My final entry for now.

Posted at Thu Mar 22 22:59:00 +0000 2007

This is a test

My test entry goes here..

Posted at Tue Mar 20 22:59:00 +0000 2007

Another test entry

This is a second entry

Posted at Tue Mar 20 22:59:00 +0000 2007

Add New entry

Figure 13-5. *The* view_all *action showing some test items from your* entries *table*

Let's take a look at what the code in your new action and view does. When you request http://localhost/entries/view_all, the view_all method in the entries controller is run:

```
def view_all
  @entries = Entry.find(:all, :order => 'created_at DESC')
end
```

All the items from the entries table are obtained through the Entry model as Entry objects and placed into an array assigned to @entries, which is then passed through to the associated view—app/views/entries/view_all.rhtml—which contains this code:

```
<% @entries.each do |entry| %>
  <h1><%= link_to entry.title, :action => 'show', :id => entry.id %></h1>
  <p><%= entry.content %></p>
  <p><em>Posted at <%= entry.created_at %></em></p>
<% end %>

<%= link_to 'Add New entry', :controller => 'entries', :action => 'new' %>
```

The first line starts by using the each method on the @entries array to iterate through each element and place each constituent entry into the entry local variable. Within the loop, you show the entry's title (from entry.title) within an <h1> HTML heading, and then the entry's content and creation date. Once the loop is over, all the entries from the database have been rendered, and finally you render a link to the new action of the entries controller so that the user can post new entries to the system.

Parameters

In the last section you created an action and view to show all the diary entries in your system on a single blog-like Web page. Within your view_all view was this line:

```
<h1><%= link_to entry.title, :action => 'show', :id => entry.id %></h1>
```

This line creates a heading that contains a link to the show action for that entry and would render into final HTML like this:

```
<a href="/entries/show/1">This is a test</a>
```

If you were to click the link, you would be redirected to the show action for the entries controller, and an ID of 1 would be passed through. Let's look at what the show action does with this:

```
def show
  @entry = Entry.find(params[:id])
end
```

The show action is simple, as all it does is retrieve a single entry from the database (using, as always, the find method provided by the Entry model from ActiveRecord::Base). You retrieve the ID from the URL through the params hash, a hash that is automatically populated by any data passed to the Rails application via the URL.

If you use find with a single parameter containing an integer ID, then that row will be retrieved from the relevant table for the associated model, and returned as a single object. In this case, the entry retrieved is associated with @entry, then the view at app/views/entries/show.rhtml renders the page you see.

Here are some examples of how some URLs relate to parameters that are found in the params hash:

```
http://localhost/entries/show/1
```

```
params[:controller] == 'entries'
params[:action] == 'show'
params[:id] == '1'
```

```
http://localhost/entries/another_method/20?formfield1=test&formfield2=hello
```

```
params[:controller] == 'entries'
params[:action] == 'another_method'
params[:id] == '20'
params[:formfield1] == 'test'
params[:formfield2] == 'hello'
```

```
http://localhost/test/test2/?formfield1=test&formfield2=hello
```

```
params[:controller] == 'test'
params[:action] == 'test2'
params[:formfield1] == 'test'
params[:formfield2] == 'hello'
```

These examples demonstrate how you can pass data into methods within the URL (or, in the case of POST requests—such as those that can be made from an HTML form—within the HTTP request directly) and then access it by the controllers (or views) through the params hash.

If you look at the code for the create action—an action used to create the new entries as supplied by the form at http://localhost/entries/new—you'll see how params is used to create new entries:

```
def create
  @entry = Entry.new(params[:entry])
  if @entry.save
    flash[:notice] = 'Entry was successfully created.'
    redirect_to :action => 'list'
  else
    render :action => 'new'
  end
end
```

In this method, you create a new entry with `Entry.new(params[:entry])`. The `new` method provided by ActiveRecord accepts the entire `params` hash and makes a new row of data from it. On the next line you save that row to the database using `@entry.save`, which returns `true` or `false`. If `true` (that is, the attempt is successful), the user will be redirected to the `list` action (try changing this to `view_all`). If the save isn't successful, the view for the `new` action is rendered using `render :action => 'new'`. Note how you can use `redirect_to` and `render` to perform operations that don't necessarily fit in with the usual controller ➤ action ➤ view life cycle, such as redirecting users elsewhere or rendering views associated with other controller actions.

Concluding Thoughts

This section has covered only the basics of using controllers and views, but these are the most essential parts to learn. Other features provided by views and controllers rely on the concepts covered in this section. URLs are parsed into the desired controller and action, any other supplied data is passed through the action via the `params` hash, and once the action code has completed, a view is rendered.

In the next section you'll take a look at how you can customize the URL parsing system so that URLs of your own formatting can be converted into any controller and method patterns that you wish. This technique is known as *routing*.

Routing

When you request a page from a Rails application that isn't present within the `public` folder, the Rails application tries to work out which controller and action you are trying to use. In the previous sections, you've seen how a URL such as `http://localhost/entries/view_all` means that the request is put through to the `entries` controller's `view_all` action.

You can use routing to override this default assumption that all URLs are of the form *controller_name/action_name/id*.

Routing configurations for a Rails application are located in `config/routes.rb`. Let's look at what ours contains by default:

```
ActionController::Routing::Routes.draw do |map|
  # The priority is based upon order of creation: first created -> highest priority

  # Sample of regular route:
  # map.connect 'products/:id', :controller => 'catalog', :action => 'view'
  # Keep in mind you can assign values other than :controller and :action
```

```
  # Sample of named route:
  # map.purchase 'products/:id/purchase', :controller => 'catalog',
                                          :action => 'purchase'
  # This route can be invoked with purchase_url(:id => product.id)

  # You can have the root of your site routed by hooking up ''
  # -- just remember to delete public/index.html.
  # map.connect '', :controller => "welcome"

  # Allow downloading Web Service WSDL as a file with an extension
  # instead of a file named 'wsdl'
  map.connect ':controller/service.wsdl', :action => 'wsdl'

  # Install the default route as the lowest priority.
  map.connect ':controller/:action/:id'
end
```

A lot of lines in this file are comments describing how to use routes. It's worth reading this documentation to gain an understanding of how routing works in the version of Rails you're running. However, we'll look at a basic example here.

Note this line near the end of the file:

```
map.connect ':controller/:action/:id'
```

This is the default route that's present within all new Rails applications. It simply defines URLs as being of the format *controller_name/action_name/id*, as we looked at earlier. Notice that symbols `:controller`, `:action`, and `:id` are used, and how these relate to the data in the `params` hash. You can use this technique yourself when creating your own routes so that different sections of the URL are passed to your controller through params using certain element keys.

Let's say that you want to create a route that means requests directly to `http://localhost/` will be passed through to your `entries` controller's `view_all` method. You can write it like so:

```
map.connect '', :controller => 'entries', :action => 'view_all'
```

This route defines that if there's nothing in the URL (that is, nothing supplied after the hostname, in the path of the URL), to apply the `entries` controller name and `view_all` action name to the request automatically, thus passing it to the correct place.

■**Note** Your new route must be located on a line above the default route of `map.connect ':
controller/:action/:id'` so that your new route takes precedence. Routes are processed in order of
precedence from the top of `routes.rb` downwards.

Make sure to delete the `index.html` file from `public` before trying to use your new
route. Otherwise, `http://localhost/` results in `public/index.html` being rendered instead,
as files in `public` that match the requested URL have precedence over the Rails application. However, once this file is gone, routing will do its job and pass a request to
`http://localhost/` through to your `view_all` action.

Routing gets a lot more advanced than this, but the techniques used vary wildly
depending on what you want to do. There's a lengthy guide to how routing works and how
to create your own advanced routes at `http://manuals.rubyonrails.com/read/chapter/65`.

Model Relationships

So far your application only has a single model, `Entry`, that relates to diary entries. However, one major benefit the ActiveRecord library provides is the ability to relate models
easily to one another. For example, you could create another model called `User` that
relates to different people who can post diary entries within your system.

The full depth of ActiveRecord and model relationships (also known as *associations*)
can, and does, take up entire books, so is beyond the scope of this introduction, but in
this section we'll look at a basic example of how ActiveRecord models can relate to one
another.

In earlier sections of this chapter you saw how ActiveRecord objects work at a basic
level. For example:

```
entry = Entry.find(1)
entry.title = 'Title of the first entry'
entry.save
```

The way ActiveRecord relates data to objects is logical and straightforward. Columns
become attributes that you can get and set on the objects, and you can then save those
objects back to the database with the object's `save` method.

However, let's imagine that you have a `User` model that contains columns including a
user's name, e-mail address, and other user-related information. Now let's imagine that
you directly relate users and entries within your application. You might expect to be able
to do things like this:

```
entry = Entry.find(1)
entry.user.name = 'Name of whoever posted the entry'
entry.user.email = 'Their e-mail address'
```

This is, indeed, what one-to-many relationships with ActiveRecord enable. Setting up such a relationship between models is easy. Consider the two models, located in app/models/entry.rb and app/models/user.rb respectively:

```
class Entry < ActiveRecord::Base
  belongs_to :user
end
```

You would use this code for the User model:

```
class User < ActiveRecord::Base
  has_many :entries
end
```

ActiveRecord was designed to allow an almost natural language mechanism of defining model relationships. In our Entry model we say that Entry objects "belong_to" User objects. In the User model we say that User objects has_many associated Entry objects.

The only thing you need to set up, other than the relationship itself, is a column in the entries table that enables the relationship to work. You need to store the id of the associated user with each Entry object, so you need to add an integer column to entries called user_id. You could do this by creating a new migration and using a directive such as add_column :entries, :user_id, :integer or by adding the column manually with SQL (or another client).

Once the model relationship has been defined and relationships between data have been made—which is as easy as, say, entry.user = User.find(1) —you can then access data across the relationship. For example, in a view showing an entry, you might have some view code such as this:

```
<p>Posted by <%= entry.user.name %> at <%= entry.created_at %></p>
```

ActiveRecord also supports *many-to-many* relationships. For example, consider the relationship between fictional Student and Class models. Students can be associated with more than one class at a time, and each class can contain many students. With ActiveRecord, you can define these relationships using a join table and a has_and_belongs_to_many relationship, or through an intermediary model such as Enrollment, which defines the links between Students and Classes.

Note It's worth pointing out that a model called Class wouldn't be allowed in Rails, because there's already a class called Class built in to Ruby. Beware of reserved words and using names that are already used elsewhere!

The variety of relationships possible are documented in the official Ruby on Rails documentation at `http://www.rubyonrails.org/api/classes/ActiveRecord/Associations/ClassMethods.html`.

Sessions and Filters

A useful feature provided by Rails applications "out of the box" is support for sessions. When a Web browser makes a request to your application, Rails silently sends back a cookie containing a unique identifier for that browser. Whenever that browser makes further requests, it sends back the cookie with the unique identifier, so the application always knows when a certain previous visitor is making another request. You can use the session's ability to store information that's specific to a particular visitor for use on future requests.

Sessions are commonly used on Web sites for features such as shopping carts or keeping track of what pages you've visited. For example, if you add an item to your cart at an e-commerce site, the item chosen is stored in a data store associated with your session's ID. When you come to check out, your session ID is used to look up data specific to your session in the session system's data store and find out what you have in your cart.

To demonstrate basic session storage in your Rails application, you'll count and show a user how many times he or she has accessed actions within your application. To do this, you need to have some way of performing this logic on each request made to the application. You could add logic to every controller action, but an easier way is to use a filter method called `before_filter`.

`before_filter` is a method you can use at the controller class level to define that a method (or, indeed, many methods) should be executed before the method for the controller action of the current request. Filters make it possible to perform generic activities before every request (or before requests to certain groups of methods or to certain controllers).

█Note A common use for filters within Rails is to make sure visitors are authenticated and authorized to visit certain controllers and perform certain actions. If you have a controller class called `AdminController`, you might want to add a `before_filter` that ensures a visitor is logged in to the site as an admin user before you let him or her use the potentially dangerous actions within!

In this example, you'll use `before_filter` to perform some logic before every request to the application. To do this, you'll add some code to `app/controllers/application.rb`, so that every controller in your application (although there is only one in this case, `entries`) will be subjected to the filter.

Here's `app/controllers/application.rb` before the new code:

```
# Filters added to this controller will be run for all controllers in the
# application.
# Likewise, all the methods added will be available for all controllers.
class ApplicationController < ActionController::Base
end
```

Tip Pay attention to the comments left in default files as they are usually quite informative, as in the preceding code.

Here's the same file after implementing your request-counting code:

```
class ApplicationController < ActionController::Base
  before_filter :count_requests_in_session

  def count_requests_in_session
    session[:requests] ||= 0
    session[:requests] += 1
  end
end
```

You use `before_filter` with a symbol as a parameter, where the symbol represents the `count_requests_in_session` method.

Within the `count_requests_in_session` method, a hash provided by Rails called `session` is used. Automatically, `session` is always a data store associated with the current session, so anything you write to it or read from it is always associated with the current session.

In this case, you initialize `session[:requests]` with 0 if it not already defined, and then you increase the count on the next line. You can access this information from your views now quite easily. Go to `app/views/entries/view_all.rhtml` and add this line to the top of the file:

```
<%= session[:requests] %>
```

If you now load `http://localhost/entries/view_all` (or just `http://localhost/` if you followed the "Routing" section earlier), you'll see "1" at the top of the page. Reload the page, and the number increases for each reload. Sessions in action!

If you totally shut down your Web browser, reload it, and do the same again, you'll notice the number has gone back to 1. This is because, by default, sessions are only stored until the Web browser is closed. You can override this if you want to, though, with some settings placed in `config/environment.rb`. You can learn more at `http://errtheblog.com/post/24`. (There is further documentation on how sessions operate independently of Rails, at a deeper level, in the "CGI" section of Chapter 16.)

Other Features

Although you've managed to create a basic, working Rails application so far, I've only covered the basics. In this section I'll go into a little more depth in a few key areas that make Rails even more powerful.

Layouts

In the Rails application developed earlier in this chapter, you let scaffolding do the work of creating views for you. You then looked through the views created to see how they work. While doing this, you might have noticed the HTML code used was very basic. The code used was only that specifically required to render that particular page or view. There was no header or footer code, as you usually get with HTML. For example, most HTML documents would start off something like this:

```
<!DOCTYPE html PUBLIC "-//W3C//DTD XHTML 1.0 Transitional//EN"
        "http://www.w3.org/TR/xhtml1/DTD/xhtml1-transitional.dtd">

<html xmlns="http://www.w3.org/1999/xhtml" xml:lang="en" lang="en">
  <head>
    <title>Page Title Here</title>
    <meta http-equiv="Content-Type" content="text/html; charset=UTF-8" />
    <link rel="stylesheet" href="styles.css" type="text/css" media="screen" />
  </head>
  <body>
```

And, at the very least, a typical HTML document would end somewhat like this:

```
</body>
</html>
```

None of this code was included in any of the views you looked at. However, if you use your browser's "View Source" option while using the Rails application, you can clearly see the header and footer code is present. This is because the views you're using are being rendered inside a *layout*.

In Rails, layouts are special, generic wrapper templates that multiple views can use. Instead of repeating the HTML header and footer code within every view, you can simply embed each view's output into a layout instead. By default, if there's a file with the same name as the current controller in `app/views/layouts` with an RHTML extension, it's used as a layout.

Here are the contents of `app/views/layouts/entries.rhtml` from your earlier application:

```
<html>
<head>
  <title>Entries: <%= controller.action_name %></title>
  <%= stylesheet_link_tag 'scaffold' %>
</head>
<body>

<p style="color: green"><%= flash[:notice] %></p>

<%= yield  %>

</body>
</html>
```

This layout demonstrates the use of layouts perfectly. It includes the basic HTML header and footer items, but also uses some special Rails code to include the name of the current action, whatever it might be, into the title of the page. It also uses an ActionPack-supplied helper method called `stylesheet_link_tag` to include a `<link>` tag that loads the `scaffold.css` file from `public/stylesheets/scaffold.css` for use within the page.

The `<p style="color: green"><%= flash[:notice] %></p>` code renders, if present, the contents of `flash[:notice]`, where `flash` is a special Rails-supplied data store (somewhat like a session) that's used for returning messages that arise during controller actions. Placing this code into the layout rather than the view means that messages raised anywhere within your `entries` controller will display correctly on any page rendered by the `entries` controller.

Last, the `<%= yield %>` code yields the rendering process to the view for the current action, so the contents of the current view are rendered at that location.

The `entries` layout is automatically used because its filename is `entries.rhtml`, so views resulting from an `entries` controller action automatically use it. However, you can force a view to be displayed without a layout by adding a line at the point of render (that is, in the relevant method or action) in the `entries` controller, like so:

```
render :layout => false
```

For example, let's create an action with a view that's entirely independent of the layout. Within the `entries` controller, you'd add this:

```
def special_method_without_layout
  render :layout => false
end
```

In `app/views/entries/special_method_without_layout.rhtml` you could have this code:

```
<html>
<body>
<h1>This is a standalone page!</h1>
</body>
</html>
```

When the `entries/special_method_without_layout` action is rendered, only the code within the view is used and the layout is ignored.

You can also specify a different layout to use in this way by supplying a layout name to `render` instead:

```
render :layout => 'some_other_layout'
```

This would then use `app/views/layouts/some_other_layout.rhtml` for that action's view's layout.

Note You can learn more about layouts at `http://api.rubyonrails.org/classes/ ActionController/Layout/ClassMethods.html`.

Testing

In Chapter 8 you looked at Ruby's unit testing abilities, and in Chapter 12 you used them to test a library you developed. Tests allow you to specify expected outcomes and then to have various elements of functionality (mostly results from methods) tested to see if the actual outcomes match the expectations. If they match, you assume the code is perfect (or as close as it can get!), but if you get errors, you can use the results to debug your code.

Rails is particularly well known for its testing features, and a lot of this is due to Ruby's fine unit testing library that you looked at in Chapters 8 and 12. Test suites are run using Rake commands from the root directory of the application, and tests take place under the "test" environment, meaning that testing operations can take place upon a different database from live data.

At present, Rails supports three main types of testing as follows:

- *Unit testing*: You use unit testing within Rails to test your models. You supply the Rails testing system with "fixtures" (that is, dummy data with which to populate the test database) and a test suite for each model where you perform operations against the data and then perform assertions against the results of these operations. These test suites are located in `test/unit`, and the fixtures are in YAML format in `test/fixtures`.

- *Functional testing*: You use this to test your controllers. You have a test suite for each controller, whereupon you make certain requests to controller actions (in code) and then assert against the responses. You define functional tests in `test/functional`.

- *Integration testing*: The highest level of testing, integration tests let you test your entire application. You can make requests to controller actions, follow redirects, assert against the responses, and then continue making more requests of different types. Integration tests are often considered *story level* tests, as you can test an entire branch of functionality from start to finish, in the same way a real user would while interacting with the application with a Web browser. Integration tests are defined in `test/integration`.

The use of the preceding testing techniques varies from developer to developer. It's common to download open source Rails applications to see no testing used at all. It can be hard to develop the habit to test consistently, and harder still to learn to write the tests before you write the code to produce the results. However, it's still encouraged, because once you perfect the technique, your code will shine, and you'll be able to rest secure in the knowledge that your code is easily testable and guaranteed.

Note You can learn about the special types of assertions Rails adds to the standard Test::Unit assertions at `http://api.rubyonrails.org/classes/Test/Unit/Assertions.html`.

In practice, it tends to be that more-advanced Rails developers write tests whereas beginners tend not to. This is why testing isn't covered in depth here, although a good resource to learn about the ins and outs of testing Rails applications is "A Guide to Testing The Rails," available online at `http://manuals.rubyonrails.com/read/book/5`. The guide is a little old, but covers all the basics. As integration tests were added at a later stage, they are not covered at this time.

However, it's best to learn how to develop Rails applications in full first, produce a few "throwaway" applications, and then retreat to look at testing once the framework is entirely familiar to you.

Plugins

In Rails, plugins are special libraries that add functionality to the Rails framework within the scope of the application they are installed under or the Rails application itself. The Rails application can then use the functionality added by the plugin.

There are hundreds of Rails plugins, and the number is growing all the time as Rails developers come up with new ideas. You can get plugins to make it easy to create graphs from your application, to add tagging functionality to your code, and even to add large chunks of functionality, such as an entire authentication system, to your app.

Installing a plugin is even easier than installing a gem. You use the `script/plugin` script, like so:

```
ruby script/plugin install <url of plugin here>
```

■**Note** Like gem, the plugin script supports operations such as `install`, `remove`, and `update` to perform the relevant action upon the plugin. You can learn all about the various supported operations by running `ruby script/plugin -h`.

The URL for the plugins you want to install is provided by the author of that plugin on his or her Web page, or wherever you learn about the plugin.

Here's a demonstration of installing a plugin called `acts_as_commentable`:

```
ruby script/plugin install http://juixe.com/svn/acts_as_commentable/
```

```
+ ./acts_as_commentable/MIT-LICENSE
+ ./acts_as_commentable/README
+ ./acts_as_commentable/init.rb
+ ./acts_as_commentable/install.rb
+ ./acts_as_commentable/lib/acts_as_commentable.rb
+ ./acts_as_commentable/lib/comment.rb
+ ./acts_as_commentable/tasks/acts_as_commentable_tasks.rake
+ ./acts_as_commentable/test/acts_as_commentable_test.rb
```

The result from running `script/plugin` shows which files were added to the project. Plugins are stored in the `vendor/plugins` folder, so this plugin is now found at `vendor/plugins/acts_as_commentable`.

When your Rails application next starts, the `acts_as_commentable` plugin will be loaded automatically (as all plugins located in `vendor/plugins` are), and you can use its functionality within your application.

Plugin usage varies significantly from plugin to plugin, but good places to find plugins to use are `http://www.agilewebdevelopment.com/plugins` and `http://plugins.radrails.org/`.

■**Note** You can learn more about plugins at `http://wiki.rubyonrails.org/rails/pages/Plugins`.

References and Demo Applications

Rails has been in popular use since the end of 2004, and it has attracted the interest of thousands of developers, many of whom blog about the framework or release the source of their own Rails applications for free. You can also look to some large-scale Rails applications for inspiration.

The best way to learn Rails, beyond the basics, is to keep up with the new features being added to the framework as it is being developed, to read the source code of other people's applications, and to experiment. Rails isn't something that you can master quickly.

This section provides links to several useful references and example applications you can investigate.

Reference Sites and Tutorials

Following are some useful reference sites and tutorials to help you get started using Rails:

- *Official Ruby on Rails API* (`http://api.rubyonrails.org/`): The official documentation for the Ruby on Rails framework. Almost every class and method provided by Rails is documented.

- *Official Ruby on Rails Wiki* (`http://wiki.rubyonrails.org/rails`): A useful set of visitor-updateable documentation for Ruby on Rails. Features hundreds of articles about various aspects of Rails.

■**Caution** Because a wiki can be updated by any visitor, pages on the wiki might have been vandalized or contain bad language. Be aware of this before visiting.

- *Ruby on Rails screencasts* (http://www.rubyonrails.org/screencasts): Videos demonstrating how Rails applications can be put together. These are valuable refreshers of the content covered in this chapter, and can even show different ways of approaching the same problems.

- *Rolling with Ruby on Rails* (http://www.onlamp.com/pub/a/onlamp/2006/12/14/ revisiting-ruby-on-rails-revisited.html): A basic introduction to Ruby on Rails by Bill Walton and Curt Hibbs that covers similar ground to that of the first few sections of this chapter. This might be useful for a refresher, however.

Example Rails Applications

Here are some applications you can download, play with, and edit to learn more about Ruby on Rails:

- *Tracks* (http://www.rousette.org.uk/projects/): An open source time-management system developed in Rails. A great early example to read through to learn more about Rails.

- *Typo* (http://www.typosphere.org/): An open source blogging engine developed with Ruby on Rails.

- *Mephisto* (http://mephistoblog.com/): Another open source Rails blogging engine.

- *Instiki* (http://www.instiki.org/): A wiki system developed in Ruby on Rails initially by the creator of Rails, David Heinemeier Hansson.

- *Ruby Asset Manager* (http://www.locusfoc.us/ram/): An asset manager developed in Ruby on Rails. Features examples of file upload, RSS, storage, and export features.

Summary

In this chapter we've looked at how to develop a basic Web application using the Ruby on Rails framework. The Rails framework has given you a lot of power "out of the box" and enabled you to develop a fully working Web application in a short period of time.

We've merely scratched the surface in this chapter, as Ruby on Rails is a large and complex framework (though simple to use, it has many details that are complex for advanced usage). Entire books larger than this one have been written about Rails, so this chapter merely provides a taste. You can use the references in the previous section to learn more about the framework, or you might like to investigate the selection of Apress books available about Rails.

Rails can seem complex initially, but the complexity of the directory structure and default files created by the `rails` tool are only there to make your job as a developer easier. Once you're familiar with the layout and the tools Rails makes available, developing Web applications is a simple, organized process.

Let's reflect on the main concepts covered in this chapter:

- *Ruby on Rails*: A Ruby-based Web application development framework developed by David Heinemeier Hansson. See Chapter 5 for the history behind Ruby on Rails.

- *Framework*: A set of libraries and tools that can be used as a foundation for developing applications.

- *Models*: Classes that represent forms of data used by the application and that contain the logic to manipulate and retrieve that data.

- *Views*: Templates and HTML code (more accurately, code that includes both HTML and embedded Ruby code) that produce the pages that users of the Web application will see. Views can output data as HTML for Web browsers, XML, RSS, and other formats.

- *Controllers*: Classes that process user input and control what data is sent to the views to output. Controllers contain the logic that binds together models, data, and views.

- *Actions*: Methods contained within controllers.

- *CRUD*: Create, Read, Update, Delete. These are four basic actions you can perform upon discrete items and that are common to most Web applications. In Rails 1.2 and later, these operations can correspond with the PUT, GET, POST, and DELETE HTTP verbs.

- *ActiveRecord*: A library that abstracts databases, rows, columns, and SQL into standard Ruby syntax using classes and objects. It's a major part of the Ruby on Rails framework.

- *Routing*: The process of translating a URL into the desired controller and action by using routing patterns.

- *Session*: A process where a unique ID is given to a new user to an application, and this unique ID is given back and forth on each further request, thereby making it possible to track that user.

- *Plugins*: Libraries for the Ruby on Rails framework that "plug in" to your applications. Plugins can override Rails' default behaviors or extend the framework with new features you can easily use from your application, such as authentication systems. Plugins are installed on a per-application basis rather than for the Rails framework as a whole.

In this chapter we've looked at developing Web applications under an organized framework, but in the next chapter we'll look at using Internet protocols more directly. You can combine the techniques covered in Chapter 14 with your Rails applications so that they can communicate with other services available online, such as e-mail, FTP, and data from other Web sites.

## CHAPTER 14

Ruby and the Internet

In this chapter we're going to look at how to use Ruby with the Internet and with the various services available on the Internet, from the Web to e-mail and file transfers.

The Internet has recently become an inescapable part of software development, and Ruby has a significant number of libraries available to deal with the plethora of Internet services available. In this chapter we'll focus on a few of the more popular services: the Web, e-mail (POP3 and SMTP), and FTP, along with how to process the data we retrieve.

In Chapter 15, we'll look at how to develop actual server or daemon code using Ruby along with lower-level networking features, such as *pinging*, *TCP/IP*, and *sockets*. However, this chapter focuses on accessing and using data from the Internet, rather than on the details of Ruby's networking features.

HTTP and the Web

HyperText Transfer Protocol (HTTP) is an Internet protocol that defines how Web servers and Web clients (such as Web browsers) communicate with each other. The basic principle of HTTP, and the Web in general, is that every resource (such as a Web page) available on the Web has a distinct Uniform Resource Locator (URL), and that Web clients can use HTTP "verbs" such as GET, POST, PUT, and DELETE to retrieve or otherwise manipulate those resources. For example, when a Web browser retrieves a Web page, a GET request is made to the correct Web server for that page, which then returns the contents of the Web page.

In Chapter 10 we looked briefly at HTTP and developed some simple Web server applications to demonstrate how Ruby applications could make their features available on the Internet. In this section we're going to look at how to retrieve data from the Web, parse it, and generate Web-compatible content.

Downloading Web Pages

One of the most basic actions you can perform on the Web is downloading a single Web page or document. First we'll look at how to use the most commonly used Ruby HTTP library, *net/http*, before moving on to a few notable alternatives.

The net/http Library

The net/http library comes standard with Ruby and is the most commonly used library to access Web sites. Here's a basic example:

```
require 'net/http'

Net::HTTP.start('www.rubyinside.com') do |http|
  req = Net::HTTP::Get.new('/test.txt')
  puts http.request(req).body
end
```

```
Hello Beginning Ruby reader!
```

This example loads the net/http library, connects to the Web server www.rubyinside.com (the semi-official blog associated with this book; take a look!), and performs an HTTP GET request for /test.txt. This file's contents are then returned and displayed. The equivalent URL for this request is http://www.rubyinside.com/test.txt, and if you load that URL in your Web browser, you'll get the same response as Ruby.

Note http://www.rubyinside.com/test.txt is a live document that you can use in all the HTTP request tests safely, and has been created specifically for readers of this book.

As the example demonstrates, the net/http library is a little raw in its operation. Rather than simply passing it a URL, you have to pass it the Web server to connect to and then the local filename upon that Web server. You also have to specify the GET HTTP request type and trigger the request using the request method. You can make your work easier by using the URI library that comes with Ruby, which provides a number of methods to turn a URL into the various pieces needed by net/http. Here's an example:

```
require 'net/http'

url = URI.parse('http://www.rubyinside.com/test.txt')

Net::HTTP.start(url.host, url.port) do |http|
  req = Net::HTTP::Get.new(url.path)
  puts http.request(req).body
end
```

In this example, you use the URI class (automatically loaded by net/http) to parse the supplied URL. An object is returned whose methods host, port, and path supply different parts of the URL for Net::HTTP to use. Note that in this example you provide two parameters to the main Net::HTTP.start method: the URL's hostname and the URL's port number. The port number is optional, but URI is clever enough to return the default HTTP port number of 80.

It's possible to produce an even simpler example:

```ruby
require 'net/http'

url = URI.parse('http://www.rubyinside.com/test.txt')
response = Net::HTTP.get_response(url)
puts response.body
```

Instead of creating the HTTP connection and issuing the GET explicitly, Net::HTTP.get_response allows you to perform the request in one stroke. There are situations where this can prove less flexible, but if you simply want to retrieve documents from the Web, it's an ideal method to use.

Checking for Errors and Redirects

Our examples so far have assumed that you're using valid URLs and are accessing documents that actually exist. However, Net::HTTP will return different responses based on whether the request is a success or not or if the client is being redirected to a different URL, and you can check for these. In the following example, a method called get_web_document is created that accepts a single URL as a parameter. It parses the URL, attempts to get the required document, and then subjects the response to a case/when block:

```ruby
require 'net/http'

def get_web_document(url)
  uri = URI.parse(url)
  response = Net::HTTP.get_response(uri)

  case response
    when Net::HTTPSuccess:
      return response.body
    when Net::HTTPRedirection:
      return get_web_document(response['Location'])
    else
      return nil
  end
end
```

```
puts get_web_document('http://www.rubyinside.com/test.txt')
puts get_web_document('http://www.rubyinside.com/non-existent')
```

```
Hello Beginning Ruby reader!
nil
```

If the response is of the Net::HTTPSuccess class, the content of the response will be returned; if the response is a redirection (represented by a Net::HTTPRedirection object being returned) then get_web_document will be called again with the URL specified as the target of the redirection by the remote server. If the response is neither a success nor a redirection request, an error of some sort has occurred and nil will be returned.

If you wish, you can check for errors in a more granular way. For example, the error 404 means "File Not Found" and is specifically used when trying to request a file that does not exist on the remote Web server. When this error occurs, Net::HTTP returns a response of class Net::HTTPNotFound. However, when dealing with error 403, "Forbidden," Net::HTTP returns a response of class Net::HTTPForbidden.

■**Note** A list of HTTP errors and their associated Net::HTTP response classes is available at http://www.ruby-doc.org/stdlib/libdoc/net/http/rdoc/classes/Net/HTTP.html.

Basic Authentication

As well as basic document retrieval, net/http supports the *Basic Authentication* scheme used by many Web servers to protect their documents behind a password-protected area. This demonstration shows how the flexibility of performing the entire request with Net::HTTP.start can come in useful:

```
require 'net/http'

url = URI.parse('http://www.rubyinside.com/test.txt')

Net::HTTP.start(url.host, url.port) do |http|
  req = Net::HTTP::Get.new(url.path)
  req.basic_auth('username', 'password')
  puts http.request(req).body
end
```

This demonstration still works with the Ruby Inside URL, because authentication is ignored on requests for unprotected URLs, but if you were trying to access a URL protected by Basic Authentication, `basic_auth` allowsyou to specify your credentials.

Posting Form Data

In our examples so far, we have only been retrieving data from the Web. Another form of interaction is to send data *to* a Web server. The most common example of this is when you fill out a *form* on a Web page. You can perform the same action from Ruby. For example:

```
require 'net/http'

url = URI.parse('http://www.rubyinside.com/test.cgi')

response = Net::HTTP.post_form(url,{'name' => 'David', 'age' => '24'})
puts response.body
```

```
You say David is 24 years old.
```

In this example, you use `Net::HTTP.post_form` to perform a `POST` HTTP request to the specified URL with the data in the hash parameter to be used as the form data.

■**Note** `test.cgi` is a special program that returns a string containing the values provided by the `name` and `age` form fields, resulting in the preceding output. We looked at how to create CGI scripts in Chapter 10.

As with the basic document retrieval examples, there's a more complex, low-level way to achieve the same thing by taking control of each step of the form submission process:

```
require 'net/http'

url = URI.parse('http://www.rubyinside.com/test.cgi')

Net::HTTP.start(url.host, url.port) do |http|
  req = Net::HTTP::Post.new(url.path)
  req.set_form_data({ 'name' => 'David', 'age' => '24' })
  puts http.request(req).body
end
```

This technique allows you to use the basic_auth method if needed, too.

Using HTTP Proxies

Proxying is when HTTP requests do not go directly between the client and the HTTP server, but through a third party en route. In some situations it might be necessary to use an HTTP proxy for your HTTP requests. This is a common scenario in schools and offices where Web access is regulated or filtered.

net/http supports proxying by creating an HTTP proxy class upon which you can then use and perform the regular HTTP methods. To create the proxy class, use Net::HTTP::Proxy. For example:

```
web_proxy = Net::HTTP::Proxy('your.proxy.hostname.or.ip', 8080)
```

This call to Net::HTTP::Proxy generates an HTTP proxy class that uses a proxy with a particular hostname on port 8080. You would use such a proxy in this fashion:

```
require 'net/http'

web_proxy = Net::HTTP::Proxy('your.proxy.hostname.or.ip', 8080)

url = URI.parse('http://www.rubyinside.com/test.txt')

web_proxy.start(url.host, url.port) do |http|
  req = Net::HTTP::Get.new(url.path)
  puts http.request(req).body
end
```

In this example, web_proxy replaces the reference to Net::HTTP when using the start method. You can use it with the simple get_response technique you used earlier, too:

```
require 'net/http'

web_proxy = Net::HTTP::Proxy('your.proxy.hostname.or.ip', 8080)
url = URI.parse('http://www.rubyinside.com/test.txt')

response = web_proxy.get_response(url)
puts response.body
```

These examples demonstrate that if your programs are likely to need proxy support for HTTP requests, it might be worth generating a proxy-like system even if a proxy isn't required in every case. For example:

```
require 'net/http'

http_class = ARGV.first ? Net::HTTP::Proxy(ARGV[0], ARGV[1]) : Net::HTTP
url = URI.parse('http://www.rubyinside.com/test.txt')

response = http_class.get_response(url)
puts response.body
```

If this program is run and an HTTP proxy hostname and port are supplied on the command line as arguments for the program, an HTTP proxy class will be assigned to http_class. If no proxy is specified, http_class will simply reference Net::HTTP. This allows http_class to be used in place of Net::HTTP when requests are made, so that both proxy and nonproxy situations work and are coded in exactly the same way.

Secure HTTP with HTTPS

HTTP is a plain text, unencrypted protocol, and this makes it unsuitable for transferring sensitive data such as credit card information. HTTPS is the solution, as it's the same as HTTP but routed over Secure Socket Layer (SSL), which makes it unreadable to any third parties.

Ruby's net/https library makes it possible to access HTTPS URLs, and you can make net/http use it semi-transparently by setting the use_ssl attribute on a Net::HTTP instance to true, like so:

```
require 'net/http'
require 'net/https'

url = URI.parse('https://example.com/')

http = Net::HTTP.new(url.host, url.port)
http.use_ssl = true if url.scheme == 'https'

request = Net::HTTP::Get.new(url.path)
puts http.request(request).body
```

Note that you use the scheme method of url to detect if the remote URL is in fact one that requires SSL to be activated.

It's trivial to mix in the form-posting code to get a secure way of sending sensitive information to the remote server:

```
require 'net/http'
require 'net/https'

url = URI.parse('https://example.com/')

http = Net::HTTP.new(url.host, url.port)
http.use_ssl = true if url.scheme == 'https'

request = Net::HTTP::Post.new(url.path)
request.set_form_data({ 'credit_card_number' => '1234123412341234' })
puts http.request(request).body
```

net/https also supports associating your own client certificate and certification directory with your requests, as well as retrieving the server's peer certificate. However, these are advanced features only required in a small number of cases, and are beyond the scope of this section. Refer to Appendix C for links to further information.

The open-uri Library

open-uri is a library that wraps up the functionality of net/http, net/https, and net/ftp into a single package. Although it lacks some of the raw power of using the constituent libraries directly, open-uri makes it a lot easier to perform all the main functions.

A key part of open-uri is the way it abstracts common Internet actions and allows file I/O techniques to be used upon them. Retrieving a document from the Web becomes much like opening a text file on the local machine:

```
require 'open-uri'

f = open('http://www.rubyinside.com/test.txt')
puts f.readlines.join
```

```
Hello Beginning Ruby reader!
```

As with `File::open`, `open` returns an I/O object (technically, a `StringIO` object), and you can use methods such as `each_line`, `readlines`, and `read`, as you did in Chapter 9.

```
require 'open-uri'

f = open('http://www.rubyinside.com/test.txt')

puts "The document is #{f.size} bytes in length"

f.each_line do |line|
  puts line
end
```

```
The document is 29 bytes in length
Hello Beginning Ruby reader!
```

Also, in a similar fashion to the File class, you can use open in a block style:

```
require 'open-uri'

open('http://www.rubyinside.com/test.txt') do |f|
  puts f.readlines.join
end
```

■**Note** HTTPS and FTP URLs are treated transparently. You can use any HTTP, HTTPS, or FTP URL with open.

As well as providing the open method as a base method that can be used anywhere, you can also use it directly upon URI objects:

```
require 'open-uri'

url = URI.parse('http://www.rubyinside.com/test.txt')
url.open { |f| puts f.read }
```

Or you could use this code if you were striving for the shortest open-uri code possible:

```
require 'open-uri'
puts URI.parse('http://www.rubyinside.com/test.txt').open.read
```

■**Note** Ruby developers commonly use quick hacks, such as in the prior example, but to catch errors successfully, it's recommended to surround such one-liners with the begin/ensure/end structure to catch any exceptions.

In addition to acting like an I/O object, open-uri enables you to use methods associated with the object it returns to find out particulars about the HTTP (or FTP) response itself. For example:

```
require 'open-uri'

f = open('http://www.rubyinside.com/test.txt')

puts f.content_type
puts f.charset
puts f.last_modified
```

```
text/plain
iso-8859-1
Sun Oct 15 02:24:13 +0100 2006
```

Last, it's possible to send extra header fields with an HTTP request by supplying an optional hash parameter to open:

```
require 'open-uri'

f = open('http://www.rubyinside.com/test.txt',
        {'User-Agent' => 'Mozilla/4.0 (compatible; MSIE 6.0; Windows NT 5.0)'})

puts f.read
```

In this example, a "user agent" header is sent with the HTTP request that makes it appear as if you're using Internet Explorer to request the remote file. Sending a user agent header can be a useful technique if you're dealing with a Web site that returns different information to different types of browsers. Ideally, however, you should use a User-Agent header that reflects the name of your program.

Generating Web Pages and HTML

Web pages are created using a variety of technologies; the most popular is HyperText Markup Language (HTML). HTML is a language that can be represented in plain text and is composed of numerous *tags* that indicate the meaning of each part of the document. For example:

```
<html>
  <head>
    <title>This is the title</title>
  </head>
  <body>
    <p>This is a paragraph</p>
  </body>
</html>
```

A tag begins like so:

```
<tag>
```

And it ends like so:

```
</tag>
```

Anything between a start tag and an end tag belongs, semantically, to that tag. So, the text in between the <p> and </p> tags is part of a single paragraph (where <p> is the HTML tag for a paragraph). This explains why the entire document is surrounded by the <html> and </html> tags, as the entire document is HTML.

Web applications, and other applications that need to output data to be shown on the Web, usually need to produce HTML to render their output. Ruby provides a number of libraries to make this easier than simply producing HTML in a raw fashion using strings. In this section we'll look at two such libraries, *Markaby* and *RedCloth*.

Markaby—Markup As Ruby

Markaby is a library developed by Tim Fletcher (http://tfletcher.com/) and "why the lucky stiff" (http://whytheluckystiff.net/) that allows you to create HTML by using Ruby methods and structures. Markaby is distributed as a gem, so it's trivial to install using the gem client, like so:

```
gem install markaby
```

Once Markaby is installed, the following example should demonstrate the basic principles of generating HTML with it:

```ruby
require 'rubygems'
require 'markaby'


m = Markaby::Builder.new


m.html do
  head { title 'This is the title' }

  body do
    h1 'Hello world'
    h2 'Sub-heading'
    p %q{This is a pile of stuff showing off Markaby's features}
    h2 'Another sub-heading'
    p 'Markaby is good at:'
    ul do
      li 'Generating HTML from Ruby'
      li 'Keeping HTML structured'
      li 'Lots more..'
    end
  end
end


puts m
```

```
<html><head><meta content="text/html; charset=utf-8" http-equiv="Content-
Type"/><title>This is the title</title></head><body><h1>Hello world</h1><h2>Sub-
heading</h2><p>This is a pile of stuff showing off Markaby's features</p><h2>
Another sub-heading</h2><p>Markaby is good at:</p><ul><li>Generating HTML from
Ruby</li><li>Keeping HTML structured</li><li>Lots more..</li></ul></body></html>
```

The output is basic HTML that could be viewed in any Web browser. Markaby works by interpreting method calls as HTML tags, so that you can create HTML tags merely by using method calls. If a method call is passed a code block (as with `m.html` and `body` in the previous example), then the code within the code block will form the HTML that goes within the start and stop tags of the parent.

Because Markaby offers a pure Ruby way to generate HTML, it's possible to integrate Ruby logic and flow control into the HTML generation process:

```ruby
require 'rubygems'
require 'markaby'

m = Markaby::Builder.new

items = ['Bread', 'Butter', 'Tea', 'Coffee']

m.html do
  body do
    h1 'My Shopping List'
    ol do
      items.each do |item|
        li item
      end
    end
  end
end

puts m
```

```
<html><body><h1>My Shopping
List</h1><ol><li>Bread</li><li>Butter</li><li>Tea</li>
<li>Coffee</li></ol></body></html>
```

If you viewed this output in a typical Web browser, it'd look somewhat like this:

```
My Shopping List

1. Bread
2. Butter
3. Tea
4. Coffee
```

A common feature of HTML that you might want to replicate is to give elements class or ID names. To give an element a class name, you can use a method call attached to the element method call. To give an element an ID, you can use a method call attached to the element method call that ends with an exclamation mark (!). For example:

```
div.posts! do
  div.entry do
    p.date Time.now.to_s
    p.content "Test entry 1"
  end

  div.entry do
    p.date Time.now.to_s
    p.content "Test entry 2"
  end
end
```

```
<div id="posts"><div class="entry"><p class="date">Mon Oct 16 02:48:06 +0100
2006</p><p class="content">Test entry 1</p></div><div class="entry"><p
class="date">Mon Oct 16 02:48:06 +0100 2006</p><p class="content">Test entry
2</p></div></div>
```

In this case, a parent `div` element is created with the id of `"posts"`. Child `div`s with the class name of `"entry"` are created, containing paragraphs with the class names of `"date"` and `"content"`.

It's important to note that the HTML generated by Markaby is not necessarily strictly valid HTML. Using tags and structure correctly is your responsibility as a developer.

■Note To learn more about Markaby, refer to the official Markaby homepage and documentation at `http://markaby.rubyforge.org/`.

RedCloth

RedCloth is a library that provides a Ruby implementation of the *Textile* markup language. The Textile markup language is a special way of formatting plain text to be converted into HTML.

Here's a demonstration of Textile, followed by the HTML that a Textile interpreter would generate from it:

```
h1. This is a heading.

This is the first paragraph.

This is the second paragraph.

h1. Another heading

h2. A second level heading

Another paragraph
```

```
<h1>This is a heading.</h1>
<p>This is the first paragraph.</p>
<p>This is the second paragraph.</p>
<h1>Another heading</h1>
<h2>A second level heading</h2>
<p>Another paragraph</p>
```

Textile provides a more human-friendly language that can be converted easily to HTML. RedCloth makes this functionality available in Ruby.

RedCloth is available as a RubyGem and can be installed in the usual way (such as with gem install redcloth), or see Chapter 7 for more information. To use RedCloth, create an instance of the RedCloth class and pass in the Textile code you want to use:

```
require 'rubygems'
require 'redcloth'

text = %q{h1. This is a heading.

This is the first paragraph.

This is the second paragraph.

h1. Another heading

h2. A second level heading
```

```
Another paragraph}

document = RedCloth.new(text)
puts document.to_html
```

The `RedCloth` class is a basic extension of the `String` class, so you can use regular string methods with `RedCloth` objects, or you can use the `to_html` method to convert the RedCloth/Textile document to HTML.

The Textile language is a powerful markup language, but its syntax is beyond the scope of this chapter. It supports easy ways to convert plain text to complex HTML containing tables, HTML entities, images, and structural elements. To learn more about RedCloth and Textile, refer to the official RedCloth Web site at `http://redcloth.rubyforge.org/`.

■**Note** BlueCloth is another markup library for Ruby that also exists as a gem. You can learn more about its operation in Chapter 16 or at the official BlueCloth Web site at `http://www.deveiate.org/projects/BlueCloth`.

Processing Web Content

As you saw earlier, retrieving data from the Web is a snap with Ruby. Once you've retrieved the data, it's likely you'll want to do something with it. Parsing data from the Web using regular expressions and the usual Ruby string methods is an option, but several libraries exist that make it easier to deal with different forms of Web content specifically. In this section we'll look at some of the best ways to process HTML and XML (including feed formats such as RSS and Atom).

Parsing HTML with Hpricot

In previous sections we used Markaby and RedCloth to generate HTML from Ruby code and data. In this section, we'll look at doing the reverse by taking HTML code and extracting data from it in a structured fashion.

Hpricot is a Ruby library by "why the lucky stiff" designed to make HTML parsing fast, easy, and fun. It's available as a RubyGem via `gem install hpricot`. Though it relies on a compiled extension written in C for its speed, a special Windows build is available via RubyGems with a precompiled extension.

Once installed, Hpricot is easy to use. The following example loads the Hpricot library, places some basic HTML in a string, creates a `Hpricot` object, and then searches for H1 tags (using `search`). It then retrieves the first (using `first`, as `search` returns an array), and looks at the HTML within it (using `inner_html`):

```
require 'rubygems'
require 'hpricot'

html = <<END_OF_HTML
<html>
<head>
  <title>This is the page title</title>
</head>

<body>
  <h1>Big heading!</h1>
  <p>A paragraph of text.</p>
  <ul><li>Item 1 in a list</li><li>Item 2</li><li class="highlighted">Item
3</li></ul>
</body>
</html>
END_OF_HTML

doc = Hpricot(html)
puts doc.search("h1").first.inner_html
```

```
Big heading!
```

Hpricot can work directly with open-uri to load HTML from remote files, as in the following example:

```
require 'rubygems'
require 'hpricot'
require 'open-uri'

doc = Hpricot(open('http://www.rubyinside.com/test.html'))
puts doc.search("h1").first.inner_html
```

■Note http://www.rubyinside.com/test.html contains the same HTML code as used in the prior example.

Using a combination of search methods, you can search for the list within the HTML (defined by the `<ul>` tags, where the `<li>` tags denote each item in the list) and then extract each item from the list:

```
list = doc.search("ul").first
list.search("li").each do |item|
  puts item.inner_html
end
```

```
Item 1 in a list
Item 2
Item 3
```

As well as searching for elements and returning an array, Hpricot can also search for the first instance of an element only, using at:

```
list = doc.at("ul")
```

However, Hpricot can search for more than element or tag names. It also supports XPath and CSS expressions. These querying styles are beyond the scope of this chapter, but here's a demonstration of using CSS classes to find certain elements:

```
list = doc.at("ul")
highlighted_item = list.at("/.highlighted")
puts highlighted_item.inner_html
```

```
Item 3
```

This example finds the first list in the HTML file, then looks for a child element that has a class name of `highlighted`. The rule `.highlighted` looks for a class name of highlighted, whereas a rule of `#highlighted` would search for an element with the ID of highlighted.

■**Note** You should prefix CSS expressions with a forward slash (/).

You can learn more about Hpricot and the syntaxes and styles it supports at the official site at `http://code.whytheluckystiff.net/hpricot/`. Hpricot is a work in progress, and its feature set is likely to have grown since the publishing of this book.

Parsing XML with REXML

Extensible Markup Language (XML) is a simple, flexible, plain-text data format that can represent many different structures of data. An XML document, at its simplest, looks a little like HTML:

```
<people>
  <person>
    <name>Peter Cooper</name>
    <gender>Male</gender>
  </person>
  <person>
    <name>Fred Bloggs</name>
    <gender>Male</gender>
  </person>
</people>
```

This extremely simplistic XML document defines a set of people containing two individual persons, each of whom has a name and gender. In previous chapters we've used YAML in a similar way to how XML is used here, but although YAML is simpler and easier to use with Ruby, XML is more popular outside the Ruby world.

XML is prevalent when it comes to sharing data on the Internet in a form that's easy for machines to parse, and is especially popular when using APIs and machine-accessible services provided online, such as Yahoo!'s search APIs and other programming interfaces to online services. Due to XML's popularity, it's worthwhile to see how to parse it with Ruby.

Ruby's primary XML library is called *REXML* and comes with Ruby by default as part of the standard library.

REXML supports two different ways of processing XML files: tree parsing and stream parsing. Tree parsing is where a file is turned into a single data structure that can then be searched, traversed, and otherwise manipulated. Stream parsing is when a file is processed and parsed on the fly by calling special *callback* functions whenever something in the file is found. Stream parsing is less powerful in most cases than tree parsing, although it's slightly faster. In this section we'll focus on tree parsing, as it makes more sense for most situations.

Here's a basic demonstration of parsing an XML file looking for certain elements:

```
require 'rexml/document'

xml = <<END_XML
<people>
  <person>
    <name>Peter Cooper</name>
```

```
    <gender>Male</gender>
  </person>
  <person>
    <name>Fred Bloggs</name>
    <gender>Male</gender>
  </person>
</people>
END_XML

tree = REXML::Document.new(xml)

tree.elements.each("people/person") do |person|
  puts person.get_elements("name").first
end
```

```
<name>Peter Cooper</name>
<name>Fred Bloggs</name>
```

You built the tree of XML elements by creating a new REXML::Document object. Using the elements method of tree returns an array of every element in the XML file. each accepts an XPath query (a form of XML search query), and passes matching elements into the associated code block. In this example you look for each <person> element within the <people> element.

Once you have each <person> element in person, you use get_elements to retrieve any <name> elements into an array, and then pull out the first one. Because there's only one name per person in your XML data, the correct name is extracted for each person in the data.

REXML has support for most of the basic XPath specification, so if you become familiar with XPath, you can search for anything within any XML file that you need.

■**Note** You can learn more about XPath and its syntax at http://en.wikipedia.org/wiki/XPath. REXML also has support for XQuery, which you can learn more about at http://en.wikipedia.org/wiki/XQuery.

Further resources relating to processing XML and using REXML and XPath within Ruby are provided in Appendix C.

Parsing Web Feeds with FeedTools

Web feeds (sometimes known as news feeds, and more commonly as just "feeds") are special XML files designed to contain multiple items of content (such as news). They're commonly used by blogs and news sites as a way for users to subscribe to them. A feed reader reads RSS and Atom feeds (the two most popular feed formats) from the sites the user is subscribed to, and whenever a new item appears within a feed, the user is notified by his or her feed client, which monitors the feed regularly. Most feeds allow users to read a synopsis of the item and to click a link to visit the site that has updated.

■**Note** Another common use for feeds has been in delivering *podcasts*, a popular method of distributing audio content online in a radio subscription–type format.

Processing RSS and Atom feeds has become a popular task in languages such as Ruby. As feeds are formatted in a machine-friendly format, they're easier for programs to process and use than scanning through inconsistent HTML.

FeedTools (`http://sporkmonger.com/projects/feedtools/`) is a Ruby library for handling RSS and Atom feeds. It's available as a RubyGem with `gem install feedtools`. It's a liberal feed parser, which means it tends to excuse as many faults and formatting problems in the feeds it reads as possible. This makes it an ideal choice for processing feeds, rather than creating your own parser manually with REXML or another XML library.

For the examples in this section you'll use the RSS feed provided by RubyInside.com, a popular Ruby weblog. Let's look at how to process a feed rapidly by retrieving it from the Web and printing out various details about it and its constituent items:

```
require 'rubygems'
require 'feed_tools'

feed = FeedTools::Feed.open('http://www.rubyinside.com/feed/')

puts "This feed's title is #{feed.title}"
puts "This feed's Web site is at #{feed.link}"

feed.items.each do |item|
  puts item.title + "\n---\n" + item.description + "\n\n"
end
```

Parsing feeds is even easier than downloading Web pages, because FeedTools handles all the technical aspects for you. It handles the download of the feed and even caches the contents of the feed for a short time so you're not making a large number of requests to the feed provider.

In the preceding example you opened a feed, printed out the title of the feed, printed out the URL of the site associated with the feed, and then used the array of items in `feed.items` to print the title and description of each item in the feed.

As well as `description` and `title`, feed items (objects of class `FeedTools::FeedItem`) also offer methods such as `author`, `categories`, `comments`, `copyright`, `enclosures`, `id`, `images`, `itunes_author`, `itunes_duration`, `itunes_image_link`, `itunes_summary`, `link`, `published`, `rights`, `source`, `summary`, `tags`, `time`, and `updated`.

A full rundown of feed terminology is beyond the scope of this book, but if you want to learn more, refer to the Web feed section on Wikipedia at `http://en.wikipedia.org/wiki/Web_feed`. You can find feeds for most major Web sites nowadays, so processing news with your Ruby scripts can be an easy reality.

E-Mail

E-mail predates the invention of the Internet, and is still one of the most important and popular technologies used online. In this section you'll look at how to retrieve and manage e-mail located on POP3 servers, as well as how to send e-mail using an SMTP server.

Receiving Mail with POP3

Post Office Protocol 3 (POP3) is the most popular protocol used to retrieve e-mail from a mail server. If you're using an e-mail program that's installed on your computer (as opposed to webmail, such as HotMail or Yahoo! Mail) it probably uses the POP3 protocol to communicate with the mail server that receives your mail from the outside world.

With Ruby it's possible to use the *net/pop* library to do the same things that your e-mail client can, such as preview, retrieve, or delete mail. If you were feeling creative, you could even use net/pop to develop your own anti-spam tools.

■**Note** In this section our examples won't run without adjustments, as they need to operate on a real mail account. If you wish to run them, you would need to replace the server name, username, and passwords with those of a POP3/mail account that you have access to. Ideally, you'll be able to create a test e-mail account if you want to play with the examples here, or have a backup of your mail first, in case of unforeseen errors. That's because although you cannot delete mail directly from your local e-mail program, you might delete any new mail waiting on your mail server. Once you're confident of your code and what you want to achieve, then you change your settings to work upon a live account.

The basic operations you can perform with a POP3 server are to connect to it, receive information about the mail an account contains, view that mail, delete the mail, and disconnect. First, you'll connect to a POP3 server to see if there are any messages available for download, and if so, how many:

```
require 'net/pop'

mail_server = Net::POP3.new('mail.mailservernamehere.com')

begin
  mail_server.start('username','password')
  if mail_server.mails.empty?
    puts "No mails"
  else
    puts "#{mail_server.mails.length} mails waiting"
  end
rescue
  puts "Mail error"
end
```

This code first creates an object referring to the server and then uses the `start` method to connect. The entire section of the program that connects to and works with the mail server is wrapped within a `begin/ensure/end` block so that connection errors are picked up without the program crashing out with an obscure error.

Once `start` has connected to the POP3 server, `mail_server.mails` contains an array of `Net::POPMail` objects that refer to each message waiting on the server. You use Array's `empty?` method to see if any mail is available, and if so, the size of the array is used to tell how many mails are waiting.

You can use the `Net::POPMail` objects' methods to manipulate and collect the server-based mails. Downloading all the mails is as simple as using the `pop` method for each `Net::POPMail` object:

```
mail_server.mails.each do |m|
  mail = m.pop
  puts mail
end
```

As each mail is retrieved (or popped, if you will) from the server, the entire contents of the mail, with headers and body text, are placed into the `mail` variable, before being displayed onscreen.

To delete a mail, you can use the `delete` method, although mails are only *marked* for deletion later, once the session has ended:

```
mail_server.mails.each do |m|
  m.delete if m.pop =~ /\bthis is a spam e-mail\b/i
end
```

This code goes through every message in the account and marks it for deletion if it contains the string `this is a spam e-mail`.

You can also retrieve *just* the headers. This is useful if you're looking for a mail with a particular subject or a mail from a particular e-mail address. Whereas `pop` returns the entire mail (which could be up to many megabytes in size), `header` only returns the mail's header from the server. The following example deletes messages if their subject contains the word "medicines":

```
mail_server.mails.each do |m|
  m.delete if m.header =~ /Subject:.+?medicines\b/i
end
```

To build a rudimentary anti-spam filter, you could use a combination of the mail retrieval and deletion techniques to connect to your mail account and delete unwanted mails before your usual mail client ever sees them. Consider what you could achieve by downloading mail, passing it through several regular expressions, and then choosing to delete depending on what you match.

Sending Mail with SMTP

Where POP3 handles the client-side operations of retrieving, deleting, and previewing e-mail, Simple Mail Transfer Protocol (SMTP) handles sending e-mail and routing e-mail between mail servers. In this section you won't be looking at this latter use, but will use SMTP simply to send mails to an e-mail address.

The net/smtp library allows you to communicate with SMTP servers directly. On many Unix machines, especially servers on the Internet, you can send mail to the SMTP server running on the local machine and it will be delivered across the Internet. In these situations, sending e-mail is as easy as this:

```
require 'net/smtp'

message = <<MESSAGE_END
From: Private Person <me@privacy.net>
To: Author of Beginning Ruby <test@rubyinside.com>
Subject: SMTP e-mail test

This is a test e-mail message.
MESSAGE_END

Net::SMTP.start('localhost') do |smtp|
  smtp.send_message message, 'me@privacy.net', 'test@rubyinside.com'
end
```

You place a basic e-mail in `message`, using a *here document*, taking care to format the headers correctly (e-mails require a From, To, and Subject header, separated from the body of the e-mail with a blank line, as in the preceding code). To send the mail you use Net::SMTP to connect to the SMTP server on the local machine and then use the `send_message` method along with the message, the from address, and the destination address as parameters (even though the from and to addresses are within the e-mail itself, these aren't always used to route mail).

If you're not running an SMTP server on your machine, you can use Net::SMTP to communicate with a remote SMTP server. Unless you're using a webmail service (such as Hotmail or Yahoo! Mail), your e-mail provider will have provided you with outgoing mail server details that you can supply to Net::SMTP, as follows:

```
Net::SMTP.start('mail.your-domain.com')
```

This line of code connects to the SMTP server on port 25 of `mail.your-domain.com` without using any username or password. If you need to, though, you can specify port number and other details. For example:

```
Net::SMTP.start('mail.your-domain.com', 25, 'localhost', 'username', 'password',➡
:plain)
```

This example connects to the SMTP server at `mail.your-domain.com` using a username and password in plain text format. It identifies the client's hostname as `localhost`.

Note Net::SMTP also supports LOGIN and CRAM-MD5 authentication schemes. To use these, use `:login` or `:cram_md5` as the sixth parameter passed into `start`.

Sending Mail with ActionMailer

ActionMailer (`http://wiki.rubyonrails.org/rails/pages/ActionMailer`) makes sending e-mail more high-level than using the SMTP protocol (or net/smtp) *directly*. Instead of talking directly with an SMTP server, you create a descendent of `ActionMailer::Base`, implement a method that sets your mail's subject, recipients, and other details, and then you call that method to send e-mail.

ActionMailer is a part of the Ruby on Rails framework (as covered in Chapter 13), but can be used independently of it. If you don't have Ruby on Rails installed on your computer yet, you can install the ActionMailer gem with `gem install actionmailer`.

Here's a basic example of using ActionMailer:

```
require 'rubygems'
require 'action_mailer'

class Emailer < ActionMailer::Base
  def test_email(email_address, email_body)
    recipients(email_address)
    from "me@privacy.net"
    subject "This is a test e-mail"
    body email_body
  end
end


Emailer.deliver_test_email('me@privacy.net', 'This is a test e-mail!')
```

A class, `Emailer`, is defined and descends from `ActionMailer::Base`. The `test_email` method uses ActionMailer's helper methods to set the recipient, from address, subject, and body of the e-mail, but you never call this method directly. To send the mail, you call a dynamic class method on the `Emailer` class called `deliver_test_email` (or `deliver_` followed by whatever you called the method in the class).

In the preceding example, ActionMailer uses the default settings for mail output, and that is to try to connect to an SMTP server on the local machine. If you don't have one installed and running, you can instruct ActionMailer to look for an SMTP server elsewhere, like so:

```
ActionMailer::Base.server_settings = {
  :address => "mail.your-domain.com",
  :port => 25,
  :authentication => :login,
  :user_name => "username",
  :password => "password",
}
```

These settings are similar to those you used to set up Net::SMTP and can be changed to match your configuration.

File Transfers with FTP

File Transfer Protocol (FTP) is a basic networking protocol for transferring files on any TCP/IP network. Although files can be sent back and forth on the Web, FTP is still commonly used for large files, or for access to large file repositories that have no particular relevance to the Web. One of the benefits of FTP is that authentication and access control is built in.

The core part of the FTP system is an FTP server, a program that runs on a file server that allows FTP clients to download and/or upload files to that machine.

In a previous section of this chapter, "The open-uri Library," we looked at using the open-uri library to retrieve files easily from the Internet. The open-uri supports HTTP, HTTPS, and FTP URLs, and is an ideal library to use if you want to download files from FTP servers with as little code as possible. Here's an example:

```
require 'open-uri'

output = File.new('1.8.2-patch1.gz', 'w')
open('ftp://ftp.ruby-lang.org/pub/ruby/1.8/1.8.2-patch1.gz') do |f|
  output.print f.read
end
output.close
```

This example downloads a file from an FTP server and saves its contents into a local file.

■Note The example might fail for you, as your network connection might not support active FTP and might require a passive FTP connection. This is covered later in this section.

However, for more complex operations, the net/ftp library is ideal, as it gives you lower-level access to FTP connections, as net/http does to HTTP requests.

Connection and Basic FTP Actions

Connecting to an FTP server with net/ftp using an FTP URL is a simple operation:

```
require 'net/ftp'
require 'uri'

uri = URI.parse('ftp://ftp.ruby-lang.org/')

Net::FTP.open(uri.host) do |ftp|
  ftp.login 'anonymous', 'me@privacy.net'
  ftp.passive = true
  ftp.list(uri.path) { |path| puts path }
end
```

```
drwxrwxr-x   2 0        103              6 Sep 10  2005 basecamp
drwxrwxr-x   3 0        103             41 Oct 13 04:53 pub
```

You use URI.parse to parse a basic FTP URL, and connect to the FTP server with Net::FTP.open. Once the connection is open, you have to specify login credentials (much like the authentication credentials when using Net::HTTP) with the ftp object's login method. Then you set the connection type to be passive (this is an FTP option that makes an FTP connection more likely to succeed when made from behind a firewall—the technical details are beyond the scope of this book), and then ask the FTP server to return a list of the files in the directory referenced in your URL (the root directory of the FTP server in this case).

Net::FTP provides a login method that you can use against a Net::FTP object, like so:

```
require 'net/ftp'

ftp = Net::FTP.new('ftp.ruby-lang.org')
ftp.passive = true
ftp.login
ftp.list('*') { |file| puts file }
ftp.close
```

Note If you know you're going to be connecting to an anonymous FTP server (one that is public and requires only generic credentials to log in), you don't need to specify any credentials with the login method. This is what happens in the preceding example.

This example demonstrates a totally different way of using Net::FTP to connect to an FTP server. As with Net::HTTP and File classes, it's possible to use Net::FTP within a structural block or by manually opening and closing the connection by using the reference object (ftp in this case).

As no username and password are supplied, the login method performs an anonymous login to ftp.ruby-lang.org. Note that in this example you connect to an FTP server by its hostname rather than with a URL. However, if a username and password are required, use this code:

```
ftp.login(username, password)
```

Once connected, you use the list method on the ftp object to get a list of all files in the current directory. Because you haven't specified a directory to change to, the current directory is the one that the FTP server puts you in by default. However, to change directories, you can use the chdir method:

```
ftp.chdir('pub')
```

It's also possible to change to any directory in the remote filesystem:

```
ftp.chdir('/pub/ruby')
```

If you have permission to do so (this depends on your account with the FTP server) you might also be able to create directories. This is done with mkdir:

```
ftp.mkdir('test')
```

Performing this operation on an FTP server where you don't have the correct permissions causes an exception, so it's worth wrapping such volatile actions within blocks to trap any exceptions that arise.

Likewise, you can delete and rename files:

```
ftp.rename(filename, new_name)
ftp.delete(filename)
```

These operations will only work if you have the correct permissions.

Downloading Files

Downloading files from an FTP server is easy if you know the filename and what type of file you're trying to download. Net::FTP provides two useful methods to download files, getbinaryfile and gettextfile. Plain text files and binary files (such as images, sounds, or applications) are sent in a different way, so it's essential you use the correct method. In most situations you'll be aware ahead of time which technique is required. Here's an example showing how to download a binary file from the official Ruby FTP server:

```
require 'net/ftp'

ftp = Net::FTP.new('ftp.ruby-lang.org')
ftp.passive = true
ftp.login
ftp.chdir('/pub/ruby/1.8')
ftp.getbinaryfile('1.8.2-patch1.gz')
ftp.close
```

getbinaryfile accepts several parameters, only one of which is mandatory. The first parameter is the name of the remote file (1.8.2-patch1.gz in this case), an optional second parameter is the name of the local file to write to, and the third optional parameter is a block size that specifies in what size chunks (in bytes) the file is downloaded. If you omit the second parameter, the downloaded file will be written to the same filename in the local directory, but if you want to write the remote file to a particular local location, you can specify this.

One problem with using `getbinaryfile` in this way is that it locks up your program until the download is complete. However, if you supply `getbinaryfile` with a code block, the downloaded data will be supplied into the code block as well as saved to the file:

```
ftp.getbinaryfile('stable-snapshot.tar.gz', 'local-filename', 102400) do |blk|
  puts "A 100KB block of the file has been downloaded"
end
```

This code prints a string to the screen whenever another 100 kilobytes of the file have been downloaded. You can use this technique to provide updates to the user, rather than make him or her wonder whether the file is being downloaded or not.

You could also download the file in blocks such as this and process them on the fly in the code block, like so:

```
ftp.getbinaryfile('stable-snapshot.tar.gz', 'local-filename', 102400) do |blk|
  .. do something with blk here ..
end
```

Each 100KB chunk of the file that's downloaded is passed into the code block. Unfortunately, the file is still saved to a local file, but if this isn't desired, you could use Tempfile (as covered in Chapter 9) to use a temporary file that's then immediately deleted.

Downloading text or ASCII-based files uses the same technique as in the preceding code, but demands using `gettextfile` instead. The only difference is that `gettextfile` doesn't accept the third block size parameter, and instead returns data to the code block line by line.

Uploading Files

Uploading files to an FTP server is only possible if you have write permissions on the server in the directory to which you want to upload. Therefore, none of the examples in this section will work unedited, as you can't provide an FTP server with write access (for obvious reasons!).

Uploading is the exact opposite of downloading, and net/ftp provides `putbinaryfile` and `puttextfile` methods that accept the same parameters as `getbinaryfile` and `gettextfile`. The first parameter is the name of the local file you want to upload, the optional second parameter is the name to give the file on the remote server (defaults to the same as the uploaded file's name if omitted), and the optional third parameter for putbinaryfile is the block size to use for the upload. Here's an upload example:

```
require 'net/ftp'

ftp = Net::FTP.new('ftp.domain.com')
ftp.passive = true
ftp.login
ftp.chdir('/your/folder/name/here')
ftp.putbinaryfile('local_file')
ftp.close
```

As with getbinaryfile and gettextfile, if you supply a code block, the uploaded chunks of the file are passed into it, allowing you to keep the user informed of the progress of the upload.

```
require 'net/ftp'

ftp = Net::FTP.new('ftp.domain.com')
ftp.passive = true
ftp.login
ftp.chdir('/your/folder/name/here')

count = 0

ftp.putbinaryfile('local_file', 'local_file', 100000) do |block|
  count += 100000
  puts "#{count} bytes uploaded"
end

ftp.close
```

If you need to upload data that's just been generated by your Ruby script and isn't within a file, you need to create a temporary file with Tempfile and upload from that. For example:

```
require 'net/ftp'
require 'tempfile'

tempfile = Tempfile.new('test')

my_data = "This is some text data I want to upload via FTP."
tempfile.puts my_data
```

```
ftp = Net::FTP.new('ftp.domain.com')
ftp.passive = true
ftp.login
ftp.chdir('/your/folder/name/here')

ftp.puttextfile(tempfile.path, 'my_data')

ftp.close
tempfile.close
```

Summary

In this chapter we've looked at Ruby's support for using various Internet systems and protocols, how Ruby can work with the Web, and how to process and manipulate data retrieved from the Internet.

Let's reflect on the main concepts covered in this chapter:

- *HTTP*: HyperText Transfer Protocol. A protocol that defines the way Web browsers (clients) and Web servers talk to each other across a network such as the Internet.

- *HTTPS*: A secure version of HTTP that ensures data being transferred in either direction is only readable at each end. Anyone intercepting an HTTPS stream cannot decipher it. It's commonly used for e-commerce and for transmitting financial data on the Web.

- *HTML*: HyperText Markup Language. A text formatting and layout language used to represent Web pages.

- *WEBrick*: An HTTP server toolkit that comes as standard with Ruby. WEBrick makes it quick and easy to put together basic Web servers.

- *Mongrel*: Another HTTP server library, developed by Zed Shaw, that's available as a gem and is faster and more scalable in operation than WEBrick.

- *Markaby*: A Ruby library that makes it possible to produce HTML directly from Ruby methods and logic.

- *RedCloth*: A Ruby implementation of the Textile markup language that makes it easy to produce HTML documents from specially formatted plain text.

* *Hpricot*: A self-proclaimed "fast and delightful" HTML parser developed to make it easy to process and parse HTML with Ruby. It is noted for its speed, with intensive sections written in C.

* *POP3*: Post Office Protocol 3. A mail server protocol commonly used when retrieving e-mail.

* *SMTP*: Simple Mail Transfer Protocol. A mail server protocol commonly used to transfer mail to a mail server or between mail servers. SMTP is used for sending mail, rather than receiving it.

* *FTP*: File Transfer Protocol. An Internet protocol for providing access to files located on a server and allowing users to download and upload to it.

In this chapter we've covered a variety of Internet-related functions, but in Chapter 15 we're going to look more deeply at networking, servers, and network services. Most of what is covered in Chapter 15 is also applicable to the Internet, but is at a much lower level than FTP or using the Web.

■ ■ ■

Networking, Sockets, and Daemons

In this chapter we're going to look at how to use Ruby to perform network-related operations, how to create servers and network services, and how to create persistent processes that can respond to queries over a network.

Chapter 14 examined Ruby's Internet capabilities from a high level, such as dealing with making requests to Web sites, processing HTML, working with XML, and managing files over FTP. In contrast, this chapter looks at networking and network services at a lower level, and works through to creating your own basic protocols and permanently running service processes.

Let's start with a look at the basic networking concepts we'll be using in this chapter.

Networking Concepts

A *network* is a group of computers connected in some fashion. If you have several computers at home all sharing a wired or wireless router, this is called your *local area network* (LAN). Your computers are probably also connected to the Internet, another form of network. *Networking* is the overall concept of communications between two or more computers or devices, and this chapter looks at how you can use Ruby to perform operations relating to a network, whether a local or global one.

■**Note** If you are experienced with networks and TCP, UDP, and IP protocols, you might wish to skip this section.

TCP and UDP

There are many types of networks, but the type of network we're most interested in is one that uses *TCP/IP*. TCP/IP is the collective name for two protocols: Transmission Control Protocol (TCP) and Internet Protocol (IP). TCP defines the concept of computers *connecting* to one another, and it makes sure *packets* of data are transmitted and successfully received by machines, in the correct order. IP, on the other hand, is the protocol that's concerned with actually routing the data from one machine to another. IP is the base of most local networks and the Internet, but TCP is a protocol that sits on top and makes the connections reliable.

User Datagram Protocol (UDP) is another protocol like TCP, but unlike TCP it isn't considered reliable and it doesn't ensure that a remote machine receives the data you sent. When you send data using UDP, you simply have to hope it reached its destination, as you'll receive no acknowledgment of failure. Despite this, UDP is still used for various non-mission-critical tasks, as it's fast and has a low overhead.

Commonly, operations that require a permanent connection (whether over a long period of time or not) between two machines use TCP and TCP-based protocols. For example, almost all services that require authentication to work, such as e-mail access, use TCP-based protocols so that the authentication information can be sent only once— at the start of the connection—and then both ends of the connection are satisfied that connection has been authenticated.

Quick operations where a connection is unimportant or easily repeatable, such as converting domain names and hostnames into IP addresses, and vice versa, can run on UDP. If an answer to a query isn't received in sufficient time, another query can simply be issued. UDP is sometimes also used for streaming video and audio due to its low overhead and latency.

IP Addresses and DNS

A machine on an IP-based network has one or many unique *IP addresses*. When data is sent across the network to a particular IP address, the machine with that address will receive the data.

When you use the Web and access a Web site such as http://www.apress.com, your computer first asks a Domain Name Service (DNS) server for the IP address associated with the hostname www.apress.com. Once it gets the raw address in response (in this case 65.19.150.101), your Web browser makes a connection to that machine on *port* 80. Machines can make and receive connections on different TCP (or UDP) ports (from a range of 65,536), and different ports are assigned to different types of services. For example, port 80 is the default port used for Web servers.

Next in this chapter we're going to look at how to perform operations over an IP-based network, such as checking the availability of machines on the network, and we'll create basic TCP and UDP clients and servers.

Basic Network Operations

Network programming is usually a difficult process. At the lowest levels it involves a lot of arcane terminology and interfacing with antique libraries. However, Ruby is not usual, and Ruby's libraries take away most of the complexities usually associated with network programming.

In this section we're going to look at how to achieve a few basic networking operations, such as checking whether a server is present on a network, looking at how data is routed across the network between two points, and how to connect directly to a service offered on a remote machine.

Checking Machine and Service Availability

One of the most basic network operations you can perform is a *ping*, a simple check that another machine is available on the network or that a service it offers is available. Ruby's standard library includes *ping*, a basic library for checking a machine's network availability:

```
require 'ping'

puts "Pong!" if Ping.pingecho('localhost', 5)
```

```
Pong!
```

The ping library is very rudimentary, offering a single class, `Ping`, with a single class method, `pingecho`. The first argument is the hostname, domain name, or IP address of the machine you want to check, and the second argument is the maximum number of seconds to wait for a response. Because pings could take up to a few seconds to respond, you might consider using Ruby's thread support to run multiple pings at once if you have many to do.

On many systems, the previous program will respond with "Pong!" as `pingecho` will be able to ping the local machine. On some systems you might need to change `'localhost'` to `'127.0.0.1'`, a default IP address that always resolves to the local machine you're using. However, you might find that you get no response. Let's look at one other example before we investigate why.

Let's use the ping library to check servers that are online:

```
require 'ping'

puts "Pong!" if Ping.pingecho('www.google.com', 5)
```

At the time of writing, this ping receives no response, and after five seconds the program exits silently. Yet, if you ping www.google.com with a command line tool, there is a response.

The reason is that the ping library only performs a TCP echo ping rather than an ICMP (Internet Control Message Protocol) echo. TCP echoes are less used and are blocked by many machines (or by some networks as a whole), particularly those on the Internet. Although TCP echoes might work on your local network, they are less likely to be supported online. Therefore, you need to find other techniques.

Another ping library available is *net-ping*, which is available as a gem with gem install net-ping. net-ping supports TCP echoes too, but can also interface with your operating system's ping command to get a response with a more reliable technique. It can also connect directly to services offered by a remote machine to gauge whether it's responding to requests or not.

```
require 'rubygems'
require 'net/ping'

if Net::PingExternal.new('www.google.com').ping
  puts "Pong!"
else
  puts "No response"
end
```

```
Pong!
```

However, if you want to check whether a particular service is available, rather than a machine in general, you can use net-ping to connect to a specific port using TCP or UDP:

```
require 'rubygems'
require 'net/ping'

if Net::PingTCP.new('www.google.com', 80).ping
  puts "Pong!"
else
  puts "No response"
end
```

In this instance you connect directly to www.google.com's HTTP port as if you were a Web browser, but once you get a connection you immediately disconnect again. This allows you to verify that www.google.com is accepting HTTP connections.

Performing DNS Queries

Most Ruby networking libraries allow you to specify domain names and hostnames when you want to interact with a remote server, and automatically *resolve* these names into IP addresses. However, this adds a small overhead, so in some situations you might prefer to resolve IP addresses ahead of time yourself.

You might also use DNS queries to check for the existence of different hostnames and to check whether a domain is active or not, even if it's not pointing to a Web server.

resolv is a library in the Ruby standard library, and it offers several methods that are useful for converting between hostnames and IP addresses:

```
require 'resolv'

puts Resolv.getaddress("www.google.com")
```

```
66.102.9.104
```

This code returns an IP address of 66.102.9.104 for the main Google Web site. However, if you run the same code several times you might get several different responses. The reason for this is that large Web sites such as Google spread their requests over multiple Web servers to increase speed. If you want to get all the addresses associated with a hostname, you can use the each_address method instead:

```
require 'resolv'

Resolv.each_address("www.google.com") do |ip|
  puts ip
end
```

```
66.102.9.104
66.102.9.99
66.102.9.147
```

You can also turn IP addresses into hostnames using the getname method:

```
require 'resolv'

ip = "192.0.34.166"
```

```
begin
  puts Resolv.getname(ip)
rescue
  puts "No hostname associated with #{ip}"
end
```

`www.example.com`

It's important to note that not all IP addresses resolve back into hostnames, as this is an optional requirement of the DNS system.

As well as converting between IP addresses and hostnames, resolv can also retrieve other information from DNS servers, such as the mail server(s) associated with a particular host or domain name. Whereas the record of which IP addresses are associated with which hostnames are called *A records*, the records of which mail servers are associated with a hostname are called *MX records*.

In the previous examples you've used special helper methods directly made available by the Resolv class, but to search for MX records you have to use the Resolv::DNS class directly so you can pass in the extra options needed to search for different types of records:

```
require 'resolv'

Resolv::DNS.open do |dns|
  mail_servers = dns.getresources("google.com", Resolv::DNS::Resource::IN::MX)
  mail_servers.each do |server|
    puts "#{server.exchange.to_s} - #{server.preference}"
  end
end
```

```
smtp2.google.com - 10
smtp3.google.com - 10
smtp4.google.com - 10
smtp1.google.com - 10
```

In this example you've performed a DNS request in a more detailed way using Resolv::DNS directly, rather than the convenient Resolv.getname and Resolv.getaddress helpers, so that you could specify the MX request using the Resolv::DNS::Resource::IN::MX option.

■**Note** Readers who are savvy with DNS terminology might like to try using CNAME, A, SOA, PTR, NS, and TXT variations of the preceding option, as these are all supported.

MX records are useful if you want to send e-mail to people but you have no SMTP server you can send mail through, as you can use Net::SMTP (as shown in Chapter 14) directly against the mail servers for the domain name of the e-mail address you want to send to. For example, if you wanted to e-mail someone whose e-mail address ended with @google.com, you could use Net::SMTP to connect directly to smtp2.google.com (or any of the other choices) and send the mail directly to that user:

```
require 'resolv'
require 'net/smtp'

from = "your-email@example.com"
to = "another-email@example.com"

message = <<MESSAGE_END
From: #{from}
To: #{to}
Subject: Direct e-mail test

This is a test e-mail message.
MESSAGE_END

to_domain = to.match(/\@(.+)/)[1]

Resolv::DNS.open do |dns|
  mail_servers = dns.getresources(to_domain, Resolv::DNS::Resource::IN::MX)
  mail_server = mail_servers[rand(mail_servers.size)].exchange.to_s

  Net::SMTP.start(mail_server) do |smtp|
    smtp.send_message message, from, to
  end
end
```

■**Note** You can learn more about DNS at http://en.wikipedia.org/wiki/Domain_Name_System.

Connecting to a TCP Server Directly

One of the most important networking operations is connecting to a service offered by another machine (or in some cases, even your local machine!) and interacting with it in some way. In Chapter 14 we looked at some high-level ways to do this, such as using the Web or FTP through Ruby libraries that made the operation of these tools easier.

However, it's possible to connect directly to remote services at the TCP level and talk to them in their raw format. This can be useful to investigate how different protocols work (as you'll need to use and understand the protocol's raw data) or to create simple protocols of your own.

To connect to a TCP port directly you can use a tool called Telnet. Telnet is a protocol to provide a general, bi-directional, 8-bit, byte-oriented communications facility. Its name comes from "*tele*communication *net*work". You're only concerned with its ability to let you easily connect to raw TCP ports. As you'd expect, Ruby comes with a Telnet library in the standard library, *net/telnet*.

Let's use net/telnet to connect to a Web site and retrieve a Web page using the HTTP protocol directly:

```ruby
require 'net/telnet'

server = Net::Telnet::new('Host' => 'www.rubyinside.com',
                          'Port' => 80,
                          'Telnetmode' => false)

server.cmd("GET / HTTP/1.1\nHost: www.rubyinside.com\n") do |response|
  puts response
end
```

```
HTTP/1.1 200 OK
Date: Wed, 01 Nov 2006 03:46:11 GMT
Server: Apache
X-Powered-By: PHP/4.3.11
X-Pingback: http://www.rubyinside.com/xmlrpc.php
Status: 200 OK
Transfer-Encoding: chunked
Content-Type: text/html; charset=UTF-8

.. hundreds of lines of HTML source code for the page removed ..
```

■**Note** After several seconds, there will be a timeout error. This is because you don't know when the data has been fully received from the Web server. Usually, if no more data is forthcoming, you would close the connection at the timeout. This is one good reason to use a proper HTTP library that handles all of this for you!

Net::Telnet connects to `www.rubyinside.com` on port 80 (the standard HTTP port) and issues these commands:

```
GET / HTTP/1.1
Host: www.rubyinside.com
```

These commands are part of the HTTP protocol and tell the remote Web server to return you the home page for `www.rubyinside.com`. The response is then printed to the screen where the first eight or so lines are HTTP headers, another part of the HTTP protocol.

All these technicalities are shielded from you when you use the open-uri and Net::HTTP libraries, as you did in Chapter 14, as those libraries create the correct HTTP commands and process the HTTP responses for you. However, if you need to create a library to deal with a new or currently unsupported protocol in Ruby, you'll probably need to use Net::Telnet or a similar library to get access to the raw TCP data.

Servers and Clients

Clients and *servers* are the two major types of software that use networks. Clients connect to servers, and servers process information and manage connections and data being received from and sent to the clients. In this section you're going to create some servers that you can connect to using net/telnet and other client libraries covered in both this chapter and Chapter 14.

UDP Client and Server

In the previous section we looked at creating a basic TCP client using net/telnet. However, to demonstrate a basic client/server system, UDP is an ideal place to start. Unlike with TCP, UDP has no concept of connections, so it works on a simple system where messages are passed from place to another with no guarantee of them arriving. Whereas TCP is like making a phone call, UDP is like sending a postcard in the mail.

Creating a UDP server is easy. Let's create a script named `udpserver.rb`:

```
require 'socket'

s = UDPSocket.new
s.bind(nil, 1234)

5.times do
  text, sender = s.recvfrom(16)
  puts text
end
```

This code uses Ruby's *socket* library, a library that provides the lowest-level access to your operating system's networking capabilities. socket is well suited for UDP, and in this example you create a new UDP socket and *bind* it to port 1234 on the local machine. You loop five times, accepting data in 16-byte chunks from the socket and printing it to the screen.

■Note The reason for looping just five times is so that the script can end gracefully after it receives five short messages. Later, however, we'll look at ways to keep servers running permanently.

Now that you have a server, you need a client to send data to it. Let's create `udpclient.rb`:

```
require 'socket'

s = UDPSocket.new
s.send("hello", 0, 'localhost', 1234)
```

This code creates a UDP socket, but instead of listening for data, it sends the string "hello" to the UDP server on `localhost` at port 1234. If you run `udpserver.rb` at the same time as `udpclient.rb`, "hello" should appear on the screen where `udpserver.rb` is running. You have successfully sent data across a network (albeit on the same machine) from a client to a server using UDP.

It's possible, of course, to run the client and server on different machines, and if you have multiple machines at your disposal, all you need to do is change `'localhost'` on the `send` method to the hostname or IP address of the machine where `udpserver.rb` is running.

As you've seen, UDP is simple, but it's possible to layer more-advanced features on top of it. For example, because there is no connection involved, you can alternate between client and server modes with a single program, accomplishing a two-way effect.

You can demonstrate this easily by making a single program send and receive UDP data to and from itself:

```ruby
require 'socket'

host = 'localhost'
port = 1234

s = UDPSocket.new
s.bind(nil, port)
s.send("1", 0, host, port)

5.times do
  text, sender = s.recvfrom(16)
  remote_host = sender[3]

  puts "#{remote_host} sent #{text}"

  response = (text.to_i * 2).to_s
  puts "We will respond with #{response}"

  s.send(response, 0, host, port)
end
```

```
127.0.0.1 sent 1
We will respond with 2
127.0.0.1 sent 2
We will respond with 4
127.0.0.1 sent 4
We will respond with 8
127.0.0.1 sent 8
We will respond with 16
127.0.0.1 sent 16
We will respond with 32
```

Note In a real-world situation you would typically have two scripts, each on a different machine and communicating between each other, but this example demonstrates the logic necessary to achieve that result on a single machine for ease of testing.

UDP has some benefits in speed and the amount of resources needed, but because it lacks a state of connection and reliability in data transfer, TCP is more commonly used. Next we'll look at how to create some simple TCP servers to which you can connect with net/telnet and other applications.

Building a Simple TCP Server

TCP servers are the foundation of most Internet services. Although lightweight time servers and DNS servers can survive with UDP, when sending Web pages and e-mails around it's necessary to build up a connection with a remote server to make the requests and send and receive data. In this section you're going to build a basic TCP server that can respond to requests via Telnet before moving on to creating something more complex.

Let's look at a basic server that operates on port 1234, accepts connections, prints any text sent to it from a client, and sends back an acknowledgment:

```ruby
require 'socket'

server = TCPServer.new(1234)

while connection = server.accept
  while line = connection.gets
    break if line =~ /quit/
    puts line
    connection.puts "Received!"
  end

  connection.puts "Closing the connection. Bye!"
  connection.close
end
```

As well as being used to create UDP servers and clients, socket can also create TCP servers and clients. In this example you create a TCPServer object on port 1234 of the local machine and then enter a loop that processes whenever a new connection is accepted using the accept method on the TCPServer object. Once a connection has been made, the server accepts line after line of input, only closing the connection if any line contains the word quit.

To test this client, you can use your operating system's telnet client (built in to OS X, Linux, and Windows, and accessible from the command line as telnet) as follows:

```
telnet 127.0.0.1 1234
```

```
Trying 127.0.0.1...
Connected to localhost.
Escape character is '^]'.
Hello!
Received!
quit
Connection closed by foreign host.
```

Alternatively, you can create your own basic client using net/telnet:

```ruby
require 'net/telnet'

server = Net::Telnet::new('Host' => '127.0.0.1',
                          'Port' => 1234,
                          'Telnetmode' => false)

lines_to_send = ['Hello!', 'This is a test', 'quit']

lines_to_send.each do |line|
  server.puts(line)

  server.waitfor(/./) do |data|
    puts data
  end
end
```

As with the UDP client and server example, the client and server applications can (and usually would) be placed on different machines. These test applications would work in exactly the same way if the server were located on the other side of the world and the client were running from your local machine, as long as both machines were connected to the Internet.

However, one downside to your TCP server is that it can only accept one connection at a time. If you telnet to it once and begin typing, but then another connection is attempted, it might begin to connect, but no responses will be forthcoming for anything sent. The reason for this is that your TCP server can work with only one connection at a time in its current state. In the next section we're going to look at how to create a more advanced server that can deal with multiple clients at the same time.

Multi-Client TCP Servers

Most servers on the Internet are designed to deal with large numbers of clients at any one time. A Web server that can only serve one file at once would quickly result in the world's slowest Web site as users began to stack up waiting to be served! The TCP server in the previous section operated in this way, and would be commonly known as a "single threaded" or "sequential" server.

Ruby's Thread class makes it easy to create a multithreaded server—one that accepts requests and immediately creates a new thread of execution to process the connection while allowing the main program to await more connections:

```
require 'socket'

server = TCPServer.new(1234)

loop do
  Thread.start(server.accept) do |connection|
    while line = connection.gets
      break if line =~ /quit/
      puts line
      connection.puts "Received!"
    end

    connection.puts "Closing the connection. Bye!"
    connection.close
  end
end
```

In this example you have a permanent loop, and when server.accept responds, a new thread is created and started immediately to handle the connection that has just been accepted, using the connection object passed into the thread. However, the main program immediately loops back and awaits new connections.

Using Ruby threads in this way means the code is portable and will run in the same way on Linux, OS X, and Windows. However, threading is not without its disadvantages. Ruby threads aren't true operating-system–level threads and can seize up in situations where the program is waiting on the system for data. There's also an overhead on each connection to create the new thread and pass execution to it.

On POSIX-compliant operating systems (such as OS X and Linux, but not Windows—though Windows users should still read this section) it's possible to *fork* a program so that a separate process is created, as opposed to a separate thread. However, rather than fork at the time of receiving a connection, you can fork a number of listening processes in advance to increase the maximum number of connections you can handle at once:

```ruby
require 'socket'

server = TCPServer.new(1234)

5.times do
  fork do
    while connection = server.accept
      while line = connection.gets
        break if line =~ /quit/
        puts line
        connection.puts "Received!"
      end

      connection.puts "Closing the connection. Bye!"
      connection.close
    end
  end
end
```

■**Note** This code won't run on operating systems that don't support POSIX-style forking, such as Windows. However, servers that use Ruby threads will operate on all operating systems that Ruby supports.

This example forks off five separate processes that can each accept connections in sequence, allowing five clients to connect to the server at the same time. Each of these processes runs separately from the main process, so even though the main process ends immediately after performing the forks, the client processes continue to run.

■**Note** Because the forked processes are continuing to run, to shut them down you need to kill them, such as with `killall ruby` (on Linux and OS X).

Although you get the ability to run multiple, identical servers in parallel using forking, managing the child processes is clumsy. You have to kill them manually, and if any of them die or run into errors, they won't be replaced with new servers. This means that if all the child processes die for whatever reason, you're left with a nonoperational service!

It's possible to code all the logic and housekeeping necessary to maintain child processes yourself, but Ruby comes with a library called *GServer* that makes life a lot easier and works across all platforms.

GServer

GServer is a Ruby library that comes in the standard library and implements a "generic server" system. It features thread pool management, logging, and tools to manage multiple servers at the same time. GServer is offered as a class, and you produce server classes that inherit from it.

Other than simple management, GServer also allows you to run multiple servers at once on different ports, allowing you to put together an entire suite of services in just a few lines of code. Threading is entirely handled by GServer, although you can get involved with the process if you like. GServer also implements logging features, although again, you can provide your own code for these functions if you wish.

Let's look at the simplest TCP server possible with GServer:

```
require 'gserver'

class HelloServer < GServer
  def serve(io)
    io.puts("Hello!")
  end
end

server = HelloServer.new(1234)
server.start
server.join
```

This code implements a basic server that simply outputs the word "Hello!" to any client connecting to port 1234. If you telnet to connect to port 1234 (or even a Web browser, using http://127.0.0.1:1234/) you'll see the string "Hello!" returned to you before the connection is closed.

In this example, you create a server class called HelloServer that descends from GServer. GServer implements all the thread and connection management, leaving you with only a handful of technicalities to worry about. In this simple example you only create a single server process, tell it to use port 1234, and start it immediately.

However, even this simple example will work with multiple clients, and if you telnet to it multiple times in parallel you'll find that all requests are processed successfully.

However, it's possible to set a maximum number of allowed connections by supplying more parameters to new:

```ruby
require 'gserver'

class HelloServer < GServer
  def serve(io)
    io.puts("Say something to me:")
    line = io.gets
    io.puts("You said '#{line.chomp}'")
  end
end


server = HelloServer.new(1234, '127.0.0.1', 1)
server.start
server.join
```

The new method for GServer accepts several parameters. In order, they are the port number to run the server(s) on, the name of host or interface to run the server(s) on, the maximum number of connections to allow at once (set to 1 in this example), a file handle of where to send logging messages, and a true or false flag to turn logging on or off.

As mentioned earlier, you can create multiple servers at once:

```ruby
require 'gserver'

class HelloServer < GServer
  def serve(io)
    io.puts("Say something to me:")
    line = io.gets
    io.puts("You said '#{line.chomp}'")
  end
end

server = HelloServer.new(1234, '127.0.0.1', 1)
server.start

server2 = HelloServer.new(1235, '127.0.0.1', 1)
server2.start
sleep 10
```

Creating multiple servers is as easy as creating a new instance of HelloServer (or any GServer descendent class), assigning it to a variable, and calling its start method.

Another difference between this example and the last is that at the end you don't call server.join. With GServer objects, join works in the same way as with Thread objects, where calling join waits for that thread to complete before continuing execution. In the first GServer examples, your programs would wait forever until you exited them manually (using Ctrl+C, for example). However, in the preceding example, you didn't call any join methods and only slept for 10 seconds using sleep 10. This means the servers you created are only available on ports 1234 and 1235 for 10 seconds after running the program, at which point the program and its child threads all exit at once.

Because GServer allows multiple servers to run at the same time without impeding the execution of the main program, you can manage the currently running servers by using several methods GServer makes available to start, stop, and check servers:

```ruby
require 'gserver'

class HelloServer < GServer
  def serve(io)
    io.puts("To stop this server, type 'shutdown'")
    self.stop if io.gets =~ /shutdown/
  end
end

server = HelloServer.new(1234)
server.start

loop do
  break if server.stopped?
end

puts "Server has been terminated"
```

This time you put the main program into a loop waiting for the server to be stopped. The server is stopped if someone connects and types **shutdown**, which triggers that server's stop method, leading to the whole server program ending.

You can also check whether a GServer is running on a port without having the object reference to hand by using the in_service? class method:

```ruby
if GServer.in_service?(1234)
  puts "Can't create new server. Already running!"
else
  server = HelloServer.new(1234)
end
```

A GServer-Based Chat Server

With the knowledge picked up in the previous section, only a small jump in complexity is required to build a practical application using GServer. You'll build a simple chat server that allows a number of clients to connect and chat amongst each other.

The first step is to subclass GServer into a new class, ChatServer, and override the new method with your own so that you can set up class variables to store client IDs and the chat log for all the clients to share:

```
class ChatServer < GServer
  def initialize(*args)
    super(*args)

    # Keep an overall record of the client IDs allocated
    # and the lines of chat
    @@client_id = 0
    @@chat = []
  end
end
```

The main part of your program can be like your other GServer-based apps, with a basic initialization and a loop until the chat server shuts itself down:

```
server = ChatServer.new(1234)
server.start

loop do
  break if server.stopped?
end
```

■**Note** Remember that you can specify the hostname to serve from as the second parameter to ChatServer.new. If you want to use this chat server over the Internet, you might need to specify your remotely accessible IP address as this second parameter, otherwise your server might only be available to machines on your local network.

Now that you have the basics in order, you need to create a serve method that assigns the connection the next available client ID (by using the class variable @@client_id), welcomes the user, accepts lines of text from the user, and shows him or her the latest lines of text entered by other users from time to time.

As the serve method is particularly long in this case, the complete source code of the chat server is shown here, including comments:

```ruby
require 'gserver'

class ChatServer < GServer
  def initialize(*args)
    super(*args)

    # Keep an overall record of the client IDs allocated
    # and the lines of chat
    @@client_id = 0
    @@chat = []
  end

  def serve(io)
    # Increment the client ID so each client gets a unique ID
    @@client_id += 1
    my_client_id = @@client_id
    my_position = @@chat.size

    io.puts("Welcome to the chat, client #{@@client_id}!")

    # Leave a message on the chat queue to signify this client
    # has joined the chat
    @@chat << [my_client_id, "<joins the chat>"]

    loop do
      # Every 5 seconds check to see if we are receiving any data
      if IO.select([io], nil, nil, 2)
        # If so, retrieve the data and process it...
        line = io.gets

        # If the user says 'quit', disconnect them
        if line =~ /quit/
          @@chat << [my_client_id, "<leaves the chat>"]
          break
        end
```

```ruby
      # Shut down the server if we hear 'shutdown'
      self.stop if line =~ /shutdown/

      # Add the client's text to the chat array along with the
      # client's ID
      @@chat << [my_client_id, line]
    else
      # No data, so print any new lines from the chat stream
      @@chat[my_position..(@@chat.size - 1)].each_with_index do |line, index|
        io.puts("#{line[0]} says: #{line[1]}")
      end

      # Move the position to one past the end of the array
      my_position = @@chat.size
    end
  end

  end
end


server = ChatServer.new(1234)
server.start

loop do
  break if server.stopped?
end
```

The chat server operates primarily within a simple loop that constantly checks whether any data is waiting to be received with the following line:

```ruby
if IO.select([io], nil, nil, 2)
```

IO.select is a special function that can check to see if an I/O stream has any data in its various buffers (receive, send, and exceptions/errors, in that order). IO.select([io], nil, nil, 2) returns a value if the connection with the client has any data received that you haven't processed, but you ignore whether there is any data to send or any errors. The final parameter, 2, specifies that you have a timeout of two seconds, so you wait for two seconds before either succeeding or failing. This means that every two seconds the else block is executed, and any new messages in the chat log are sent to the client.

If you use telnet to connect to this chat server, a session would look somewhat like this:

```
$ telnet 127.0.0.1 1234

Trying 127.0.0.1...
Connected to localhost.
Escape character is '^]'.
Welcome to the chat, client 1!
1 says: <joins the chat>
2 says: <joins the chat>
Hello 2!
1 says: Hello 2!
2 says: Hello 1!
2 says: I'm going now.. bye!
2 says: <leaves the chat>
quit
Connection closed by foreign host.
```

With the basic GServer principles covered in this and the previous sections, you can create servers that operate to protocols of your own design, or even create server programs that can respond to preexisting protocols. All it requires is being able to receive data, process it, and send back the data required by the client. Using these techniques, it's possible to create a mail server, Web server, or any other type of server necessary online.

Web/HTTP Servers

As hinted at in the previous section, Web servers are also TCP servers, and use many of the same techniques covered in the last few sections, such as forking and threading. A Web server is a normal TCP server that *talks* HTTP.

However, you're not going to look at HTTP servers directly here, as I covered them previously in Chapter 10, so if you want to recap how to construct a basic Web server in Ruby using WEBrick or Mongrel, refer to the latter sections of that chapter.

Daemon Processes

In our previous examples, our servers have all run as normal applications at the command line. They can print to the screen, and if you use Ctrl+C you can close them. However, servers typically run as *daemon* processes that operate independently of any shell or terminal.

> **■Note** This section is not relevant to Windows users, as Windows has the concept of services rather than daemons. Information about creating a Windows service is available at `http://www.tacktech.com/` `display.cfm?ttid=304.`

A daemon process is one that runs continually and silently in the background on a machine and is not run directly by a user. Daemon processes are often used to run servers, as they run consistently without any interaction requirements on the local machine.

In the "Multi-Client TCP Servers" section of this chapter you created a basic server that forked five separate processes to listen for and process client connections. It resulted in processes running in the background, but they weren't truly separate. The processes still output their error messages to the current screen, and they were still attached to the parent process, even though it had died.

To make a program truly run as a background daemonized process, it's necessary to perform a few operations:

1. Fork the process to allow the initial process to exit.

2. Call the operating system's `setsid` function to create a new session separate from any terminal or shell.

3. Fork the process again to ensure the new daemon process is an orphan process, totally in control of itself.

4. Change the working directory to the root directory so that the daemon process isn't blocking erase access to the original present working directory.

5. Ensure that standard output, standard input, and standard error file handles (`STDIN`, `STDOUT`, and `STDERR`) aren't connected to any streams.

6. Set up a signal handler to catch any `TERM` signals so that the daemon will end when requested.

Let's look at how this is done in Ruby:

```ruby
def daemonize
  fork do
    Process.setsid
    exit if fork
    Dir.chdir('/')
    STDIN.reopen('/dev/null')
    STDOUT.reopen('/dev/null', 'a')
```

```
    STDERR.reopen('/dev/null', 'a')
    trap("TERM") { exit }
    yield
  end
end

daemonize do
  # You can do whatever you like in here and it will run in the background
  # entirely separated from the parent process.
end

puts "The daemon process has been launched!"
```

The `daemonize` method performs all the operations covered in the preceding list and then yields to a supplied code block. This means the code inside the code block following the `daemonize` call makes up the activity of the daemonized process. In here you could create GServer servers, create threads, and do anything in Ruby that you like, independent of the shell or terminal with which you launched the initial program.

Summary

In this chapter we've looked at Ruby's support for building lower-level networking tools and servers, as well as using Ruby to develop daemons and other persistently running processes.

Let's reflect on the main concepts covered in this chapter:

- *Network*: A collection of computers connected in such a way that they can send and receive data between one another.

- *TCP*: Transmission Control Protocol. A protocol that handles connections between two machines over an IP-based network, and ensures packets are transmitted and received successfully and in the correct order.

- *UDP*: User Datagram Protocol. A protocol that allows two computers to send and receive messages between each other where no "connection" is made and no assurances are made whether the data is received by the remote party.

- *IP*: Internet Protocol. A packet-based protocol for delivering data across networks. IP also makes provisions for each machine connected to the network to have one or many IP addresses.

- *DNS*: Domain Name Service. A system of referencing host or machine names against different IP addresses and converting between the two. For example, a DNS server will convert `apress.com` into the IP address `65.19.150.101`.

- *Ping*: The process of verifying whether a machine with a particular IP is valid and accepting requests by sending it a small packet of data and waiting for a response.

- *Server*: A process that runs on a machine and responds to clients connecting to it from other machines, such as a Web server.

- *Client*: A process that connects to a server, transmits and receives data, and then disconnects once a task is completed. A Web browser is a basic example of a client.

- *GServer*: A Ruby library that makes developing network servers and services easy. It handles the thread and connection management and allows servers to be created by simply subclassing the `GServer` class.

- *Daemon*: A process that runs continually and silently in the background on a machine and isn't run directly by a user. Daemon processes are often used to run servers, as they run consistently without any interaction requirements on the local machine. A process that is then turned into a daemon is often said to be *daemonized*.

This marks the last chapter of narrated, instructional content, with Chapter 16 being a reference-style guide to a large collection of Ruby libraries (both in the standard library and those available as gems). With this in mind, all of us involved in the production of this book would like to thank you for reading so far and hope you find the following reference chapters and appendixes useful.

I wish you the best on your continuing journey into the world of Ruby! Be sure to look at the following reference chapter and appendixes to flesh out your Ruby knowledge further.

■■■

## CHAPTER 16

Useful Ruby Libraries and Gems

This chapter is a basic reference to a collection of useful Ruby libraries and RubyGems that you might want to use in your programs. We're going to look at libraries covering a vast array of functionality, from networking and Internet access to file parsing and compression. The libraries in this chapter are in alphabetical order, and each library starts on a new page with the name as the page header for easy browsing. Below each library's title, several subsections follow:

- *Overview*: A description of what the library does, its basic functionality, and why you would want to use it. The overview has no header, but is directly beneath the library name.

- *Installation*: Information on where the library is found, how to install it, and how to get it running on most systems.

- *Examples*: One or more examples of how to use the library that demonstrate its various elements of functionality. Example results are included too. This section can be split into multiple subsections, each containing a single example of how to use a particular branch of functionality.

- *Further Information*: Links and pointers to further information about the library, including online references and tutorials.

Unlike the other main chapters in this book, this is a reference chapter, one that you might not necessarily need right away, but that will become useful over time when you want to find out how to perform a certain function. In any case, make sure at least to scan through the list of libraries to get a feel for the variety of Ruby libraries available so that you don't unnecessarily reinvent the wheel when you want to do something a library already does!

Note I've tried my best to ensure that references made to the Web are to sites that are likely to be running for many years yet, but it is possible that some of the references might have moved or been taken offline. In this case, the best solution is to use a search engine, such as Google, to search for "ruby" and the library's name.

---

abbrev

The *abbrev* library offers just a single method that calculates a set of unique abbreviations for each of a supplied group of strings.

Installation

abbrev is in the standard library, so it comes with Ruby by default. To use it, you only need to place this line near the start of your program:

```
require 'abbrev'
```

Examples

abbrev provides a single method that's accessible in two ways: either directly through Abbrev::abbrev, or as an added method to the Array class. Let's look at the most basic example first:

```
require 'abbrev'
require 'pp'

pp Abbrev::abbrev(%w{Peter Patricia Petal Petunia})
```

```
{"Patrici"=>"Patricia",
 "Patric"=>"Patricia",
 "Petal"=>"Petal",
 "Pat"=>"Patricia",
 "Petu"=>"Petunia",
 "Patri"=>"Patricia",
 "Patricia"=>"Patricia",
 "Peter"=>"Peter",
 "Petun"=>"Petunia",
 "Petuni"=>"Petunia",
 "Peta"=>"Petal",
 "Pa"=>"Patricia",
 "Patr"=>"Patricia",
 "Petunia"=>"Petunia",
 "Pete"=>"Peter"}
```

abbrev can be useful if you have an input requirement with a number of guessable answers, as you can detect partially entered or erroneous entries more easily. For example:

```
require 'abbrev'

abbrevs = %w{Peter Paul Patricia Petal Pauline}.abbrev
puts "Please enter your name:"
name = gets.chomp

if a = abbrevs.find { |a, n| a.downcase == name.downcase }
  puts "Did you mean #{a.join(' or ')}?"
  name = gets.chomp
end
```

```
Please enter your name:
paulin
Did you mean Paulin or Pauline?
pauline
```

Because the results given by abbrev are the longest unique abbreviations possible, it's viable to rely on them more if the entry data set is smaller.

Further Information

- *Official documentation for abbrev*: http://www.ruby-doc.org/stdlib/libdoc/abbrev/rdoc/index.html

base64

Base64 is a way to encode 8-bit binary data into a format that can be represented in 7 bits. It does this by using only the characters A–Z, a–z, 0–9, +, and / to represent data (= is also used to pad data). Typically, three 8-bit bytes are converted into four 7-bit bytes using this encoding, resulting in data that's 33 percent longer in length. The main benefit of the Base64 technique is that it allows binary data to be represented in a way that looks and acts like plain text, so it can more reliably be sent in e-mails, stored in databases, or used in text-based formats such as YAML and XML.

■**Note** The Base64 standard is technically specified in RFC 2045 at `http://www.faqs.org/rfcs/rfc2045.html`.

Installation

The *base64* library is a part of the standard library, so it comes with Ruby by default. To use it, you only need to place this line near the start of your program:

```
require 'base64'
```

Examples

The following two examples show how to convert binary data to Base64 notation and back again. Then we'll look at a third example showing how to make your use of Base64 notation more efficient through compression.

Converting Binary Data to Base64

The base64 library makes a single module, Base64, available, which provides `encode64` and `decode64` methods. To convert data into Base64 format, use `encode64`:

```
require 'base64'
puts Base64.encode64('testing')
```

```
dGVzdGluZw==
```

In this example you only encode data that's already printable data (though it's still, technically, 8-bit data internally), but this is acceptable. However, generally you'd encode binary data from files or that generated elsewhere:

```
require 'base64'
puts Base64.encode64(File.read('/bin/bash'))
```

yv66vgAAAAIAAAAHAAAAAwAAEAAAB4xQAAAADAAAABIAAAAAAAegAAAIrywA
AAAMAAAAAAAAAAAAAAAAAAAAAAAAAAAAAAAAAAAAAAAAAAAAAAAAAAAAAAAAAA
AAAAAAAAAAAAAAAAAAAAAAAAAAAAAAAAAAAAAAAAAAAAAAAAAAAAAAAAAAAAAA
<hundreds of lines skipped for brevity>

■**Note** This example works on OS X and Linux operating systems. On a Windows machine, you could try replacing /bin/bash with c:\windows\system\cmd.exe to get a similar result.

Convert Base64 Data to Binary Data

To convert Base64-encoded data back to the original data, use decode64:

```
require 'base64'
puts Base64.decode64(Base64.encode64('testing'))
```

testing

Note that if you attempt to decode data that isn't Base64 format, you'll receive no error in response. Instead, you'll just end up with no legitimate data coming back from decode64.

Using Compression to Make Base64 Efficient

Even though Base64 adds 33 percent to the length of a piece of data, it's possible to overcome this by compressing the data before converting it to Base64, and then uncompressing it when you want to convert it back to binary data.

■**Note** Not all binary data compresses well, although in most cases you'll achieve a reduction of at least 5 percent, usually more.

To compress and uncompress, you can use the *zlib* library, which is covered later in this chapter, like so:

```ruby
require 'base64'
require 'zlib'

module Base64
  def Base64.new_encode64(data)
    encode64(Zlib::Deflate.deflate(data))
  end

  def Base64.new_decode64(data)
    Zlib::Inflate.inflate(decode64(data))
  end
end

test_data = 'this is a test' * 100

data = Base64.encode64(test_data)
puts "The uncompressed data is #{data.length} bytes long in Base64"

data = Base64.new_encode64(test_data)
puts "The compressed data is #{data.length} bytes long in Base64"
```

```
The uncompressed data is 1900 bytes long in Base64
The compressed data is 45 bytes long in Base64
```

In this example, two new methods have been added to the Base64 module that use zlib to compress the data before converting it to Base64, and then to uncompress the data after converting it back from Base64. In this way you've received significant space savings.

Read the "zlib" section in this chapter for more information about zlib's operation.

Further Information

The following are some links to good information on the base64 library, and on Base64 in general:

- *Standard library documentation for base64*: http://www.ruby-doc.org/stdlib/ libdoc/base64/rdoc/index.html

- *General information about the Base64 standard*: http://en.wikipedia. org/wiki/Base64

- *A practical look at how Base64 works*: http://email.about.com/cs/standards/a/ base64_encoding.htm

BlueCloth

BlueCloth is a library that converts specially formatted text documents (in a formatting known as *Markdown*) into valid HTML. The reasoning behind languages such as Markdown is that most users prefer to write their documents in a clean format, rather than be forced to use HTML tags everywhere and create documents that don't read well as plain text. Markdown allows you to format text in a way that makes documents look good as plain text, but that also allows the text to be converted quickly to HTML for use on the Web. This makes languages such as Markdown popular for use with posting and commenting systems online, and many blog authors even first write their posts in languages such as Markdown before converting them for publication.

Installation

BlueCloth isn't part of the Ruby standard library, and is available as a RubyGem. To install it, use the typical gem installation process (as covered in Chapter 7), like so:

```
gem install BlueCloth
```

or

```
sudo gem install BlueCloth
```

Examples

An example Markdown document might look like this:

```
This is a title
===============

Here is some _text_ that's formatted according to [Markdown][1]
*specifications*. And how about a quote?

 [1]: http://daringfireball.net/projects/markdown/

> This section is a quote.. a block quote
> more accurately..

Lists are also possible:

* Item 1
* Item 2
* Item 3
```

In the following example, we'll assume this document is already assigned to the variable markdown_text to save space on the page.

BlueCloth works by subclassing String and then adding a to_html method that converts from Markdown markup to HTML. This allows you to use the standard String methods on the BlueCloth object.

Here's how to convert Markdown syntax to HTML:

```
require 'rubygems'
require 'bluecloth'

bluecloth_obj = BlueCloth.new(markdown_text)
puts bluecloth_obj.to_html
```

```
<h1>This is a title</h1>

<p>Here is some <em>text</em> that's formatted according to <a
href="http://daringfireball.net/projects/markdown/">Markdown</a>
<em>specifications</em>. And how about a quote?</p>

<blockquote>
    <p>This section is a quote.. a block quote
    more accurately..</p>
</blockquote>

<p>Lists are also possible:</p>

<ul>
<li>Item 1</li>
<li>Item 2</li>
<li>Item 3</li>
</ul>
```

The output HTML correctly resembles the Markdown syntax when viewed with a Web browser.

To learn more about the Markdown format and its syntax, visit the official Markdown home page, as linked in the following section.

Further Information

- *Official BlueCloth home page*: http://www.deveiate.org/projects/BlueCloth

- *Official Markdown format home page*: http://daringfireball.net/projects/markdown/

cgi

CGI stands for Common Gateway Interface (although it is rarely called such), and is a system for running scripts from a Web server that allows data to be passed to and from a script to produce a response for people accessing the script via a Web browser.

Less commonly used than it once was, CGI is still used in situations where a small script is desired to perform a simple task, and the overhead of loading Ruby for each request isn't a significant issue.

The Ruby CGI library not only offers page header and CGI data-management methods, but also tools to make managing cookies and sessions easy.

Installation

The *cgi* library is a part of the standard library, so it comes with Ruby by default. To use it, you only need to place this line near the start of your program:

```
require 'cgi'
```

Examples

In this section you'll look at several distinct things the cgi library can do. You'll create a few simple CGI scripts that demonstrate how you can use the cgi library to produce Ruby scripts that can respond to Web-based input and perform dynamic operations within the scope of a Web page. (CGI execution is also covered in Chapter 10.)

A Basic CGI Script

Let's create a basic CGI script that could be uploaded to a Web space provided by a Linux-based Web hosting provider (as most are). Here's an example of a CGI script that generates a trivial Web page:

```
#!/usr/bin/ruby

require 'cgi'

cgi = CGI.new

puts cgi.header
puts "<html><body>This is a test</body></html>"
```

If this Ruby script were named `test.cgi`, uploaded to the aforementioned Web host, and made executable, it would be possible to access `http://www.your-website.com/test.cgi` and see "This is a test" in response.

■Note The preceding script uses a shebang line that assumes the Ruby interpreter is located at `/usr/bin/ruby`. If it isn't, the script will fail. If this happens, change the pathname to the correct one, and/or refer to the documentation in Chapter 10 for how to work around it.

The way the prior example works is that the Web server provided by the Web host recognizes requests for CGI files and executes them. The first line tells the Web server to run the file as a Ruby script. You then load the cgi library and use it to print out the header to return to the Web server, before you send some HTML of your own creation.

You can also use the cgi library in a more direct way by feeding in a string of the data you want to return to the Web browser and then letting the cgi library handle the output of the headers and any other data relevant to the request. Here's an example:

```ruby
#!/usr/bin/ruby

require 'cgi'
cgi = CGI.new

cgi.out do
  "<html><body>This is a test</body></html>"
end
```

A major benefit of using `cgi.out` to return data to a visiting Web browser is that `out` handles the output of headers without you having to remember to do it. You'll use this technique more in the "Cookies" section, where `out` will also automatically send other forms of data back through the request.

■Note Learn more about `out` and what features it supports at `http://www.ruby-doc.org/stdlib/libdoc/cgi/rdoc/classes/CGI.html#M000078`.

Accepting CGI Variables

A benefit of CGI scripts is that they can process information passed to them from a form on an HTML page or merely specified within the URL. For example, if you had a Web form with an `<input>` element with a name of "text" that posted to `test.cgi`, you could access the data passed to it like this:

```
#!/usr/bin/ruby

require 'cgi'
cgi = CGI.new

text = cgi['text']

puts cgi.header
puts "<html><body>#{text.reverse}</body></html>"
```

In this case, the user would see the text he or she entered on the form reversed. You could also test this CGI script by passing the text directly within the URL, such as with *http://www.mywebsite.com/test.cgi?text=this+is+a+test*.

Here's a more complete example:

```
#!/usr/bin/ruby

require 'cgi'
cgi = CGI.new

from = cgi['from'].to_i
to = cgi['to'].to_i

number = rand(to - from + 1) + from

puts cgi.header
puts "<html><body>#{number}</body></html>"
```

This CGI script responds with a random number that's between the number supplied in the `from` CGI variable and the `to` CGI variable. An associated, but basic, form that could send the correct data would have HTML code like so:

```
<form method="POST" action="http://www.mywebsite.com/test.cgi">
For a number between <input type="text" name="from" value="" /> and
<input type="text" name="to" value="" /> <input type="submit"
value="Click here!" /></form>
```

Cookies

Cookies are small fragments of data that can be sent to and received from Web browsers. If you send a cookie from your program to a Web browser, the cookie will (usually—some people disable their cookie functions) be stored in the user's Web browser and sent back on any subsequent requests.

For example, cookies make it possible to store a number on a user's computer, which is then sent back on every future request the user makes to the same page (or the same site, in most situations). You could increment this number by one for each request to show how many times the user has accessed a certain page.

Creating and manipulating cookies with the cgi library is simple. In this example you set a cookie on the user's computer and then retrieve that cookie if it's present on future requests:

```ruby
#!/usr/bin/ruby

require 'cgi'
cgi = CGI.new

cookie = cgi.cookies['count']

# If there is no cookie, create a new one
if cookie.empty?
  count = 1
  cookie = CGI::Cookie.new('count', count.to_s)
else
  # If there is a cookie, retrieve its value (note that cookie.value results
  # in an Array)
  count = cookie.value.first

  # Now send back an increased amount for the cookie to store
  cookie.value = (count.to_i + 1).to_s
end

cgi.out("cookie" => [cookie]) do
  "<html><body>You have loaded this page #{count} times</body></html>"
end
```

On the first request to this example script, you'd see:

```
You have loaded this page 1 times
```

On subsequent requests, the one would increase to two, and so on for each further request. This is because if the script detects a cookie called count, the script will retrieve it and adjust its value, and then the cookie will be sent back out with each request using the parameter to cgi.out.

Cookies are used for many things beyond simple examples such as this. They're often used to store things such as usernames, locations, and other pieces of information that could dictate what is displayed on a given Web page. They're commonly used to track "sessions," which we'll look at next.

Sessions

Cookies act like dumb fragments of data going to and from the client and Web server on every request. However, sessions provide a better-managed and more abstracted relationship between a Web browser and Web server. Instead of sending actual data back and forth, the client only needs to send a *session ID*, and any data associated with that user or session is stored on the Web server and managed by the CGI script itself. Sessions, in effect, make it possible to "maintain state" between requests, where a state can be a large collection of data rather than the tiny amount a cookie can contain.

The cgi library makes it easy to add session functionality to your CGI scripts. Rather than use the cookie features and implement sessions manually with files or a database (though that's still an option, if you need that level of control), you can use the CGI::Session class to handle it all for you.

Here's an example of using CGI::Session to assign a data store for each unique visitor to the page:

```ruby
#!/usr/bin/ruby

require 'cgi'
require 'cgi/session'
require 'cgi/session/pstore'

cgi = CGI.new
session = CGI::Session.new(cgi,
                           :session_key => 'count_app',
                           :database_manager => CGI::Session::PStore,
                           :prefix => 'session_id'
                           )

if session['count'] && session['count'].to_i > 0
  session['count'] = (session['count'].to_i + 1).to_s
else
```

```
  session['count'] = 1
end

cgi.out do
  "<html><body>You have loaded this page #{session['count']} times</body></html>"
end

session.close
```

In this example, you perform the same counting operation as with the cookie code, although you could, effectively, store many kilobytes of data alongside each session, such as shopping cart information, binary data, or other forms of metadata such as YAML and XML documents.

Notice that the prior code is similar to that used in Ruby on Rails to work with sessions. The `session` variable acts like a special hash that's created and saved for each unique user. However, unlike in Rails, you use the `close` method after you've finished using the session so that any new data is written to disk safely.

■Note You can test the prior example's effectiveness by loading different Web browsers (for example, Firefox and Internet Explorer, not different windows of the *same* browser).

You can learn more about `CGI::Session` at `http://www.ruby-doc.org/core/classes/ CGI/Session.html`, including how to make `CGI::Session` store session data in different ways (such as in memory or in a plain text format).

Further Information

- *Standard library documentation for cgi*: `http://www.ruby-doc.org/stdlib/libdoc/ cgi/rdoc/index.html`

- *Further information about CGI*: `http://www.w3.org/CGI/`

- *Further information about HTTP cookies*: `http://en.wikipedia.org/wiki/ HTTP_cookie`

chronic

The *chronic* library makes it easy to convert dates and times written in almost any format into dates and times that Ruby recognizes correctly internally. It accepts strings such as 'tomorrow' and 'last tuesday 5pm' and turns them into valid Time objects.

Installation

The chronic library isn't part of the Ruby standard library and is available as a RubyGem. To install it, use the typical gem installation process (as covered in Chapter 7), like so:

```
gem install chronic
```

or

```
sudo gem install chronic
```

Examples

chronic is designed to accept dates and times written in a natural language format and to return valid Time objects. Here are some basic examples:

```
puts Chronic.parse('last tuesday 5am')
```

```
Tue Nov 07 05:00:00 +0000 2006
```

```
puts Chronic.parse('last tuesday 5:33')
```

```
Tue Nov 07 17:33:00 +0000 2006
```

```
puts Chronic.parse('last tuesday 05:33')
```

```
Tue Nov 07 05:33:00 +0000 2006
```

```
puts Chronic.parse('last tuesday lunchtime')
```

```
Tue Nov 07 17:33:00 +0000 2006
```

```
puts Chronic.parse('june 29th at 1am')
```

```
Fri Jun 29 01:00:00 +0100 2007
```

```
puts Chronic.parse('in 3 years')
```

```
Thu Nov 12 03:50:00 +0000 2009
```

```
puts Chronic.parse('sep 23 2033')
```

```
Fri Sep 23 12:00:00 +0100 2033
```

```
puts Chronic.parse('2003-11-10 01:02')
```

```
Mon Nov 10 01:02:00 +0000 2003
```

`Chronic.parse` will return `nil` if a date or time isn't recognized.

■**Note** An extension to the `Time` class provided by the standard library can also parse times, though at a more preformatted level. See `http://stdlib.rubyonrails.org/libdoc/time/rdoc/index.html` for information. There's also a library in the standard library called `ParseDate` that provides a method that converts textually formatted dates into an array of values representing different aspects of the supplied date. You can learn more about `ParseDate` at `http://www.ruby-doc.org/stdlib/libdoc/parsedate/rdoc/index.html`.

Further Information

- *Documentation for chronic*: `http://chronic.rubyforge.org/`

- *Further chronic examples*: `http://www.yup.com/articles/2006/09/10/a-natural-language-date-time-parser-for-ruby-chronic`

Digest

A *digest* (more commonly known as a *hash*—though not the same type of hash as you've used to store data structures in Ruby)—is a number or string of data that's generated from another collection of data. Digests are significantly shorter than the original data and act as a form of checksum against the data. Digests are generated in such a way that it's unlikely some other valid data would produce the same value, and that it's difficult, if not "impossible," to create valid data that would result in the same hash value.

A common use for hashes or digests is to store passwords in a database securely. Rather than store passwords in plain text where they could potentially be seen, you can create a digest of the password that you then compare against when you need to validate that the password is correct. You'll look at an example of this in the "Examples" section.

Installation

The libraries to produce digests in Ruby are called *digest/sha1* and *digest/md5*. Both are a part of the standard library, so they come with Ruby by default. To use them, you only need to place this line near the start of your program:

```
require 'digest/sha1'
```

or

```
require 'digest/md5'
```

Examples

Let's look at what a digest of some data can look like:

```
require 'digest/sha1'
puts Digest::SHA1.hexdigest('password')
```

```
5baa61e4c9b93f3f0682250b6cf8331b7ee68fd8
```

You can use `hexdigest` (on both `Digest::SHA1` and `Digest::MD5`—more about this later in this section) to produce a digest of any data. The digest is a string of 20 hexadecimal 8-bit numbers. In this case, the digest is significantly longer than the input data. In real-world use, the input data is generally longer than the resulting digest. Whatever the case, any digest generated via `Digest::SHA1` is exactly the same length. For example, here's a digest of a 4,000-character input string:

```
require 'digest/sha1'
puts Digest::SHA1.hexdigest('test' * 1000)
```

```
52fcb8acabb0a5ad7865350249e52bb70666751d
```

Digest::SHA1 operates using the SHA-1 hashing algorithm, currently known and used as a reasonably secure hashing operation. It results in a 160-bit output (as with the 20 hexadecimal numbers from hexdigest), meaning there are some 1,461,501,637,330, 902,918,203,684,832,716,283,019,655,932,542,976 possible hash values. This almost guarantees there will be no clashing hash values for legitimate data within a single domain.

Another hashing mechanism provided by Ruby is based on the MD5 hashing algorithm. MD5 produces a 128-bit hash value, giving 340,282,366,920,938,463,463,374,607, 431,768,211,456 combinations. MD5 is considered to be less secure than SHA-1, as it's possible to generate "hash collisions," where two sets of valid data can be engineered to get the same hash value. Hash collisions can be used
to break into authentication systems that rely on MD5 hashing. However, MD5 is still a popular hashing mechanism, so the Ruby support is useful. You can use Digest::MD5 in exactly the same way as SHA-1:

```
require 'digest/md5'
puts Digest::MD5.hexdigest('test' * 1000)
```

```
b38968b763b8b56c4b703f93f510be5a
```

Using digests in place of passwords is easily done:

```
require 'digest/sha1'

puts "Enter the password to use this program:"
password = gets
if Digest::SHA1.hexdigest(password) == ➥
                      '24b63c0840ec7e58e5ab50d0d4ca243d1729eb65'
  puts "You've passed!"
else
  puts "Wrong!"
  exit
end
```

In this case, the password is stored as an SHA-1 hex digest, and you hash any incoming passwords to establish if they're equal. Yet without knowing what the password is, there's no way you could succeed with the preceding program even by looking at the source code!

■**Note** A prize of $50 awaits the first (and only the first!) person to contact me via http://www.rubyinside.com/ with the unhashed version of the password used in the previous example!

You can also generate the raw digest without it being rendered into a string of hexadecimal characters by using the digest method, like so:

```
Digest::SHA1.digest('test' * 1000)
```

As the result is 20 bytes of 8-bit data, it's unlikely you would be satisfied with the output if you printed it to the screen as characters, but you can prove the values are there:

```
Digest::SHA1.digest('test' * 1000).each_byte do |byte|
  print byte, "-"
end
```

```
82-252-184-172-171-176-165-173-120-101-53-2-73-229-43-183-6-102-117-29-
```

It's worth noting that if you want to store digests in text format, but want something that takes up less space than the 40 hexadecimal characters, the base64 library can help:

```
require 'base64'
require 'digest/sha1'

puts Digest::SHA1.hexdigest('test')
puts Base64.encode64(Digest::SHA1.digest('test'))
```

```
a94a8fe5ccb19ba61c4c0873d391e987982fbbd3
qUqP5cyxm6YcTAhzO5Hph5gvu9M=
```

Further Information

- *Further information about SHA-1*: http://en.wikipedia.org/wiki/SHA-1

- *Further information about MD5*: http://en.wikipedia.org/wiki/MD5

English

Throughout this book you've often used special variables provided by Ruby for various purposes. For example, $! contains a string of the last error message raised in the program, $$ returns the process ID of the current program, and $/ lets you adjust the default line or record separator as used by the gets method. The *English* library allows you to access Ruby's special variables using names expressed in English, rather than symbols. This makes the variables easier to remember.

Installation

The English library is a part of the standard library, so it comes with Ruby by default. To use it, you only need to place this line near the start of your program:

```
require 'English'
```

Examples

Using require 'English' (note the capitalization of the first letter, as opposed to the standard, all-lowercase names adopted by the filenames of other libraries) creates English-language aliases to Ruby's special variables, some of which are covered in the following list:

- $DEFAULT_OUTPUT (alias for $>) is an alias for the destination of output sent by commands such as print and puts. By default it points to $stdout, the standard output, typically the screen or current terminal (see the sidebar "Standard Input and Output" in Chapter 9 for more information).

- $DEFAULT_INPUT (alias for $<) is an object that acts somewhat like a File object for data being sent to the script at the command line, or if the data is missing, the standard input (usually the keyboard or current terminal). It is read-only.

- $ERROR_INFO (alias for $!) refers to the exception object passed to raise or, more pragmatically, can contain the most recent error message. In the initial form, it can be useful when used within a rescue block.

- $ERROR_POSITION (alias for $@) returns a stack trace as generated by the previous exception. This is in the same format as the trace provided by Kernel.caller.

- $OFS and $OUTPUT_FIELD_SEPARATOR (aliases for $,) can be set or read, and contain the default separator as used in output from the print method and Array's join method. The default value is nil, as can be confirmed with %w{a b c}.join, which results in "abc."

- ORS and $OUTPUT_RECORD_SEPARATOR (aliases for $\) can be set or read, and contain the default separator as used when sending output with methods such as print and IO.write. The default value is nil, as typically you use puts instead when you want to append a newline to data being sent.

- $FS and $FIELD_SEPARATOR (aliases for $;) can be set or read, and contain the default separator as used by String's split method. Changing this and then calling split on a string without a split regex or character can give different results than expected.

- $RS and $INPUT_RECORD_SEPARATOR (aliases for $/) can be set or read, and contain the default separator as used for input, such as from gets. The default value is a newline (\n) and results in gets receiving one line at a time. If this value is set to nil, then gets would read an entire file or data stream in one go.

- $PID and $PROCESS_ID (alias for $$) return the process ID of the current program. This ID is unique for every program or instance of a program running on a computer, which is why tempfile uses it when constructing names for temporary files. It is read-only.

- $LAST_MATCH_INFO (alias for $~) returns a MatchData object that contains the results of the last successful pattern match.

- $IGNORECASE (alias for $=) is a flag that you can set or read from that determines whether regular expressions and pattern matches performed in the program will be case insensitive by default. This special variable is deprecated and might be removed in Ruby 2. Typically, if you required this feature you'd use the /i flag on the end of a regular expression instead.

- $MATCH (alias for $&) contains the entire string matched by the last successful regular expression match in the current scope. If there has been no match, its value is nil.

- $PREMATCH (alias for $`) contains the string preceding the match discovered by the last successful regular expression match in the current scope. If there has been no match, its value is nil.

- $POSTMATCH (alias for $') contains the string succeeding the match discovered by the last successful regular expression match in the current scope. If there has been no match, its value is nil.

Further Information

- *Standard library documentation for English*: http://www.ruby-doc.org/stdlib/ libdoc/English/rdoc/index.html

ERB

ERB is a templating library for Ruby that allows you to mix content and Ruby code. ERB is used as the main template system in Ruby on Rails when rendering RHTML views (see Chapter 13 for more information). Mixing Ruby code with other content results in a powerful templating system that's a little reminiscent of PHP.

Installation

The ERB library is a part of the standard library, so it comes with Ruby by default. To use it, you only need to place this line near the start of your program:

```
require 'erb'
```

Examples

ERB works by accepting data written in ERB's template language, converting it to Ruby code that can produce the desired output, and then executing that code.

Basic Templates and Rendering

A basic ERB script might look like this:

```
<% 1.upto(5) do |i| %>
  <p>This is iteration <%= i %></p>
<% end %>
```

In this template, Ruby and HTML code are mixed. Ruby code that's meant to be executed is placed within <% and %> tags. Ruby code that's to be evaluated and "printed" is placed within <%= and %> tags, and normal content is left as is.

Running the preceding template through ERB would result in this output:

```
<p>This is iteration 1</p>
<p>This is iteration 2</p>
<p>This is iteration 3</p>
<p>This is iteration 4</p>
<p>This is iteration 5</p>
```

■**Note** Due to the spacing in the template, the spacing in the output can look odd. Usually added whitespace isn't an issue with HTML or XHTML, but if you're using ERB to output other forms of data, you might need to develop your templates with whitespace in mind.

You use the ERB library to render ERB code from Ruby:

```
require 'erb'

template = <<EOF
<% 1.upto(5) do |i| %>
  <p>This is iteration <%= i %></p>
<% end %>
EOF

puts ERB.new(template).result
```

The `result` method doesn't print the data directly, but returns the rendered template to the caller, so you then print it to the screen with `puts`. If you'd rather have ERB print the output directly to the screen, you can use the `run` method:

```
ERB.new(template).run
```

Accessing Outside Variables

ERB templates can also access variables in the current scope. For example:

```
require 'erb'

array_of_stuff = %w{this is a test}

template = <<EOF
<% array_of_stuff.each_with_index do |item, index| %>
  <p>Item <%= index %>: <%= item %></p>
<% end %>
EOF

puts ERB.new(template).result
```

```
<p>Item 0: this</p>
<p>Item 1: is</p>
<p>Item 2: a</p>
<p>Item 3: test</p>
```

■**Note** The `result` and `run` methods also accept a binding as an optional parameter if you want ERB to have access to variables that are defined in a different scope, or if you want to "sandbox" the variables to which templates have access. If you allow them access to your main binding, as is default, remember that code within templates could change the value of the current variables if the author of the template so wished.

Safe Levels

Due to ERB allowing Ruby code to be executed among other content, it's not wise to allow users you cannot trust to be able to create or edit ERB templates on systems under your control. That's because they could execute arbitrary code that could access the file system, delete data, or otherwise damage your system (remember that Ruby can use backticks to run any program on the system accessible to the current user).

In Chapter 11 you looked at the concept of "safe levels" provided by Ruby, which allow you to restrain the capabilities of code, particularly in relation to running arbitrary programs or using tainted data with "dangerous" commands such as `eval`.

`ERB.new` accepts a safe level as an optional second parameter, which goes a long way toward making your template rendering a safer process:

```
require 'erb'

template = <<EOF
Let's try to do something crazy like access the filesystem..
<%= `ls` %>
EOF

puts ERB.new(template, 4).result    # Using safe level 4!
```

```
/usr/local/lib/ruby/1.8/erb.rb:739:in `eval': Insecure: can't modify
trusted binding (SecurityError)
```

The safe level applies only to the code executed to run the code for the ERB template, whereas when you've previously used safe levels, you've been unable to lower them. The way this works is that when a safe mode is used with ERB, ERB creates a new thread for the processing of the ERB code, which allows a separate safe level to be set from that of the main code.

Refer to Chapter 11 or Appendix B for a refresher on what capabilities each safe level provides.

Further Information

- *Standard library documentation for ERB*: `http://www.ruby-doc.org/stdlib/libdoc/erb/rdoc/index.html`

- *Merb—a lightweight app server using ERB*: `http://merb.rubyforge.org/`

FasterCSV

In Chapter 9 you looked at Comma-Separated Value databases. An extremely crude way of storing data, CSV delimits fields of data with commas and separates records by newlines. For example:

```
Clive,53,male,UK
Ann,55,female,France
Eugene,29,male,California
```

You looked at the csv library provided with Ruby and used it to work with this form of data. The *FasterCSV* library, created by James Edward Gray II, performs similar functions to the csv library and is intended as a faster replacement. It has a slightly different interface from the standard csv library, though it can mimic it if necessary.

Installation

FasterCSV isn't part of the Ruby standard library (although this is likely to change in future) and is available as a RubyGem. To install it, use the typical gem installation process (as covered in Chapter 7), like so:

```
gem install fastercsv
```

or

```
sudo gem install fastercsv
```

Examples

In these examples we'll assume this CSV data is present in a file called data.csv:

```
Clive,53,male,UK
Ann,55,female,France
Eugene,29,male,California
```

Parsing a String Line by Line

If you want to iterate over CSV data line by line and parse the data as you go, it's easy to do so from a regular string:

```
require 'rubygems'
require 'fastercsv'
```

```
FasterCSV.parse(File.read("data.csv")) do |person|
  puts person.inspect
end
```

Parsing a String to an Array of Arrays

In the prior example you processed CSV data in "real time," but it's also possible for
FasterCSV to convert CSV data into another data structure—an array of arrays—making it
easy to compare and process datasets in one go:

```
require 'rubygems'
require 'fastercsv'
array_of_arrays = FasterCSV.parse(File.read("data.csv"))
array_of_arrays.each do |person|
  puts person.inspect
end
```

Parsing CSV Data from a File Line by Line

In a previous example you iterated over CSV data in a string line by line, but FasterCSV
can also operate directly upon a file:

```
require 'rubygems'
require 'fastercsv'
FasterCSV.foreach("data.csv") do |person|
  puts person.inspect
end
```

Parsing a Whole CSV File to an Array of Arrays

One technique that FasterCSV makes extremely easy is the ability to read in an entire CSV
file and convert it into an array of arrays with a single method call:

```
require 'rubygems'
require 'fastercsv'
array_of_arrays = FasterCSV.read("data.csv")
```

Generating CSV Data

As well as being able to read data, FasterCSV lets you create data in CSV format. To do this, you must have the data you want to write in an array in the correct order. This example demonstrates how you can convert an array of hashes into CSV-formatted output:

```ruby
require 'rubygems'
require 'fastercsv'

people = [
  {:name => "Fred", :age => 10, :gender => :male},
  {:name => "Graham", :age => 34, :gender => :male},
  {:name => "Lorraine", :age => 29, :gender => :female}
]

csv_data = FasterCSV.generate do |csv|
  people.each do |person|
    csv << [person[:name], person[:age], person[:gender]]
  end
end

puts csv_data
```

```
Fred,10,male
Graham,34,male
Lorraine,29,female
```

The FasterCSV class also provides an open method that lets you write direct to file as you go:

```ruby
FasterCSV.open("data.csv", "w") do |csv|
  people.each do |person|
    csv << [person[:name], person[:age], person[:gender]]
  end
end
```

■**Note** If you open the file with mode "a" instead of "w", then any data would be appended to the end of the existing data. With mode "w", the data is entirely replaced.

FasterCSV also provides convenience methods on `String` and `Array` so you can convert single lines to and from CSV easily:

```
puts ["Fred", 10, "male"].to_csv
```

```
Fred,10,male
```

```
puts "Fred,10,male".parse_csv.inspect
```

```
["Fred", 10, "male"]
```

FasterCSV Tables

FasterCSV also supports table data structures. It can use the first row of the CSV file as a list of column names so that you can use those column names to get easier access to the rest of the data in the table. To make FasterCSV read data in as a table with the first line as the header, set the `:headers` option to `true` on any of the FasterCSV class's reader methods.

To make the following example work, assume `data.csv` contains these lines:

```
Name,Age,Gender,Location
Clive,53,male,UK
Ann,55,female,France
Eugene,29,male,California
```

Now, use this code to read in `data.csv` as a table:

```
require 'rubygems'
require 'fastercsv'
require 'pp'

csv = FasterCSV.read("data.csv", :headers => true)
pp csv
```

```
#<FasterCSV::Table:0x5b7ed0
 @mode=:col_or_row,
 @table=
```

```
[#<FasterCSV::Row:0x5b72f0
  @header_row=false,
  @row=
   [["Name", "Clive"],
    ["Age", "53"],
    ["Gender", "male"],
    ["Location", "UK"]]>,
 #<FasterCSV::Row:0x5b6c60
  @header_row=false,
  @row=
   [["Name", "Ann"],
    ["Age", "55"],
    ["Gender", "female"],
    ["Location", "France"]]>,
 #<FasterCSV::Row:0x5b651c
  @header_row=false,
  @row=
   [["Name", "Eugene"],
    ["Age", "29"],
    ["Gender", "male"],
    ["Location", "California"]]>]>
```

Note In the preceding example you used pp to display the table structure more nicely than puts csv.inspect would, although other than the spacing, the output is roughly the same. The pp library is covered later in this chapter.

Rather than importing an array of arrays, when you use headers it creates a FasterCSV::Table object containing a FasterCSV::Row object for each row. You can also see that each column name is associated with the correct piece of data on each row.

FasterCSV::Table provides a number of useful methods (these examples assume csv contains a FasterCSV::Table object, as in the previous example) as follows:

- csv.to_s returns a string containing the entire table in CSV format. You can use this to rewrite the data back to file.

- csv.to_a returns the table as an array of arrays, as FasterCSV.read would if you hadn't used the :headers option.

- csv << can be used to push a new row onto the end of the table (for example, csv << ['Chris', 26, 'male', 'Los Angeles']).

- csv.headers returns an array of the header row.

- csv.delete('Name') removes the Name column from every row.

- csv.delete(n) deletes the *n*th row.

- csv[n] returns the *n*th row.

- csv.each iterates through each row using a code block.

The rows within the table (FasterCSV::Row objects) also have their own methods to access their data, as this example demonstrates:

```
csv.each do |row|
  puts row['Name']
end
```

```
Clive
Ann
Eugene
```

As a FasterCSV::Row, rather than an array, it's possible to use the column header name to retrieve the information you want on each row. Likewise, it's also possible to set columns to equal something else:

```
csv.each do |row|
  row['Location'] = "Nowhere"
end

puts csv.to_csv
```

```
Name,Age,Gender,Location
Clive,53,male,Nowhere
Ann,55,female,Nowhere
Eugene,29,male,Nowhere
```

■**Note** You can find other lesser-used methods in the official FasterCSV documentation, linked in the "Further Information" section.

Further Information

- *Official documentation for FasterCSV*: http://fastercsv.rubyforge.org/

- *More information about CSV formats*: http://en.wikipedia.org/wiki/ Comma-separated_values

iconv

iconv is an interface between Ruby and the Unix iconv utility that can translate strings between character encodings. In Chapter 11 you looked at character encodings and how you can use them from within Ruby, and iconv provides the functionality for *converting* strings between encodings within Ruby.

■**Note** The iconv utility and library (the operating system library, not the Ruby library) is provided as standard with all distributions of Linux (and often on BSDs, such as Mac OS X), but is not provided with Windows. Although iconv comes with the Cygwin environment on Windows, this library isn't likely to work otherwise, due to limitations of the standard Windows environment.

Installation

The iconv library is a part of the standard library, so it comes with Ruby by default. To use it, you only need to place this line near the start of your program:

```
require 'iconv'
```

Examples

There are three main ways to use iconv to convert strings from one character encoding to another. You can use it in a handle form, in an immediate form, or in a block form. For example, you can convert from the UTF-8 encoding to the ISO-8859-1 encoding using the handle form like this:

```
require 'iconv'
converter = Iconv.new('utf-8', 'iso-8859-1')
utf8_string = "This is a test"
iso_string = converter.iconv(utf8_string)
```

■**Note** The source encoding is provided as the first argument to `Iconv.new`, and the destination encoding is provided as the second argument.

Using iconv in a block form works in a similar way to using a `File` object in block form, as demonstrated here:

```
require 'iconv'
Iconv.open('utf-8', 'iso-8859-1') do |converter|
  utf8_string = "This is a test"
  iso_string = converter.iconv(utf8_string)
end
```

You can also use iconv in an immediate form to convert strings on a single line:

```
require 'iconv'
Iconv.iconv("utf-8", "iso-8859-1", "This is a test").to_s
```

Further Information

- *Standard library documentation for iconv*: http://www.ruby-doc.org/stdlib/libdoc/iconv/rdoc/index.html

- *Wikipedia article with more general information about iconv*: http://en.wikipedia.org/wiki/Iconv

logger

logger is a library developed by Hiroshi Nakamura and Gavin Sinclair that provides sophisticated logging features to Ruby applications. It supports automatic log rotation and multiple urgency levels, and can output to file, to standard output, or to standard error handles. Ruby on Rails uses logger as its main logging system, but you can use it from any Ruby application.

Installation

The logger library is a part of the standard library, so it comes with Ruby by default. To use it, you only need to place this line near the start of your program:

```
require 'logger'
```

Examples

To use logger, you create Logger objects and then use the methods provided by the objects to report events that occur while your program is running. The first step is to get a Logger object.

Setting up a Logger

Loggers can write to standard output, standard error, or to a file. Just specify a file handle or filename to Logger.new. For example, here's how to write log messages directly to the screen or terminal:

```
require 'logger'
logger = Logger.new(STDOUT)
```

Use this code to write log messages to file:

```
logger = Logger.new('mylogfile.log')
logger = Logger.new('/tmp/some_log_file.log')
```

You can also specify that a log file ages daily, weekly, or monthly (old log files are suffixed with date indicators):

```
logger = Logger.new('mylogfile.log', 'daily')
logger = Logger.new('mylogfile.log', 'weekly')
logger = Logger.new('mylogfile.log', 'monthly')
```

Last, it's possible to create a logger that only creates a log file up to a certain size. Once the log file hits that size, logger copies the existing log file to another filename, then starts a new log file. This is known as log rotation:

```
logger = Logger.new('mylogfile.log', 10, 100000)
```

This logger logs files to `mylogfile.log` until it reaches 100,000 bytes in length, whereupon the logger renames the log file (by suffixing it with a number) and creates a new `mylogfile.log`. It keeps the ten most recent, but unused, log files available.

Logging Levels

There are five different logging levels that are ranked in order of severity as follows:

- `DEBUG`: The lowest severity, used for debugging information for the developer.
- `INFO`: General information about the operation of the program, library, or system.
- `WARN`: A nonfatal warning about the state of the program.
- `ERROR`: An error that can be handled (as with a rescued exception).
- `FATAL`: An error that is unrecoverable and that forces an immediate end to the program.

Whenever you start a logger, you can specify the level of messages it should track. If a message is of that level or above, it will be logged. If it's below that level, it will be ignored. This is useful so that during development you can log every debug message, whereas when your program is being used for real, you only log the important messages.

To set the severity level of a logger, use the logger's `sev_threshold` method. This level ensures *only* `FATAL` messages are logged:

```
logger.sev_threshold = Logger::FATAL
```

This level ensures every message of all levels is logged:

```
logger.sev_threshold = Logger::DEBUG
```

Logging Messages

Each `Logger` object provides several methods to allow you to send a message to the log. The most commonly used way is to use the `debug`, `info`, `warn`, `error`, and `fatal` methods, which all create log messages of their respective severity:

```
require 'logger'
logger = Logger.new(STDOUT)
```

```
logger.debug "test"
logger.info "test"
logger.fatal "test"
```

```
D, [2007-03-12T11:06:06.805072 #9289] DEBUG -- : test
I, [2007-03-12T11:06:06.825144 #9289]  INFO -- : test
F, [2007-03-12T11:06:06.825288 #9289] FATAL -- : test
```

Log messages are notated by their severity as a single letter, the date and time of their creation, the process ID of which process created them, their severity label, followed by the actual message. Optionally, the program name might be present, if it was specified in the logging method, with the normal message coming from a block, like so:

```
logger.info("myprog") { "test" }
```

```
I, [2007-03-12T11:09:32.284956 #9289]  INFO -- myprog: test
```

You can also assign a severity to a log message dynamically, like so:

```
logger.add(Logger::FATAL) { "message here" }
```

```
F, [2007-03-12T11:13:06.880818 #9289] FATAL -- : message here
```

To use different severities, just pass the severity's class (Logger::FATAL, Logger::DEBUG, Logger::INFO, and so on) as the argument to add.

Closing a Logger

You close a logger as you would a file or any other I/O structure:

```
logger.close
```

Further Information

- *Standard library documentation for logger:* http://www.ruby-doc.org/stdlib/ libdoc/logger/rdoc/index.html

- *Log4r—another, more complex, Ruby logging library:* http://log4r. sourceforge.net/

pp

pp is a "pretty printer" that provides nicer output than a simple `puts something.inspect`. It gives you a nice, clean look at data structures that are properly tabulated and spaced, unlike `inspect`'s output.

Installation

The pp library is a part of the standard library, so it comes with Ruby by default. To use it, you only need to place this line near the start of your program:

```
require 'pp'
```

Examples

To use pp, simply use the `pp` method, followed by the object whose structure you wish to display. Here's a basic comparison of `inspect` and `pp`:

```
person1 = { :name => "Peter", :gender => :male }
person2 = { :name => "Laura", :gender => :female }
people = [person1, person2, person1, person1, person1]
puts people.inspect
```

```
[{:name=>"Peter", :gender=>:male}, {:name=>"Laura", :gender=>:female},
 {:name=>"Peter", :gender=>:male}, {:name=>"Peter", :gender=>:male},
 {:name=>"Peter", :gender=>:male}]
```

```
pp people
```

```
[{:name=>"Peter", :gender=>:male},
 {:name=>"Laura", :gender=>:female},
 {:name=>"Peter", :gender=>:male},
 {:name=>"Peter", :gender=>:male},
 {:name=>"Peter", :gender=>:male}]
```

As demonstrated, pp is mostly useful when dealing with complex objects whose data cannot fit on a single line. Here's a more contrived example:

```
require 'pp'

class TestClass
  def initialize(count)
    @@a = defined?(@@a) ? @@a + 1 : 0
```

```
    @c = @@a
    @d = [:a => {:b => count }, :c => :d] * count
  end
end

pp TestClass.new(2), STDOUT, 60
pp TestClass.new(3), $>, 60
pp TestClass.new(4), $>, 60
```

```
#<TestClass:0x357000
 @c=0,
 @d=[{:a=>{:b=>2}, :c=>:d}, {:a=>{:b=>2}, :c=>:d}]>
#<TestClass:0x354364
 @c=1,
 @d=
  [{:a=>{:b=>3}, :c=>:d},
   {:a=>{:b=>3}, :c=>:d},
   {:a=>{:b=>3}, :c=>:d}]>
#<TestClass:0x3503f4
 @c=2,
 @d=
  [{:a=>{:b=>4}, :c=>:d},
   {:a=>{:b=>4}, :c=>:d},
   {:a=>{:b=>4}, :c=>:d},
   {:a=>{:b=>4}, :c=>:d}]>
```

Where it's practical, pp fits data onto a single line, but when more data is to be shown than could fit on a single line, pp formats and spaces that data accordingly.

Note that in the preceding example the pp calls are in this format:

```
pp TestClass.new(4), $>, 60
```

With no parameters, pp assumes a display width of 79 characters. However, pp supports two optional parameters that set the destination for its output, and the width of the output field. In this case you output to the standard output and assume a wrapping width of 60 characters.

Further Information

- *Standard library documentation for pp*: http://www.ruby-doc.org/stdlib/libdoc/pp/rdoc/index.html

RedCloth

RedCloth is a library that converts specially formatted text documents (in a formatting known as *Textile*) into valid HTML. In many ways it's similar to the BlueCloth library featured earlier in this chapter.

The reasoning behind languages such as Textile is that most users prefer to write their documents in a clean format, rather than be forced to use HTML tags everywhere and create documents that don't read well as plain text. Textile allows you to format text in a way that makes documents look good as plain text, but that also allows the text to be converted quickly to HTML for use on the Web.

Compared to the Markdown markup language used by BlueCloth, Textile gives you a little more control over the HTML output and provides easy access to certain advanced features. However, in my opinion it's more technical and doesn't flow quite as well as Markdown, although it certainly has its uses.

RedCloth was developed by "why the lucky stiff" and Textile by Dean Allen.

Installation

RedCloth isn't part of the Ruby standard library and is available as a RubyGem. To install it, use the typical gem installation process (as covered in Chapter 7), like so:

```
gem install RedCloth
```

or

```
sudo gem install RedCloth
```

Examples

RedCloth works in an almost identical way to BlueCloth, as covered previously in this chapter. It makes a RedCloth class available that directly inherits from String, so you can use all the usual String methods on a RcdCloth object.

The basic example for RedCloth is similar to that for BlueCloth:

```
require 'rubygems'
require 'redcloth'

redcloth_text = <<EOF
h1. This is a title

Here is some _lext_ that's formatted according to
"Textile":http://hobix.com/textile/ *specifications*.
And how about a quote?
```

```
bq. This section is a quote.. a block quote
more accurately..

Lists are also possible:

* Item 1
* Item 2
* Item 3
EOF

redcloth_obj = RedCloth.new redcloth_text
puts redcloth_obj.to_html
```

```
<h1>This is a title</h1>
        <p>Here is some <em>text</em> that&#8217;s formatted according to
<a href="http://hobix.com/textile/">Textile</a> <strong>specifications</strong>.
And how about a quote?</p>

        <blockquote>
                <p>This section is a quote.. a block quote
more accurately..</p>
        </blockquote>

        <p>Lists are also possible:</p>

        <ul>
        <li>Item 1</li>
                <li>Item 2</li>
                <li>Item 3</li>
        </ul>
```

Note Some line spacing has been removed in the preceding output, but the horizontal formatting has been left intact.

It's worth noting that RedCloth's output isn't immediately as clean as that from Blue-Cloth, but it's still valid HTML.

Further Information

- *Official RedCloth home page*: http://whytheluckystiff.net/ruby/redcloth/

- *Official Textile home page*: http://www.textism.com/tools/textile/

StringScanner

StringScanner is a library that lets you "walk through" a string, matching patterns one at a time, while only applying them to the remainder of the data that you haven't yet matched. This is in stark contrast to the standard `scan` method that automatically returns all matching patterns immediately.

Installation

StringScanner is in the standard library, so it comes with Ruby by default. To use it, you only need to place this line near the start of your program:

```
require 'strscan'
```

Note It's important to recognize that the filename doesn't match the name of the library, or class in this case. Although most library developers tend to keep names consistent, not all do!

Examples

The best way to see StringScanner's feature set is to see it in action:

```
require 'strscan'

string = StringScanner.new "This is a test"
puts string.scan(/\w+/)
puts string.scan(/\s+/)
puts string.scan(/\w+/)
puts string.scan(/\s+/)
puts string.rest
```

```
This

is

a test
```

In this example you step through the string by first matching a word with scan, then whitespace, then another word, then more whitespace, before asking StringScanner to give you the rest of the string with the rest method.

However, scan will only return content if the specified pattern matches at the current position in the string. For example, this doesn't retrieve each word:

```
puts string.scan(/\w+/)
puts string.scan(/\w+/)
puts string.scan(/\w+/)
puts string.scan(/\w+/)
```

```
This
nil
nil
nil
```

After the first scan, the pointer for string is waiting at the whitespace after "This," and scan must match the whitespace for it to continue. One way to get around this would be like so:

```
puts string.scan(/\w+\s*/)
puts string.scan(/\w+\s*/)
puts string.scan(/\w+\s*/)
puts string.scan(/\w+\s*/)
```

In the preceding example, you'd retrieve the words and any whitespace located after each word. Of course, this might not be desirable, so StringScanner also provides other useful methods for scanning through strings.

scan_until scans through the string from the current position until the specified pattern matches. All the data from the start of the scan, until and including the match, is then returned. In this example, you perform a normal scan and pick off the first word, but then you use scan_until to scan all text until you reach a number:

```
string = StringScanner.new "I want to live to be 100 years old!"
puts string.scan(/\w+/)
puts string.scan_until(/\d+/)
```

```
I
want to live to be 100
```

You can also use scan_until to give a different solution to the previous "scan for each word" problem:

```
require 'strscan'
string = StringScanner.new("This is a test")
puts string.scan_until(/\w+/)
puts string.scan_until(/\w+/)
puts string.scan_until(/\w+/)
puts string.scan_until(/\w+/)
```

Another useful method is unscan, which gives you the opportunity to roll back a single scan:

```
string = StringScanner.new "I want to live to be 100 years old!"
puts string.scan(/\w+/)
string.unscan
puts string.scan_until(/\d+/)
string.unscan
puts string.scan_until(/live/)
```

```
I
I want to live to be 100
I want to live
```

You can also retrieve the current position of the scanner in the string:

```
string = StringScanner.new "I want to live to be 100 years old!"
string.scan(/\w+/)
string.unscan
puts string.pos
string.scan_until(/\d+/)
puts string.pos
string.unscan
string.scan_until(/live/)
puts string.pos
```

```
0
24
14
```

You can use pos to set or override the position of the scanner too:

```
string = StringScanner.new "I want to live to be 100 years old!"
string.pos = 12
puts string.scan(/...../)
```

```
ve to
```

■Note StringScanner isn't a subclass of String, so typical methods provided by String won't necessarily work. However, StringScanner does implement some of them, such as <<, which concatenates data
onto the end of the string.

Further Information

- *Standard library documentation for StringScanner*: http://www.ruby-doc.org/
  stdlib/libdoc/strscan/rdoc/index.html

tempfile

Temporary files are files that are intended for a single one-time purpose. They're ephemeral files that you use to store information temporarily, but that are quickly erased. In Chapter 9 you looked at the creation of temporary files using several techniques, but *tempfile* provides an easy and standard way to create and manipulate them.

Installation

tempfile is in the standard library, so comes with Ruby by default. To use it, you only need to place this line near the start of your program:

```
require 'tempfile'
```

Examples

tempfile manages the creation and manipulation of temporary files. It creates temporary files in the correct place for your operating system, and gives them unique names so that you can concentrate on the main logic of your application.

To create a temporary file, use `Tempfile.new`:

```
require 'tempfile'
f = Tempfile.new('myapp')
f.puts "Hello"
puts f.path
f.close
```

```
/tmp/myapp1842.0
```

`Tempfile.new` creates a temporary file using the given string as a prefix in the format of `<supplied name>-<program's process ID>.<unique number>`. The returned object is a `Tempfile` object that delegates most of its methods to the usual `File` and `IO` classes, allowing you to use the file methods you're already familiar with, as with `f.puts` earlier.

To use the data in your temporary file, you can close it and reopen it quickly:

```
f.close
f.open
```

If you specify no arguments to f.open, it will reopen the temporary file associated with that object. At that point you can continue to write to the temporary file or read from it.

```
require 'tempfile'
f = Tempfile.new('myapp')
f.puts "Hello"
f.close
f.open
puts f.read
f.close!
```

```
Hello
```

The preceding code creates a temporary file, writes data to it, closes the temporary file (which flushes the written data out to disk from the memory buffers), and then reopens it for reading.

The last line uses close! instead of close, which forces the temporary file to be closed and permanently deleted.

Of course, you can flush the buffers manually so you can use the same temporary file for reading and writing without having to close it at any point:

```
require 'tempfile'

f = Tempfile.new('myapp')
f.puts "Hello"
f.pos = 0
f.print "Y"
f.pos = f.size - 1
f.print "w"
f.flush
f.pos = 0
puts f.read
f.close!
```

```
Yellow
```

■Note By default, temporary files are opened in the w+ mode.

In some situations, you might want to use temporary files, but not allow tempfile to put them in a place that can be seen by other programs or users. `Tempfile.new` accepts an optional second argument that specifies where you want temporary files to be created:

```
f = Tempfile.new('myapp', '/my/secret/temporary/directory')
```

As with other file-related classes, you can use `Tempfile` in block form:

```
require 'tempfile'

Tempfile.open('myapp') do |f|
  f.puts "Hello"
  f.pos = 0
  f.print "Y"
  f.pos = f.size - 1
  f.print "w"
  f.flush
  f.pos = 0
  puts f.read
end
```

```
Yellow
```

Note You use `Tempfile.open` instead of `Tempfile.new` when using a block.

The benefit of using block form in this case is that the temporary file is removed automatically and no closing is required. However, if you want to use a temporary file throughout the scope of a whole program, block form might not be suitable.

Further Information

- *Standard library documentation for tempfile*: http://www.ruby-doc.org/stdlib/libdoc/tempfile/rdoc/index.html

uri

You use the *uri* library to manage Uniform Resource Identifiers (URIs), which are typically referred to as Uniform Resource Locators (URLs). A URL is an address such as `http://www.rubyinside.com/`, `ftp://your-ftp-site.com/directory/filename`, or even `mailto:your-email-address@privacy.net`. uri makes it easy to detect, create, parse, and manipulate these addresses.

Installation

uri is in the standard library, so it comes with Ruby by default. To use it, you only need to place this line near the start of your program:

```
require 'uri'
```

Examples

In this section you'll look at a few examples of how to use the uri library to perform basic URL-related functions.

Extracting URLs from Text

`URI.extract` is a class method that extracts URLs from a given string into an array:

```
require 'uri'
puts URI.extract('Check out http://www.rubyinside.com/ or e-mail ➥
mailto:me@privacy.net').inspect
```

```
["http://www.rubyinside.com/", "mailto:me@privacy.net"]
```

You can also limit the types of URLs that `extract` should find:

```
require 'uri'
puts URI.extract('http://www.rubyinside.com/ and mailto:me@privacy.net', ➥
['http']).inspect
```

```
["http://www.rubyinside.com/"]
```

If you immediately want to use the URLs one by one, you can use `extract` with a block:

```
require 'uri'

email = %q{Some cool Ruby sites are http://www.ruby-lang.org/ and ➥
http://www.rubyinside.com/ and http://redhanded.hobix.com/}

URI.extract(email, ['http', 'https']) do |url|
  puts "Fetching URL #{url}"
  # Do some work here...
end
```

Parsing URLs

A URL in a string can be useful, particularly if you want to use that URL with open-uri or net/http, for example, but it can also be useful to split URLs into their constituent sections. Doing this with a regular expression would give inconsistent results and be prone to failure in uncommon situations, so the URI class provides the tools necessary to split URLs apart easily.

```
URI.parse('http://www.rubyinside.com/')
```

```
=> #<URI::HTTP:0x2d071c URL:http://www.rubyinside.com/>
```

URI.parse parses a URL provided in a string and returns a URI-based object for it. URI has specific subclasses for FTP, HTTP, HTTPS, LDAP, and MailTo URLs, but returns a URI::Generic object for an unrecognized URL that's in a URL-type format.

The URI objects have a number of methods that you can use to access information about the URL:

```
require 'uri'
a = URI.parse('http://www.rubyinside.com/')
puts a.scheme
puts a.host
puts a.port
puts a.path
puts a.query
```

```
http
www.rubyinside.com
80
/
nil
```

Note that URI::HTTP is smart enough to know that if no port is specifically stated in an HTTP URL, the default port 80 must apply. The other URI classes, such as URI::FTP and URI::HTTPS, also make similar assumptions.

With more complex URLs, you can access some extended data:

```
require 'uri'
url = 'http://www.x.com:1234/test/1.html?x=y&y=z#top'
puts URI.parse(url).port
puts URI.parse(url).path
puts URI.parse(url).query
puts URI.parse(url).fragment
```

```
1234
/test/1.html
x=y&y=z
top
```

The uri library also makes a convenience method available to make it even easier to parse URLs:

```
u = URI('http://www.test.com/')
```

In this case, URI(url) is synonymous with URI.parse.

As well as URI.parse, you can use URI.split to split a URL into its constituent parts without involving a URI object:

```
URI.split('http://www.x.com:1234/test/1.html?x=y&y=z#top')
```

```
=> ["http", nil, "www.x.com", "1234", nil, "/test/1.html", nil,
    "x=y&y=z", "top"]
```

URI.split returns, in order, the scheme, user info, hostname, port number, registry, path, opaque attribute, query, and fragment. Any elements that are missing are nil.

■Note The only benefit of URI.split is that no URI object is created, so there can be minimal gains in memory and processor usage. However, generally it's more acceptable to use URI() or URI.parse so that you can address the different elements by name, rather than rely on the order of elements in an array (which could change between versions of the library).

Creating URLs

You can also use uri to create URLs that meet the accepted specifications. At their simplest, you can use the URI subclasses for each protocol to generate URLs by passing in a hash of the elements you want to make up the URL:

```
require 'uri'
u = URI::HTTP.build( :host => 'rubyinside.com', :path => '/' )
puts u.to_s
puts u.request_uri
```

```
http://rubyinside.com/
/
```

Note that to_s returns the entire URL, whereas request_uri returns the portion of the URL that follows the hostname. This is because libraries such as net/http would use the data from request_uri, whereas libraries such as open-uri can use the entire URL.

You could also pass in :port, :query, :fragment, :userinfo, and other elements to the URI subclasses to generate more complex URLs.

Here's an example of creating an FTP URL:

```
ftp_url = URI::FTP.build( :userinfo => 'username:password',
:host => 'ftp.example.com',
:path => '/pub/folder',
:typecode => 'a')

puts ftp_url.to_s
```

```
ftp://username:password@ftp.example.com/pub/folder;type=a
```

Also note that uri is good at adjusting URLs in a safe manner, as you can set the various attributes to new values, as well as read them:

```
require 'uri'
my_url = "http://www.test.com/something/test.html"
url = URI.parse(my_url)
url.host = "www.test2.com"
url.port = 1234
puts url.to_s
```

```
http://www.test2.com:1234/something/test.html
```

Further Information

- *Standard library documentation for uri*: http://www.ruby-doc.org/ stdlib/libdoc/uri/rdoc/index.html

- *Information about URLs and URIs*: http://en.wikipedia.org/wiki/URL

zlib

zlib is an open source data-compression library. It's a significant standard in data compression, and you can manipulate zlib archives on almost every platform. Notably, zlib is often used to compress Web pages between servers and Web browsers, is used in the Linux kernel, and forms a key part of many operating system libraries.

You can use zlib from Ruby as a mechanism to compress and uncompress data.

Installation

zlib is in the standard library, so comes with Ruby by default. To use it, you only need to place this line near the start of your program:

```
require 'zlib'
```

Examples

Under zlib, compression and uncompression are called *deflating* and *inflating*. The quickest way to compress (*deflate*) data is by using the Zlib::Deflate class directly:

```
require 'zlib'

test_text = 'this is a test string' * 100
puts "Original string is #{test_text.length} bytes long"
compressed_text = Zlib::Deflate.deflate(test_text)
puts "Compressed data is #{compressed_text.length} bytes long"
```

```
Original string is 2100 bytes long
Compressed data is 46 bytes long
```

This test text compresses extremely well, as it's the same string repeated 100 times over. However, on normal data, it's more practical to see compression rates of around 10 to 50 percent.

Restoring compressed data requires Zlib::Inflate:

```
require 'zlib'

test_text = 'this is a test string' * 100
puts "Original string is #{test_text.length} bytes long"
```

```
compressed_text = Zlib::Deflate.deflate(test_text)
puts "Compressed data is #{compressed_text.length} bytes long"
uncompressed_text = Zlib::Inflate.inflate(compressed_text)
puts "Uncompressed data is back to #{uncompressed_text.length} bytes in length"
```

```
Original string is 2100 bytes long
Compressed data is 46 bytes long
Uncompressed data is back to 2100 bytes in length
```

■**Note** The compressed data returned by zlib is full 8-bit data, so might not be suitable to use in e-mails or in formats where regular plain text is necessary. To get around this, you can compress your data using zlib as usual, and then use the base64 library to turn the compressed results into plain text.

zlib also comes with classes to help you work directly with compressed files. Files compressed with the zlib algorithm are often known as *gzipped* files, and Zlib::Gzip-Writer and Zlib::GzipReader make it easy to create, and read from, these files:

```
require 'zlib'

Zlib::GzipWriter.open('my_compressed_file.gz') do |gz|
  gz.write 'This data will be compressed automatically!'
end

Zlib::GzipReader.open('my_compressed_file.gz') do |my_file|
  puts my_file.read
end
```

```
This data will be compressed automatically!
```

Further Information

- *Standard library documentation for zlib*: http://www.ruby-doc.org/stdlib/libdoc/zlib/rdoc/index.html

APPENDIX A

■■■

Ruby Primer and Review for Developers

This appendix is designed to act as both a Ruby primer and review, useful both to developers who want to brush up rapidly on their Ruby knowledge, and to those who are new to the language but who have existing programming knowledge and want to get a quick overview.

If you're a new programmer, or at least are new to concepts such as object orientation, scripting languages, and dynamic languages, you'll want to read through Chapter 2 and continue with the rest of the book instead of depending on this appendix to teach you about Ruby. This appendix is designed for those who have either finished reading the rest of this book and who want to brush up on the basics, or those who want to look quickly through some basic elements of Ruby syntax in the flesh.

With that in mind, this appendix isn't instructional, as most of the other chapters in this book are. A lot of concepts will be covered at a quick pace with succinct code examples. References to more explanatory detail found in this book are given where possible.

The Basics

In this section I'll give a brief overview of the Ruby programming language, its concepts, and how to use the Ruby interpreter.

Definition and Concepts

Ruby is an open source, object-oriented programming language created and maintained by Yukihiro Matsumoto (among others). Languages such as Perl, LISP, Smalltalk, and Python have inspired the syntax and styling of the language. It is cross platform and runs on several different architectures, although its "home" architecture is Linux on x86.

Among other things, Ruby has automatic garbage collection, is easily portable, supports cooperative multitasking on all supported platforms using its own threading system, has a large standard library, and supports most features associated with dynamic languages (such as closures, iterators, exceptions, overloading, and reflection).

Ruby is an interpreted language. This is in opposition to languages that are *compiled*. Code developed in languages such as C and C++ has to be compiled into *object code* that represents instructions supported by a computer's processor. Ruby, however, is compiled down into platform-independent bytecode that is run by a virtual machine. Python, Java, and C# share this characteristic, although they all run upon different virtual machine implementations and have different execution characteristics. Table A-1 highlights some key differences between several popular programming languages.

Table A-1. *Feature Comparison Between Several Popular Programming Languages*

Language	Object-Oriented?	Reflective?	Dynamically Typed?	Interpreted?
Ruby	Yes	Yes	Yes	Yes
C	No	No	No	No
C++	Yes	No	No	No
C#	Yes	Yes	Yes	Yes, through VM
Perl	Partially	Partially	Yes	Yes
Java	Yes, mostly	Not generally	No	Yes, through VM
Python	Yes	Yes	Yes	Yes

Ruby has been developed with the "principle of least surprise" in mind, so the way you'd expect things to work is usually a valid way of doing something. This means Ruby is very much a "There's More Than One Way To Do It" type of language, in the same vein as Perl but quite different in philosophy from languages such as Python, where having one clear process to achieve something is seen as the best way to do things.

■**Note** A useful resource is the official Ruby site's "Ruby From Other Languages" section at http://www.ruby-lang.org/en/documentation/ruby-from-other-languages/, where in-depth comparisons of Ruby against C, C++, Java, Perl, PHP, and Python are given.

One important concept in Ruby is that almost everything is an object. For example, the following line of code calls a primitive, internal method called `puts` with a single argument of `10`. `puts` prints its arguments to the screen:

```
puts 10
```

```
10
```

The following line of code calls the `class` method on the numeric object 10. Even the literal number 10 is an object in this situation. The result demonstrates that `10` is an object of the `Fixnum` class.

```
puts 10.class
```

```
Fixnum
```

Ruby's reflection, overriding, object orientation, and other dynamic features make it possible for developers to entirely override the behaviors of even built-in classes such as `Fixnum`. It's possible to make `Fixnum` objects work in totally different ways. You can override `Fixnum` to the point that 2 + 2 could well equal 5. Although some developers already experienced with languages such as Java and C see this as a downside, this level of control over the internals of the language gives Ruby developers a significant amount of power. The key is to use that power carefully.

The Ruby Interpreter and Running Ruby Code

As Ruby is an interpreted language, Ruby code is executed using the Ruby interpreter. On most platforms, that makes running a Ruby script as easy as this:

```
ruby name_of_script.rb
```

▪**Note** Ruby program files usually end with the extension of RB, although this isn't a strict requirement.

The Ruby interpreter has a number of options. You can ask the Ruby interpreter to print out its version details using the -v (version) option:

```
ruby -v
```

```
ruby 1.8.5 (2006-08-25) [i686-darwin8.8.1]
```

You can also execute Ruby commands directly from the command line, using -e:

```
ruby -e "puts 2 + 2"
```

```
4
```

You can learn more about the Ruby interpreter's command line options by typing **man ruby** (on Unix-related platforms) or by visiting a Web-based version of the Ruby *man* page at http://www.linuxcommand.org/man_pages/ruby1.html.

■**Note** In Microsoft Windows, you might choose to associate the Ruby interpreter directly with any RB files so that you can double-click Ruby files to execute them.

On Unix-related platforms, it's possible to add a "shebang" line as the first line of a Ruby script so that it can be executed without having to invoke the Ruby interpreter explicitly. For example:

```
#!/usr/bin/ruby
puts "Hello, world!"
```

You can take this script, give it a simple filename such as hello (no RB extension needed), make the file executable (using chmod), and run it directly using its filename rather than having to invoke the Ruby interpreter explicitly. Chapter 10 covers this technique in more depth. More information about the shebang line specifically is available at http://en.wikipedia.org/wiki/Shebang_(Unix).

Interactive Ruby

With the normal Ruby interpreter also comes an interactive Ruby interpreter called *irb*. This allows you to write Ruby code in an immediate, interactive environment where the results of your code are given as soon as you type it. Here's an example irb session:

```
# irb
irb(main):001:0> puts "test"
test
=> nil
irb(main):002:0> 10 + 10
=> 20
irb(main):003:0> 10 == 20
=> false
irb(main):004:0> exit
```

irb gives you the results of methods and expressions immediately. This makes it an ideal tool for debugging or putting together quick snippets of code, and for testing concepts.

Expressions, Logic, and Flow Control

Expressions, logic, and flow control make up a significant part of any developer's tools in any programming language. This section looks at how Ruby implements them.

Basic Expressions

Ruby supports expressions in a style familiar to almost any programmer:

```
"a" + "b" + "c"
```

```
abc
```

```
10 + 20 + 30
```

```
60
```

```
("a" * 5) + ("c" * 6)
```

```
aaaaacccccc
```

```
a = 10
b = 20
a * b
```

```
200
```

You can assign the results of expressions to variables, which you can then use in other expressions.

Method calls, variables, literals, brackets, and operators can all combine so long as subexpressions always feed values of the correct type into their parent expressions or provide methods that allow them to be *coerced* into the right types. The next section covers this topic in more depth. (Expressions are covered in depth in Chapter 3.)

Class Mismatches

Ruby is a dynamic language, but unlike Perl, objects aren't converted between different classes automatically. For example, this expression is valid in Perl:

```
"20" + 10
```

```
30
```

However, in Ruby, you get an error response with the same expression:

```
TypeError: can't convert Fixnum into String
        from (irb):1:in `+'
        from (irb):1
```

In Ruby, you can only use objects that are of the same class or that support automatic translation between classes (*coercion*) in operations with one another.

However, Ruby comes with a set of methods that exist on many types of objects, which make conversion easy. For example:

```
"20" + 10.to_s
```

```
2010
```

In this example, the number 10 is converted to a string "10" in situ with the to_s method.

Consider this inverse example, where you convert the string "20" into an integer object using the to_i method before adding 10 to it:

```
"20".to_i + 10
```

```
30
```

> **Note** Methods are covered in depth in Chapters 2, 3, and 6, as well as later in this appendix.

The to_s method provided by all number classes in Ruby results in a number being converted into a String object. C and C++ programmers might recognize this concept as similar to *casting*.

Other conversions that can take place are converting integers to floats using to_f, and vice versa with to_i. You can convert strings and numbers using to_s, to_i, and to_f. Many other classes support to_s for converting their structure and other data into a string (the Time class provides a good demonstration of this). This topic is covered in Chapter 3 in the section "Converting Between Classes."

Comparison Expressions

Comparison expressions in Ruby, as in most other languages, return true or false, except that in some situations comparisons might return nil, Ruby's concept of "null" or nonexistence. For example:

```
2 == 1
```

```
false
```

```
2 == 2
```

```
true
```

```
(2 == 2) && (1 == 1)
```

```
true
```

```
x = 12
x * 2 == x + 1
```

```
false
```

```
x * x == x ** 2
```

```
true
```

In each of the preceding examples, you test whether variables, literals, or other expressions are equal to one another using == (symbolizing "is equal to"). You can check that multiple expressions result in true (logical "and"—if x and y are true) using && (symbolizing "and").

As in other languages, the concept of a logical "or" is symbolized by ||:

```
(2 == 5) || (1 == 1)
```

```
true
```

This expression is true because even though 2 is not equal to 5, the other subexpression *is* true, meaning that one *or* another of the expressions is true, so the whole comparison is also true.

Last, it can be useful to negate expressions. You can do this with the ! operator, as in many other programming languages. For example, you might want to see if one thing is true but another thing is false. Here's an example:

```
(2 == 2) && !(1 == 2)
```

```
true
```

The expression is true because both subexpressions are true. 2 is equal to 2, and 1 is *not* equal to 2.

You can also check that one thing is not equal to another with the inequality operator !=:

```
(2 == 2) && (1 != 2)
```

```
true
```

Flow

Ruby supports a few different forms of flow control. In this section you'll see several techniques you can use for branching and looping. (All the topics in this section are covered in more depth in Chapter 3.)

Branching and Conditional Execution

The simplest form of conditional execution is with just a single line using if or unless:

```
puts "The universe is broken!" if 2 == 1
```

This example won't print anything to the screen because 2 is not equal to 1. In this case, if performs the comparison before the rest of the line is executed. This usage will be familiar to Perl programmers (indeed, that's where this construction came from), but might appear back-to-front to developers from languages such as C.

Ruby also supports a multiline construction that's more familiar to non-Perl or Ruby coders:

```
if 2 == 1
  puts "The universe is broken!"
end
```

This multiline construction is less space efficient than the previous, single-line construction, but it allows you to put multiple lines between the condition and the end of the block, which isn't possible with the "end of line" technique. Pascal coders should note the absence of a begin, though otherwise the style is similar to that in Pascal.

You can also write the preceding conditional logic in a single-line way, but it's a messy style and rarely seen:

```
if 2 == 1: puts "The universe is broken!" end
```

This technique is only shown for completeness. Try not to use it!

■**Note** unless is the opposite of if. It executes code if the expression is false (or nil), rather than true. Some coders think of it as "if not," because unless acts like if with the expression negated.

Ruby also supports the else directive, as found in languages such as C, Perl, and Pascal:

```
if 2 == 1
  puts "The universe is broken!"
else
  puts "The universe is okay!"
end
```

```
The universe is okay!
```

If the expression (2 == 1 in this example) is true, the main block of code is executed, *else* the other block of code is. There's also a feature called elsif that lets you chain multiple ifs together:

```
if x == 1 || x == 3 || x == 5 || x == 7 || x == 9
  puts "x is odd and under 10"
elsif x == 2 || x == 4 || x == 6 || x == 8
  puts "x is even and under 10"
else
  puts "x is over 10 or under 1"
end
```

The preceding rather obtuse example demonstrates how you can use if, elsif, and else in tandem. The only thing to note is that end always finishes an if (or unless) block, whether end is on its own or features elsif and else blocks too. In some languages there's no need to delimit the end of if blocks if they only contain a single line. This isn't true of Ruby.

Note C coders will be used to else if. Ruby's variation is based on the Perl standard of elsif.

Ruby also supports another construction familiar to C, C++, Java, and Pascal coders, case (known as switch in C, C++, and Java):

```
fruit = "orange"
case fruit
  when "orange"
    color = "orange"
  when "apple"
    color = "green"
  when "banana"
    color = "yellow"
  else
    color = "unknown"
end
```

This code is similar to the if block, except that the syntax is a lot cleaner. A case block works by processing an expression first (supplied after case), and then the case block finds and executes a contained when block with an associated value matching the result of that expression. If no matching when block is found, then the else block within the case block will be executed instead.

case is, essentially, a substitution for a large, messy clump of if and elsif statements.

The Ternary Operator (Conditional Expressions)

Ruby supports a construction called the *ternary operator*. Its usage is simple:

```
x = 10
puts x > 10 ? "Higher than ten" : "Lower or equal to ten"
```

```
Lower or equal to ten
```

The ternary operator works like so:

```
expression ? true_expression : false_expression
```

It works like an expression, but with built-in flow control. If the initial expression is true, then the first following expression will be evaluated and returned. If the initial expression is false, then the final following expression will be evaluated and returned instead.

Loops

Ruby supports loops in a similar way to other programming languages. For example, while, loop, until, next, and break features will be familiar (although with possibly different names) to most programmers.

■**Note** Ruby also supports iteration and code blocks, which can prove a lot more powerful than regular loops. These are covered later in this appendix and in Chapters 2, 3, and 6.

Loop techniques are covered in Chapter 3, but some basic demonstrations follow. Here's a permanent loop that you can break out of using break:

```
i = 0
loop do
  i += 1
  break if i > 100
end
```

■**Note** It's worth noting that unlike in C or Perl, you cannot increment variables by 1 with variable++ in Ruby. variable = variable + 1 or variable += 1 are necessary instead.

Here's a while loop, using next to skip even numbers (using the % modulo operator):

```
i = 0
while (i < 15)
  i += 1
  next if i % 2 == 0
  puts i
end
```

```
1
3
5
7
9
11
13
15
```

> ■**Note** until is the opposite to while. until (i >= 15) is equivalent to while (i < 15).

Further looping techniques are covered in Chapter 3 and throughout the book.

Object Orientation

Ruby is considered a *pure* object-oriented language, because everything appears, to Ruby, as an object. An earlier example in this appendix demonstrated this:

```
puts 10.class
```

```
Fixnum
```

Even literal data within code is considered to be an object, and you can call the methods made available by those objects (and/or their parent classes).

> ■**Note** Object orientation, classes, objects, methods, and their respective techniques are covered in full in Chapters 2 and 6. This section presents merely a brief overview.

Ruby implements object orientation in a simple way (syntax-wise), but offers more dynamic features than other major languages (see Chapter 6 for many examples of such features).

Objects

Objects in Ruby have no special qualities beyond objects that exist in any other object-oriented programming language. However, the key difference between Ruby and most other major object-oriented languages is that in Ruby everything is an object. With this in mind, you can call methods on almost everything, and even chain methods together.

In C or Perl it would be common practice to write code in this form:

```
function1(function2(function3(something)))
```

However, in Ruby you'd do this:

```
something.function3.function2.function1
```

Periods are used between an object and the method to call, as in C++ or Java (as opposed to -> used in Perl). In this example, you call the function3 method upon the something object, then the function2 method upon the result of that, and then the function1 method on the result of that. A real-world demonstration can illustrate:

```
"this is a test".reverse
```

```
tset a si siht
```

```
"this is a test".reverse.upcase.split(' ').reverse.join('-')
```

```
SIHT-SI-A-TSET
```

This example is deliberately long to demonstrate the power of method chaining in Ruby. The syntax is a lot cleaner than the equivalent in Perl, C, or C++, and almost reads like English. This example takes your string "this is a test", reverses it, converts it to upper case, splits it into words (splitting on spaces), reverses the position of the words in an array, then joins the array back into a string with each element separated by dashes. (Objects are covered in depth in Chapters 2, 3, and 6.)

Classes and Methods

Ruby classes are similar in style to those in Perl, C++, or Java, but keep the benefits of Ruby's dynamic features. Let's look at an example class definition:

```ruby
class Person
  def initialize(name, age)
    @name = name
    @age = age
  end

  def name
    return @name
  end

  def age
    return @age
  end
end
```

This class features an `initialize` method that is called automatically when you create a new instance of that class. Two parameters or arguments are accepted (name and age) and assigned to instance variables. Instance variables are variables associated with a particular instance of a class and begin with an @ sign (as in @name). Java developers should recognize @name as being similar to `this.name`.

After the initializer come two methods (name and age) that act as basic accessors. They simply return the value of their respective instance variables.

Note In Ruby, if no value is explicitly returned from a method, the value of the last expression is returned instead. Therefore, `return @name` and just @name as the last line in the name method would be equivalent.

With the preceding class definition, it's trivial to create new objects:

```ruby
person1 = Person.new('Chris', 25)
person2 = Person.new('Laura', 23)
puts person1.name
puts person2.age
```

```
Chris
23
```

One benefit of Ruby is that you can add features to classes even if they've already been defined. Within the same program as before, you can simply "reopen" the class and add more definitions:

```ruby
class Person
  def name=(new_name)
    @name = new_name
  end

  def age=(new_age)
    @age = new_age
  end
end
```

These new methods are added to the Person class and are automatically made available to any existing instances of that class. These new methods are *setter* methods, as signified by the equal sign following their names. They allow you to do this:

```ruby
person1.name = "Barney"
person2.age = 101
puts person1.name
puts person2.age
```

```
Barney
101
```

Ruby can simplify most of the preceding work for you though, as it provides the attr_accessor helper method that automatically creates accessors and setter methods within a class for you.

```ruby
class Person
  attr_accessor :name, :age
end
```

You can also create *class methods*: methods that don't exist within the scope of a single object, but that are bound directly to the class. For example:

```ruby
class Person
  @@count = 0

  def initialize
    @@count += 1
  end
```

```
  def Person.count
    @@count
  end
end

a = Person.new
b = Person.new
c = Person.new
puts Person.count
```

3

This Person class implements a count class method (notice that it is defined as Person.count, rather than just count, making it a class method). The count class method returns the value of a class variable (@@count) that stores the total number of Person objects created so far. Class variables begin with two @ signs and exist within the scope of a class and all its objects, but not within the scope of any specific object. Therefore, @@count equals 3 and only 3 once you've created three Person objects.

This section has given only a brief overview of classes, objects, and their special variables. For a detailed look at classes and objects, refer to Chapter 6.

Reflection

Ruby is often called a *reflective* language, as it supports reflection. Reflection is a process that allows a computer program to observe and modify its own structure and behavior during execution. This functionality can seem like a novelty to developers experienced with C, C++, and Perl, but it's incredibly important in terms of Ruby's operation and Ruby's ability to define domain-specific languages, making other forms of development easier.

A brief demonstration of reflection is the ability to programmatically retrieve a list of all the methods associated with any object or class in Ruby. For example, here's how to display a list of all methods of the Hash class:

```
Hash.methods
```

```
["methods", "instance_eval", "display", "dup", "object_id",
"instance_variables",
"include?", "private_instance_methods", "instance_of?",
```

```
"protected_method_defined?", "extend", "const_defined?", "eql?", "name",
"public_class_method", "new", "hash", "id", "singleton_methods", "taint",
"constants", "autoload", "frozen?", "instance_variable_get", "kind_of?",
"ancestors", "to_a", "private_class_method", "const_missing", "type",
"instance_method", "instance_methods", "protected_methods", "superclass",
"method_defined?", "instance_variable_set", "const_get", "is_a?", "respond_to?",
"to_s", "module_eval", "class_variables", "allocate", "class", "<=>", "<",
"tainted?", "private_methods", "==", "public_instance_methods", "__id__",
"autoload?", "===", "public_method_defined?", ">", "included_modules", "nil?",
"untaint", "const_set", ">=", "method", "<=", "send", "inspect", "class_eval",
 "clone", "=~", "protected_instance_methods", "public_methods",
"private_method_defined?", "__send__", "equal?", "freeze", "[]"]
```

Similarly, you can retrieve a list of methods available on a `String` object directly:

`"testing".methods`

```
["methods", "instance_eval", "%", "rindex", "map", "<<", "display", "split",
"any?", "dup", "object_id", "sort", "strip", "size", "instance_variables",
 "downcase", "min", "gsub!", "count", "include?", "succ!", "instance_of?",
 "extend", "downcase!", "intern", "squeeze!", "eql?", "*", "next", "find_all",
 "each", "rstrip!", "each_line", "+", "id", "sub", "slice!", "hash",
"singleton_methods", "tr", "replace", "inject", "reverse", "taint", "sort_by",
 "lstrip", "frozen?", "instance_variable_get", "capitalize", "max", "chop!",
 "kind_of?", "capitalize!", "scan", "select", "to_a", "each_byte", "type",
"casecmp", "gsub", "protected_methods", "empty?", "to_str", "partition", "tr_s",
 "tr!", "match", "grep", "rstrip", "to_sym", "instance_variable_set", "next!",
"swapcase", "chomp!", "is_a?", "swapcase!", "ljust", "respond_to?", "between?",
"reject", "to_s", "upto", "hex", "sum", "class", "reverse!", "chop", "<=>",
"insert", "<", "tainted?", "private_methods", "==", "delete", "dump", "===",
"__id__", "member?", "tr_s!", ">", "concat", "nil?", "succ", "find", "untaint",
"strip!", "each_with_index", ">=", "method", "to_i", "rjust", "<=", "send",
"index", "collect", "inspect", "slice", "oct", "all?", "clone", "length",
"entries", "chomp", "=~", "public_methods", "upcase", "sub!", "squeeze",
"__send__", "upcase!", "crypt", "delete!", "equal?", "freeze", "unpack",
"detect",
"zip", "[]", "lstrip!", "center", "[]=", "to_f"]
```

The results given by the `methods` method might seem overwhelming at first, but over time they become incredibly useful. Using the `methods` method on any object allows you to learn about methods that aren't necessarily covered in this book (or other books), or that are new to the language. You can also use methods to retrieve a list of class methods, because classes are also objects in Ruby!

This section provides only a taste of reflection, but the topic is covered in more detail in Chapter 6.

Reopening Classes

It's trivial to override already defined methods on classes. Earlier in this appendix I mentioned that, if you so wish, you can adjust the Fixnum class so that 2 + 2 would equal 5. Here's how you do that:

```
class Fixnum
  alias_method :old_plus, :+

  def +(other_number)
    return 5 if self == 2 && other_number == 2
    old_plus other_number
  end
end

puts 2 + 2
```

5

The first thing this code does is to enter the Fixnum class, so you can define methods and perform actions within it. Next you make an alias from the addition operator/method (+) to a new method called old_plus. This is so you can still use the normal addition feature, though with a different name.

Next you redefine (or "override") the + method and return 5 if the current number is 2 and the number you're adding to the current number is also 2. Otherwise, you simply call old_plus (the original addition function) with the supplied argument. This means that 2 + 2 now equals 5, but all other addition is performed correctly.

You can redefine nearly any method within Ruby. This can make testing essential because you (or another developer) might incorporate changes that affect classes and objects being used elsewhere within your program. Testing is covered in Chapters 8 and 12.

Method Visibility

It's possible to change the visibility of methods within Ruby classes in one of three ways. Methods can be public (callable by any scope within the program), private (callable only within the scope of the instance the methods exist upon), and protected (callable by any object of the same class). Full details about method visibility are available in Chapter 6.

To encapsulate methods as public, private, or protected, you can use two different techniques. Using the words `public`, `private`, and `protected` within a class definition causes the methods defined thereafter to be encapsulated in the respective fashion:

```ruby
class MyClass
  def public_method
  end

  private
  def private_method1
  end

  def private_method2
  end

  protected
  def protected_method
  end
end
```

You can also explicitly set methods to be encapsulated in one way or another, but only after you've first defined them. For example:

```ruby
class MyClass
  def public_method
  end

  def private_method1
  end

  def private_method2
  end

  def protected_method
  end

  public :public_method
```

```
  private :private_method1, :private_method2
  protected :protected_method
end
```

Declarations such as this should come after you define the methods, as otherwise Ruby won't know what you're referring to.

Data

As everything is an object in Ruby, all forms of data represented within Ruby are also objects, just of varying classes. Therefore, some Ruby developers will try to correct you if you refer to *types* rather than *classes*, although this is merely pedantry.

In this section we'll take a quick look at some of the basic data classes in Ruby.

Strings

Strings in Ruby are generally unexceptional, except for the object-oriented benefits you gain. Previously in this appendix we looked at how powerful classes and methods can be when working upon strings:

```
"this is a test".reverse.upcase.split(' ').reverse.join('-')
```

```
SIHT-SI-A-TSET
```

The `String` class offers a plethora of useful methods for managing text. I'll cover several of these in the following "Regular Expressions" section. However, if you want to see what other methods strings offer, it's easy: just execute `"test".methods`!

Regular Expressions

In Ruby, regular expressions are implemented in a reasonably standard way, being somewhat aligned with the Perl style. If you're familiar with regular expressions, Ruby's techniques shouldn't seem alien:

```
"this is a test".sub(/[aeiou]/, '*')
```

```
th*s is a test
```

```
"this is a test".gsub(/[aeiou]/, '*')
```

```
th*s *s * t*st
```

```
"THIS IS A TEST".gsub(/[aeiou]/, '*')
```

```
THIS IS A TEST
```

```
"THIS IS A TEST".gsub(/[aeiou]/i, '*')
```

```
TH*S *S * T*ST
```

---

sub performs a single substitution based on a regular expression, whereas gsub performs a global substitution. As in Perl, you use the /i option to make the regular expression case insensitive.

Ruby also makes matching easy, with the match method of String returning a special MatchData array you can query:

```
m = "this is a test".match(/\b..\b/)
m[0]
```

```
is
```

```
m = "this is a test".match(/\b(.)(.)\b/)
m[0]
```

```
is
```

```
m[1]
```

```
i
```

```
m[2]
```

```
s
```

The latter example demonstrates how you can parenthesize elements of the regular expression to separate their contents in the results. `m[0]` contains the full match, whereas `m[1]` onwards matches each set of parentheses. This behavior is similar to that of $1, $2, $.. in Perl (note that these special variables also exist in Ruby, but their use is generally frowned upon unless there are no other solutions).

You can also scan through a string, returning each match for a regular expression:

```
"this is a test".scan(/[aeiou]/)
```

```
['i', 'i', 'a', 'e']
```

```
"this is a test".scan(/\w+/)
```

```
['this', 'is', 'a', 'test']
```

Methods such as `split` also accept regular expressions (as well as normal strings):

```
"this is a test".split(/\s/)
```

```
['this', 'is', 'a', 'test']
```

Regular expressions are covered in more depth in Chapter 3, and are used throughout the book.

Numbers

Integers and floating point numbers are available in Ruby and operate mostly as you'd expect. Numbers support all common operators such as modulus (%), addition, subtraction, division, multiplication, and powers (**).

Note You can produce roots easily by raising a number to the power of *1/n*. For example, you can find the square root of 25 with `25 ** 0.5`.

A key consideration with numbers in Ruby is that unless you explicitly define a number as a floating point number, it won't be one unless it contains a decimal point. For example:

```
10 / 3
```

```
3
```

In this situation, 10 and 3 are both considered integers, so integer division is used. If integer division is what you're after—and it might be in some cases—then you're fine. But if you're after floating point division, you need to do something to ensure that at least one of the values involved is recognized as a floating point number. You can generate a floating point value in one of three ways as follows:

- By invoking the `to_f` method, to convert an integer to its floating point equivalent

- By writing the number with a decimal point, even if you just add ".0" to the end

- By invoking the `Float()` initializer method to convert an integer to a floating point value

Here are some examples:

```
10.to_f / 3
```

```
3.33333333333333
```

```
10.0 / 3
```

```
3.33333333333333
```

```
10 / Float(3)
```

```
3.33333333333333
```

Which method you choose to make the 10 be recognized as a Float object can be largely influenced by the situation, so it's useful to see all your options.

Another useful feature in Ruby is that even though whole numbers are typically stored as 32-bit integers internally, Ruby automatically converts integer Fixnum objects into Bignum objects when the 32-bit barrier is breached. For example:

```
(2 ** 24).class
```

```
Fixnum
```

```
(2 ** 30).class
```

```
Bignum
```

```
2 ** 100
```

```
1267650600228229401496703205376
```

Ruby appears to have no problem in dealing with numbers of up to about 78,000 digits in length, certainly enough to solve any mathematical problems you might face! However, clearly there are limits:

```
2 ** 263000
```

```
Infinity
```

Numbers are covered in depth in Chapter 3.

Arrays

As in other programming languages, arrays act as ordered collections. However, in Ruby specifically, arrays are ordered collections of *objects*, because everything in Ruby is an object! Arrays can contain any combination of objects of any class.

At first sight, Ruby arrays work much like arrays in any other language, although note that you work upon an array using methods, because an array itself is an object. The following example shows the invocation of the Array class's push method:

```
a = []
a.push(10)
a.push('test')
a.push(30)
a << 40
```

```
[10, 'test', 30, 40]
```

Notice the use of a different form of pushing objects to an array with the << operator on the last line of the preceding example.

Note Although [ ] defines an empty literal array, you can also use Array.new to generate an empty array if you prefer to stick to object orientation all the way. Java and C++ developers might prefer this syntax initially.

Arrays are objects of class Array and support a plethora of useful methods, as covered in full in Chapter 3.

Hashes (Associative Arrays)

Hashes (also known as associative arrays) exist as a concept in many programming languages, such as Perl, Java, and Python (where they are called *dictionaries*). Hashes are data structures that let you associate keys with values.

Ruby's implementation of hashes is straightforward and should be familiar to both Perl and Python developers, despite some minor syntax changes. For example:

```ruby
fred = {
  'name' => 'Fred Elliott',
  'age' => 63,
  'gender' => 'male',
  'favorite painters' => ['Monet', 'Constable', 'Da Vinci']
}
```

fred refers to a basic hash that contains four elements that have keys of 'name', 'age', 'gender', and 'favorite painters'. You can refer back to each of these elements easily:

```ruby
puts fred['age']
```

```
63
```

```ruby
puts fred['gender']
```

```
male
```

```ruby
puts fred['favorite painters'].first
```

```
Monet
```

Hashes are objects of class Hash and come with a large number of helpful methods to make hashes easy to navigate and manipulate, much like regular arrays. It's important to note that both hash element keys and values can be objects of any class themselves, as long as each element key is distinct. Otherwise, previously existing values will be overwritten. Hashes and associated methods and techniques are covered in detail in Chapter 3.

Complex Structures

Because hashes and arrays can contain other objects, it's possible to create complex structures of data. Here's a basic example of a hash containing other hashes (and another hash containing an array at one point):

```ruby
people = {
  'fred' => {
    'name' => 'Fred Elliott',
    'age' => 63,
    'gender' => 'male',
    'favorite painters' => ['Monet', 'Constable', 'Da Vinci']
  },
  'janet' => {
    'name' => 'Janet S Porter',
    'age' => 55,
    'gender' => 'female'
  }
}

puts people['fred']['age']
puts people['janet']['gender']
puts people['janet'].inspect
```

```
63
female
{"name"=>"Janet S Porter", "gender"=>"female", "age"=>55}
```

This example presents a hash called `people` that contains two entries with keys of `'fred'` and `'janet'`, each of which refer to another hash containing information about each person. These sorts of structures are common in Ruby (as well as in Perl and C++). They are covered in more depth in Chapter 3 and throughout this book. Typically, compared to other languages, the syntax is simple, and in Ruby, the simplest answer is usually the right one.

Input/Output

Ruby has powerful Input/Output (I/O) support, from the ability to create, read, and manipulate files through to database support, external devices, and network connectivity. These topics are covered in full in this book (primarily in Chapters 9, 14, and 15), but this section presents a basic overview of the most important forms of I/O.

Files

Ruby's support for file I/O is powerful compared to that of other languages. Although Ruby supports traditional techniques for reading and manipulating files, its object-oriented features and tight syntax offer more exciting possibilities. First, here is the traditional way you'd open and read a file (as when using a more procedural language):

```
lines = []
file_handle = File.new("/file/name/here", "r")

while line = file_handle.gets
  lines << line
end
```

This example opens a file in read-only mode, then uses the file handle to read the file line by line before pushing it into an array. This is a reasonably standard technique in, say, C or Pascal. Let's look at a Ruby-specific technique:

```
lines = File.readlines('/file/name/here')
```

Ruby's file handling and manipulation support is particularly deep and extensive, so is out of the scope of this chapter. However, the preceding examples should have provided a glimpse into what's possible, and files are covered in full in Chapter 9 of this book.

Databases

There are several ways to connect to database systems such as MySQL, PostgreSQL, Oracle, SQLite, and Microsoft SQL Server from Ruby. Typically, a "driver" library is available for each of the main database systems, although these don't come with Ruby by default. You typically install database driver libraries using the RubyGems Ruby library packaging system, or you might need to download and install them manually. Explaining how to use such libraries is beyond the scope of this appendix, but they are covered in full in Chapter 9.

Ruby also has a DBI library that can provide a more standardized interface to all the various driver libraries. Because each driver library is mostly based on the official library for each database system, they're extremely inconsistent and differ in their implementation. DBI makes many of the features provided by these drivers available in a consistent manner.

Note Ruby's DBI library is not exactly like Perl's DBI library, but is heavily influenced by it, and Perl developers will feel at home using it. It's covered in Chapter 9 of this book.

Web Access

Ruby comes with libraries that make accessing data on the Web incredibly easy. At a high level is the open-uri library, which makes it easy to access data from the Web. This example retrieves a Web page and returns an array containing all the lines on that page:

```
require 'open-uri'
open('http://www.rubyinside.com/').readlines
```

open-uri is a convenience library that provides an open method that allows you to load data from URLs. open returns a File handle (technically a Tempfile object) that works in the same way as any other File object, allowing you to use methods such as readlines to read all the lines of the data into an array. (This topic is covered in significantly more depth in Chapter 14.)

Ruby also provides lower-level libraries, such as net/http. Here's an example of retrieving a file from a Web site and displaying it on the screen:

```
require 'net/http'

Net::HTTP.start('www.rubyinside.com') do |http|
  req = Net::HTTP::Get.new('/test.txt')
  puts http.request(req).body
end
```

```
Hello Beginning Ruby reader!
```

This example connects to the Web server at www.rubyinside.com and performs an HTTP GET request for /test.txt. This file's contents are then returned and displayed. The equivalent URL for this request is http://www.rubyinside.com/test.txt, and if you load that URL in your Web browser, you'll get the same response as this Ruby program.

net/http also lets you make requests using other HTTP verbs such as POST and DELETE, and is the most flexible HTTP library for Ruby. As it's included with the standard library, it's usually the first choice for most Ruby developers. Refer to Chapter 14 for full information.

Libraries

This section looks at how you can organize code into multiple files and manage libraries within Ruby.

File Organization

Ruby libraries don't need to be packaged in any special way (unlike, say, Java's JAR archives). Ruby does have a library packaging system called RubyGems (covered in the next section), but its use is entirely optional. The simplest way to create a library is to create a Ruby file containing classes and methods and use `require` to load it. This technique will be familiar to Perl (using `use`), C (using `#include`), Pascal (using `uses`), and other developers.

Let's assume you have a file called `mylib.rb` containing the following:

```ruby
class MyLib
  def MyLib.hello_world
    puts "Hello, world!"
  end
end
```

And then you have another file like so:

```ruby
require 'mylib'
MyLib.hello_world
```

This program loads in `mylib.rb` and includes its classes, methods, and other particulars into the current runtime environment, meaning that `MyLib.hello_world` calls the correct routine.

Ruby searches through its library folders in a specific order (and, usually, the current directory too, as in the previous example) as dictated by the special variable `$:`. This variable is an array that can be manipulated like any other array. You can push, pop, and otherwise change the order and directories in which your program searches for libraries.

Here's an example of what `$:` contains on an Intel Mac running Ruby 1.8.5:

```ruby
["/usr/local/lib/ruby/site_ruby/1.8", "/usr/local/lib/ruby/site_ruby/1
.8/i686-darwin8.8.1", "/usr/local/lib/ruby/site_ruby", "/usr/local/lib
/ruby/1.8", "/usr/local/lib/ruby/1.8/i686darwin8.8.1", "."]
```

This topic is covered in depth in Chapter 7, and demonstrations of several Ruby libraries are offered in Chapter 16. A basic Ruby library is also created from scratch in Chapter 12.

Packaging

RubyGems (`http://rubygems.org/`) is a packaging system for Ruby libraries and applications. Each package within the RubyGems universe is called a *gem* or RubyGem (in this book both terms are used interchangeably). RubyGems makes it easier to distribute, update, install, and remove libraries and applications on your system.

Before the advent of RubyGems, Ruby libraries and applications were distributed in a basic fashion in archive files, or even as source code to copy and paste from the Web. RubyGems makes it easier and more centralized, and also takes care of any prerequisites and dependencies required when installing a library. For example, here's how to install the Ruby on Rails system:

```
gem install rails
```

■**Note** On some platforms, `sudo gem install rails` would be required so as to install the libraries as a super-user.

This installs the Rails gems along with all their dependencies. The gem application prompts at each step of the way so you know exactly what's being installed (you can override this with command line options). For example, `gem install rails -y` installs Rails and its dependencies without questioning you at all.

You can uninstall gems in as simple a fashion:

```
gem uninstall rails
```

If you have multiple versions of the same gem(s) installed, gem will ask you which version(s) you want to remove.

By default, gems are searched for in the default repository, hosted by RubyForge (`http://www.rubyforge.org/`) at `http://gems.rubyforge.org/`. Any gem files uploaded to Ruby projects hosted on the RubyForge site are made available in the default repository, making a RubyForge account a necessity if you want to distribute your libraries to the widest audience possible in an easy fashion.

However, you can run your own gems repository on your own Web site or by using the RubyGems server software. This is less common and requires users of your gems to specify your server name at the same time as installing the gem.

RubyGems is covered in full in Chapter 7 and several RubyGems are documented in Chapter 16.

APPENDIX B

■■■■

Ruby Reference

This appendix provides several reference sections that you'll find useful from time to time while developing applications with Ruby. More specifically, what's in this appendix is limited to direct reference information that you might find useful while otherwise using this book. For a list of external resources, such as Web sites and mailing lists you can query for more detailed or up-to-date information, refer to Appendix C. Over time, it's essential you learn to use Ruby's online references, as they'll be updated in line with how the Ruby language develops. They'll also open your mind to new possibilities and advanced techniques not covered in this book.

Useful Classes and Methods

The following subsections highlight several of the basic classes and their most useful methods.

Note *This section is not designed to be an exhaustive reference.* Only the most useful methods of several key classes are covered. For a complete, easy-to-search reference of the Ruby core classes, refer to http://www.ruby-doc.org/core/.

Array

See Enumerable, a module that's mixed in with Array, for more methods. The following are the most commonly used methods available on Array objects:

- &: Intersects the contents of one array with another. For example: [1, 2, 3] & [2, 3, 4] == [2, 3].

- *: Repeats the elements of an array a certain number of times if an integer is supplied; otherwise, joins the array elements together if a string is supplied. For example: [1, 2, 3] * 2 == [1, 2, 3, 1, 2, 3] and [1, 2, 3] * " " == "1 2 3".

- +: Concatenates two arrays together into a new array. For example: `[1, 2, 3] + [2, 3, 4] == [1, 2, 3, 2, 3, 4]`.

- -: Returns a new array with elements removed. For example: `[1, 2, 2, 3] - [2] == [1, 3]`.

- `<<`: Pushes or appends objects on to the end of the array. Equivalent to `push`.

- `compact` (and `compact!`): Returns a copy of the array with any `nil` elements removed. For `compact!`, `nil` elements are removed from the current array in place.

- `delete_if`: Invokes the supplied code block for each element of the array and deletes any elements that result in the code block evaluating to `true`. For example: `[1, 11, 20].delete_if { |i| i > 10 } == [1]`.

- `each`: Invokes the supplied code block for each element of the array, passing in each element as a parameter.

- `each_index`: Invokes the supplied code block for each element of the array, passing in the index of each element as a parameter.

- `empty?`: Returns `true` if the array contains no elements.

- `first`: Returns the first element of the array. If none, then `nil`.

- `flatten` (and `flatten!`): Returns the array with all subarrays flattened. For example: `[[1, 2], [2, 3], [4, 5]].flatten == [1, 2, 2, 3, 4, 5]`.

- `include?`: Returns `true` if the supplied object is also found within the array.

- `index`: Returns the index of the first instance of the supplied object within the array, if any. For example: `%w{a b c d e}.index("d") == 3`.

- `join`: Joins the array elements together using an optionally supplied string as a separator.

- `last`: Returns the last element of the array. If none, then `nil`.

- `length`: Returns the total number of elements within the array.

- `pop`: Removes the last element of the array and returns it.

- `push`: Pushes or appends the supplied object to the array (as with `<<`).

- `reverse` (and `reverse!`): Reverses the elements of the array and returns a new array. With `reverse!` the elements are reversed in the current array in place.

- `reverse_each`: The same as `each`, but going through each element in reverse order.

- `shift`: Removes the first element of the array and returns it. Therefore, every other element of the array is moved one element toward the start of the array, to compensate for the newly missing element.

- `sort` *(and* `sort!`*)*: Sorts the elements of the array, returning a new array or in place (with `sort!`). The sorting uses the `<=>` comparison operator of each object. You can also supply an optional code block with which to perform custom sorts.

- `uniq` *(and* `uniq!`*)*: Returns the array with duplicate values removed (`uniq!` removes them in place).

- `unshift`: Pushes objects onto the start of the array (whereas `push` appends to the end of the array).

Bignum and Fixnum

The `Bignum` and `Fixnum` classes represent integers of differing sizes (see Chapter 3 for the full details of how this works). Both classes descend from `Integer` (and therefore `Numeric`). You'll want to refer to the "Integer" and "Numeric" sections for further methods you can use.

Arithmetic Methods

`Bignum` and `Fixnum` objects support the following arithmetic methods:

- `+`: Adds one number to another. For example: `10 + 5 == 15`.

- `-`: Subtracts one number from another. For example: `10 - 5 == 5`.

- `*`: Multiplies one number with another. For example: `10 * 5 == 50`.

- `/`: Divides one number by another. For example: `10 / 3 == 3` (but `10.0 / 3.0 == 3.3333333`).

- `**`: Multiplies a number by itself a certain number of times. Known as *exponentiation* or *raising to the power of*. For example: `5 ** 2 == 25`.

- `%`: Divides one number by another and returns the modulus (remainder). For example: `10 % 3 == 1` because 10 divides into 3 cleanly three times, leaving 1 as a remainder.

Bitwise Methods

Bignum and Fixnum objects also support the following bitwise methods:

- &: Bitwise AND. Be careful not to confuse with the && Boolean operator!

- |: Bitwise OR. Be careful not to confuse with the || Boolean operator!

- ^: Bitwise XOR (eXclusive OR).

- <<: Shifts the bits within the integer a certain number of places to the left. This usually has the effect of doubling the value for each bit shifted. For example: 10 << 2 == 40.

- >>: Shifts the bits within the integer a certain number of places to the right. This has the opposite effect of shifting to the left. For example: 40 >> 2 == 10.

- ~: Inverts the bits within the integer. Also known as a bitwise NOT.

Enumerable

Enumerable is a module that's automatically mixed in to Array and Hash classes. Therefore, you can also use the methods in this section upon arrays and hashes. In these references, the parent array or hash is referred to as a *collection*. The following methods are available and are the most commonly used:

- all?: Invokes the supplied code block for every element of the collection. It ultimately returns true or false depending on whether, for every element, each call to the code block returned true.

- any?: Invokes the code block for every element of the collection and ultimately returns true or false depending on whether, for *any* element, a code block returned true.

- collect: Returns an array of the results obtained by passing each element of the collection into a supplied code block. For example: %w{this is a test}.collect { |i| i * 2 } == ["thisthis", "isis", "aa", "testtest"].

- find *(or* detect*)*: Passes each element of the collection to a supplied code block and returns the first for which the code block evaluates to true.

- find_all *(or* select*)*: Passes each element of the collection to a supplied code block and returns all for which the code block evaluates to true.

- `include?`: Returns `true` if the supplied object is also found within the collection.

- `min`: Returns the object within the collection with the smallest (minimum) value.

- `max`: Returns the object within the collection with the largest (maximum) value.

- `sort` *(and* `sort!`*)*: Sorts the elements of the collection, returning a new collection or in place (with `sort!`). The sorting uses the `<=>` comparison operator of each object. You can also supply an optional code block with which to perform custom sorts.

- `sort_by`: Sorts the collection using the values generated by an invoked code block (to which each element of the collection is passed).

Float

Objects of the `Float` class represent floating point or decimal numbers. They have the same arithmetic methods as `Bignum` and `Fixnum` (see the section "Bignum and Fixnum"), but don't have any bitwise methods, as they are internally represented in an entirely different way to integers. Refer to `Bignum` and `Fixnum` for arithmetic methods, and to `Numeric` for other inherited methods.

Hash

See `Enumerable`, a module that's mixed in with `Array`, for more methods. The following are some of the most popular methods made available by `Hash` objects:

- `clear`: Removes all key and value pairs from the hash.

- `delete`: Deletes the hash entry whose key is equal to the supplied object.

- `delete_if`: Deletes all hash entries where, for a code block invoked with the key and value, true is returned. For example: `{ :a => 10, :b => 20, :c => 30 }.delete_if { |k, v| v > 10 } == { :a => 10 }`.

- `each`: Invokes a supplied code block once for each entry in the hash, passing in the key and value of that element as two parameters.

- `each_key`: Invokes a supplied code block once for each entry in the hash, passing in the key only.

- `each_value`: Invokes a supplied code block once for each entry in the hash, passing in the value only.

- empty?: Returns true if the hash has no entries (that is, pairs of keys and values).

- has_key?: Returns true if the hash has an entry with the supplied key.

- keys: Returns an array containing all the keys from the hash's entries.

- length (or size): Returns the number of entries within the hash.

- to_a: Returns an array representing the hash with each entry given an array containing its key and value.

- values: Returns an array containing all the values from the hash's entries.

Integer

Integer is the parent class of Fixnum and Bignum and is not generally used on its own. However, its methods are made available to both classes. The following are some of the most commonly used methods:

- chr: Returns a string containing an ASCII character of the code represented by the integer. For example: 65.chr == "A".

- downto(end_integer): Invokes the code block for each integer between that represented by the current object down to end_integer, passing each integer into the code block as i.

- next: Returns the next integer in ascending sequence from the current one. For example: 5.next == 6.

- times: Invokes the code block the number of times represented by the current object. The number of each iteration is passed to i. For example: 10.times { |i| puts "This is iteration #{i}" }.

- upto(end_integer): Invokes the code block for each integer between that represented by the current object up to end_integer, passing each integer into the code block as i.

Numeric

Float and Integer (and therefore Fixnum and Bignum) are subclasses of Numeric, and so inherit all Numeric's methods. Numeric objects aren't instantiated on their own. The following are the most commonly used methods available to objects whose classes inherit from Numeric:

- `abs`: Returns the absolute value of the object as another instance of that object. For example, the absolute value of -3 and 3 is 3. Therefore, `-3.abs == 3`.

- `ceil`: Rounds up a value to the nearest integer. For example: `1.2.ceil == 2`.

- `integer?`: Returns `true` if the object is of class `Integer`, otherwise `false`. Note that floats might contain integer values, but they aren't necessarily of class `Integer`.

- `floor`: Rounds down a value to the nearest integer. For example: `1.2.floor == 1`.

- `round`: Rounds a value to the nearest integer. Note: `0.5` rounds up to 1.

- `step(end_number, step_amount)`: Invokes the supplied code block, passing in numbers (to i) starting from the value of the object and going in steps of `step_amount` to `end_number`.

- `zero?`: Returns `true` if the object represents zero, otherwise `false`.

Object

`Object` is a "superclass." All other classes in Ruby descend from it. Therefore, all its methods—several of which are described in the following list—are made available to all other classes and objects via inheritance. Some classes and objects *might* choose to override `Object`'s methods, but generally they all work.

- `class`: Returns the name of the class of an object. For example: `"test".class == String`.

- `clone`: Copies an object to create a new one. However, it's only a shallow copy, so objects referenced by instance variables might still be the same as those referenced by any copies.

- `freeze`: Freezes the object so that no more changes can be made to it. A `TypeError` exception will be raised if any attempts are made to change the object.

- `frozen?`: Returns `true` if the object is frozen.

- `instance_eval`: Evaluates a supplied string or code block in the scope of the object.

- `is_a?` *(or* `kind_of?`*)*: Returns `true` if the object is of a supplied class. For example: `10.is_a?(Integer) == true`.

- `methods` *(or* `public_methods`*)*: Returns an array of the methods publicly accessible on the object.

- `nil?`: Returns `true` if the object is `nil`.

- `object_id`: Returns an integer that uniquely identifies the object internally to Ruby.

- `private_methods`: Returns an array of all private methods associated with the object.

- `protected_methods`: Returns an array of all protected methods associated with the object.

- `send`: Invokes the method represented by a symbol passed as the first argument. All other arguments are passed through to the destination method. For example: `10.send(:+, 20) == 30`.

- `taint`: Taints the object, making it impossible to perform certain operations under certain safe levels (see Chapter 8).

- `untaint`: Untaints the object.

String

The following commonly used methods are available on `String` objects:

- `*`: Returns a new string representing the current string multiplied by a certain number of times. For example: `"abc" * 3 == "abcabcabc"`.

- `<<`: Appends data to the end of the string. If the supplied argument is an integer between 0 and 255, the ASCII character represented by that number is appended instead.

- `=~`: Matches a supplied regular expression against the string. The position of the first match is returned, otherwise `nil`. This technique is commonly used as a comparison expression to see if a string matches a regular expression.

- `capitalize` *(and* `capitalize!`*)*: Capitalizes the first letter of the string, with the remainder converted to lower case. `capitalize!` performs the operation in place on the current string.

- `chop` *(and* `chop!`*)*: Removes the last character of a string (or two characters if equal to `'\r\n'`).

- `count`: Counts the occurrences of the supplied strings within the string. For example: `"this is a test".count("i") == 2`.

- delete *(and* delete!*)*: Removes instances of the supplied strings from the string. For example: "this is a test".delete("i") == "ths s a test".

- downcase *(and* downcase!*)*: Converts all letters in the string to lower case.

- each_byte: Invokes the supplied code block for each byte within the string, passing in the ASCII code of the character.

- empty?: Returns true if the string is empty.

- gsub *(and* gsub!*)*: Substitutes all occurrences of the first supplied parameter (or that match a supplied regular expression) with the second supplied parameter. For example: "this is a test".gsub(/[aeiou]/, "X") == "thXs Xs X tXst".

- gsub(exp) *(and* gsub!*) with a following code block*: Invokes the code block for each occurrence of exp (whether a String or Regexp), substituting each occurrence within the result of the code block.

- include?: Returns true if the string contains the supplied string.

- length: Returns the length of the string.

- lstrip *(and* lstrip!*)*: Removes whitespace from the start of the string. lstrip! removes the whitespace in place on the string.

- reverse *(and* reverse!*)*: Returns a reversed copy of the string (or reverses the current string in place, with reverse!).

- rstrip *(and* rstrip!*)*: Removes whitespace from the end of the string. rstrip! removes the whitespace in place on the string.

- scan: Iterates through the string, finding each match against a supplied string or regular expression. All matches are returned as an array.

- scan(pattern): Iterates through the string, invoking the code block and passing in each match found against a supplied string or regular expression.

- split: Splits the string into an array using a supplied pattern as a delimiter, or if none is supplied, $;. See the "Special Variables" section of this appendix.

- strip *(and* strip!*)*: Removes whitespace from the start and end of the string. strip! removes the whitespace in place on the string.

- sub *(and* sub!*)*: Substitutes only the first occurrence of the first supplied parameter (or the first match of a supplied regular expression) with the second supplied parameter. For example: "this is a test".sub(/[aeiou]/, "X") == "thXs is a test".

- sub(exp) *(and* sub!*) with following code block*: Invokes the code block for the first occurrence of exp (whether a String or Regexp), substituting that occurrence with the result of the code block.

- to_f: Attempts to return a Float representing a value depicted in the string. For example: "3.141592 is equal to pi".to_f == 3.141592.

- to_i: Attempts to return an integer representing a value depicted in the string. For example: "100".to_i == 100.

- to_sym: Converts the string into a Symbol object.

- upcase *(and* upcase!*)*: Converts all characters into upper case.

Regular Expression Syntax

Regular expressions are special expressions that can be used to match patterns within strings, and were covered in depth in Chapter 3. This section provides a reference for the main elements of regular expression syntax.

Regular expressions are usually represented as strings contained within forward slashes, like so:

```
/regular expression here/
```

Regular expressions can also be contained within %r{ and }, like so:

```
%r{regular expression here}
```

Regular expression syntax is reasonably standard between programming languages, and Ruby supports most of the standard POSIX regular expression syntax. Therefore, many examples of regular expressions you might find online are also likely to work within Ruby.

Regular Expression Options

When using the forward-slash notation for regular expressions, you can set options for the regular expression by placing letters after the last forward slash, as follows:

- i: Makes the regular expression case insensitive. Therefore, /test/i matches positively against strings containing 'TEST', 'TeSt', 'tESt', 'test', or any other combination of lower- and upper case letters making up the word "test."

- m: Puts the regular expression into multiline mode where the special character "." (usually meaning "any character except newline") matches newlines. Therefore, /.*/m matches the whole of a multiline string, whereas /.*/ alone would only match the first line within that string.

- x: Makes the regular expression ignore whitespace. This allows you to format the regular expression in a more readable way without worrying about whitespace becoming part of the regular expression. For example, /t e s t/x matches against "test." This option is particularly useful if you want to spread out your regular expression over multiple lines for easier reading.

Special Characters and Formations

Regular expressions can contain normal characters (such as letters or digits) and match against these, but you can use special characters to represent more abstract concepts such as "any character" or "any digit." The following are some of the special characters that you can use in regular expressions or to create sub-expressions:

- .: Matches any character except the newline character.

- []: Matches a character range or set. See Chapter 3 for full details.

- (): Denotes a sub-expression. For example, (abc)+ matches 'abcabcabc'.

- |: Separates alternate choices. For example, t|x matches 't' or 'x'.

- \w: Matches any alphanumeric character or underscore.

- \W: Matches anything \w doesn't match.

- \b: Matches a word *boundary* (but not a specific character).

- \B: Matches anything \b doesn't match.

- \d: Matches digits (0 through 9).

- \D: Matches anything \d doesn't match (nondigits).

- \s: Matches whitespace characters (spaces, tabs, newlines, form feeds).

- \S: Matches anything \S doesn't match (non-whitespace).

- \A: Matches the beginning of a string.

- \Z: Matches the end of a string.

- ^: Matches the beginning of a line (or string).

- $: Matches the end of a line (or string).

Character and Sub-Expression Suffixes

You can use the following characters after a character, character range, or a sub-expression (as provided within parentheses) to modify how that element is matched by the regular expression:

- +: Matches one or more of the previous.

- +?: Matches one or more, but as few as possible, of the previous.

- ?: Matches zero or one of the previous.

- *: Matches zero or more of the previous.

- *?: Matches zero or more, but as few as possible, of the previous.

Note You can learn more about regular expressions, and more advanced syntax, at `http://en.wikipedia.org/wiki/Regular_expression`.

Exception Classes

Exceptions are covered in Chapter 8, but this section gives a hierarchical list of all standard exception classes within Ruby. You can raise these for your own purposes using `raise`. This list might also be useful if you want to catch certain exceptions. For example, `IOError` is useful to rescue in many situations.

To get more information about certain exceptions, you can raise them from irb to get a more complete error message. For example:

```
irb(main):001:0> raise Errno::EAGAIN
```

```
Errno::EAGAIN: Resource temporarily unavailable
        from (irb):1
        from :0
```

Here's the exception class list:

```
Exception
  fatal
  NoMemoryError
  ScriptError
    LoadError
    NotImplementedError
    SyntaxError
    Interrupt
  SignalException
  StandardError
    ArgumentError
    IndexError
      EOFError
    IOError
    LocalJumpError
    NameError
      NoMethodError
      FloatDomainError
    RangeError
    RegexpError
    RuntimeError
    SecurityError
      Errno::E2BIG
      Errno::EACCES
      Errno::EADDRINUSE
      Errno::EADDRNOTAVAIL
      Errno::EAFNOSUPPORT
      Errno::EAGAIN
      Errno::EALREADY
      Errno::EBADF
```

```
Errno::EBADMSG
Errno::EBUSY
Errno::ECHILD
Errno::ECONNABORTED
Errno::ECONNREFUSED
Errno::ECONNRESET
Errno::EDEADLK
Errno::EDESTADDRREQ
Errno::EDOM
Errno::EDQUOT
Errno::EEXIST
Errno::EFAULT
Errno::EFBIG
Errno::EHOSTDOWN
Errno::EHOSTUNREACH
Errno::EIDRM
Errno::EILSEQ
Errno::EINPROGRESS
Errno::EINTR
Errno::EINVAL
Errno::EIO
Errno::EISCONN
Errno::EISDIR
Errno::ELOOP
Errno::EMFILE
Errno::EMLINK
Errno::EMSGSIZE
Errno::EMULTIHOP
Errno::ENAMETOOLONG
Errno::ENETDOWN
Errno::ENETRESET
Errno::ENETUNREACH
Errno::ENFILE
Errno::ENOBUFS
Errno::ENODATA
Errno::ENODEV
Errno::ENOENT
Errno::ENOEXEC
Errno::ENOLCK
Errno::ENOLINK
Errno::ENOMEM
Errno::ENOMSG
```

```
            Errno::ENOPROTOOPT
            Errno::ENOSPC
            Errno::ENOSR
            Errno::ENOSTR
            Errno::ENOSYS
            Errno::ENOTBLK
            Errno::ENOTCONN
            Errno::ENOTDIR
            Errno::ENOTEMPTY
            Errno::ENOTSOCK
            Errno::ENOTTY
            Errno::ENXIO
            Errno::EOPNOTSUPP
            Errno::EOVERFLOW
            Errno::EPERM
            Errno::EPFNOSUPPORT
            Errno::EPIPE
            Errno::EPROTO
            Errno::EPROTONOSUPPORT
            Errno::EPROTOTYPE
            Errno::ERANGE
            Errno::EREMOTE
            Errno::EROFS
            Errno::ESHUTDOWN
            Errno::ESOCKTNOSUPPORT
            Errno::ESPIPE
            Errno::ESRCH
            Errno::ESTALE
            Errno::ETIME
            Errno::ETIMEDOUT
            Errno::ETOOMANYREFS
            Errno::ETXTBSY
            Errno::EUSERS
            Errno::EXDEV
        SystemCallError
        SystemStackError
        ThreadError
        TypeError
        ZeroDivisionError
    SystemExit
```

Special Variables

Throughout this book you've used special variables provided automatically by Ruby for various purposes. For example, $! is a string of the last error message raised in the program, $$ returns the process ID of the current program, and $/ lets you adjust the default line or record separator as used by the gets method.

The English library (used by simply placing require 'English' in your program) allows you to access Ruby's special variables using names expressed in English, rather than symbols. This makes the variables easier to remember. The following are the main ones:

- $DEFAULT_OUTPUT (or $>) is an alias for the destination of output sent by commands such as print and puts. By default it points to $stdout, the standard output (see the sidebar "Standard Input and Output" in Chapter 9 for more information), typically the screen or current terminal.

- $DEFAULT_INPUT (or $<) is an object that acts somewhat like a File object for data being sent to the script at the command line. It's read-only.

- $ERROR_INFO (or $!) refers to the exception object passed to raise or, more pragmatically, can contain the most recent error message. In the initial form, it can be useful when used within a rescue block.

- $ERROR_POSITION (or $@) returns a stack trace as generated by the previous exception. This is in the same format as the trace provided by Kernel.caller.

- $OFS and $OUTPUT_FIELD_SEPARATOR (or $,) can be set or read, and contain the default separator as used in output from the print method and Array's join method. The default value is nil, as can be confirmed with %w{a b c}.join, which results in 'abc'.

- $ORS and $OUTPUT_RECORD_SEPARATOR (or $\) can be set or read, and contain the default separator as used when sending output with methods such as print and IO.write. The default value is nil, as typically you use puts instead when you want to append a newline to data being sent.

- $FS and $FIELD_SEPARATOR (or $;) can be set or read, and contain the default separator as used by String's split method. Changing this and then calling split on a string without a split regex or character can give different results than expected.

- $RS and $INPUT_RECORD_SEPARATOR (or $/) can be set or read, and contain the default separator as used for input, such as from gets. The default value is a newline (\n), and results in gets receiving one line at a time. If you set this value to nil, then an entire file or data stream would be read by gets in one go.

- `$PID` and `$PROCESS_ID` (or `$$`) returns the process ID of the current program. This ID is unique for every program or instance of a program running on a computer, which is why Tempfile uses it when constructing names for temporary files. It is read-only.

- `$LAST_MATCH_INFO` (or `$~`) returns a `MatchData` object that contains the results of the last successful pattern match.

- `$IGNORECASE` (or `$=`) is a flag that you can set or read from that determines whether regular expressions and pattern matches performed in the program will be case insensitive by default. This special variable is deprecated and might be removed in Ruby 2. Typically, if you required this feature you'd use the `/i` flag on the end of a regular expression instead.

- `$MATCH` (or `$&`) contains the entire string matched by the last successful regular expression match in the current scope. If there has been no match, its value is `nil`.

- `$PREMATCH` (or `` $` ``) contains the string preceding the match discovered by the last successful regular expression match in the current scope. If there has been no match, its value is `nil`.

- `$POSTMATCH` (or `$'`) contains the string succeeding the match discovered by the last successful regular expression match in the current scope. If there has been no match, its value is `nil`.

Ruby License

From time to time you might need to check on some detail of Ruby's licensing to be sure that you're in compliance. The following is the exact text of the Ruby license as of January 2007:

> *Ruby is copyrighted free software by Yukihiro Matsumoto <matz@netlab.co.jp>. You can redistribute it and/or modify it under either the terms of the GPL (see COPYING.txt file), or the conditions below:*

> *1. You may make and give away verbatim copies of the source form of the software without restriction, provided that you duplicate all of the original copyright notices and associated disclaimers.*

2. You may modify your copy of the software in any way, provided that you do at least ONE of the following:

a) place your modifications in the Public Domain or otherwise make them Freely Available, such as by posting said modifications to Usenet or an equivalent medium, or by allowing the author to include your modifications in the software.

b) use the modified software only within your corporation or organization.

c) rename any non-standard executables so the names do not conflict with standard executables, which must also be provided.

d) make other distribution arrangements with the author.

3. You may distribute the software in object code or executable form, provided that you do at least ONE of the following:

a) distribute the executables and library files of the software, together with instructions (in the manual page or equivalent) on where to get the original distribution.

b) accompany the distribution with the machine-readable source of the software.

c) give non-standard executables non-standard names, with instructions on where to get the original software distribution.

d) make other distribution arrangements with the author.

4. You may modify and include the part of the software into any other software (possibly commercial). But some files in the distribution are not written by the author, so that they are not under this terms. They are gc.c(partly), utils.c(partly), regex.[ch], st.[ch] and some files under the ./missing directory. See each file for the copying condition.

5. The scripts and library files supplied as input to or produced as output from the software do not automatically fall under the copyright of the software, but belong to whomever generated them, and may be sold commercially, and may be aggregated with this software.

6. THIS SOFTWARE IS PROVIDED "AS IS" AND WITHOUT ANY EXPRESS OR IMPLIED WARRANTIES, INCLUDING, WITHOUT LIMITATION, THE IMPLIED WARRANTIES OF MERCHANTABILITY AND FITNESS FOR A PARTICULAR PUR-POSE.

Note The latest copy of the Ruby license is always available at `http://www.ruby-lang.org/en/LICENSE.txt`.

■ ■ ■

Useful Resources

This appendix provides links to useful Ruby resources that are available online, from Web sites to chatrooms and mailing lists.

Note that because the Internet is ever-changing, some resources that were available at the time of writing might no longer be available to you. When you find that to be the case, it's worth using a search engine to search for the keywords involved, as the site you're looking for might have simply changed URLs.

References

The resources covered in this section are general references to Ruby and Ruby on Rails. For specific tutorials and guides to doing certain things, you need to refer instead to the "Tutorials and Guides" section later on in this appendix.

Ruby

Official Ruby home page (http://www.ruby-lang.org/): The official Ruby home page.

Ruby-Doc.org (http://www.ruby-doc.org/): Ruby-Doc.org is a documentation site built by the Ruby community that features documentation for the core API, standard libraries, and other miscellaneous Ruby bits and pieces. Its primary maintainer is James Britt, who has been involved with Ruby documentation for many years.

Ruby core documentation (http://www.ruby-doc.org/core/): Documentation for the core elements of Ruby, such as the included classes (Array, Hash, and so on), as well as much of the standard library. The documentation is presented in the standard RDoc format.

Ruby 1.9 documentation (http://www.ruby-doc.org/core-1.9/index.html): Documentation for the cutting-edge (at the time of writing) 1.9 developer-only version of Ruby. Prior to the release of Ruby 2.0, this documentation is useful to get a glimpse into what 2.0 may contain.

"Ruby Standard Library Documentation" (http://www.ruby-doc.org/stdlib/): Documentation for the Ruby standard libraries. Each library is presented separately, making it easier to read than the core documentation.

RubyForge (http://rubyforge.org/): The home for open source Ruby projects. Any Ruby developer can sign up and promote his or her own libraries, or simply download existing libraries for free. RubyForge hosts the default RubyGems repository (see Chapter 7).

"Ruby Application Archive" (http://raa.ruby-lang.org/): A repository of applications and libraries for Ruby. It has largely been superseded by RubyForge, but is still used to host a large number of projects.

Thomas, David and Andrew Hunt. Programming Ruby: The Pragmatic Programmer's Guide, First Edition. *Addison Wesley Longman, 2001* (http://www.rubycentral.com/book/): A free, online copy of the first edition of a Ruby book, targeted to an old version of Ruby (1.6).

"Ruby Quickref" (http://www.zenspider.com/Languages/Ruby/QuickRef.html): A quick-fire set of references and reminders that act as a cheat sheet for Ruby, listing reserved words, regular expression syntax, language constructions, special variables, and more.

"6 Ruby and Rails Job Sites" (http://www.rubyinside.com/6-ruby-and-rails-job-sites-312.html): A list of Ruby- and Rails-related job sites. Ideal if you're looking for employment with your newly found Ruby skills!

Ruby on Rails

Official Rails home page (http://www.rubyonrails.org/): The official home page for the Ruby on Rails framework. It features screencasts, tutorials, and links to many useful Rails references.

Rails documentation (http://api.rubyonrails.org/): API documentation for the entire Ruby on Rails framework in RDoc format. This is the most useful reference documentation for Ruby on Rails, as almost all Rails techniques and methods are covered.

Rails edge documentation (http://caboo.se/doc.html): API documentation for the most cutting-edge releases of Rails. Unlike the typical Rails documentation, all the methods available in Ruby have been exposed, even if there's no full documentation for them. This makes this reference ideal for advanced users.

Rails wiki (`http://wiki.rubyonrails.com/`): A publicly updateable site with random reference information about Ruby on Rails. At one time well updated and popular, at the time of writing it's a little neglected. There's still some useful content available on the wiki, but much of the advice has been written for old versions of Rails and might not be relevant by the time you read this.

Blogs

Blogs (or "weblogs") are frequently updated "journal"-style Web pages where content is displayed in reverse time order (the most recently posted content is at the top of the front page). Blogs have become important places to go for the latest Ruby news, and the thoughts and latest projects of developers in the Ruby community.

Aggregators and Community Blogs

"Ruby Inside" (`http://www.rubyinside.com/`): The semi-official blog associated with this book, but also the most often updated, central blog for Ruby- and Rails-related announcements, along with occasional editorial and tutorial posts.

"PlanetRubyOnRails" (`http://www.planetrubyonrails.com/`): An automatic aggregator of many of the top Ruby and Rails weblogs.

Ruby on Rails podcast (`http://podcast.rubyonrails.com/`): Although it isn't strictly a blog, the Ruby on Rails podcast is a regular presentation of audio programs related to both Ruby and Rails, produced by Geoffrey Grosenbach.

"RubyCorner" (`http://rubycorner.com/`): A site that automatically posts links to the latest posts from Ruby and Rails blogs. Unlike Planet Ruby on Rails, Ruby Corner only provides quick links to each blog post, rather than republishing them in full.

"Riding Rails" (`http://weblog.rubyonrails.org/`): The official blog for Ruby on Rails, updated by several core Rails developers along with Rails creator David Heinemeier Hansson. This blog focuses on sporadic announcements of interesting uses or deployments of Rails, along with new Rails features.

"The Unofficial Ruby on Rails Blog" (`http://www.rubyonrailsblog.com/`): An unofficial blog attempting to cover the full gamut of Ruby on Rails topics.

Personal Blogs

"RedHanded" (http://redhanded.hobix.com/): "why the lucky stiff," author of this book's foreword, blogs at RedHanded, covering exciting new Ruby developments and numerous advanced topics. RedHanded is not a generalist blog, but one packed with humor, wit, and an eclectic range of Ruby knowledge.

Yukihiro Matsumoto (http://www.rubyist.net/~matz/): A blog from the creator of Ruby himself, Yukihiro "Matz" Matsumoto. The blog is in Japanese, although you can run it through BabelFish or Google Translate to get the basic gist. Some Ruby users read the blog simply for the code examples.

Pat Eyler: "On Ruby" (http://on-ruby.blogspot.com/): A blog about general Ruby topics and things that take the interest of Pat Eyler. This blog is great for its many interviews and detail on topics.

"Loud Thinking" (http://www.loudthinking.com/): The blog from the creator of Ruby on Rails, David Heinemeier Hansson. Posts are infrequent, but are usually related to the future of Rails, making it a popular read nonetheless.

"eigenclass" (http://eigenclass.org/): A blog by Ruby guru Mauricio Fernandez focusing on particularly advanced Ruby topics.

"has_many :through" (http://blog.hasmanythrough.com/): Josh Susser, a popular commentator and writer about Ruby on Rails, blogs here.

"err.the_blog" (http://errtheblog.com/): A blog by PJ Hyett and Chris Wanstrath presenting regular tutorials, hints, and tips relevant to both Ruby and Rails.

Forums and Newsgroups

A forum is a site that acts as an online discussion system. You make posts to which other users can respond with comments, making forums ideal for discussing topics, sharing code, and having debates of all kinds.

comp.lang.ruby newsgroup (http://groups.google.com/group/comp.lang.ruby): comp.lang.ruby is a Usenet newsgroup you can access through any Usenet server, or on the Web via Google Groups.

"comp.lang.ruby FAQ" (http://rubyhacker.com/clrFAQ.html): Frequently asked questions, and their answers, about the Ruby newsgroup.

"Rails Weenie" (`http://rails.techno-weenie.net/`): A questions-and-answers forum for Rails-related questions. This forum has been popular for quite some time, and is a great place to ask questions.

"Rails Forum" (`http://railsforum.com/`): A popular Ruby on Rails help and discussion forum. There are more than 1,000 registered members and many posts each day.

SitePoint Ruby forum (`http://www.sitepoint.com/forums/forumdisplay.php?f=227`): A Ruby forum provided by the SitePoint webmaster resources site. Unlike with the Rails Forum, all posts to the SitePoint Ruby Forum are within a single category, making it easier to scan through.

Mailing Lists

Mailing lists are like forums, but based upon e-mail. People subscribe to a "list," and then all messages sent to that list are received by all the subscribers. There are also archives of e-mail lists available on the Web for reference or for those who don't want to sign up for the list.

Ruby mailing lists (`http://www.ruby-lang.org/en/community/mailing-lists/`): The official page on the Ruby site that provides information about the official Ruby mailing lists.

Ruby-Talk mailing list: Ruby-Talk is the most popular Ruby mailing list, where all aspects of Ruby development are discussed. To join the Ruby-Talk mailing list, send an e-mail to `ruby-talk-ctl@ruby-lang.org` with the first line as **subscribe YourFirstName YourLastName**, replacing the relevant parts as necessary.

Ruby-Talk Web gateway (`http://www.ruby-forum.com/forum/4`): The Ruby-Talk Web Gateway mirrors messages from the Ruby-Talk mailing list onto the Web in a forum-style format, and also allows messages to be posted *to* the list from the Web.

Ruby-Talk mailing list archives (`http://blade.nagaokaut.ac.jp/ruby/ruby-talk/index.shtml`): Offers Web access to more than 200,000 posts made to the Ruby-Talk mailing list, including a search feature.

"ruby-core" (`http://blade.nagaokaut.ac.jp/ruby/ruby-core/index.shtml`): Ruby-Core is a mailing list dedicated to discussing implementation details and the development of Ruby itself. Those who are developing the Ruby language use this list. However, it isn't a list on which to ask general Ruby questions.

■**Note** It's important when using a mailing list that you look at the format and tone of other posts and don't offend anyone. If your postings sound too demanding or are of the wrong tone, you might not get any responses.

Real-Time Chat

On the Internet there are several ways you can discuss topics with other users in real time. For example, Web sites can contain Flash or Java chatrooms. Alternatively, you can use instant messenger or Internet Relay Chat (IRC) clients. Ruby is the primary focus of discussion in only a few real-time chat systems at present:

#ruby-lang (`irc://irc.freenode.net/%23ruby-lang`): #ruby-lang is an IRC channel on the `irc.freenode.net` server, and is used for general discussion about Ruby. Ruby on Rails isn't covered here. The number of people in the channel can vary, although there are usually a few hundred or so. Despite this, not many tend to talk at the same time.

#rubyonrails (`irc://irc.freenode.net/%23rubyonrails`): #rubyonrails is the official Ruby on Rails IRC channel. You can ask questions about Ruby on Rails here, and most people are willing to help. As with #ruby-lang, the channel has many visitors, but isn't too noisy.

#ruby (`irc://irc.freenode.net/%23ruby`): #ruby is a more generic Ruby IRC channel, and far less busy than either #ruby-lang or #rubyonrails, with fewer than a hundred people at once.

"Ruby Inside Chatroom" (`http://www.lingr.com/room/5Rfd8nM5tMF`): The official chatroom for the Ruby Inside blog. It's Web-based, but isn't as consistently busy as the preceding IRC channels. Chats are scheduled here from time to time, and you can learn about these by subscribing to the Ruby Inside blog.

■**Note** If you aren't familiar with IRC, you can learn more at `http://en.wikipedia.org/wiki/Internet_Relay_Chat`.

Tutorials and Guides

The Internet is host to a significant number of tutorials and guides on how to use various features of Ruby and its libraries. Often there are multiple tutorials on how to do the same thing in different ways, and tutorials can appear quickly after libraries are released. This is why it's worth subscribing to a few Ruby blogs so that you can learn about the latest action as it happens.

However, in this section are links to a number of useful tutorials and guides that have already proven useful.

Installation

In this section I present links to a collection of guides to installing Ruby and/or Rails on multiple platforms.

■**Note** Full instructions for Windows, Linux, and Mac OS X are provided in Chapter 1. These resources are only provided if you want to get more specific information.

Linux

"Install Ruby Rails on Ubuntu Dapper Drake" (http://www.urbanpuddle.com/articles/2006/06/10/install-ruby-rails-on-ubuntu-dapper-drake): A guide to installing Ruby and Rails on Ubuntu Dapper Drake.

"Ruby, Gems and RMagick on Ubuntu Edgy" (http://www.digitalblueprint.co.uk/articles/2006/10/26/ruby-gems-and-rmagick-on-ubuntu-edgy/): Step-by-step instructions for installing Ruby, Rails, and the RMagick image-processing gem on Ubuntu Edgy.

"Ruby on Rails on Fedora Core 6" (http://felipec.wordpress.com/2006/11/06/ruby-on-rails-on-fedora-core-6/): Installation of Ruby on Rails on Fedora. These details will likely be relevant even on future releases of Fedora.

"Ruby on Rails on Red Hat" by David Berube (http://www.redhat.com/magazine/025nov06/features/ruby/?sc_cid=bcm_edmsept_007): An article published by Red Hat about getting Ruby on Rails running on the Red Hat Enterprise Linux OS.

"Ruby on Rails on Debian" (http://www.debian-administration.org/articles/329): Covers the installation of Ruby, Rails, and the RadRails IDE on Debian.

Mac OS X

"Building Ruby, Rails, LightTPD, and MySQL on Tiger" by Dan Benjamin (http://hivelogic.com/articles/2005/12/01/ruby_rails_lighttpd_mysql_tiger): A comprehensive guide to installing Ruby, Rails, and a Web and database server on Mac OS X.

"Using Ruby on Rails for Web Development on Mac OS X" (http://developer. apple.com/tools/rubyonrails.html): Official documentation provided by Apple about installing Ruby on Rails on Mac OS X.

Other Platforms

"Installing Rails on Solaris 9" (http://www.hydrus.org.uk/journal/rails-sun.html): Notes on installing Ruby on Rails on Sun's Solaris OS.

"RubyOnRails + FastCGI in OpenBSD 4.0 Apache-chroot" (http://bsd.phoenix.az. us/faq/openbsd/rails-chroot-fastcgi): A guide to installing Ruby on Rails in OpenBSD 4.0.

"RailsOnFreeBSD" (http://wiki.rubyonrails.org/rails/pages/RailsOnFreeBSD): Notes on setting up Ruby on Rails on FreeBSD.

Ruby and Techniques

"Learning Ruby" (http://rubylearning.com): A collection of short tutorials on various aspects of Ruby by Satish Talim. Ideal as a quick recap on various topics.

"Mr. Neighborly's Humble Little Ruby Book" by Jeremy McAnally (http:// humblelittlerubybook.com/): An up-to-date Ruby book available in both print (for a nominal fee) and online (for free).

"Try Ruby!" (http://tryruby.hobix.com/): An online Ruby interpreter with a built-in tutorial.

"Getting Started with Ruby on Windows IIS Tutorial" (http://www.tutorialized.com/ tutorial/eRuby-Getting-Started-with-Ruby-on-Windows-IIS/17025): A tutorial demonstrating how to hook up Ruby with Windows IIS and eRuby to provide another dynamic templating system.

"Using Ruby, PostgreSQL, and MySQL on Windows" (`http://www.tutorialized.com/ tutorial/eRuby-Using-Ruby-PostgreSQL-and-MySQL-on-Windows/17026`): A guide to using two popular database systems alongside Ruby on Windows.

"Why's (Poignant) Guide to Ruby" (`http://poignantguide.net/ruby/`): An amazingly quirky and exciting Ruby tutorial written by "why the lucky stiff," the author of this book's foreword.

"Ruby in Twenty Minutes" (`http://www.ruby-lang.org/en/documentation/quickstart/`): A basic primer to the bare essentials of Ruby. This guide won't be of any use to readers of this book, but might be useful to forward to others who are interested in Ruby and want to get a quick look at the language from a beginner's point of view.

Ruby on Rails

"Time For A Grown-Up Server: Rails, Mongrel, Apache, Capistrano, and You" (`http://blog.codahale.com/2006/06/19/ time-for-a-grown-up-server-rails-mongrel-apache-capistrano-and-you/`): An excellent walkthrough of several key technologies for deploying and maintaining Ruby on Rails applications.

"Rolling with Ruby on Rails Revisited" by Bill Walton and Curt Hibbs (`http://www.onlamp.com/pub/a/onlamp/2006/12/14/ revisiting-ruby-on-rails-revisited.html`): A tutorial walking through the creation of a basic Ruby on Rails application.

"Rails Security Checklist" (`http://rubythis.blogspot.com/2006/11/ rails-security-checklist.html`): A list of important security considerations when developing and deploying Rails applications.

"Subversion Primer for Rails projects" (`http://blog.teksol.info/articles/ 2006/03/09/subversion-primer-for-rails-projects`): An introduction to using Subversion source control and management with your Rails projects.

"PeepCode Screencasts for Ruby on Rails Developers" (`http://www.peepcode.com/`): A series of Rails-related screencasts (videos that show you how to accomplish certain tasks), by Geoffrey Grosenbach.

"HOWTO: Make A Rails Plugin From Scratch" (`http://www.railsforum.com/ viewtopic.php?id=682`): An excellent tutorial demonstrating how to create a Rails plugin.

Other

"REXML Tutorial" (`http://www.germane-software.com/software/rexml/docs/tutorial.html`): A tutorial giving lots of quick code snippets showing how to use the REXML XML–processing library that comes in the Ruby standard library.

"Ruby/Tk Tutorial" (`http://members.chello.nl/~k.vangelder/ruby/learntk/`): A tutorial demonstrating how to use Tk, a GUI toolkit for Ruby that makes it possible to build graphical applications.

"Verifying Server Certificates in Ruby" (`http://brianellin.com/blog/2006/03/18/verifying-server-certificates-in-ruby/`): A blog post demonstrating how to use net/http and OpenSSL to verify HTTPS security certificates in Ruby.

"Using the Rake Build Language" by Martin Fowler (`http://www.martinfowler.com/articles/rake.html`): A comprehensive run through the Ruby "Rake" (Ruby Make) system, as briefly covered in Chapter 13 of this book.

"SQL Tutorial" (`http://www.w3schools.com/sql/`): A comprehensive SQL tutorial, extending upon what was covered in Chapter 9 of this book.

"XML Matters: The REXML library" (`http://www-128.ibm.com/developerworks/xml/library/x-matters18.html`): It's several years old, but this IBM article about using REXML is still relevant.

Index

Find it faster at http://superindex.apress.com/

Find it faster at http://superindex.apress.com/

Y

Z

forums.apress.com

JOIN THE APRESS FORUMS AND BE PART OF OUR COMMUNITY. You'll find discussions that cover topics of interest to IT professionals, programmers, and enthusiasts just like you. If you post a query to one of our forums, you can expect that some of the best minds in the business—especially Apress authors, who all write with *The Expert's Voice*™—will chime in to help you. Why not aim to become one of our most valuable participants (MVPs) and win cool stuff? Here's a sampling of what you'll find:

DATABASES
Data drives everything.

Share information, exchange ideas, and discuss any database programming or administration issues.

INTERNET TECHNOLOGIES AND NETWORKING
Try living without plumbing (and eventually IPv6).

Talk about networking topics including protocols, design, administration, wireless, wired, storage, backup, certifications, trends, and new technologies.

JAVA
We've come a long way from the old Oak tree.

Hang out and discuss Java in whatever flavor you choose: J2SE, J2EE, J2ME, Jakarta, and so on.

MAC OS X
All about the Zen of OS X.

OS X is both the present and the future for Mac apps. Make suggestions, offer up ideas, or boast about your new hardware.

OPEN SOURCE
Source code is good; understanding (open) source is better.

Discuss open source technologies and related topics such as PHP, MySQL, Linux, Perl, Apache, Python, and more.

PROGRAMMING/BUSINESS
Unfortunately, it is.

Talk about the Apress line of books that cover software methodology, best practices, and how programmers interact with the "suits."

WEB DEVELOPMENT/DESIGN
Ugly doesn't cut it anymore, and CGI is absurd.

Help is in sight for your site. Find design solutions for your projects and get ideas for building an interactive Web site.

SECURITY
Lots of bad guys out there—the good guys need help.

Discuss computer and network security issues here. Just don't let anyone else know the answers!

TECHNOLOGY IN ACTION
Cool things. Fun things.

It's after hours. It's time to play. Whether you're into LEGO® MINDSTORMS™ or turning an old PC into a DVR, this is where technology turns into fun.

WINDOWS
No defenestration here.

Ask questions about all aspects of Windows programming, get help on Microsoft technologies covered in Apress books, or provide feedback on any Apress Windows book.

HOW TO PARTICIPATE:
Go to the Apress Forums site at **http://forums.apress.com/**.
Click the New User link.